BEYOND THE BOOK

Unique and Rare Primary Sources
for East Asian Studies Collected
in North America

Cover Images:

Front cover: page from *Izumi nikki* with reading notations by Ozawa Suien Keijirō 小澤醉園圭次郎 (1842–1932). From chapter 13, "Revealing the Hidden: Uncataloged Japanese Manuscripts at the C.V. Starr East Asian Library, University of California, Berkeley" by Toshie Marra, University of California, Berkeley.

Back cover: Devil dance at a lama temple in Beijing. From chapter 5, "Making the Sidney D. Gamble Photographs Digital Collection" by Luo Zhou, Duke University.

Beyond the Book

Unique and Rare Primary Sources
for East Asian Studies Collected
in North America

Jidong Yang, Editor

Asia Past & Present

Published by the Association for Asian Studies.
Asia Past & Present: New Research from AAS, Number 16

The Association for Asian Studies (AAS)

Formed in 1941, the Association for Asian Studies (AAS)—the largest society of its kind, with over 5,000 members worldwide—is a scholarly, non-political, non-profit professional association open to all persons interested in Asia. For further information, please visit www.asianstudies.org.

Published by Association for Asian Studies, Inc.
825 Victors Way, Suite 310, Ann Arbor, MI 48108 USA

Library of Congress Cataloging-in-Publication Data

Names: Yang, Jidong, 1966– editor.
Title: Beyond the book : unique and rare primary sources for East Asian Studies collected in North America / Jidong Yang.
Other titles: Unique and rare primary sources for East Asian Studies collected in North America
Description: Ann Arbor, MI : Association for Asian Studies, [2022] | Series: Asia past & present: new research from AAS ; number 16 | Includes bibliographical references. | Summary: "Beyond the Book is the first ever book dedicated to the studies of rare East Asian materials collected by individuals and institutions in North America. Most of the materials discussed in this volume are in a non-book format, such as archives, maps, prints, photographs, motion pictures, sound recordings, diaries, correspondence, posters, and unofficial publications. Beyond the Book not only reveals many interesting and forgotten stories in the two centuries of cultural exchanges between East Asia and North America, but also provides fresh clues for East Asian studies scholars in their search for important research materials"— Provided by publisher.
Identifiers: LCCN 2021057364 | ISBN 9780924304989 (hardcover)
Subjects: LCSH: East Asia—Bibliography. | Libraries—Special collections—East Asia. | Archives—North America.
Classification: LCC Z3001 .B44 2022 DS504.5 | DDC 025.2/95—dc23/eng/20220203
LC record available at https://lccn.loc.gov/2021057364

Contents

Acknowledgments

The essays collected in this volume were originally presented to Beyond the Book: A Conference on Unique and Rare Primary Sources for East Asian Studies Collected in North America, held at the East Asia Library of Stanford University, July 1–2, 2015. I am grateful to all the parties that contributed to the organization of the conference and the publication of this volume, including East View Information Services (Minneapolis, MN), China National Knowledge Infrastructure (Beijing, China), Superstar Digital Library (Beijing, China), the Asian Culture Press (Seoul, Korea), Kinokuniya Bookstores of America Co., Ltd. (San Francisco, CA), and the following departments of Stanford University: Stanford University Libraries, Department of East Asian Languages and Cultures, Center for East Asian Studies, Hoover Institution Library and Archives, and the Walter H. Shorenstein Asia-Pacific Research Center.

Jidong Yang
Head, East Asia Library, Stanford University

Contributors to this Volume

YOUNG-MEE YU CHO, Associate Professor, Department of East Asian Languages and Cultures, Rutgers University

MICHAEL J. DABRISHUS, Associate University Librarian for Archives and Special Collections, University of Pittsburgh

MIKYUNG KANG, Librarian for the Korean Collection, Harvard-Yenching Library, Harvard University

HANA KIM, Director, Cheng Yu Tung East Asian Library, University of Toronto

SHIGERU KOBAYASHI, Professor Emeritus, Graduate School of Letters, Osaka University

RIA KOOPMANS-DE BRUIJN, Head of Public Services / East Asian Studies Librarian, C. V. Starr East Asian Library, Columbia University

HYE-EUN LEE, Assistant Professor, Sookmyung Women's University

HSIAO-TING LIN, Curator, Modern Chinese Collection / Research Fellow, Hoover Institution Library and Archives

TOSHIE MARRA, Librarian for the Japanese Collection, C. V. Starr East Asian Library, University of California, Berkeley

HARUKO NAKAMURA, Librarian for Japanese Studies, East Asia Library, Yale University

SUNGMIN PARK, Special Formats Cataloger / Repository Librarian, The College of New Jersey

ROBERT C. PROVINE, Professor Emeritus, School of Music, University of Maryland

FABIANO TAKASHI ROCHA, Japanese Studies / Collection and Services Librarian, Cheng Yu Tung East Asian Library, University of Toronto

HEE-SOOK SHIN, Korean Studies Librarian, C. V. Starr East Asian Library, Columbia University Columbia

YUWU SONG, Reference Specialist, Asian Division, Library of Congress

AZUSA TANAKA, Japanese Studies Librarian, East Asia Library, University of Washington

ZHAOHUI XUE, Chinese Studies Librarian, East Asia Library, Stanford University

KUNIKO YAMADA MCVEY, Librarian for the Japanese Collection, Harvard-Yenching Library, Harvard University

JIDONG YANG, Head, East Asia Library, Stanford University

KEIKO YOKOTA-CARTER, Japanese Studies Librarian, Asia Library, University of Michigan

HAIHUI ZHANG, Head of the East Asian Library, University of Pittsburgh

LUO ZHOU, Chinese Studies Librarian, Duke University Libraries

PREFACE

Jidong Yang, Stanford University

The chapters included in this volume were originally presented in July 2015 at a conference held at the East Asia Library of Stanford University, which had recently moved into a renovated building and become one of the most spacious and resourceful libraries in the United States for teaching, learning, and research focused on East Asia. Titled "Beyond the Book: A Conference on Unique and Rare Primary Sources for East Asian Studies Collected in North America," it drew librarians, archivists, and scholars from all over the United States and Canada to present their research on collections of materials that were still little known to the academic world yet potentially valuable for scholarly research. The vast majority of the resources presented at the conference are in a nonbook format such as manuscripts, archival materials, photographs, sound and video recordings, maps, and so on.

Just like all other disciplines of the humanities and social sciences, the scholarship of East Asian studies is shaped, defined, and limited first of all by the scholarly resources that are available and accessible to researchers. To put it simply, the type and quantity of primary materials that a researcher can gather is oftentimes the deciding factor in the quality of his or her research. East Asian peoples and their civilizations have survived for thousands of years, but the vast majority of information about those peoples and civilizations, especially in the premodern age, has been lost forever. History, as historians have pointed out over and over again, is never a comprehensive account of all the things that happened in the past. Instead, it is a collection of fragmentary human memories that have survived in written and various other forms. Generation after generation, East Asian studies scholars have lamented the scarcity of primary sources for their research. Taking Chinese history as an example, while China has perhaps the world's longest continuous tradition of state-sponsored history writing, its recorded past is almost an exclusive account of the events that took place inside the capital city and between the emperor and his closest ministers. From the so-called twenty-four dynastic or official histories, modern scholars can scarcely draw anything useful when they attempt to restore the daily lives of ordinary Chinese people living in the provinces, especially those far from the capital. In the case of early Japanese history, to take another example, although today's researchers are fortunate enough to have classical historiographies such as the *Nihon Shoki* and *Kojiki*, they are very clear in their view that all those texts are a mixture of legends, myths, and historical facts. To find the true origin of a country's civilization, one cannot rely on those sources alone and so must look for new materials.

If we take an overview of the history of East Asian studies over the past one and a half centuries—starting in the mid-nineteenth century when Sinology and Japanology were gradually transformed from Christian missionary learning into college academic programs in Europe and modern humanities and social sciences began to be introduced into East Asia—we can confidently conclude that the discovery of new research materials has played an essential role in the development of the field. During the period, large numbers of ancient sites in East Asia have been scientifically and systematically investigated by archaeologists; thousands of premodern texts have been excavated from underground; numerous government archives have opened their doors to the public; and many private writings, such as diaries, manuscripts, and correspondences, have also been made available to researchers. As the scholarship has been transformed, the very notion of "primary sources" has also undergone dramatic changes. Materials in nonbook formats are now being equally valued by scholars. Needless to say, all these changes have greatly expanded the frontiers of East Asian studies. Taking a quick look at the fields with which I am most familiar, namely, the history of premodern China and the Silk Road, we can see that they were fundamentally reshaped and redefined thanks to the abundance of newly discovered research materials. Beginning with the last years of the nineteenth century, a vast number of ancient manuscripts and inscriptions in Chinese, Tibetan, Tangut, Khitan, Sanskrit, Tocharian, Sogdian, Khotanese, Old Uighur, Old Turkic, and many other languages and scripts were discovered first by European explorers and then by Chinese archaeologists in Northwest China. Those manuscripts and inscriptions, dated from the third century BCE to the twelfth century CE, completely transformed our knowledge of ancient China and the Silk Road, which was previously reliant entirely on the official histories written by Chinese court historiographers. They have allowed scholars around the world to understand the local societies and economies of the medieval Chinese empire and the international and intercultural exchanges between China and other parts of the Eurasian world, as well as the languages and literatures of many historical Sino-Tibetan, Indo-European, and Altaic peoples who used to live in the territories now belonging to the People's Republic of China, and whose traces would have been utterly lost without the discovery of their written records. In the study of Korean and Japanese history, the same kinds of breakthroughs have also been brought about by numerous exciting discoveries. The uncovering of the

Goguryeo Kingdom inscribed steles in Manchuria, for instance, has thoroughly rewritten the early history of the Korean people and their civilization. In short, new resources are the life support for East Asian studies, and the development of the discipline depends on the continuous supply of fresh primary sources. Only against this background of academic history from the nineteenth century on can we fully comprehend the significance of the cause we are pursuing throughout this volume.

Our articles focus on resources collected by North American institutions. As relatively young countries, both the United States and Canada have a shorter history of cultural communication with East Asia than Europe does. When Jesuit missionaries arrived in East Asia in waves and began to bring Chinese and Japanese woodblock-printed books back to Europe in the sixteenth century, French and Spanish expeditions to the North American coastlines and inland valleys had only just begun. When the Chinese and Japanese styles became a major theme of European decorative arts and architecture during the seventeenth and eighteenth centuries, colonial America's imagination of East Asia was still limited to the fine porcelains imported from South China by way of Europe. Entering the nineteenth century, however, North America's interest in East Asia grew quickly. Soon after the country gained its independence, and especially after the War of 1812, a growing number of US citizens, most of whom were Protestant missionaries, embarked on the long journey to East Asia. Sailing mostly from New York, they had to endure more hardship than the Asia-bound Europeans because they had to overcome the heavy seas of the North Atlantic before entering the maritime route along the African coastline. The American Oriental Society, the first learned society in the United States devoted to a particular field of scholarship, was founded in 1842 to promote the study of Asian civilizations. After California joined the United States, America's distance from East Asia was significantly reduced. In the late nineteenth and early twentieth centuries, as the United States became an economic and political power on a global scale, succeeding generations of Americans displayed a much stronger interest in other parts of the world and began to collect East Asian books and arts on a large scale. Several vivid examples of that booming interest can be found right across the street from the East Asia Library of Stanford University in the exhibition hall under the Hoover Tower. They are the Chinese vases collected by President Herbert Hoover, one of the first graduates of Stanford, and his wife Lou Henry, both of whom spent several years in China and were fluent in Mandarin. During the entire first half of the twentieth century, East Asia was in constant turmoil. With their rapidly accumulating wealth, the United States and Canada played an important role in collecting and preserving the cultural heritages of the East Asian peoples. After World War II, thanks to the generous funding support from both public and private sources, East Asian studies flourished in North America. Meanwhile, the collection of primary sources for the field underwent the fastest period of development ever seen in the history of the West.

Scholars' interests are always changing. Raw research materials collected by insightful archivists and librarians do not necessarily draw scholarly attention right away. Over time, precious materials can end up being buried in dust-covered boxes in the corner of the storage room. It is hard to estimate how many such boxes of East Asian materials are still waiting to be discovered and studied across North America, but I can tell from my own career that quite a lot of them are out there. Several years ago, when I was working for the University of Pennsylvania Libraries, I found quite a number of interesting and valuable items among unprocessed materials, such as a textbook of the Shanghai dialect written in the Latin alphabet and published in 1860. It was clearly used by Christian missionaries to teach the local language to their coworkers. Today it is an important piece of primary source material for studying the language of Shanghai, my hometown, during the nineteenth century when the city underwent dramatic social and cultural changes. I made an even greater discovery at Penn when I noticed that quite a few old Chinese and Japanese books displayed a bookplate bearing the name "the McCartee Library," which does not exist in Penn's library system today. After conducting some research, I found that D. B. McCartee was a Presbyterian missionary born in 1820. After graduating from Penn's medical school, he arrived in China in 1842 and spent the better part of his life in China and Japan. As one of the very few Americans in the nineteenth century who mastered two East Asian languages, McCartee left numerous legacies in China and Japan. He donated more than a thousand East Asian books to Penn to establish one of the earliest East Asian libraries on this continent. As part of my research on McCartee, I visited a number of institutions in Philadelphia, including the University of Pennsylvania Archives, the Academy of Natural Sciences, American Philosophical Society, Presbyterian Historical Society, and the Free Library of Philadelphia. In all of those places, I found exciting new materials related to East Asia and worthy of scholarly research. It is my firm belief that, throughout North America, treasures like these are everywhere, and we do not need to look too far away from each of us to find some of them.

That is why we held the conference at Stanford in 2015 and are publishing this book today. By presenting a whole set of little-known yet valuable materials at once, we are showing the scholarly world that the potential for digging out new East Asian studies resources is still endless and that we librarians and archivists are fully behind scholars to help them in developing groundbreaking research ideas. The vast majority of the resources presented in this volume are in a nonbook format. I believe this will make them even more special and meaningful in pushing the boundaries of East Asian studies.

1

MISSIONARY FAMILIES AND THE CHINA CONNECTION

AN INTRODUCTION TO THE R. STUART HUMMEL FAMILY PAPERS

Zhaohui Xue, Stanford University

The late nineteenth and early twentieth centuries witnessed a great expansion of foreign missionaries, particularly Protestants, traveling from the United States to China "to change Chinese minds and hearts."[1] However, for a long time the missionaries were not widely known or discussed. As John K. Fairbank once put it, "The missionary in foreign parts seems to be the invisible man of history." He pointed out that missionaries "went out from most of Europe and the British Commonwealth as well as from the United States; they came from various sections, as well as various denominations, with all their regional-cultural diversity; they worked in the most diverse lands abroad, encountering widely different societies and institutions. Mission history is a great and underused research laboratory for the comparative observation of cultural stimulus and response in both directions."[2]

Today this group of "invisible men of history" is no longer invisible. A large number of studies have produced a rich literature on the different missions in China, individual missionaries, their families and social networks, educational and medical missionaries, missionary publishing, and interactions and conflicts between missionaries and Chinese, as well as missionaries in different geographic localities (the coastal areas vs. in the heartland). There are also abundant primary sources and reference tools, online and in print, for research on missionary movements, especially in the realm of American Protestant missionary movements in China. Of course, there are still many areas to be explored and stories to be told.

The newly acquired and digitized R. Stuart Hummel Family Papers in the Special Collections of the Stanford University Library, is a major collection of significant primary sources that can shed new light on the lives and works of two missionary families and fill some gaps and historical details in the larger picture of missionary history in China. These two families, connected through marriage, had deep China connections. Most family members, spanning three generations, either worked in China or held China- or East Asia–related government or academic jobs after they returned to the United States.

The first to go was George Arthur Stuart (1858–1911), a Methodist medical missionary, who, with his wife Rachel Anna Golden Stuart (1859–1972) and newborn daughter, went to China in 1886. He worked as missionary doctor and educator in Wuhu, Nanjing, and Shanghai from 1886 till his death in 1911. His missionary work spanned for about twenty-five years. The couple gave birth to five more children in China.

Figure 1.1: Photo of George Stuart family with servants in Wuhu.

Then came the second generation, many of whom continued the China connection. George A. Stuart's first son, George Golden, practiced medicine in China throughout the 1920s. The first daughter, Mildred, worked as a teacher in a Chinese missionary school. In 1912 she married another missionary, William Frederick Hummel, who was teaching at the University of Nanking. After returning to the United States in 1927, William F. Hummel earned a PhD in Chinese history and taught at a number of institutions. He had a twin brother, Arthur William Hummel Sr. (恆慕義), who was a well-known missionary and a noted Sinologist. Arthur William Hummel Sr. was in China from 1914 to 1927. He taught first in Fenzhou, Shanxi, then at Yenching University, and then served as the head of the newly established Division of Chinese Literature of the Library of Congress (the name was changed to the Orientalia Division later) from 1928 till his retirement in 1954. Alcy Orma Stuart, the second daughter of George A. Stuart and Rachel Anna Golden Stuart, married an optometrist, Otto Durham Rasmussen, in 1912 (the couple later divorced). Otto and George G. Stuart once jointly operated a business called the Stuart-Rasmussen Optical Company (雷師眼鏡公司) in Hankow (Hankou) and Shanghai. Otto also authored a number of books on Chinese history.

In the third generation, R. Stuart Hummel, a son of William F. Hummel and Mildred Stuart, first worked as a cryptographer for the US Navy during World War II and then joined the State Department, where he worked in the Department of Chinese Affairs, overseeing US information centers throughout Asia and directing Chinese-language broadcasts for the Voice of America in the 1950s. Arthur W. Hummel Jr. (恆安石), a son of Arthur W. Hummel Sr. and Ruth Bookwalter Hummel, was a career diplomat and US ambassador to China from 1981 to 1985. He was born in Fenzhou, Shanxi. In 1927 the family returned to United States. Hummel went back to Beijing in 1940 to study at the California College of Chinese Studies and also taught English at the Catholic University of Peking 輔仁大學. He was taken prisoner by the Japanese after the Pearl Harbor attack in 1941 and held in a Japanese camp in Shandong. In 1944 he fled and joined the Chinese Nationalist forces, where he remained until the end of the war. After returning to the United States, he worked in various US foreign service positions in the Asia and Pacific regions. The chart below illustrates the relationships among these two families.

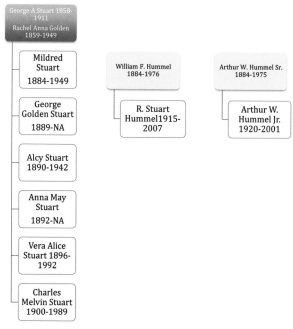

The Collection

This collection was compiled and preserved by R. Stuart Hummel. In 2007 the family donated the collection to the Stanford University Library. The collection has been digitized and is now available for public access via the finding aid in the Online Archive of California. It is a valuable collection that consists of 279 boxes. It includes an extensive collection of correspondence between family members and friends in China, as well as in the United States, and other items such as photographs, diaries, ephemera, artworks, and audiovisual materials.

The collection is arranged by family, type of material, and subject matter in fifteen series. Series 1 to 7 contain family papers, arranged chronologically for each family member and including extensive personal letters, and diaries, as well as some business letters and documents. Series 8 holds R. Stuart Hummel's research materials on the genealogical lines of his family. Series 9 to 11 contain photographs, a rich collection on family life and friends in China and United States; ten Chinese woodblock prints (*nianhua*); a few missionary posters; and audiovisual materials that were recorded by R. Stuart Hummel and others on the family's history. Series 12 to 14 contain early missionary publications, photocopies of books on the subject of missionaries in China, and the Muriel Boone files (a missionary who worked in China from 1917 to 1950 and a friend in the social circle of the Stuart and Hummel families), which include her typescripts of an unpublished book, *Four Flags over a Changing China,* and correspondence in her late years from 1983 to 1990, the year of her death. Series 15 holds oversized materials such as diplomas and newspapers.

A few characteristics of this collection can be noted. First, private letters, diaries, and other memorabilia form a large part of the collection. The handwritten letters in the late nineteenth century are well preserved and survived over the generations. More than seventy years of the diaries by R. Stuart Hummel is an especially significant holding and occupies eighty-two manuscript boxes. He wrote diaries diligently almost every day from 1932 to 2006 on his works, family matters, and current events in rich detail. These personal writings deserve careful attention. The correspondence and diaries provide a unique lens through which to look into the lives of the Stuart and Hummel families in China, and they provide valuable information for the study of family history, their social network and social life, and their interaction with Chinese people and culture. Their personal recordings, observations, and comments on life events provide valuable historical texts of their times and places, different from official documents, for the historians to explore.

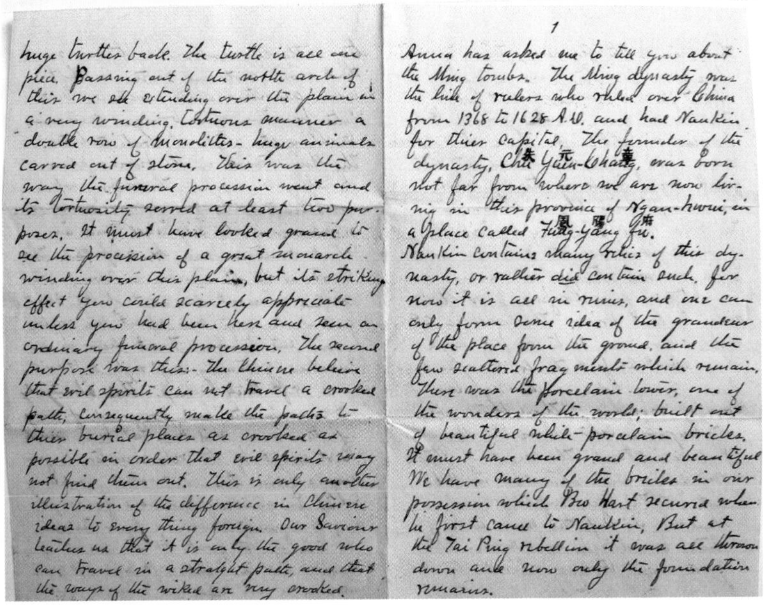

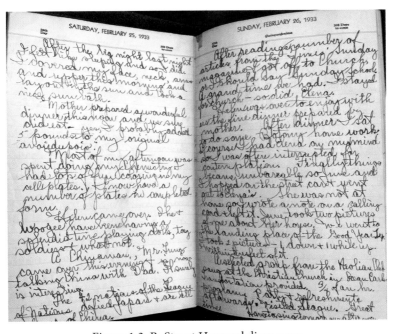

Figure 1.2: George Author Stuart's letter to the family.

Figure 1.3: R. Stuart Hummel diary page.

The timeline of this collection spans more than one hundred years, from the late nineteenth to the twenty-first century. The subject matter covers a variety of topics on China and East Asia ranging from early missionary life in Wuhu, then a remote inland port city in the late nineteenth century, and Nanking, a political and cultural center in the early twentieth century; to the Boxer Uprising in 1900; the Nanking Incident in 1927; family members' lives and work after the war and back in the United States; events such as the attack on Pearl Harbor and World War II; their social connections and family circles in China and the United States; and R. Stuart Hummel's career experiences in the State Department and Voice of America. There are also materials on fellow missionaries such as Muriel Boone.

There are extensive early historical photographs of the Wuhu General Hospital, Nanking University, colleagues and friends in the United States and China, and family vacations in Kuling (Lushan). There are also photos of many students, early buildings, faculty members, and various activities at Nanking University. The historical photographs provide powerful visual representations of people, times, and places related to the two families.

Some highlights of the photograph collection include the following:

Figure 1.4: A Wuhu Chinese family in late 19th century.

Figure 1.5: British custom officers in Wuhu.

Figure 1.6: George A. Stuart at work in Wuhu office.

Figure 1.7: George A. Stuart with students in Nanking University.

Figure 1.8: George A. Stuart with Chinese officials.

In addition to the original materials from the Stuart and Hummel families, this collection contains photocopies of archival materials from the collections kept in other institutions that pertain to the Stuart and Hummel families. There are photocopies from the United Methodist Archives and History Center at Drew University in New York that are related to George A. Stuart's work in Wuhu and Nanking. There are photocopies of the diaries of Arthur W. Hummel Sr. from 1901 to 1904. The collector, Stuart Hummel, has tried to put together as many documents as possible from various archives and resource centers for the collection. Throughout the collection, duplicate photocopies of the original documents and photographs and photocopies of official publications on related topics are added to the multiple subject files in an attempt to provide background information and the larger context in which these files are situated.

It is worth noting that there are other archival collections pertaining to the Stuart and Hummel families held by other institutions. For example, Arthur W. Hummel Sr.'s archive in Harvard-Yenching Library and the Arthur W. Hummel Family and Professional Papers, 1905–1975, in the Harold B. Lee Library, Brigham Young University, are two collections that contain some correspondence between William F. Hummel and his family.

To highlight the historical and research value of this collection, the following discussion focuses on the materials pertaining to George A Stuart's missionary work in China.

George A. Stuart and His Life in China

Among the many early missionaries, Catholic or Protestant, George A. Stuart, whose Chinese name is 师图尔, is not a well-known figure, nor has he been studied before to the best of my knowledge. This is in sharp contrast to another well-known missionary educator and diplomat, whose last name was also Stuart, John Leighton Stuart. Nevertheless, George A. Stuart had a distinguished career in China that deserves special attention.

Figure 1.9: George A. Stuart.

Dr. George A. Stuart grew up in Iowa, attended Simpson College, and received his medical degree from the Iowa College of Physicians and Surgeons. He married Rachel Anna Golden in 1882. The Stuart couple arrived at Nanjing on July 25, 1886, and worked for a very short time at the Methodist hospital under the direction of Dr. Robert C. Beebe. He was soon charged with the responsibility of building another hospital in Wuhu. He built the first western hospital, Wuhu General Hospital, in Anhui Province, the former Yijishan Hospital 弋矶山医院, in 1888 and worked there for nearly ten years. He returned to Nanjing in 1896 to establish a medical school at Nanking University 汇文书院. He was appointed the president in the same year, a position he held till 1908, when he was appointed as the general editor for the Methodist Episcopal Church in China and moved to Shanghai. He served as editor of the *Chinese Christian Advocate* 兴华报 till his death in 1911. He was also active in professional missionary organizations. In 1905 he was chosen as the president of the Educational Association of China 中国教育会, and two years later he became the president of the China Medical Missionary Association 中华医学会. Both missionary associations had a great impact on the modernization of Chinese education and medicine. For several years he served as the editor of the *China Medical Journal*. He translated numerous religious and medical texts from English into Chinese. One of his major works was translation of the *Compendium of Materia Medica* 本草纲目 into English. He died on July 25, 1911, and was buried in the Pahsienjao cemetery (Baxianqiao 八仙桥外国坟山) in Shanghai.

The Wuhu Years, 1887-1895

Wuhu was one of the five trading ports established after the Sino-British Yantai Treaty in 1876 (historically known as the Chefoo Conversion). As noted above, Wuhu General Hospital was the first western hospital built in Anhui Province. Studies on this topic have attributed the building of the hospital to the American Methodist Episcopal Church. However, questions such as when or who built the hospital, how it was built, and the kind of difficulties encountered in the building process, remain unexplored or certainly not well examined in these studies.[3] On the website of the International Mission Photography Archive (IMPA) at University of Southern California Digital Library, some photographs of Wuhu General Hospital are presented, but they were all taken after the 1920s–30s.[4] What is the story of its early days? The documents in Stuart Hummel Papers provide rich information on this set of questions. The papers also reveal internal struggles that occurred during the building process.

Some sources credit Virgil C. Hart 赫怀仁, who came to Wuhu in 1881, with the building of the hospital.[5] The documents in the collection provide evidence that it was Hart who secured the land on which Stuart later designed and built the hospital.

George A. Stuart arrived at Wuhu in the spring of 1887. On May 23, in an article published on the *Inland Advocate*, a missionary publication, Stuart wrote:

> About April 1st I was appointed by our superintendent, Rev. V. C. Hart, to take charge of the medical work at Wuhu, with a view to establishing it upon some permanent basis.

> At this important port, some four years ago, our church established a mission, purchasing as building site, a hill about two miles down river

Figure 1.10: Wuhan General Hospital 1.

Figure 1.11: Wuhan General Hospital 2.

from the city. Every one who has seen our site, says it is the best situated of any missionary property he has seen in China. The hill rises directly from the river's edge and is visible for fifteen miles either up or down the river. The steamers daily pass within a few rods of our grounds, and multitudes of native freight and passenger boats are almost constantly passing under the shadow of our houses. Here we have at present two 'houses' and the W.F.M.S. have a chapel, and a girl's boarding school. We have also land upon which to erect other buildings.[6]

However, Stuart faced the daunting challenge of carrying out his medical duties and building the hospital. He had neither resources for building the hospital nor basic medical equipment and medicine. He described this difficult situation in his report.

Since my arrival I have been appealed to by a large number of persons for relief from suffering, including several who desire to be cured of the opium habit. But I came without drugs or instruments and there is no money in the treasury with which to buy, there being no appropriation for medical work last year. I have endeavored to relieve such as I was able from my own resources, but this number has been very small compared to the number of applicants.

Understandably, Stuart was frustrated. "Here a great opportunity for daily preaching and enforcing the gospel of Christ upon these thousands of people is being lost for want of what is necessary to carry on this work" and impatient with the slow process of obtaining funding from the missionary board. "If we wait for the action of the board, nothing can be done for nearly a year, and many souls will never hear of the gospel thereby."

He listed the basic medical items in desperate need and continued to seek support for the hospital, estimating that "From $7,000 to $10,000 would give us a building of which we need not to be ashamed, and being set on the very top of the hill, would be a constant reminder to the Chinese world around us that Christ came to relieve the 'sick.'"

As a result of Stuart's persistence, the church approved $5,000 for the hospital. However, what followed was a very interesting twist in the internal struggles around where to build the hospital. It was part of a personal clash between Stuart and John R. Hykes, the treasurer of the mission, and was mostly a struggle over financial control and decision-making power.

We can piece together the story of the contention using a series of urgent letters sent by George A. Stuart in 1889 to the secretaries of the missionary society of the Methodist Episcopal Church,[7] as I will try to outline below.

The site initially purchased and decided upon for the hospital was two miles outside the city and on the hillside of Yijishan. G. A. Stuart considered it the best-situated missionary property for building the hospital. After funding was secured in 1887, he began preparing immediately for construction. But in February 1888, because of the lack of an official document, a "red deed," for the land on the hillside, he had to suspend construction and spend almost eight months going through the bureaucratic process of obtaining the document, which he viewed as unnecessary and a waste of time. Furthermore, he had to pay the fee and tax for the document from the fund he deemed should only be used for the hospital's construction. This delay and extra cost made him incredibly anxious. When he finally obtained the document in September 1888, a decision was made at the annual meeting of the Central China Mission in October 1888 to find another hospital site inside Wuhu city, which surprised him and completely upset his plans. The treasurer of the mission, John R. Hykes, insisted on finding a new site, even though Stuart was strongly against the decision.

Without another option, he tried to implement the decision and find a new, suitable site, but to no avail.

> The price was very high for all. The reason for this is, the Jesuits and Li Hung Chang are buying up all the available land, because it is thought that at some time in the near future, Wuhu will be a port of considerable importance, from a commercial point of view. Other foreigners, especially the Russians, are desirous of purchasing here, and as the amount of available land is quite limited, this demand has run the price up, and parties do not seem anxious to sell unless they can get their price.

Only one site was available, but:

> This piece is within a few rods of the District Magistrate's office, and he would never allow us to build there, in the first place, it being so close to his "ya-men." (the office and residence of the District Magistrate). It is also between and close to the principal Buddhist and Confucian temples of the city. The worshipers would be apt to come there some night and tear the houses down for us. This is not my opinion alone, but I have asked many of our Chinese, and they say that both of these facts that I have just stated are true.

To be sure, Stuart was not exaggerating about the fight for land that had played out in Wuhu since its opening as the trading port in 1867. The Yangtze River connects Wuhu with the most prosperous cities in southern China such as Shanghai, Suzhou, Wuxi, Nanjing, and Hangzhou. After the treaty went into effect, Wuhu became an important channel through which a large number of western commodities entered the hinterland. Foreign companies and missionaries from Britain, the United States, Russia, Japan, and other countries came one after another. Eyeing an expansion of his family business and wealth, Li Hongzhang and his extended families also seized the opportunity. In 1877 he persuaded the emperor to move the rice-industry market from Zhejiang to Wuhu and played a major role in its development. The Li family invested heavily in property there and owned a lot of real estate in the city. Stuart's report on the Wuhu real estate market provides us with a glimpse of the economic conditions in and historical background of Wuhu in the late nineteenth century.

With insufficient funds for the purchase of new land and limited choices in the real estate market, Stuart wrote several urgent letters first to V. C. Hart and then directly to the secretaries of the missionary society of the Methodist Episcopal Church in New York, asking them to reverse the decision and allow him to build the hospital on the initial site outside the city. In the letters, he explicitly expressed his frustration with the political struggles over decision-making power and authority. He made clear that, if his suggestion was not accepted, he would like to be transferred to Nanking or another city or even sent back to the United States. If the bishop would not do it, he threatened, "I will transfer myself." He specifically accused Hykes of abuse of authority in creating obstacles to his work: "I can safely say that when the Treasurer of a Mission sets himself up as Dictator to the Mission, there is going to be trouble."

On receiving the letter, the board quickly decided in Stuart's favor in March 1889. Even though the matter was settled to his satisfaction, the internal struggle over power and financial control of the construction of the hospital left Stuart with a bitter feeling. He wrote, "Yet at every turn I made I had, such apparently insuperable obstacles seemed to arise. . . . I could not help feeling discouraged."[8] This episode on the surface seems a small dispute over a small issue, but it allows us a deeper view of the internal decision-making and power struggle in the Methodist church's Central China Mission in its early years.

The construction was completed in October 1889 and consisted of one large building and two small ones, with a ward accommodation of seventy beds.

The hospital and a dispensary clinic in the city attracted patients. In a report Stuart wrote to the mission in 1890, in the roughly fifteen months from the opening of the hospital to the end of 1890, the number of new patients had risen to 2,670, and there were 8,020 visits paid to the hospital and dispensary. "These came from all parts of this rice-growing district, and by far the larger number of patients were farmers who were actively engaged in the principal industry of the province." There is also detailed report on the diseases he treated.

In particular, Stuart treated a large number of patients with chronic bronchitis or phthisis. From his description, we learn that respiratory diseases were common and serious in the Wuhu region at the time. Stuart wrote, "I once visited a small market town in that district, and in a few minutes had seen about fifteen cases of advanced consumption. Chronic Bronchitis is also caused and kept up by the heavy, moist atmosphere of this district, which constantly remains in this condition on account of the evaporation from the paddy-fields and stagnant supply-lagoons plentifully found through this country."

A large proportion of hospital patients were farmers. But rich merchants were also paying visits, which motivated Stuart to attract more patients from this community for the financial benefit. He told a story of a Guangdong merchant.

> The patient is the head man of the Canton Club of this place. One day, when out shooting with a coolie, the latter managed to lodge two charges of iron shot in his master's back: one striking between the shoulders, and the other in the left lumbar region. He was brought to the hospital, and we put him under Chloroform and removed all the shot that we could

find. He was highly pleased with our method of treatment, and later wrote a full account of the matter, which was published in the "Shen Pao." Through this case we gained the good opinion and good will of all the Cantoness rice-merchants and other business men of the place. This is of no small advantage to our work in a port where these men control so large a part of the commerce. The number of operations performed been (sic) amply repaid by their gratitude and good will. We hope to be able to do more for this class in the future.[9]

Stuart also made interesting observations about female patients, writing, "The customs of different places vary; and I find that the women here at Wuhu are not as averse to having a male physician to attend them, as they are at other places. A very large per cent of my patients are women" and "a large percent of these women come for diseases particular to their sex." As we know, in the traditional principals and custom, even in the late Qing, Chinese women would rarely see male doctors "不就男医." Stuart's remark here raises a very interesting question about women's responses to western medicine in the late Qing period in Wuhu.

Stuart saw this as a great opportunity for spreading the Gospel: "There are so many come, and their difficulties are usually so easily relieved, and they are so grateful and teachable, and the mothers, wives and daughters are so important a factor in the family, that I regard this work as the most hopeful for speedy results, of any."

From these documents we have learned that, in addition to his medical practice, Stuart was also very active in evangelical works: "I regard it as necessary that the medical missionary be not only a physician, but an evangelist in the most extended sense of that term. He has an influence up on the minds of his patients that no one else can have. I think that physicians who are not thoroughly consecrated to evangelistic side of missionary work, should not under any circumstances be sent out." He adopted a particular system, which he called the "itinerating dispensary."

> I have made up medicines in a concentrated form, which can be readily diluted with water. I carry these with books, scriptures and tracts in a basket upon my arm, and go out through the villages, (of which there are scores within the radius of a few miles from our home.), and dispense medicines to the sick, sell books to those who want them, and preach and talk to the people. In this way, I am enabled to have an "itinerating dispensary."[10]

There is no record showing how many locals converted to Christianity because of his efforts, but he made the following observation:

> Even among those who apparently take no interest in the Gospel, there is a better feeling towards us. While formerly we could not go outside of our gage without being called "foreign devil," now we very seldom hear it. Much of this good feeling can be traced to opening the dispensary here and on the street.[11]

Nevertheless, this "good feeling" was fragile. On May 12, 1891, an antimissionary riot broke out in Wuhu. A French Jesuit church and a school were burned down, and the British consulate was attacked. Fortunately, the Stuart family escaped to Shanghai without any harm. A series of antimissionary riots and his frightening Wuhu experience deepened Stuart's belief that the Chinese people were not "civilized" in the western sense and therefore a greater western presence was needed in order to protect those who came to save them. In a letter George Stuart sent to his parents after the Wuhu riot, he offered his own assessment of the situation.

> It is impossible to prognosticate what will be the end of these troubles. The disaffection seems to be wide-spread, and the Chinese officials seem unable to put a stop to it or to protect foreign lives and property. The ministers at Pekin [Peking] have informed the government that if they can not protect the lives and property of foreigners, they will have to take the matter into their own hands. This will mean a foreign protectorate over China, at least. It may mean the division of the country between the different foreign powers of Europe and America. No doubt this would be the best disposition of the matter, and a way to overcome some obstacles that are now in the way in the treaties. The great difficulty has been that the foreign powers have recognized China as a "civilized" nation. It stands on the same footing in the treaties as England, Germany or United States. This is not as it should be. China is not civilized in a western sense at all. Their ideas are entirely the opposite of what is usually regarded as true political economy.[12]

This perception of China and call for the application of force were typical among missionaries in China at the time. As the historian Joseph Esherick pointed out in his authoritative research on the Boxer Uprising, "Yet when the missionaries proved as unsuccessful as the merchants in turning Chinese concessions into a wider market for their spiritual wares, the frustrations turned them into leading advocates of Western firepower as a means to open China still further."[13]

Nanking Years, 1896-1910

In 1895 George A. Stuart and his family returned to the United States for a furlough, during which he studied bacteriology at the Harvard Medical School. He and his family members also gave speeches at local churches on China and their China experience. A letter from Stuart to his parents, dated July 2, 1895, described the questions asked by the audience in a church gathering in Harlan, Iowa: "The questions asked were very good ones, such as 'what is the condition of widows in China?' 'Do the Chinese believe in a future state?' 'Does conversion to Christianity change the Chinese character?' etc."

The George A. Stuart family returned to Nanjing in 1896 because he had been hired as the dean of the newly established medical department at Nanking University. He was soon appointed president of the university to replace John Calvin Ferguson (福开森), who moved to Shanghai to assist Sheng Xuanhuai in the building and management of the Nanyang Public School (南洋公学). Stuart worked in this capacity till 1908 when he moved to Shanghai to serve as the general editor of the Methodist Episcopal Church in China.

Nanking University was founded by Methodist missionary Ferguson in 1888. In 1907, it merged with the Union Christian College (宏育书院), which was a previous merger of two other missionary schools, the Christian College (基督书院) and the Presbyterian College (益智书院). The new school was renamed University of Nanking (金陵大学).

There is not much information in the collection on Stuart's work at the University of Nanking. One notable document that followed his death in 1911 is a special memorial issue of the *University of Nanking Magazine* for November 1911, in which articles written by Stuart's colleagues, fellow missionaries, and students recounted his life and his substantial achievements and lasting impact as a missionary, educator, and physician. An article by then president of the university A. J. Bowen highly praised his accomplishments.

> For ten years, under his conscientious and efficient management the School continued to grow and develop both in numbers and in real effectiveness. The standard of the school steadily improved and large additions to plant and equipment were made. The campus was enlarged to twice its former size, another story was added to the main dormitory and the YMCA building was erected,—nearly all by funds specially solicited by Dr. Stuart. During all these years, in addition to his heavy administrative work, he taught classes frequently in three departments— the theological, the College of Arts and in the Medical School."[14]

Other documents in the collection provided information on the mergers of the different schools.

Besides being a missionary doctor and educator, George A. Stuart also assumed the role of a US government official on some occasions. He was appointed US vice-consul in Chinkiang (Zhenjiang, Jiangsu) in 1901, and he accompanied USS Navy Admiral Louis Kempff's visit to Nanking in 1902. A note on the back of a photo marking this occasion (see following page) reads "Officials on the occasion of the

Figure 1.12: Officials on the occasion of the visit
of Admiral Kempff to Nanking.

visit of Admiral Kempff to Nanking, China. 1–Foreign office Tao-tai, 2–Admiral
Kempff, USN, 3–Dr. George Arthur Stuart, acting U.S. Consul at Nanking, 4–En-
Shou, Governor of Kiangsu Province."[15]

The roles missionaries played and their impact in the diplomatic and political
arenas are important topics in the study of the missionary history of China beyond
the traditional focus on their religious, educational, and medical activities. Many
missionaries served as translators or go-betweens who helped the military and the
Qing government deal with their conflicts with foreigners and the Boxer Uprising.
Some even became official diplomats, as in the case of John Leighton Stuart 司徒
雷登. George A Stuart's work as an official and state consul is certainly intriguing.
Unfortunately, the collection does not contain sufficient materials on this aspect
of his career. It will require further exploration of other sources to gain a more
comprehensive picture.

Conclusion

At the sixth triennial meeting of the Educational Association of China, held
in Shanghai in May 1909, George A Stuart delivered a lengthy and thought-
provoking presidential address. In the speech, he expressed a firm belief in the
importance and efforts of the missionaries "crossing seas and sacrificing life" in
order to "bring the evangel to those who are in greater darkness than he." However,
we see a departure from his earlier views and position and deep reflection on how

Christian education should be conducted in China. We can recall the letter he wrote to his parents after the Wuhu antimissionary riot in 1891 in which he was in favor of using political and military force to "overcome some obstacles that are now in the way in the treaties." After ten more years of living and working in China and witnessing destruction and death in the clashes between foreigners and Chinese, as well as the Boxer Uprising, he now reminded people in his speech that "Within moral and social limits, individual liberty is the highest privilege of man. Within similar limits, the development of a national life, by a people in accordance with methods of their own choice, is their inalienable right." The Chinese were "faithful to their heritage [and] they go adapting conditions as they find them to their peculiar ideals, and amalgamating their environment with their civilization. True, their ways are not our ways; their manners and customs not as ours; their civilization not our civilization. But that is no sufficient reason for wholly condemning it, or insisting in substituting Western civilization for it." Therefore, "These times call for a re-consideration, or rather for a further consideration, of our position as educators in China." What was required was "[h]earty co-operation with the Chinese educational authorities, and cordially yielding to them that which is legitimately their work; more careful study of Chinese ideals and view points; less of a determination to force upon them our methods, and to demand from them recognition of that we consider to be our rights."[16]

To George Stuart, political and military forces were no longer legitimate and effective means for Christian missions. Christian education had to respect Chinese culture and customs. This special collection provides just a glimpse of view changes and reflection by the early missionaries after many years living and working in China.

Notes

[1] Suzanne Barnett and John K. Fairbank,. *Christianity in China: Early Protestant Missionary Writings* (Cambridge, MA: Committee on American–East Asian Relations of the Department of History in collaboration with the Council on East Asian Studies, Harvard University, 1985), 2.

[2] John K. Fairbank, "Assignment for the '70's," *American Historical Review* 74, no. 3 (February 1969): 877–78.

[3] Evanston Ives Hart, *Virgil C. Hart: Missionary Statesman, Founder of the American and Canadian Missions in Central and West China* (Toronto: McClelland, Goodchild, and Stewart, [ca. 1917]).

[4] International Mission Photography Archive, University of California Digital Library, http://digitallibrary.usc.edu/cdm/landingpage/collection/p15799coll123.

[5] Shichao Tang, Guangzu Zhu and Chen Xia (唐世超, 朱光祖, 夏晨), Wuhu Yijishan yi yuan chuang yu he nian kao (芜湖弋矶山医院创于何年考), Wannan yi xue yuan xue bao (皖南医学院学报) 5, no. 2, (1986) 150–52.

[6] George A. Stuart, Our medical work at Wuhu, China. Inland Advocate, [1887?]. R. Stuart Hummel Family Papers, George Arthur Stuart and Wuhu General Hospital 1887–97. Box 11, Folder 2.

[7] R. Stuart Hummel Family Papers, George Arthur Stuart and Methodist Episcopal Mission, correspondence, 1886-1899. Box 10, Folder 6.

[8] R. Stuart Hummel Family Papers, George A. Stuart letter to the secretaries of the missionary society of the Methodist Episcopal Church, March 24, 1889. Box 10, Folder 6.

[9] R. Stuart Hummel Family Papers, Report of Wuhu General Hospital. Box 11, Folder 2.

[10] R. Stuart Hummel Family Papers, George A. Stuart letter to the secretaries of the missionary society of the Methodist Episcopal Church, March 24, 1889. Box 10, Folder 6.

[11] R. Stuart Hummel Family Papers, George A. Stuart letter to the secretaries of the missionary society of the Methodist Episcopal Church, March 29, 1889. Box 10, Folder 6.

[12] R. Stuart Hummel Family Papers, George A. Stuart letter to the parents. June 12th, 1891. Box 10, Folder 2, item 5.

[13] Joseph Esherick, *The Origins of the Boxer Uprising* (Berkeley: University of California Press, 1987), 75.

[14] A. J. Bowen, "George A. Stuart as an Educator," *University of Nanking Magazine*, special memorial issue, November 1911, 7–8, Box 10, Folder 8.

[15] R. Stuart Hummel Family Papers, George A. Stuart letter to the parents. June 12th, 1891. Box 10, Folder 2, item 5.

[16] "The Relation of Christian Schools to Racial and National Movements in China," presidential address by Rev. George A. Stuart, M.D., in *Records of the Sixth Triennial Meeting of the Educational Association of China, Held at Shanghai, May 19–22, 1909*, part 1, *Papers, Addresses, and Discussions* (Shanghai: Educational Association of China, 1909), 1–13.

2

Gaihōzu, Maps of Areas Outside the Japanese Territories Prepared by the Former Japanese Army in Libraries in the United States

Discovery and Processing

Azusa Tanaka, University of Washington
Shigeru Kobayashi, Osaka University

In the winter of 2014, a Map Collection librarian at the University of Washington, Matt Parsons, was moving the *Seattle Times* subject files from the Map Collection to the Microform and Newspaper Collections. In the process he found approximately three thousand sheets of old Japanese maps. A student assistant working under Parsons who was a Japanese native speaker noticed the value of these maps and eventually brought them to the attention of the Japanese studies librarian, Azusa Tanaka, one of the authors of this chapter.

The University of Washington (UW) Libraries is one of the largest and most innovative libraries in North America, with a collection exceeding 8 million print volumes and more than 1.35 million electronic books. It spans sixteen individual libraries in different locations such as UW Seattle, UW Bothell, UW Tacoma, and Friday Harbor.[1] One of these libraries is the East Asia Library, which holds monographs, periodicals, a selection of audiovisual materials, and other miscellaneous items mostly in the Chinese, Japanese, and Korean languages and some Tibetan and English. The collection is especially strong in areas of the humanities and social sciences. As of June 2020, the library contained close to 860,000 published volumes.[2]

In general at the UW Libraries, maps are housed in the Map Collection in the main library (Suzzallo Library). This collection is home to more than 270,000 map sheets, 86,000 aerial photographs, and 2,000 atlases.[3] Uncataloged foreign maps are stored together, and occasionally student assistants with foreign-language ability examine and sort them into drawers by language. Eventually language and subject specialists, if not the map librarian, assess these maps and decide whether or not to add them to the collection and how to process them. For some reason, this set of old Japanese maps had been deeply hidden in the huge map collection room for several decades.

The authors first met at the annual conference of the Pacific Neighborhood Consortium (PNC) in December 2013 at which Kobayashi gave a presentation on his research regarding Geographic Information Systems (GIS) usage as it relates to Gaihōzu (外邦図) and how much historical value they hold. This was a few months before the discovery of these old Japanese maps at UW Libraries. Therefore, when the maps were discovered, the Japanese Studies Librarian, Tanaka, instantly recognized them as Gaihōzu which needed to be treated with special care.

Gaihōzu are general topographic maps of areas outside former Japanese territories (Gaihō = 外邦 that were created from the beginning of the Meiji era (1870s) to the end of World War II (1945). These maps were either surveyed and drawn by Japanese surveying squads or reproduced from topographic maps drawn by the land surveys of other countries by order of the Land Survey Department of the General Staff Office of the former Japanese Army.[4]

In the middle of nineteenth century, Japan was facing a critical situation—either be colonized by western powers or colonize its own neighboring countries. Wars with neighboring countries were perceived as unavoidable. To conduct successful battles in foreign lands and effectively govern the colonies it acquired as a result of war, it became essential for Japan to create maps like the Gaihōzu.

Following Japan's military defeat in 1945, Gaihōzu were disposed of on a large scale by the Japanese military due to the highly sensitive nature of the information they contained. However, within a few weeks of the end of the war in September 1945 and through early 1946, some thousands of Gaihōzu were brought out of the places where they had been held by a group of Japanese scholars who feared that the maps would be scattered and lost.[5] These maps were gradually distributed to a number of universities, including Tohoku University, Ochanomizu University, Kyoto University, the University of Tokyo, Rikkyo University, Hiroshima University, and Osaka University. Today many Gaihōzu are also held by some public institutes, including the National Diet Library, the Gifu Public Library, the Geospatial Information Authority of Japan, and the National Institute for Defense Studies.[6]

The remaining *Gaihōzu* became the target of confiscation by the occupation forces, particularly the US Army Map Service (AMS) under the War Department, which was a map-making organization established in response to the military demand for maps of the Pacific and European theaters. Starting in 1944, the AMS focused on collecting maps of Japan and China, and after the war its focus shifted to maps of the Korean Peninsula, Manchuria, and Siberia in preparation for the approaching Cold War.

It is still unclear where and how the AMS captured Japanese military documents after Japan's defeat. It is known that many of the *Gaihōzu* now in the United States used to belong to the Land Survey Department of the Imperial Japanese Army General Staff Office (陸軍参謀本部陸地測量部, Rikugun Sanbō Honbu Rikuchi Sokuryōbu). They were collected by the occupation army, sent to US Far East Army Map Services located in Shinjuku, Tokyo.[7] It is also known that the Allied Forces issued an order that Japan reprint fifty copies of *Gaihōzu,* submit them to the Allied Forces, and then destroy the originals.[8] The surplus copies of such maps at the AMS were eventually transferred to public and academic libraries across the United States.

On the back of some of the maps held at the UW Libraries, there are stamps or handwritten notes of the original owners of the maps in Japan such as the Yokosuka Naval District (横須賀鎮守府, Yokosuka Chinjufu), the Imperial Japanese Army Narashino School (陸軍習志野学校, Rikugun Narashino Gakkō), and the Japanese East Asia Research Institute (東亜研究所, Tōa Kenkyūjo). While it is known that many maps were captured at the site of the Land Survey Department, these stamps suggests that some of the *Gaihōzu* may have been captured from or belonged to these institutions as well.

The Army Map Service Depository Program

During the Pacific War, the US Army did not have sufficient foreign country map coverage, so it made use of the resources at university and public libraries extensively.[9] Those partnering libraries informed the AMS of maps as they became available, and the military borrowed them from the libraries.[10] Partly in gratitude to the libraries that allowed the AMS to use their collections and partly to create map depositories to meet possible future needs, the AMS began discussing a potential depository program with cooperating libraries early in 1945.

Oregon State College (now Oregon State University, OSU) was selected as one such cooperating institution. A letter from Dr. W. D. Wilkinson, a member of the faculty of the Department of Geology at OSU at that time, to a map librarian at

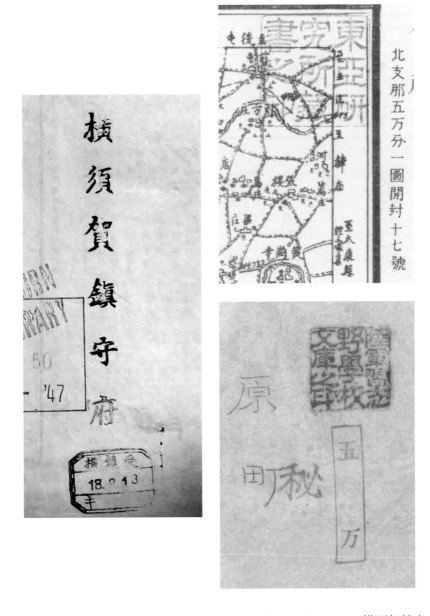

Figure 2.1. *Left*: A stamp of receipt by the Yokosuka Naval District (橫須賀鎮守府, Yokosuka Chinjufu). *Upper right*: A stamp of ownership from the Japanese East Asia Research Institute (東亜研究所, Tōa Kenkyūsho). *Lower right*: A stamp of ownership from the Imperial Japanese Army Narashino School (陸軍習志野学校, Rikugun Narashino Gakkō)

OSU dated April 3, 1945, indicates that the participation became possible thanks to Dr. Wilkinson's connection to the AMS. Wilkinson at the time was a captain in the US Army Corps of Engineers headquartered in Washington, DC, and he was in charge of the library of the AMS. He wrote:

> I have taken the liberty of seeing that Oregon State College was placed on the tentative list to receive distribution of certain maps published by the Army Map Service. You will hear from the Office Chief of Engineers in this respect. . . . I understand that approximately twenty thousand maps will be in this collection, and I am sure that it would be of great value in all sorts of research work. . . . It is my hope that the College will accept them if they are offered. If the librarian will simply leave them in the original boxes until my return, I will be more than glad to assist in cataloging and filing.[11]

In September 1945, the AMS officially invited certain institutions, including OSU, to join the depository program in which the AMS distributed maps and publications in the fields of geography, economics, geology, history, political science, agriculture, and related subjects. In return, the AMS asked the cooperating institutions to supply copies of any new maps they might receive through their own contacts.[12]

In addition to this original depository plan, later in November 1945 the AMS selected several institutions based on geography and asked if they might also be interested in accepting captured maps such as Gaihōzu. "During the course of World War II, American units captured a rather large quantity of foreign maps. These maps had been and are being shipped to the Army Map Service for evaluation and necessary incorporation in the A.M.S Library."[13] The AMS felt that some distribution of this material to civilian institutions would be both desirable and beneficial.

These geographically selected institutions were given the opportunity to request maps of the areas in which they had a particular interest. Oregon State University requested captured maps of Pacific countries, the Paris Basin, and the Alps region.[14] According to a memo exchanged in January 1949 between the librarians at OSU, the maps they received were printed in German or Japanese with some in Russian.[15]

Letters between the AMS and OSU helps us guess one potential path of custody of the Gaihōzu at UW. A letter from the AMS to OSU dated December 17, 1945, includes a list of 143 institutions that had accepted the original depository plan and were to receive twenty-five thousand map sheet pairs. Each map consisted of a set of two duplicate sheets—one for circulation and the other for preservation. UW is one of the institutions included on this list. However, this original depository plan

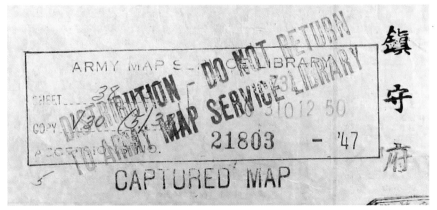

Figure 2.2. Stamps of the AMS

should not be confused with the distribution of the captured maps, as the captured maps were only furnished to select groups.[16] The AMS Depository List of February 27, 1950, is the only source we have that lists the twenty-seven universities and six public libraries in the AMS college depository program that received captured maps.[17] And this list does not include UW. Some of UW's *Gaihōzu* bear stamps of the AMS. Thus it is logical to assume that these maps came directly or via the AMS.

It is known that the captured *Gaihōzu* maps were first transferred to the United States War Department then AMS. The surplus map copies were eventually transferred to Washington Document Center, American Geographical Society Library, and the Library of Congress. Those ones transferred to LC via the Depository Program were finally distributed to the universities all over the United States.[18]

Most of UW's collection of *Gaihōzu* bear LC stamps showing accession dates between 1945 and the mid-1960s. Most likely these maps came to UW directly from LC or via AMS.

The Library of Congress Division of Maps Summer Sorting Project

After World War II, thousands of maps were being supplied to the LC Division of Maps (now the Geography and Map Division) from federal libraries and mapping agencies.[19] Duplicate maps and those not selected for the library's permanent collection totaled approximately fifty thousand copies a year.[20] To address this situation, the Special Processing Project, or Summer Sorting Project, was started in the summer of 1951.[21] It invited "qualified map librarians, faculty members and students, who were sponsored by collaborating university and college libraries and geography departments, to work with the staff of LC's Geography and Map

Division on map sorting projects."[22] Because the funding provided by LC for the project was limited, the majority of these participants were paid by their home institutions.[23]

Those faculty, staff, and graduate and undergraduate participants who were on salary from their home institutions were referred to as "cooperative participants" and were permitted to select up to 1,000 maps and/or atlases from the LC's unwanted duplicates to bring back to their home institutions for each week they worked.[24] As of 2001, LC had provided more than 2 million duplicate maps and atlases to 438 participants from 135 colleges and universities across the country, including UW.[25] The author contacted Peterson. He did participate in the Summer Sorting Project, but he didn't think he had brought back any Japanese language maps.

The earliest record of UW participation in the project (although it is possible that there had been participants from UW prior to this) appears in the Geography and Map Division's annual report of 1968 (for the fiscal year ending in September 1968) and again in 1971. According to the 1968 report, Gerald Peterson participated in the project from June 10 to July 5, 1968, as a "cooperative participant" and received 1,702 maps and 39 atlases. The report does not detail what kind of maps the participants brought back with them; however, the report does indicate that there were surplus maps in the AMS in that year: "And because of abnormally large transfer receipts (mainly from the Army Map Service) during the last 18 months, there is still a large accumulation of duplicates."[26]

The participant from UW during the summer of 1971, Patricia Mayo, worked for the project for ten weeks sometime between June 14 and September 3. She was not, however, a cooperative participant. She was one of four "LC-supported" participants that summer who received a salary from LC rather than maps or atlases in return for their time and labor.

Steve Hiller, who came tp the UW Libraries as a map librarian in 1979 recalls that the *Gaihōzu* maps were already in the Map Collection (in wooden map cases) when he arrived. He also remembers hearing that these maps came from the LC Summer Map Processing Project during the period of time when UW geography professor John C. Sherman was sending graduate students to participate. Sherman taught at UW between 1954 and 1986. Therefore, it is safe to say that these maps somehow came to the UW Libraries sometime after 1954, Professor Sherman's start date, but before 1979 when Hiller was hired.[27]

Samples of *Gaihōzu* from University of Washington's Collection

Since the discovery of *Gaihōzu* at UW Libraries, Tanaka has been contacting the recipients of AMS's captured maps mentioned earlier in order to better understand the provenance of UW's *Gaihōzu* collection. Oregon State University was the one

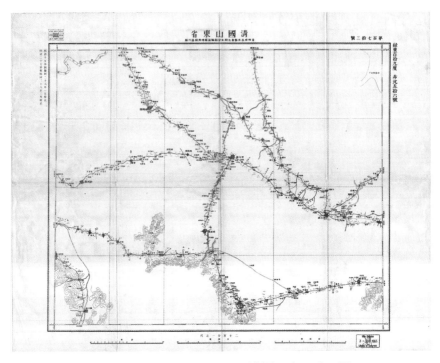

Figure 2.3. *Shinkoku nijūmanbun no ichi zu* (清國二十万分一圖), 1890s, Land Survey Department of the Imperial Japanese Army General Staff Office (陸軍參謀本部陸地測量部). Scale: 1/200,000.

positive respondent and eventually donated their entire collection of *Gaihōzu* (3,863 maps and 79 indices) to UW Libraries in July 2018.

2. The UW Libraries has discovered maps of broader areas, including Korea, Taiwan, China, and India in the east, and the Philippines and Australia in the south, as well as *Naikokuzu* (内国図), which are maps of mainland Japan (内国). The *Naikokuzu* series at the UW Libraries is nearly complete and covers most of the regions of Japan, including Hokkaidō, Tōhoku, Kantō, Chūbu, Kinki, and so on. An interesting point about this series is that each map of *Naikokuzu* actually consists of a set of two or three editions: the original prints created by the Japanese military during World War II and revised editions created after the war on the orders of the occupation forces. Because *Naikokuzu*, like *Gaihōzu*, were also captured at the same time, the UW Libraries decided to treat and catalog the two groups of maps together.

One of the unique *Gaihōzu* map sets at the UW Libraries is a partial set (twenty-four sheets) of a sixty-seven-sheet series titled *Shinkoku nijūmanbun no ichi zu* (清國二十万分一圖), which covers three provinces of the Qing dynasty

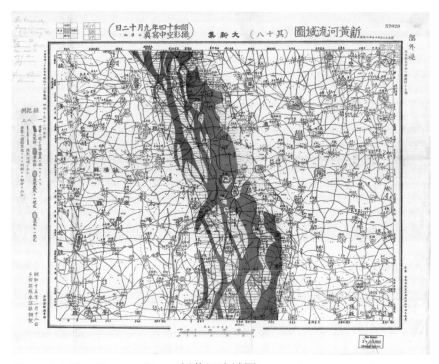

Figure 2.4. *Shin Kōga ryūiki-zu* (新黄河流域圖), 1940, Japanese Northern China Area Army, Tada Corps (日本軍北支那方面軍 (多田部隊)). Scale: 1/50,000.

(1644–1911): Shengjing Province (盛京省), which is now Liaoning Province (遼寧省); Chihli Province (直隷省), which is a part of today's Hebei Province (河北省); and Shandong Province (山東省). This set was created using the geographic data gathered by Japanese Army officers during their trips to mainland China in the 1880s. This set is rarely seen in Japan, nor is there a complete series in LC's *Gaihōzu* collection.[28] The maps at the UW Libraries show LC stamps dated 1965, indicating that these twenty-four sheets were once at LC but for some reason were donated to UW.

   Shin Kōga ryūiki-zu (新黄河流域圖) is another interesting set held by UW. This series, consisting of more than twenty sheets of maps, covers the Yellow River (黄河) basin area. In June 1938, the Chinese Nationalist Army burst the levee of the Yellow River to prevent the approach of the forces of the Japanese Army. The map series was created after this incident by the Tada Corps of the Japanese Northern China Area Army (日本軍北支那方面軍 [多田部隊]). It used Chinese maps created by the Henan Army Land Survey (河南省陸地測量局) in 1935 as a basis and modified them according to information gleaned from aerial photographs taken a year after the flood of September 1939 to detail the damage.[29]

Gaihōzu Collections in North America and the Challenges of Processing

Gaihōzu scholars in Japan have done extensive research on the *Gaihōzu* holdings in the United States, including at LC and the American Geographical Society Library (AGSL). The Library of Congress and AGSL both own unique sets of *Gaihōzu,* no copies of which remain in Japan. For example, included in LC's collection of six to seven thousand *Gaihōzu* are large-scale maps of the Kwantung Leased Territory, water supply distribution maps of northern Manchuria and northern China, Yellow River basin maps, and earlier *Gaihōzu* prints dating from the late nineteenth through early twentieth century. The AGSL holds approximately seven to ten thousand *Gaihōzu,* including maps of Korea that are coated with a sheet of film and lined with hemp cloth, maps of former Russian territories, and military maps with specific purposes such as indicating the enemy's military institutions (兵要地誌図, Heiyō chishi-zu), all of which are unique collections that Japanese institutions rarely own.[30]

So far we have found that at least the following US institutions own a collection of *Gaihōzu*; we will continue contacting other institutions to determine if any also hold *Gaihōzu.*

Auburn University; Clark University; Harvard University; Louisiana State University; Northwestern University; Stanford University, University of California, Berkeley; University of Chicago, University of Colorado; University of Georgia; University of Hawaii; University of Michigan; University of Texas; University of Washington

Among these institutions, some are merely aware of the existence of *Gaihōzu* in their library while others have conducted more in-depth processing such as digitizing, indexing, or/and cataloging their items; however, the specific ways these libraries process *Gaihōzu* are varied.

For example, the University of Hawaii owns about three thousand sheets of *Gaihōzu,* which were discovered in 2004 during the cleanup after a flood in its library. Librarians have sorted and organized them by series and entered the data in Excel; however, the cataloging process has not yet begun.[31]

At the University of Chicago, several thousand *Gaihōzu* had been in boxes for more than sixty years.[32] But as of the summer of 2014, 98 percent of them had been cataloged.[33]

The Stanford University Libraries holds a large collection of *Gaihōzu* covering a broad area, including Japan, China, Mongolia, North Korea, South Korea, the Philippines, and beyond.[34] The university has scanned all of the more than 120 sets of maps in the collection and making them available. Its portal, Gaihōzu: Japanese

Imperial Maps (http://stanford.maps.arcgis.com/apps/PublicGallery/index.htm l?appid=1ed3022fc7884690a2f137bce9dfe4fe), allows users to search for maps geographically through an index and then download the images at multiple resolutions.

As for UW, the Libraries is entering the descriptive data of these maps in Excel in a form intended for use as a finding aid. It follows the entities of the Gaihōzu Digital Archive developed by the Tohoku University Library and Institute of Geography, Graduate School of Science, Tohoku University (http://chiri. es.tohoku.ac.jp/~gaihozu/index.php?lang=en-US). We also added certain fields unique to US institutions, which show where these maps have been previously held (i.e., previous owners in Japan and the United States, such as the AMS or LC). The following are examples of the entities and possible values.

Title (図幅名)	根茂山
Surveyed country (測量機関国)	Japan
Surveyed institution (測量機関)	大日本帝國陸地測量部, 参謀本部, 陸地測量部
Survey date (測量時期)	大正4年測圖, 明治34年測圖, 大正13年修正測圖, 明治34年測圖, 大正15年修正側圖, 昭和17年第二回修正測圖, 昭和29年応急修正（行政区画）, 明治35年測圖, 昭和7年要部修正測圖, 昭和10年部分修正測圖
Plate date (製版時期)	大正6年
Code (記号)	温禰古丹嶋3號（共5面）, 温禰古丹嶋3號, 千島列島22號（共102面）[a]
Note	軍事極秘（戰地ニ在リテハ軍事秘密トス), renamed "軍事極秘（戰地ニ在リテハ軍事秘密トス" to "軍事秘密（戰地ニ限リ極秘トス）", 軍事極秘（戰地ニ限リ極祕), 応急修正版, 秘
Color (色)	1色（黒）, 3色（黒・赤・青）
Scale (縮尺)	1:50,000
Latitude/longitude (緯度経度)	E 154° 45′ 0″, E 155° 0′ 0″, N 49° 30′ 0″, N 49° 40′ 0″
Previous owners (Japan)	習志野士官学校
Previous owners (North America)	Army Map Services Map Library (1943) Library of Congress, Division of Maps (1951)

[a] *Gaihōzu* usually come in sets, such as 新黄河流域圖, 山東省十万分一地誌圖 and 荷澤方面情報圖. This entry can be used as a series title.

Cataloging maps in general can be a challenge, but cataloging a map collection more than seventy years old that was created by and for the military is even more challenging. We describe some of the challenges below.

Many *Gaihōzu* come in series that were geographically divided by the military for its own purposes. In many instances, the geographic names have changed since the time when the *Gaihōzu* were created. These divisions, moreover, do not necessarily correspond with current administrative units. For example, two of the provinces covered in the map mentioned earlier, *Shinkoku nijūmanbun no ichi zu* (清國二十万分一圖), are different from today's. Shengjing Province (盛京省) is now known as Liaoning Province (遼寧省) while what was Chihli Province (直隸省) is a part of what is now Hebei Province (河北省). The Library of Congress Subject Headings (LCSH) of course follow current administrative divisions instead of those used in the past by military organizations, so how to describe these regions on the maps can be a challenge in cataloging *Gaihōzu.*

In addition, *Gaihōzu* often include the dates of survey (測図時期) and plate making (製版時期), as well as publication (発行時期). In many cases, these maps were also revised several times. Therefore, all the dates could be important, but judgment of which actually indicate a change of edition can be difficult and requires study.

Finally, many *Gaihōzu* are marked with one of the five levels of confidentiality. From highest confidentiality to lowest, these are "military secrecy" (軍事機密), "military complete secrecy" (軍事極秘), "military secret" (軍事秘密), "complete secrecy" (極秘), and "secret" (秘).[35] Military Secrecy was typically used for the fortified zone maps of the Japanese mainland. If there are two maps with the same title but different levels of confidentiality, should they be considered two different manifestations (editions of maps)? Or should they even be considered two different works (maps) altogether? In fact, Japanese scholars have done some research regarding the level of confidentiality in *Gaihōzu,* and they have figured, by interviewing the former Japanese engineers of the Land Survey Department, that these confidentialities would have been changed over time and location.[35] However, whether or not to include the level of confidentiality in the cataloging record is a question to consider.

Some of the institutions mentioned earlier hold at least a few thousand *Gaihōzu.* It is inefficient for each institution to process these maps on their own, using different methods. With this in mind, Japanese catalogers within North America have started exchanging ideas and questions regarding *Gaihōzu* cataloging.

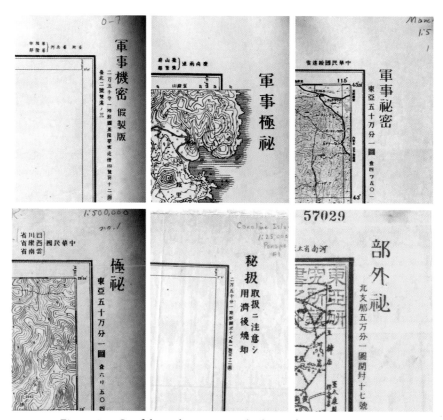

Figure 2.5. Confidentiality stamps, clockwise from upper right:
"military secret" (軍事秘密), "restricted to the department" (部外秘),
"secret" (秘), "complete secrecy" (極秘), "military secrecy" (軍事機密),
"military complete secrecy" (軍事極秘).

Usage of *Gaihōzu* and Cooperation between Librarians and Researchers

Gaihōzu, being clear records of both the physical topography and the history of much of Asia from the end of the nineteenth century through the first half of the twentieth, are of great educational and research value, far beyond their original military purposes.

For example, a recent GIS analysis tracing the development of irrigation aqueducts in the Guanyin (観音郷) area of Taiwan used materials published during the colonial period, including some statistics and topographic maps such as *Gaihōzu*. In addition to more recent maps from 1950–58 and 2003, two sheets of *Gaihōzu* from 1904 and 1925 were used to trace the development of these aqueducts.[37]

Another research group analyzed changes in land use along the Amur River watershed over the period of time from the 1930s to the 2000s. This transnational geosystem includes portions of Russia, China, Mongolia, and North Korea. In order to see the changes that have occurred in the northern part of China (previously Manchuria), these researchers examined *Gaihōzu* maps of the area dating from 1930 to 1940.[38]

The survey techniques, details, style, and contents of the maps reflect the background of the time period in which they were created. *Gaihōzu* are thus a precious resource for understanding detailed geographic and historical facts about the war and colonial territories. Discovery and accessibility of the *Gaihōzu* will accelerate a variety of research on such topics.

The *Gaihōzu* remaining in Japan are well organized. The National Diet Library's holdings are searchable via its online catalog. Tohoku University, Kyoto University, Ochanomizu University, Rikkyo University, and Komazawa University provide catalogs of several thousands items they own. Latitude and longitude information is also available on these *Gaihōzu*, thus GIS technology will allow us to easily see changes over time in the areas depicted on the maps. The *Gaihōzu* in our hands are now seventy years old, or older, and preservation is imperative. Digitization of *Gaihōzu* will be a good solution for preservation purposes and accessibility.

Because these *Gaihōzu* are scattered not only throughout Japan and the United States but also in the United Kingdom, the Netherlands, and so on, it is essential for librarians and researchers who are knowledgeable about *Gaihōzu* to communicate and develop a union catalog or database showing holdings information for the existing maps in Japan, North America, and elsewhere in the world. Before it can be accomplished, we need to identify all the institutions owning *Gaihōzu,* to create a place and opportunity to communicate with each other to understand what kinds of *Gaihōzu* each institution owns, and to coordinate methods for processing and cataloging these maps most efficiently.

Notes

[1] University of Washington Libraries, "UniversityLibraries Fact Sheet 2018," University Libraries, https://www.lib.washington.edu/assessment/stats/facts.

[2] Council on East Asian Libraries, "CEAL Statistics Data in Table," Council on East Asia Libraries Statistics, https://ceal.ku.edu/quick.

[3] University of Washington Libraries, "Map Collection and Cartographic Information Services," Map Collection, http://www.lib.washington.edu/maps/.

[4] Shigeru Kobayashi, "Japanese Mapping of Asia-Pacific Areas, 1873–1945: An Overview," *Cross-Currents: East Asian History and Culture Review* 2 (2012), http://cross-currents. berkeley.edu/e-journal/issue-2.

[5] Toshikazu Tamura, "Sanbo honbu kara no Gaihōzu kinkyū hanshutsu no keii," in *Kindai Nihon no Chizu Sakusei to Ajia Taiheiyō Chiiki: "Gaihōzu" e no Apurōchi*, ed. Shigeru Kobayashi (Suita-shi: Ōsaka Daigaku Shuppankai, 2009), 383–84.

[6] Tetsuya Hisatake and Satoshi Imazato, "Nihon oyobi kaigai ni okeru Gaihōzu no shozai jōkyō to keifu kankei," in *Kindai Nihon no Chizu Sakusei to Ajia Taiheiyō Chiiki: "Gaihōzu" e no Apurōchi*, ed. Shigeru Kobayashi (Suita-shi: Ōsaka Daigaku Shuppankai, 2009), 32–33.

[7] Masatoshi Nagaoka, "Rikuchi Sokuryōbu Gaihōzu Sakusei no Kiroku," in *Kindai Nihon no Chizu Sakusei to Ajia Taiheiyō Chiiki: "Gaihōzu" e no Apurōchi*, ed. Shigeru Kobayashi (Suita-shi: Ōsaka Daigaku Shuppankai, 2009), 102.

[8] Ibid., 103.

[9] John M. Anderson, "Forgotten Battles, Forgotten Maps: Resources for Reconstructing Historical Topographical Intelligence Using Army Map Service Materials," *Historical Geography* 29 (2001): 80.

[10] Mary Murphy, "History of the Army Map Service Map Collection," in *Federal Government Map Collection: A Brief History*, ed. Richard W. Stephenson (Washington, DC: Special Libraries Association, 1969), 4–5.

[11] E. B. Lemon to W. H. Carlson, April 3, 1945. RG009, Library Records, Special Collections and Archives Research Center, Oregon State University, Corvallis, Oregon. The following five letters also come from the same collection.

[12] W. D. Milne to Oregon State College Librarian, September 19, 1945.

[13] W. D. Milne to Oregon State College Librarian, November 15, 1945.

[14] W. H. Carlson to Commanding Officer, Army Map Service, December 8, 1945.

[15] Hanzel Saremal to Mr. Carlson, January 27, 1949.

[16] Charles F. Steele to Oregon State College, January 23, 1946.

[17] Shigeru Kobayashi, "Shiryo: Amerika Gasshukoku de Dainiji Sekai Taisen-go ni AMS (Army Map Service) kara 'Captured Maps' (Doitsu to Nihon kara sesshū shita chizu) o haibun sareta daigaku to toshokan no risuto," *Gaihōzu kenkyū nyūzuretā* 9 (2012): 70–71, http://www.let.osaka-u.ac.jp/geography/gaihouzu/newsletter9/pdf/n9_s5.pdf.

[18] Tetsuya Hisatake and Satoshi Imazato, "Nihon oyobi kaigai ni okeru Gaihōzu no shozai jōkyō to keifu kankei" in Kindai Nihon no Chizu Sakusei to Ajia Taiheiyō Chiiki: "Gaihōzu" e no Apurōchi, ed. Shigeru Kobayashi (Suita-shi: Ōsaka Daigaku Shuppankai, 2009), 39–40.

[19] Leanne, Kearns, "Summer Help for Geography and Map G&M Division Special Project Hosts Interns," *Library of Congress Information Bulletin* 60, no. 9 (2001), http://www.loc.gov/loc/lcib/0109/intern.html.

[20] Ralph E. Ehrenberg, "Administration of Cartographic Materials in the Library of Congress and National Archives of the United States." *Archivaria* 1, no. 13 (1981): 26.

[21] Library of Congress, *Report of the Librarian of Congress for the Fiscal Year Ending June 30, 1965* (Washington, DC: US Government Printing Office, 1966), 56, http://www.memory.loc.gov/service/gdc/scd0002/0014/00142141826/001421418326.pdf.

[22] Ehrenberg, "Administration of Cartographic Materials," 27.

[23] Kearns, "Summer Help."

[24] Harold M. Otness, "A Look at the Library of Congress Summer Map Processing Project," *Information Bulletin* 3, no. 1 (1971): 16.

[25] Kearns, "Summer Help."

[26] Library of Congress Geography and Map Division, "1968 Special Map Processing Project Report," in *Annual Report of the Geography and Map Division,* Appendix D, 3–4. Washington, DC: Library of Congress Geography and Map Division, 1969.

[27] Steve Hiller, email message to the author, June 16, 2015.

[28] Shigeru Kobayashi, "Washinton daigaku, Hawai daigaku kara no Gaihōzu shūzō no hōkoku," *Gaihōzu kenkyū nyuzūretā* 11 (2014): iii, http://www.let.osaka-u.ac.jp/geography/gaihouzu/newsletter11/pdf/n11_intro.pdf.

[29] Tatsuro Aratake, "1938 Yellow River Flood and 'Shin-Koga-Ryuikizu' (Maps of New Yellow River)," *Journal of Human Sciences and Arts* (Faculty of Integrated Arts and Sciences, Tokushima University) 24 (2016): 75–92.

[30] Satoshi Imazato and Tetsuya Hisatake, "Zai Amerika Gaihōzu no shozō jyōkyō: Gikai Toshokan to Amerika Chiri Gakkai Chizushitsu no chōsa kara," in *Kindai Nihon no Chizu Sakusei to Ajia Taiheiyō Chiiki: "Gaihōzu" e no Apurōchi,* ed. Shigeru Kobayashi (Suita-shi: Ōsaka Daigaku Shuppankai, 2009), 57–64.

[31] Meagan Calogeras, "Hawai daigaku Manoa-kō Hamiruton toshokan ni okeru Gaihōzu, Naikokuzu no aratana hakken to kakunin" [Captured Japanese maps: Discovery and cataloging at the University of Hawaii at Manoa Library], *Gaihōzu kenkyū nyuzūretā* 11 (2014): 9, http://www.let.osaka-u.ac.jp/geography/gaihouzu/newsletter11/pdf/n11_s2.pdf.

[32] University of Chicago Library, "Captured Japanese Maps Processed," *Map Collection News,* http://www.lib.uchicago.edu/e/collections/maps/news.html.

[33] University of Chicago Library, "Topographic Map Indexes at the University of Chicago Map Collection," Map Collection, http://www.lib.uchicago.edu/e/collections/maps/indexes/index.html.

[34] Stanford University Libraries, "Gaihōzu: Japanese Imperial Maps," *Topic Guides,* last modified October 21, 2015, http://library.stanford.edu/guides/gaihozu-japanese-imperial-maps

[35] Gaihōzu Kenkyukai, ed., "Shūsen zengo no rikuchi sokuryō-bu," *Gaihōzu kenkyū nyuzūretā* 3 (2005): 12–14, http://www.let.osaka-u.ac.jp/geography/gaihouzu/newsletter3/pdf/n3_s2_1.pdf.

[36] Kenjiro Tsukada and Akira Tomizawa, "Shusen zengo no Rikuchi sokuryobu," in *Kindai Nihon no Chizu Sakusei to Ajia Taiheiyō Chiiki: "Gaihōzu" e no Apurōchi,* ed. Shigeru Kobayashi (Suita-shi: Ōsaka Daigaku Shuppankai, 2009), 313.

[37] Shigeru Kobayashi et al., "Development of Irrigation and Land-Use Changes in the Taoyuan Tableland, Taiwan: Application of GIS Analysis," *E-Journal GEO* 9, no. 2 (2014): 175–76.

[38] Sergy S. Ganzey, Victor Srmoshin, and Natalya Mishina, "The Landscape Changes after 1930 Using Two Kinds of Land Use Maps (1930 and 2000), *Report on Amur-Okhotsk Project* (Research Institute for Humanity and Nature) 6 (2010): 252.

Bibliography

Anderson, John M. "Forgotten Battles, Forgotten Maps: Resources for Reconstructing Historical Topographical Intelligence Using Army Map Service Materials." *Historical Geography* 29 (2001): 79–91.

Aratake, Tatsuro. "1938 Yellow River Flood and 'Shin-Koga-Ryuikizu' (Maps of New Yellow River)." *Journal of Human Sciences and Arts* (Faculty of Integrated Arts and Sciences, Tokushima University) 24 (2016): 75–92.

Calogeras, Meagan. "Hawai daigaku Manoa-kō Hamiruton toshokan ni okeru Gaihōzu, Naikokuzu no aratana hakken to kakunin" [Captured Japanese maps: discovery and cataloging at the University of Hawaii at Manoa Library]. *Gaihōzu kenkyū nyuzūretā* 11 (2014): 9. Accessed February 16, 2016. http://www.let.osaka-u.ac.jp/geography/gaihouzu/newsletter11/pdf/n11_s2.pdf.

Council on East Asian Libraries. "CEAL Statistics Data in Table." Council on East Asia Libraries. Statistics. Accessed February 16, 2016. http://ceal.lib.ku.edu/ceal/php/quickview.php.

Ehrenberg, Ralph E. "Administration of Cartographic Materials in the Library of Congress and National Archives of the United States." *Archivaria* 1, no. 13 (1981): 23–39.

Gaihōzu Kenkyukai. "Shūsen Zengo no Rikuchi Sokuryō-bu." *Gaihōzu Kenkyū Nyuzūretā* 3 (2005): 11–22. Accessed February 16, 2016. http://www.let.osaka-u.ac.jp/geography/gaihouzu/newsletter3/pdf/n3_s2_1.pdf.

Ganzey, Sergy S., Victor Srmoshin, and Natalya Mishina. "The Landscape Changes after 1930 Using Two Kinds of Land Use Maps (1930 and 2000)." *Report on Amur-Okhotsk Project* (Research Institute for Humanity and Nature) 6 (2010): 251–62.

Hisatake, Tetsuya, and Satoshi Imazato. "Nihon oyobi kaigai ni okeru Gaihōzu no shozai jokyo to keifu kankei." In *Kindai Nihon no Chizu Sakusei to Ajia Taiheiyō Chiiki: "Gaihōzu" e no Apurōchi,* edited by Shigeru Kobayashi, 32–33. Suita-shi: Ōsaka Daigaku Shuppankai, 2009.

Imazato, Satoshi, and Tetsuya Hisatake. "Zai Amerika Gaihōzu no shozō jyōkyō: Gikai Toshokan to Amerika Chiri Gakkai Chizushitsu no chōsa kara." In *Kindai Nihon no Chizu Sakusei to Ajia Taiheiyō Chiiki: "Gaihōzu" e no Apurōchi*, edited by Shigeru Kobayashi, 55–69. Suita-shi: Ōsaka Daigaku Shuppankai, 2009.

Kearns, Leanne. "Summer Help for Geography and Map G&M Division Special Project Hosts Interns." *Library of Congress Information Bulletin* 60, no. 9 (2001). Accessed February 16, 2016. http://www.loc.gov/loc/lcib/0109/ intern.html.

Kobayashi, Shigeru. *Gaihōzu: Teikoku Nihon no Ajia Chizu*. Tokyo: Chuō Kōron Sha, 2011.

———. "Japanese Mapping of Asia-Pacific Areas, 1873–1945: An Overview." *Cross-Currents: East Asian History and Culture Review* 2 (2012). Accessed December 24, 2017. http://cross-currents.berkeley.edu/e-journal/issue-2.

———, ed. *Kindai Nihon no Chizu Sakusei to Ajia Taiheiyō Chiiki: "Gaihōzu" e no Apurōchi*. Suita-shi: Ōsaka Daigaku Shuppankai, 2009.

———, ed. *Kindai Nihon no Kaigai Chiri Jōhō Shūshū to Shoki gaihōzu*. Suita-shi: Ōsaka Daigaku Shuppankai, 2017.

———. "Shiryo: Amerika Gasshūkoku de Dainiji Sekai Taisen-go ni AMS (Army Map Service) kara 'Captured Maps' (Doitsu to Nihon kara Sesshū Shita Chizu) o Haibun Sareta Daigaku to Toshokan no Risuto." *Gaihōzu Kenkyū Nyūzuretā* 9 (2012): 67–71. Accessed February 16, 2016. http://www.let. osaka-u.ac.jp/geography/gaihouzu/newsletter9/pdf/n9_s5.pdf.

———. "Washinton daigaku, Hawai daigaku kara no Gaihōzu Shūzō no Hōkoku."

Gaihōzu Kenkyū Nyuzūretā 11 (2014): i–iii. Accessed February 16, 2016. http://www.let.osaka-u.ac.jp/geography/gaihouzu/newsletter11/pdf/n11_intro. pdf.

Kobayashi, Shigeru, Yusuke Morino, Hiroshi Kadono, Kenichi Tadakuma, Azusa Kojima, and Akihiko Namie. "Development of Irrigation and Land-Use Changes in the Taoyuan Tableland, Taiwan: Application of GIS Analysis." *E-Journal GEO* 9, no. 2 (2014): 172–93.

Library of Congress. *Report of the Librarian of Congress for the Fiscal Year Ending June 30, 1965*. Washington, DC: US Government Printing Office, 1966.

Library of Congress Geography and Map Division. "1968 Special Map Processing Project Report." In *Annual Report of the Geography and Map Division*, appendix D, 3–4. Washington, DC: Library of Congress Geography and Map Division, 1968.

Murphy, Mary. "History of the Army Map Service Map Collection." In *Federal Government Map Collection: A Brief History*, edited by Richard W. Stephenson, 1–6. Washington, DC: Special Libraries Association, 1969.

Nagaoka, Masatoshi. "Rikuchi Sokuryōbu Gaihōzu Sakusei no Kiroku." In *Kindai Nihon no Chizu Sakusei to Ajia Taiheiyō Chiiki: "Gaihōzu" e no Apurōchi*, edited by Shigeru Kobayashi, 82–108. Suita-shi: Ōsaka Daigaku Shuppankai, 2009.

Otness, Harold M. "A Look at the Library of Congress Summer Map Processing Project." *Information Bulletin* 3, no. 1 (1971): 16–19.

Stanford University Libraries. "Gaihōzu: Japanese Imperial Maps." Topic Guides. Last modified October 21, 2015. http://library.stanford.edu/guides/gaihozu-japanese-imperial-maps.

Tamura, Toshikazu. "Sanbo honbu kara no Gaihōzu kinkyu hanshutsu no keii." In *Kindai Nihon no Chizu Sakusei to Ajia Taiheiyō Chiiki: "Gaihōzu" e no Apurōchi*, edited by Shigeru Kobayashi, 383–84. Suita-shi: Ōsaka Daigaku Shuppankai, 2009.

Tsukada, Kenjiro, and Akira Tomizawa. "Shusen zengo no Rikuchi sokuryobu." In *Kindai Nihon no Chizu Sakusei to Ajia Taiheiyo Chiiki: "Gaihōzu" e no Apurōchi*, edited by Shigeru Kobayashi, 306–25. Suita-shi: Ōsaka Daigaku Shuppankai, 2009.

University of Chicago Library. "Captured Japanese Maps Processed." *Map Collection News*. Accessed February 16, 2016. http://www.lib.uchicago.edu/e/collections/maps/news.html.

———. "Topographic Map Indexes at the University of Chicago Map Collection." Map Collection. Accessed February 16, 2016. http://www.lib.uchicago.edu/e/collections/maps/indexes/index.html.

University of Washington Libraries. "Libraries Fact Sheet 2015." University Libraries. https://www.lib.washington.edu/assessment/stats/facts.

———. "Map Collection and Cartographic Information Services." Map Collection. http://www.lib.washington.edu/maps/.

Acknowledgements

We thank Keiko Minami and Matt Parsons for discovering the *Gaihōzu* at the UW Libraries Map Collection. We also thank University Archivist at Oregon State University Libraries, Elizabeth Nielsen for her providing the correspondence between OSU and AMS which gave us a great insight about how *Gaihōzu* maps were distributed to universities. Ms. Setsuko Means at Library of Congress Geography and Map Division has also helped us understand how *Gaihōzu* might have donated to other libraries. We thank all of the colleagues and scholars who had done tremendous research on *Gaihōzu* and developed and are maintaining *Gaihōzu* Digital Archive.Special thanks to Dr. Ryohei Sekine and Dr. Kenta Yamamoto who were in the development team of the Archive and helped UW Libraries best plan organizing its *Gaihōzu* collection and developing the inventory. Earth Sciences Library & Map Collections has developed their *Gaihōzu* collection database which also gives us guidance on how to best organize this type of map collection. We thank tremendous effort and hard work of them especially the director, Julie Sweetkind-Singer and Ms. Shizuka Nakazaki. Last but not least, we thank Dr. Jidong Yang and Dr. Regan Murphy Kao who gave us the opportunity to present at *Beyond the Book: A Conference on Unique and Rare Primary Sources for East Asian Studies Collected in North America*.

3

The First Korean Rare Manuscript in Canada

The Min Family Correspondence Collection at the University of Toronto

Hana Kim, University of Toronto

Hye-Eun Lee, Sookmyung Women's University

The University of Toronto's Cheng Yu Tung East Asian Library is a treasure trove of Korean studies research resources and unique materials. Over the years, the library has undertaken numerous initiatives to add to its holdings, and with technological advances more effort has been placed on digitization initiatives both to increase access and to help with preservation efforts. These digitization initiatives have also had an added benefit of helping to strengthen relationships between the library and the communities it serves. This chapter highlights one such digitization collection—the Min Family Correspondence Collection—and will touch on the library's evolution in building its Korean primary source collection.

The University of Toronto's Cheng Yu Tung East Asian Library and Its Korean Collection

The University of Toronto Libraries system is the largest academic library in Canada and is consistently ranked in the top ten among academic research libraries in North America, having forty-two individual libraries holding outstanding collections in 341 languages.[1] One of the remarkable libraries at the University of Toronto is the Cheng Yu Tung East Asian Library. The Cheng Yu Tung East Asian Library can trace its origins to 1933, when Bishop William C. White, a former

Anglican bishop of Henan, China, heard about an outstanding Chinese library for sale consisting of approximately forty thousand volumes. This library had been built by the scholar Mr. Mu Xuexun (慕學勛 1880-1929), former secretary at the German Legation in Beijing. The Mu Collection was purchased and reached Toronto in 1935, marking the start of the university's Chinese collection.

With holdings of more than 654,000 volumes (2020 Statistics of the Council on East Asian Libraries), mostly in the Chinese, Japanese, Korean, and Tibetan languages, the library is one of the preeminent North American East Asian studies research collections.

In 1979, the Korean Collection was established with a grant from the Korean Research Foundation. With the grant, the library purchased a number of rare Korean books—duplicates from the Harvard-Yenching Library. As Korean programs at the university expanded, the collection increased. In the late 1980s, the Foundation for the Support of Korean Studies at the University of Toronto pledged one hundred thousand dollars to assist the library in more active acquisition of Korean research materials.[2]

In 1997, the University of Toronto was the first institution in Canada to join the Korean Collections Consortium of North America. This consortium is a cooperative collection development program sponsored by the Korea Foundation for the purpose of sharing resources and supporting Korean studies teaching and research programs in North America by providing library services to optimize access to and use of the Korean studies collections.[3]

The Cheng Yu Tung East Asian Library holds the digitized collection of two significant Toronto Korean-language newspapers: the *Minjoong Shinmoon* and *New Korea Times*. The digitization was funded by the National Institute of Korean History. Since 2009, the East Asian Library has also been working with the University of British Columbia Asian Library on the Korean Canadian Heritage Archives Project, which aims to create a nationwide online database system for Korean-Canadian cultural and historical resources.

In 1971, Dr. Ross McDonald (the son of missionary parents, born in Hoeryŏng-si, Hamgyŏng-bukto) taught the first university course on Korea, "Religion in Korean Society" at the Department and Centre for the Study of Religion. In 1977, Dr. Yu Chae-sin (유재신) offered a course entitled "Introduction to Korean Civilization" in the Department of East Asian Studies. Since its inception, the Korean Studies discipline has grown into an active program. With an expansion of the Korean Studies program at the University of Toronto, the Centre for the Study of Korea was established in 2006 with the goal of promoting critical approaches to research on Korea.

Figure 3.1. Min Sŏk-hong (*left*), Yun Kyŏng-nam (*center*), and Hana Kim (*right*) in front of the Cheng Yu Tung East Asian Library on May 30, 2013. Photo by Jay Seo. Courtesy of the Cheng Yu Tung East Asian Library, University of Toronto.

The Donation Background of the Min Family Correspondence Collection

The Min Family Correspondence Collection, consisting of 260 envelopes containing 623 pieces of correspondence, was received on October 6, 2006, as a donation from Mr. Min Sŏk-hong (閔碩泓 민석홍, Samuel Sukhong Min, 1936–) and Mrs. Yun Kyŏng-nam (尹慶男 윤경남, Yunice Kyungnam Min, 1936–). Min Sŏk-hong inherited these *kanch'al* (handwritten letters) (簡札 간찰) materials (written in literary Chinese) from his father, Min Kyŏng-hwi (閔庚煇 민경휘, 1903–78), who was the former director of Namsan Public Library in Seoul (October 31, 1956, to March 27, 1958, the thirteenth director). Min Kyŏng-hwi in turn inherited them from his mother, Yu Chin-gyŏng (兪鎭卿 유진경, 1879–1973).

In early 2005, Min Sŏk-hong and Yun Kyŏng-nam, who is a translator and writer, visited the Cheng Yu Tung East Asian Library. They met with Hana Kim, then the Korea Studies Librarian, were given a tour of the Library, and were introduced to the Korean Collection. During the tour, the couple learned that the Korean Collection was the smallest and youngest of the East Asian collections (Chinese and Japanese). During an interview that Hana Kim conducted with the donors in early 2006, they mentioned that, although the correspondence might include private information about the family, the couple had decided to donate the correspondence collection to the East Asian Library at the University of Toronto. They believed that it would be better to make the material publicly accessible to scholars for research rather than let it remain unexamined.

Prior to this donation, in 2005, Min Sŏk-hong also donated the Yŏhŭng (驪興 여흥) Min Clan genealogical records, *chokpo* (族譜 족보), entitled "Yŏhŭng Min Ssi segyebo" (驪興 閔氏 世系譜 여흥 민씨 세계보). From March 17 to September 30, 2006, a photo exhibit featuring Yun Kyŏng-nam's photo collection of traditional Korean houses was organized. The exhibit was curated by Hana Kim, and this event was well received by the university community and the local community in the Greater Toronto Area.

At the invitation of the donors' daughter, Min Tong-yŏn (민동연), and her husband, Pak Chŏl-bŏm (박철범, Chul B. Park), a professor in the Department of Mechanical and Industrial Engineering, University of Toronto, and a fellow of the Royal Society of Canada, the donor couple immigrated to Canada from South Korea and settled down in Toronto in September 2001.

According to the donors, they donated the *kanch'als* to the University of Toronto in hopes that the correspondence collection would be translated from classical Chinese into the Korean language and contribute to shedding light on the social aspects and economic structure of the time. Another reason why they donated the collection was that they were hoping it might enhance the Korean Collection's position within the library, although this might be a very small addition to the East Asian Library collections.

Min Sŏk-hong (閔碩泓 민석홍) is the fourth son of Min Kyŏng-hwi (閔庚煇 민경휘, 1903–78) and Yi Kyu-suk (李奎淑 이규숙, 1905–2006), who had six sons and one daughter. Yun Kyŏng-nam (尹慶男 윤경남) is a great-niece of Yun Chi'-ho (尹致昊 윤치호, 1865–1945), who is also known by his pen name, Chwa-ong (佐翁 좌옹), and was an important politician during the late 1800s and early 1900s in the Chosŏn dynasty. He became involved with the Independence Club, one of the first modern political movements in Korea, and became president and editor of the newspaper *The Independent* (1896–98). He was the uncle of Yun Po-sŏn (尹潽善 윤보선, 1897–1990), South Korea's fourth president. Yun Kyŏng-nam is also a granddaughter of Yun Chi'-so (尹致昭 윤치소, 1871–1944), who was a councillor of Chungch'uwŏn (中樞院 중추원), the Privy Council of Korea.

According to Min Sŏk-hong, his father, Min Kyŏng-hwi, inherited *kyoji* (教旨 교지, royal edicts), *aekcha* (額字 액자, signboards), *chokcha* (簇字 족자, scrolls), *pyŏngp'ung* (屏風 병풍, folding screens), and *sŏch'al* (書札 서찰, letters) from his mother, Sukpuin (淑夫人 숙부인) Yu Chin-gyŏng (俞鎭卿 유진경,

Figure 3.2 and table 3.1, the family tree of the donor, Min Sŏk-hong (閔碩泓 민석홍), present a simplified version of the family from the twenty-ninth to the thirty-third generation.[5] Min Sŏk-hong is in the thirty-third generation.

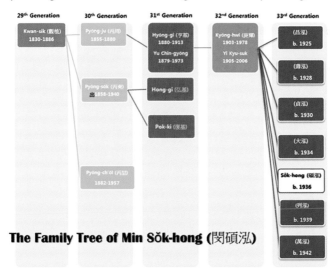

The Family Tree of Min Sŏk-hong (閔碩泓)

29th Generation	30th Generation	31st Generation	32nd Generation	33rd Generation
Kwan-sik (觀植 관식), 1825–86 Died of cholera while serving as deputy governor of the city of P'yŏngyang (平壤府 庶尹 평양부 서윤)	Pyŏng-ju (丙周 병주), 1855–80 Died in his twenties.	Hyŏng-gi (亨基 형기), 1880–1913 Married to Yu Chin-gyŏng (兪鎭卿 유진경, 1879–1973)	Kyŏng-hwi (庚輝 경휘), 1903–78 Married to Yi Kyu-suk (李奎淑 이규숙, 1905–2006)	6 sons and 1 daughter **4th son, Sŏk-hong** (碩泓 석홍, 1936–) Married to Kyŏng-nam Yun (尹慶男 윤경남, 1936–)
Buried in Yŏnghwabong, Ch'ongp'a-dong (청파동 연화봉) by his second son, Pyŏng-sŏk (丙奭 병석)		Was a *chaemugwan* (財務官, 재무관, financier) in the T'akchibu (度支部 탁지부, Ministry of Finance)		Sŏk-hong and Kyŏng-nam have two sons and one daughter
		Was a *sŭngji* (承旨 승지, royal secretary-transmitter) at the Pisŏwŏn (祕書院 비서원, Royal Secretariat) during the reigns of King Kojong and King Sunjong (純宗 순종)		

	Pyŏng-sŏk (丙奭 병석), 1858–1940 Adopted into the family of Min Kyŏng-sik (閔敬植 민경식), a member of the Sambangp'a (三房派 삼방파)	After the Ŭlsa Choyak (乙巳條約 을사조약, Protectorate Treaty), went to Japan to study forestry. Died at the age of thirty-three.		
	Was governor of the province of P'yŏngan (平安道 평안도) and a high official in the Department of the Royal Household (宮內府 궁내부) ……………………… **Pyŏng-ch'ŏl (丙喆 병철), 1882–1957**	Managed the inheritance of his grandfather, Kwan-sik, and the property of his uncle, Pyŏng-sŏk ……………………… **Hong-gi (弘基 홍기)**		
		Pok-ki (復基 복기) Former chief justice of the Supreme Court of Korea		

1879–1973), which were given to the family by the King Kojong (高宗 고종, 1852–1919, reigned 1863–1907). Later Min Sŏk-hong's siblings split the items and kept them individually. Among the items, Yu Chin-gyŏng, after Sŏk-hong's father, Min Kyŏng-hwi, passed away, gave the Min Family Correspondence *kanch'als* to Min Sŏk-hong in the late 1960s. He then brought it to Canada when he and his wife immigrated in 2001.[4]

Currently, the family heritagehome of the donor, Min Sŏk-hong remains in Seoul. The Min Hyŏng-gi's house is located at 105, Kye-dong Chongno-gu (종로구 계동 105번지). This district is called Pukch'on (北村 북촌, north village) since it is located north of Chŏnggyech'ŏn (淸溪川 청계천) and Chonggak (鐘閣 종각). It is also called Pukch'on Hanok Maŭl (북촌 한옥 마을, Pukch'on Hanok Village) and is a Korean traditional village composed of lots of alleys and *hanoks* (Korean traditional houses). Most *hanoks* are located between two palaces: the Kyŏngbokkung (景福宮 경복궁) and the Ch'angdŏkkung (昌德宮 창덕궁). This is the area where many royal families and families of high-ranking government officials used to live.[6] The Min Hyŏng-gi's Kye-dong house was designed with the floor plan of a house in a palace and built by a carpenter from a royal palace in the 1920s. The house is currently used as the Pukch'on Cultural Center, operated by the city of Seoul, and is number 229 on the Registered Cultural Properties list.[7]

The Content and Characteristics of the Min Family Correspondence Collection

The Min Family Correspondence Collection consists a total of 883 pieces (including 260 envelopes containing a total of 623 pieces of correspondence). Table 3.2 presents an overview of the collection.

Table 3.2. Status of the Min Family Correspondence Collection.

Accession Code	No. of Items	Remarks
National Library of Korea Accession Code MFC-0001 - 0235 - University of Toronto Accession Codes MFC-L-001 - 235J and MFC-E-001 - 236	236 + 536 = 772	*Kanch'al* (簡札 간찰)/letter with a *p'ibong* (皮封 피봉)/envelope including *komok* (告目 고목)/official accounts
National Library of Korea Accession Code MFC-LS-0001 - 0072 - University of Toronto Accession Code MFC-LS-001 - 072	72	*Kanch'al*/letter without a *p'ibong*/envelope MFC_LS_0006-0016 are *munjips* (文集 문집)/collected works
National Library of Korea Accession Code MFC-O-0001 - 0003 - University of Toronto Accession Codes MFC-LO-001 - 003F and MFC-EO-001 - 003	8 + 3 = 11	*Chobo* (朝報 조보)/official gazette, *chŏllyŏng* (傳令 전령)/message, *maemae munsŏ* (賣買文 매매문서)/purchase and sale documents, *p'aeji* (牌旨 패지)/master's power of attorney

National Library of Korea Accession Code MFC-P-0001 - 0004 - University of Toronto Accession Codes MFC-PL-001 - 004B and MFC-PE-001 - 004 FB	5 + 4 = 9	Personal letters with a *p'ibong*/envelope There are four *kanch'als*/letters that Min Pyŏng-sŏk sent to his biological father, Min Kwan-sik
National Library of Korea Accession Code MFC-ES-0001 - 0017 University of Toronto Accession Code MFC-ES-001 - 017	17	*P'ibongs*/envelopes without *kanch'al*/letters
National Library of Korea Accession Code MFC-PLS -0001- 0002 - University of Toronto Accession Code MFC-PLS-001 - 002	2	*P'ibongs*/envelopes without personal letters
Total	**883**	

Of the collection of 333 items (883 individual pieces, including letters and envelopes), 293 are *kanch'als*/letters and 40 are non-*kanch'al* items. Among the *kanch'als*, there are 3 letters written in Han'gŭl (한글, the Korean alphabet), and the rest are written in literary Chinese. All the letters are addressed to Min Kwan-sik (閔觀植 민관식, 1825–86) except 5 for which the recipient is not clear. In the collection, one of the earliest dated letters is from Min Kwan-sik's son, Min Pyŏng-sŏk (閔丙奭 민병석, 1858–1940), who was adopted into the family of Min Kyŏng-sik (閔敬植 민경식), a member of the Sambangp'a (三房派 삼방파), on February 21, 1881 (January 23, the eighteenth year of the reign of King Kojong). Most of the letters are concentrated between February 1884 (the twenty-first year of King Kojong) and July 1885 (the twenty-second year of King Kojong), except the letters whose dates are not identified.

By looking at the documents' issuers, it can be seen that these letters were written mostly by immediate family and other relatives of Min Kwan-sik (閔觀植 민관식), as well as by friends, acquaintances, villagers of the jurisdiction where Min Kwan-sik was positioned, and so on. Looking only at letters clearly identified by the names of their issuers, more than 44 percent were issued by other relatives—not by the immediate family members. It is also interesting to note that many of the letters were written by nephews of Min Kwan-sik.

Let us examine the characteristics of the Min Family Correspondence Collection. First of all, in general the *kanch'als* mostly concern important incidents and news of the affairs of the state. Again, the period during which Min Kwan-sik received the *kanch'als* is concentrated between 1884 and 1885, during which the major historical event was Kapsin Chŏngbyŏn (甲申政變 갑신정변), also known as the 1884 Coup. This can now also be verified using the contents of the donated *kanch'als* and is of high academic value.

Yŏng-ho Ch'oi describes the Kapsin Chŏngbyŏn in his article "The Kapsin Coup of 1884: A Reassessment" as follows.

On the night of December 4, 1884, a small group of reform-minded Koreans staged a bloody coup to seize political power in hopes of instituting drastic reforms that would transform Korea into a modern state. But unfortunately for Korea, these reformers only remained in power for three days, and their attempted coup ended in disastrous failure. This incident is known in Korea as the *kapsin chŏngbyŏn*, the political disturbance of the year *kapsin* (1884).[8]

In particular, the letter reproduced in figure 3.3. (front and back, Accession Code MFC-0066 by the National Library of Korea's call number MFC-L-066-F and MFC-L-006-B by the University of Toronto accession code system), which was sent to Min Kwan-sik, who was the Kosan Hyŏn'gam (高山縣監 고산현감, county magistrate of Kosan) by Han Kyu-dong (韓圭東 한규동) on December 13, 1884 (October 26, in the twenty-first year of King Kojong), describes in detail what happened during the 1884 Coup on December 4–6, 1884 (October 17–19 in the twenty-first year of King Kojong).

The letter in figure 3.4 (Accession Code MFC-0185 by the National Library of Korea's call numbers MFC-L-185-A and MFC-L-185-B and MFC-L-185-C by the University of Toronto Accession Code system), which was sent to Min Kwan-sik by Ch'a Pong-il (車鳳鎰 차봉일) on January 25, 1885 (December 10 in the twenty-first year of King Kojong), describes public sentiment after the 1884 Coup, which shook Seoul. Ch'a Pong-il also adds to this sentiment by explaining the uneasy political situation through the analogy that entering the palace is akin to stepping on thin ice.

In the collection, there are many letters from special interests asking (*chŏngt'ak* 請託 청탁) for favors. There are various types of requests. Among them, asking to pass the Civil Service Examination (*kwagŏ* 科擧 과거) is the most

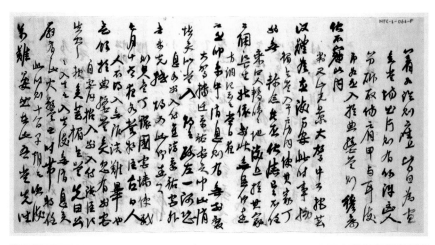

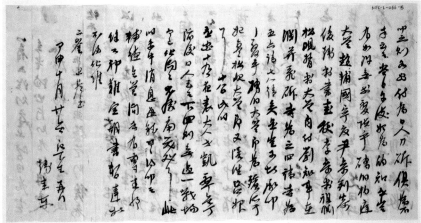

Figure 3.3. Front and back of a letter from the collection, University of Toronto Accession Code MFC-L-066-F (*top*) and MFC-L-006-B (*bottom*). Courtesy of the Cheng Yu Tung East Asian Library, University of Toronto Libraries.

common. Min Kwan-sik's female second cousin wrote a letter in Han'gŭl, asking Min Kwan-sik directly for the favor of passing the Civil Service Examination, stating, "Please take care of my son as he takes the *kwagŏ* by only counting on you." There are similar requests: asking for a government post through his son or asking for a favorable ruling or to quickly take measures to relocate enemy ancestors' graves from the petitions or lawsuits concerning graves (*sansong sakŏn* 山訟事件 산송사건) that were handled during Min's term of office as the Kosan Hyŏn'gam (高山縣監 고산현감, County Magistrate of Kosan) and the Kongju P'an'gwan (公州判官 공주판관, judge of Kongju). There are also letters asking for the district government office's protection or exemption from miscellaneous

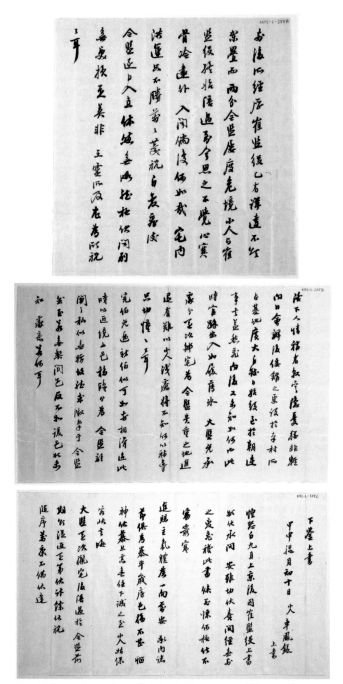

Figure 3.4. A letter from the collection, University of Toronto's Accession Code
MFC-L-185-A (*top*), MFC-L-185-B (*middle*), and MFC-L-185-C (*bottom*).
Courtesy of the Cheng Yu Tung East Asian Library, University of Toronto Libraries.

services, recommending people, and asking for the release of criminals. All these constitute historical evidence of the political power of the Yŏhŭng Min family.

Figure 3.5 is a letter written in Han'gŭl that Min Pyŏng-sŏk (閔丙奭) sent to his biological father, Min Kwan-sik. This is significant because during the nineteenth century most correspondence by well-educated male Confucian scholars (*yangban* 兩班 양반) was written in Hancha (漢字 한자, Chinese characters). The donor assumes that it was written in Han'gŭl so that Min Pyŏng-sŏk's biological mother could also read his letter, as Han'gŭl was especially used by women.

Initially the owners of the Min Family Correspondence Collection assumed that the letters were related to tenant farming, possibly written by *nonggam* (農監 농감, farm overseers), and so they believed that either Min Pyŏng-sŏk (閔丙奭 민병석) or Min Hyŏng-gi (閔亨基 민형기) may have been the recipient of the documents. However, after the National Library of Korea completed the content analysis, it was confirmed that they are *kanch'als* having all the characteristics described earlier.

Open Access to the Collection through Digitization

The National Library of Korea has conducted a reproduction project of ancient Korean publications preserved in outside countries for the purposes of surveying those publications and contributing to the collection of national publications' manuscripts by photocopying, collecting valuable ancient books, and providing researchers with academic information. Through this project, which began in 1982, the library has collected paper copies and microfilms of ancient Korean publications maintained in Japan, China, Taiwan, and France. Since 2006 the library has digitized valuable materials preserved in the US Harvard-Yenching Library, the US Library of Congress, and the Columbia University Library.

The research team of the National Library of Korea visited the University of Toronto to conduct research on the Korean rare materials of the Cheng Yu Tung East Asian Library in March 2012. Through the visit, the research team was able to prepare bibliographic records of 99 titles and 308 volumes of rare books. The basic metadata of these rare books are available on the Korean Old and Rare Collection Information System (KORCIS) which is a comprehensive list database of the ancient Korean publications preserved at the National Library of Korea. In addition, the team had a chance to examine the Min Family Correspondence Collection. After reviewing the rare manuscripts, the National Library of Korea confirmed that the collection has a distinct historical value and agreed to fund the digitization of the collection performed by the University of Toronto Libraries. For the digitization project, the National Library of Korea and the University of Toronto Libraries spent eight months evaluating and negotiating the digitization deal. During the period, the digitization project schedule, the project workflow,

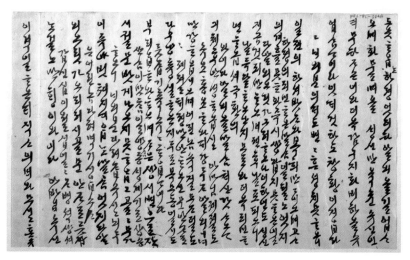

Figure 3.5. A letter from the collection, University of Toronto's Accession Code
MFC-PL-004-A. Courtesy of the Cheng Yu Tung East Asian
Library, University of Toronto Libraries.

digitization standards such as file formats of scanned images, quality control, and
the delivery of the digitized files were discussed.

Between January and March 2013, the agreement on the digitization project
was crystallized. The "Agreement for the Cooperative Project of Digitization of
Korean Rare Books between the University of Toronto Libraries and the National
Library of Korea" was concluded. The agreement carries forward the project with
the objective of providing a digital copy of a unique resource and easy access to
valuable historical documents on the libraries' websites. This, then, strengthens
the support of scholars and researchers in Korean studies.

The digitization work of the Korean rare manuscripts was carried out by
IT Services at the University of Toronto Libraries. The digitization work was
undertaken from April to December 2013. A total of 883 individual pieces,
including documents and envelopes, were created as digital copies. What follows
are the detailed digitization standards that were produced.

600 dpi, 24-bit color TIFF format scanned images.
Each complete object (letter plus envelope) was assigned a unique
identifier, and each image within the object was numbered sequentially.

JPEG files: three types of JPEG files were produced.
Thumbnail: 100 pixels on the short edge
Small: 500 pixels on the short edge
Large: 1,000 pixels on the short edge

Korean Old and Rare Collection Information System (KORCIS)

List of contributing institutions in Korea and foreign institutions

Bibliographic Record of the Min Family Correspondence Collection on KORCIS

Figure 3.6. The Korean Old and Rare Collection Information System (KORCIS) and Bibliographic Record and Image of the Min Family Correspondence Collection on it.

Although the image files of and bibliographic information about the reproduced materials of the Min Family Correspondence Collection are not yet available on the University of Toronto Libraries' website, they are currently publicly accessible through KORCIS.

Since its inception in 2004, KORCIS has played a leading role in researching ancient Korean books as a union catalog of Korean rare books and manuscripts, including records from sixty Korean and thirty-seven foreign institutions. As of 2021, it contains more than 468,000 bibliographic records and provides access to more than 53,000 full-text images. It is constantly being enhanced with new bibliographic and full-text image data.

Outcomes and Conclusion

Old documents are generally regarded as invaluable primary sources through which to study history as they provide firsthand testimony or direct evidence concerning a topic under investigation. In particular, *kanch'als* exchanged by individuals are priceless sources because one can examine at the closest distance the state, custom, or thought of a period, as they were not expected to be shared with others when they were written—especially the *kanch'als* of the Min family, which was at the center of political power during the late Chosŏn.

The donors' wish to offer access to the *kanch'al* collection by donating it to a public institution for scholars and researchers should be noted. In addition, the digitization work that provides accessibility to the resources anywhere greatly saves researchers' time and money. Through the digitization project by the two project partners and the research undertaken by the National Library of Korea, the content of the Min Family Correspondence Collection was identified, the creation of the metadata was completed, and access to the resources has been greatly enhanced.

This digitization project generated an opportunity to look back on the importance of old Korean documents and rediscover a lost cultural heritage. Libraries should continuously work to gather overseas Korean studies collections to increase the value of their collections, not as "stagnant collections" but as "living and breathing collections." At the same time, the overseas Korean studies collections should fulfill their role as essential partners in the scholarship of Korean studies.

Notes

[1] The figures are supplied by the University of Toronto Libraries Communication Office.

[2] "Our History," University of Toronto East Asian Library, accessed July 28, 2021, https://east.library.utoronto.ca/about/history.

³ "Member of Korean Collections Consortium of North America," University of Toronto East Asian Library, accessed July 28, 2021, https://east.library.utoronto.ca/content/member-korean-collections-consortium-north-america.

⁴ Hana Kim, email message to Min Sŏk-hong, May 2015.

⁵ Yŏhung Min Ssi Taejongjung Yŏhŭnghoe, *Yŏhŭng Min Ssi sebo* (Seoul: Yŏhung Min Ssi Taejongjung Yŏhŭnghoe, 2004), 450–55.

⁶ Sŏul T'ŭkpyŏlsi Sisa P'yŏnch'an Wiwŏnhoe, *Sŏul chimyŏng sajŏn* (Seoul: Sŏul T'ŭkpyŏlsi Sisa P'yŏnch'an Wiwŏnhoe, 2009).

⁷ "Munhwajae sojae," Cultural Heritage Administration, accessed July 28, 2021, https://www.heritage.go.kr/heri/cul/culSelectDetail.do?culPageNo=1&region=2&searchCondition=%eb%b6%81%ec%b4%8c&searchCondition2=&s_kdcd=00&s_ctcd=11&ccbaKdcd=79&ccbaAsno=02290000&ccbaCtcd=11&ccbaCpno=4411102290000&ccbaCndt=&ccbaLcto=00&stCcbaAsno=&endCcbaAsno=&stCcbaAsdt=&endCcbaAsdt=&cbaPcd1=99&chGubun=&header=view&returnUrl=%2fheri%2fcul%2fculSelectViewList.do&pageNo=1_1_1_0.

⁸ Ch'oi, Yŏng-ho, "The Kapsin Coup of 1884: A Reassessment," *Korean Studies* 6 (1982): 105–124.

Bibliography

Ch'oi, Yŏng-ho. "The Kapsin Coup of 1884: A Reassessment." *Korean Studies* 6 (1982): 105–124.

"Member of Korean Collections Consortium of North America." University of Toronto East Asian Library. Accessed July 28, 2021. https://east.library.utoronto.ca/content/member-korean-collections-consortium-north-america.

"Munhwajae sojae." Cultural Heritage Administration. Accessed July 28, 2021. https://www.heritage.go.kr/heri/cul/culSelectDetail.do?culPageNo=1&region=2&searchCondition=%eb%b6%81%ec%b4%8c&searchCondition2=&s_kdcd=00&s_ctcd=11&ccbaKdcd=79&ccbaAsno=02290000&ccbaCtcd=11&ccbaCpno=4411102290000&ccbaCndt=&ccbaLcto=00&stCcbaAsno=&endCcbaAsno=&stCcbaAsdt=&endCcbaAsdt=&1=99&chGubun=&header=view&returnUrl=%2fheri%2fcul%2fculSelectViewList.do&pageNo=1_1_1_0.

"Our History." University of Toronto East Asian Library. Accessed July 28, 2021. https://east.library.utoronto.ca/about/history.

Sŏul T'ŭkpyŏlsi Sisa P'yŏnch'an Wiwŏnhoe. *Sŏul chimyŏng sajŏn*. Seoul: Sŏul T'ŭkpyŏlsi Sisa P'yŏnch'an Wiwŏnhoe, 2009.

Yŏhung Min Ssi Taejongjung Yŏhŭnghoe. *Yŏhŭng Min Ssi sebo*. Seoul: Yŏhung Min Ssi Taejongjung Yŏhŭnghoe, 2004.

4

Preserving the Growing Collection of Japanese Canadian Redress Materials at the University of Toronto Libraries

Fabiano Takashi Rocha, University of Toronto

In the past couple of years, the University of Toronto Libraries has initiated dialogues with a number of members of the Japanese Canadian community regarding the preservation of archival materials related to the Japanese Canadian internment and redress. The materials are found in a variety of formats, including textual records, photographs, negatives, posters, audio recordings, video footage and other miscellaneous formats. The collecting of archival materials on the topic of Japanese Canadian internment and redress is fairly new to the University of Toronto Libraries.

In this chapter, I aim to provide a historical background to the Japanese Canadian internment experience, and the postwar redress movement, in an effort to illustrate the significance of this growing collection of archival materials.

Several key individuals, also called the "unsung heroes," are choosing the University of Toronto as a repository for their valuable documents consisting of their personal diaries, notes of numerous redress meetings, drafts of important documents, audio recordings, photographs, and other redress memorabilia. These collections highlight the significance of the events and the impact they have had on the history of the Japanese Canadian community and Canada as a nation.

From the collection development perspective, I would like to discuss the provenance of the materials, their academic value, the University of Toronto

Libraries' approach to digitization, and the provision of access to the interconnected collections.

This chapter aims to bring awareness of the existence of this unique and valuable collection of primary sources available for the support of Asian Canadian and Asian American studies programs, as well as fostering further collaboration with other academic and archival institutions.

Background and Significance of Japanese Canadian Internment and Redress

The value of the growing collection of archival materials related to internment and redress can only be understood in the context of the internment experience and the postwar redress movement.

In 1942, more than 22,000 men, women, and children of Japanese ancestry were stripped of their citizenship rights and labeled "enemy aliens." Although more than 75 percent of these individuals were naturalized or Canadian-born citizens, they were given twenty-four-hours' notice and then forcibly removed from their homes, businesses, and properties. The government would later confiscate these properties and sell them without the owners' consent. The government used the term *evacuation*, as if the people were being removed for their own protection. However, research has revealed that the internment of Japanese Canadians was highly motivated by the discriminatory attitudes directed toward Japanese Canadians since their early days of settlement.[1]

British Columbian politicians such as the then Minister of Pensions Ian Mackenzie and Minister of Labour George Pearson argued that "no Japanese could be trusted and that they must be driven out of the province and interned."[2] They took advantage of the anti-Asian sentiment that was deeply rooted in British Columbia to instigate fear of economic competition, social disruption and intermarriage, and personal and national security.[3] The loyalty of Japanese Canadians was questioned with the misguided argument that the Nisei (second-generation Japanese) with dual citizenship would be fighting for Japan instead of Canada in the event of war.[4] A meeting of political representatives from British Columbia, officials of the Department of External Affairs, and representatives of the Armed Forces and the Royal Canadian Mounted Police (RCMP) was held in Ottawa to discuss national policy on Japanese Canadians. Despite the RCMP representative's report stating that there was no indication that internment was necessary, British Columbian delegates were determined to see their wishes carried out and all persons of Japanese origin removed from the West Coast to locations east of the Rockies. From the blunt racism seen in the campaigning of British Columbian politicians and other statements from individuals, it was clear that national security was not the real reason for internment. In a private conversation, one politician from British Columbia "admitted that the war was a 'heaven-sent opportunity' to rid the province of the Japanese economic menace forever."[5] Furthermore, the Japanese were likely to not offer resistance, as their cultural norms emphasized duty and obligation, as well as the values of conformity and obedience.[6] Sadly, the continuous use of political propaganda such as false stories of sabotage at Pearl Harbor and pseudodocumentation by unidentified "eyewitnesses" of the dangers of the presence of people of Japanese origin contributed to public apprehension and exerted pressure on the government to expand its military presence in British Columbia.[7]

The War Measures Act, a federal statute adopted by the Parliament in 1914, was intended to be invoked during a crisis of wartime in order to give the governor in council (the Cabinet) the authority to respond quickly to emergencies. The Cabinet could pass orders and regulations judged necessary "for the security, defense, order and welfare of Canada."[8] The War Measures Act transferred that power from the Parliament to the Cabinet, and decisions were already being made without the awareness of Parliament. As an example, the Cabinet already had plans to sell Japanese Canadian properties, despite the fact that properties were supposed to be held by the government "in trust" to prevent them from deteriorating.[9] In addition, a series of orders-in-council were issued under the War Measures Act, which allowed the government to detain its own citizens and control their movements without being questioned.[10]

Although the main purpose of this chapter is not to draw comparisons between the internment experiences of the United States and Canada, it is valid to highlight some major differences illustrating the ways in which Japanese Canadians were treated more harshly than Japanese Americans. As noted by Roy Miki, there were a number of differences in policy between the United States and Canada: American properties were not confiscated and liquidated, families were moved together, the costs of [Americans'] internment were borne by the US government.[11]

Japanese Americans suffered severe economic losses, as they needed to evacuate and take "only what [they] could carry."[12] Evacuees were given just a day to manage the sale of their houses, properties, and businesses. Local officials and residents took advantage of their precarious situation by offering a fraction of what the properties were worth or simply taking over what the government deemed "abandoned property."[13] In contrast, the Canadian government went as far as passing an order-in-council (PC 469) that granted the Custodian of Enemy Property the right to dispose of Japanese Canadian properties without the owner's consent. The revenue generated by the auctioning of the Japanese Canadian properties was actually used to pay the expenses of their own internment.[14] The government justified the custodian's actions as an "efficient" economic policy.[15] Ian Mackenzie had a central role in the process of dispossession of Japanese

Canadians. The sale of Japanese Canadian–owned farms was very appealing to him, as he planned to use the farms in postwar restructuring programs such as the Veteran Land's Act, whereby lands would be given at a cheap price to war veterans, allowing them to become farmers. This program would not only solve the problem of providing employment to veterans once the war was over, but it would also ensure that the uprooted Japanese Canadians would not return to the Pacific Coast.[16] Thus, although it was disguised as a measure for national security, its sole purpose was to ensure that economic competition by successful Japanese Canadian fishermen and farmers was completely eradicated.[17]

One of the toughest emotional challenges that Japanese Canadians had to deal with during the period of "evacuation" was the separation of married men from their families. This measure was explicitly contrary to one of the recommendations that resulted from the meetings of January 8–9, 1942, in Ottawa.[18] Families were divided, with the men sent to road camps in Ontario and women and children to ghost towns (former mining towns) in interior British Columbia such as Kaslo, Greenwood, Sandon, New Denver, and Slocan.[19] When it was clear that evacuation in family units was not a priority for the British Columbia Securities Commission, the organization in charge of overseeing the evacuation, a group of Nisei members of the Japanese Canadian Citizens Council (JCCC) led by Fuji Tanaka broke away from the main group and resisted cooperating with the government's policy of separating males from their families.[20] More than 100 males joined the resistance movement, and the group was known as the Nisei Massive Evacuation Group (NMEG). The males who refused to comply with the commission's orders that they be moved to road camps were rounded up by RCMP officers and later sent to prisoner of war camps in Petawawa and Angler, Ontario. More than 470 Nisei were interned behind barbed wire fences, without being charged with any crime.[21]

Over time the refusal of the federal government to recognize the problems associated with the splitting of families, and in particular the Japanese Canadian imprisoned males' fear that they could not provide for their families, became increasingly hard to ignore.[22] By July 1, 1942, the British Columbia Security Commission finally instituted a policy of family reunification.[23] Some families had the financial resources to voluntarily relocate in family units to "self-supporting" projects beyond the protected area.[24] Other families signed up to work in beet fields in Alberta and Manitoba in an effort to avoid separation. The ghost towns to which women and children were moved were not ideal, but they were far better than the livestock buildings they were forced to live in at Hastings Park when they were first moved from their homes.[25]

Another contentious issue derived from the relocation of Canadians was the effect it had on the education of Japanese Canadian children. When evacuation began in the spring of 1942, children outside Vancouver were forced to leave their classes and were placed in makeshift schools at Hastings Park staffed by untrained volunteers.[26] Of the twenty-two thousand Japanese Canadians forced out of the West Coast, about three thousand were schoolchildren. The provincial government was refusing to take any responsibility for the Japanese Canadians, and the Securities Commission had not implemented policies regarding education. Some older Nisei decided to volunteer and provide schooling to the younger ones.[27] Conditions in the camp schools were difficult, as none of the teachers had formal teacher training with the exception of the Japanese Canadian camp schools supervisor, Hide Hyodo (aka Hide Shimizu), who had graduated from the Vancouver Normal School, the province's premier teacher-training institution,[28] prior to the outbreak of the war. In addition, teaching materials were scarce, school facilities inadequate, and the generally harsh living conditions and absence of fathers who had been sent to road camps had an impact on the behavior of some of the children, making teaching considerably more challenging.[29]

The actions of the Canadian government, justified by the series of orders-in-council under the War Measures Act, led to the total uprooting of Japanese Canadians, their dispossession, the traumatic separation of families, and the obstruction of Japanese Canadian children's access to education. In the 1970s, researchers finally gained access to World War II government files once the thirty-year ban on access to them was lifted. Ann Gomer Sunahara's work provided proof that the uprooting of Japanese Canadians was politically motivated and disguised as a security measure.[30] As Miki pointed out,[31] despite of the argument that such drastic measures were taken for the sake of national security, thanks to Sunahara's research on government documents, we now understand them as an abuse of the War Measures Act. While the United States recognized that citizens could not be held against their will once the military emergency had passed, Canada was figuring out ways to retain control over Japanese Canadians once the war ended. The ultimate goal of politicians such as Ian Mackenzie was to ensure that Japanese Canadians never returned to the West Coast and thus to protect the economic interests of the anti-Asian British Columbian residents.

The First Attempt to Seek Compensation

There were two issues that Japanese Canadians felt were necessary to pursue: the achievement of full citizenship rights and an assessment of the economic losses resulting from the uprooting of the Japanese Canadians during the war. In 1947, the Japanese Canadian Committee for Democracy (JCCD) evolved into the National Japanese Canadian Citizens' Association (NJCCA) with representation from five different provinces. This organization's most important objective was to represent Japanese Canadians across Canada in their struggle for the franchise and in negotiations with the Bird Commission, which had been established by the government to investigate the financial losses resulting from the interment experience.[32]

The Bird Commission was set up on July 18, 1947, with the purpose of investigating the claims of Japanese Canadians who had been dispossessed and suffered economic losses during the internment period. It was in reality a mere facade established by the government to demonstrate its accountability, and it had no intention of providing the claimants with adequate compensation.[33]

The terms of reference were deliberately restricted to economic losses from the sale of properties in the care of the Custodian of Enemy Property. That meant that other issues, such as compensation for the violation of rights, loss of income, disruption of education, and emotional and psychological trauma, were excluded from the commission's purview.[34]

From the fall of 1947 to June 1948, the commission became aware of the amount of time that would be needed to process individual cases. The solution to the problem was to offer global compensation by category of properties liquidated. By eliminating individual claims, the commission managed to speed up the claims process and get funds to claimants much faster. This weakened the position of the NJCCA's representatives.[35] The Bird Commission proposed a settlement, offering 1.2 million dollars to the twenty-three thousand uprooted Japanese Canadians (52 dollars per person) with the condition that they sign a release form waiving their rights to file further claims for compensation.[36] The Toronto Claimants' Committee (TCC), originally a group in the NJCCA, strongly opposed the NJCCA's decision to accept the recommendations and encouraged Japanese Canadians to seek further substantial compensation.[37] Having had little impact on the government's position, the TCC decided to formally disband on May 28, 1951, outlining three main points of urgency that addressed issues of increasing the Canadian public's awareness of the injustices that had been perpetrated, the inadequacy of the awards recommended by the Bird Commission, and the injustices resulting from the exclusion of a group of evacuees from substantial and justifiable compensation.[38]

Beginning of the Redress Movement

With the disappointing settlement proposed by the Bird Commission, many in the community just wanted to forget the injustices of the past and move on. Discussions about adequate compensation would not surface again until the late 1970s, when the thirty-year ban on access to World War II government files was lifted, allowing for a reassessment of the government's wartime actions. Sunahara's *Politics of Racism* (1981) brought to light the truth about the reasons behind the government's uprooting of Japanese Canadians. It became clear that, though justified as a measure of national security, the uprooting was merely a tool to move forward the racist political agenda of British Columbian politicians and individuals.[39]

The Japanese Canadian Centennial of 1977 involved a nationwide effort to celebrate the achievements and substantial contributions of Japanese Canadians to the economic development of Canada, particularly in British Columbia, in the agriculture, forestry, and fishing industries since the arrival of Manzo Nagano, the first Japanese to settle in Canada in 1877.[40] It provided a venue for many Sansei (third-generation Japanese) to become aware of their parents' and grandparents' struggles and the deplorable treatment they had received from the Canadian government during World War II. This event was also a catalyst for the younger Sansei generation to question whether anything could be done to address the suffering and injustices of the past. It also marked the birth of the redress movement.[41]

In the same year, 1977, the National Japanese Canadians Citizens' Association (NJCCA) established a Reparations Committee to investigate the question of redress. The Japanese Canadian redress movement started drawing media attention in 1980, as journalists in Canada followed the development of the redress movement in the United States and gradually realized that the treatment of individuals of Japanese ancestry had been even more severe in Canada. Members of the JCCP formed a Redress Committee in 1981, with the objective of educating Japanese Canadians and other Canadians about the wartime injustices and to advocate redress. The Redress Committee organized major community forums in 1982, which drew the attention of major media outlets, namely, the *New York Times, Los Angeles Times,* and CBC Television's *The Journal.*[42]

Toronto became an exciting center of redress activism. The Sodan Kai was a group established in 1983 by the three lawyers Shin Imai, Maryka Omatsu, and Marcia Matsui, out of concern for the lack of community input and involvement in the redress issue. It aimed at educating the Japanese Canadian public about the developments in the United States, including a government report entitled Personal Justice Denied (1983),[43] which recommended that Japanese Americans demand a public apology and individual compensation. In addition to publishing the newsletter, *Redress News,* the Sodan Kai organized informal discussions held in members' homes that quickly evolved into public meetings and educational forums.[44]

The organization that officially represented the Japanese Canadian community was the National Association of Japanese Canadians (NAJC). Its National Redress Committee (NRC) was chaired by George Imai.[45] Despite Imai's antagonism to the Sodan Kai members' idea of holding a public meeting to gather feedback from the community, he finally agreed to it. More than three hundred people attended the event on May 15, 1983, at the Japanese Canadian Cultural Centre. Two subsequent public meetings were held, and it became increasingly evident that the great majority of the people who spoke out were in favor of either individual or group compensation or a combination of both.[46] The Labour Day Conference at the Prince Hotel, held on September 2–4, 1983, was a decisive event for the future direction of the redress movement. Members of the community questioned a $103,000 federal grant to Imai's NRC. The money was intended to be used to conduct a community survey through a telephone poll and questionnaire, with the objective of reaching a Japanese Canadian collective position on redress.[47] Concerns were raised based on the fact that the telephone poll was never conducted and the questionnaire was heavily biased toward the acceptance of group compensation, which was the NRC's position.

The NRC's position released to the press was that there should be acknowledgment of wrongdoing by the government and a fifty-million-dollar community compensation fund.[48] The responses to the questionnaire were few and mostly from Toronto and did not represent the views of Japanese Canadians across Canada. Victor Ujimoto, a professor of sociology at Guelph University, cautioned about the dangers of moving forward without adequate representation.[49] A motion was passed to create a new body in the NAJC, the National Redress Council, with nationwide representation that would diminish the role of Imai as the spokesperson for redress. This motion prompted him to resign, although he later withdrew his resignation.[50]

Needless to say, redress became a very divisive issue. In an effort to increase representation of the points of view of different groups concerned about redress, the Toronto JCCA Redress Committee was established on December 14, 1983. However, any motions that were not aligned with Imai's group and its position were simply squashed through what was seemingly a democratic process. Imai's group was pushing for acknowledgment first, with negotiations for compensation left to the future.[51] In order to convince the public, Imai argued that failure to accept a settlement when the government was receptive could risk losing a deal when a new government was formed. He also created a false sense of urgency by saying it was critical to settle, as many Issei (first-generation Japanese) and Nisei were dying.[52] In the meantime, Imai was conducting negotiations behind the scenes with Minister of Multiculturalism David Collenette, who was offering a five-million-dollar settlement "Justice Institute" for all Canadians. He had organized a delegation of "selected" Japanese Canadians to attend a ceremony where Collenette would announce the fund to promote racial harmony. As this maneuver was outside the NAJC's knowledge and consent, in a conference call members voted to remove Imai and dissolve the NRC.[53] A telegram was sent to Collenette, the prime minister, leaders of the opposition parties, and other ministers to immediately protest Imai's maneuver and halt the proposed plan, which it claimed "trivialize[d] the injustices suffered by the Japanese Canadians."[54]

Wesley Fujiwara, a Toronto physician, emerged as one the most outspoken activists who fought for the redress movement. Wanting to find out more about redress, he traveled to Winnipeg at his own expense and ended up taking the seat vacated by Imai following the dissolution of the NRC. Prompted by requests from individuals in the community, Fujiwara gathered more than three hundred signatures on a petition that outlined the community's wishes concerning redress. The petition included the following points: acknowledgment of the injustices and monetary compensation, comprehensive research to assess the suffered losses, negotiations with the government based on the research findings, and transparency in the negotiations.[55]

The meetings of the JCCA Redress Committee were tense. Jack Oki, the chair of the meetings and a supporter of Imai, used what Fujiwara referred to the tactic of "tabling a motion" by using other agenda items to avoid voting on the motion. This practice ignited the anger of Fujiwara, who walked out in protest, joined by other redress activists such as Stan Hiraki, Matt Matsui, Kunio Hidaka, Roger Obata, and Harry Yonekura.[56] With no hope of reasoning with Imai and his supporters, a group of "concerned Nisei and Sansei" began meeting at Marj and Stan Hiraki's house and later at Fujiwara and his wife Misao's home.[57] The group organized a public meeting at Harbord Collegiate, which was attended by more than five hundred people who became more aware of the possibility of redress. One of the major outcomes of this effort was the decision to create an official group detached from the Toronto JCCA Redress Committee.[58] A Toronto chapter was established and later affiliated with the NAJC. Fujiwara became the first president of the Toronto chapter of the NAJC.[59]

Two documents were critical to the success of the redress movement. *Democracy Betrayed: The Case for Redress* (1984) was a brief submitted to the government that outlined how it had betrayed democratic principles when Japanese Canadians were stripped of their citizenship rights. It gave a voice to the Japanese Canadians who had suffered the injustices and whose citizenship rights had been violated.[60] The second document that gave legitimacy to the compensation claim was a study conducted by Price Waterhouse on the losses incurred by Japanese Canadians resulting from the government's actions in confiscating and selling their properties. *The Economic Losses of Japanese Canadians after 1941: A Study* (1986) examined the documents published by the Custodian of Enemy Property's files and pointed out the limitations of the Bird Commission and the injustices resulting from its recommendations.[61] The conclusions of the study were as follows.

We concluded that the Japanese Canadian community suffered a total economic loss after 1941, of not less than $443 million. This figure is expressed in 1986 dollars.

The total loss is made up of the following elements—

Japanese Canadians suffered income loss of $333 million in 1986 dollars as a result of not being able to earn their normal income levels between 1942 and 1986.

The community suffered property losses of $110 million in 1986 dollars, principally because the value of property rose quickly between 1942 (when the Canadian government seized all property belonging to Japanese Canadians) and 1949 (when some of the Japanese Canadians were able to re-enter the property market).[62]

With the figures produced by the Price Waterhouse study, it was impossible for the government to argue that the amount it was offering was sufficient to cover the actual losses Japanese Canadians had suffered. Deals in the range of five to six million dollars were offered by the successors to David Collenette, ministers of multiculturalism Jack Murta and Otto Jelinek. Even the amount offered by Minister David Crombie, a twelve-million-dollar community fund, did not constitute an acceptable settlement.[63]

Following the failed negotiations with Crombie, the National Strategy Committee and National Council decided that a show of public support was necessary to put pressure on the government to address the issue of redress. Months were dedicated to preparations for an Ottawa Rally on Parliament Hill. Toronto became a center of activity during this time, and people devoted their time and energy to producing banners, distributing and collecting signed postcards by voters across Canada in support of Japanese Canadian redress, and fundraising for transportation and overnight accommodations at hotels.[64] On April 14, 1988, busloads of senior Japanese Canadians from Montreal, Hamilton, and Toronto assembled on Parliament Hill. About five hundred gathered to voice their outrage and urge the government to address the problem. A number of activists, politicians, and civil rights organizations spoke in support of the NAJC, making the case stronger, as Canadians' perception of redress was changing into understanding it as a major human rights issue. The Ottawa Rally served as the greatest incentive for the government to reopen talks on the redress settlement.[65]

Art Miki, the president of the NAJC, received a phone call on August 23, 1988, and was summoned to a meeting with Gerry Weiner, the minister of multiculturalism. The negotiations opened with a positive tone when Lucien Bouchard, minister of the secretary of state, entered and announced that "the government had come to accept the principle of individual compensation."[66] He opened the negotiations by offering fifteen thousand dollars per individual. Weiner was in charge of negotiating the terms of the settlement with the NAJC. The final agreement included twenty-one thousand dollars for each individual and fifteen million to establish a community fund. In addition, pardons were to be issued, upon application, for those convicted under the War Measures Act, and citizenship was to be reinstated to those who had lost it through deportation.[67] Those were the terms that constituted the redress agreement of September 22, 1988.

The redress settlement was achieved thanks to the strong determination of Japanese Canadians who fought to ensure that the government would take responsibility for having violated their citizenship rights. One of the most remarkable outcomes was the support the movement gathered through the National Redress Coalition, which brought together ethnic, cultural, religious, and political organizations, as well as prominent individuals from different walks of Canadian society.

Materials and Their Provenance

The provenance of the internment and redress-related archival materials at the University of Toronto is most varied. Some materials were acquired through connections by our faculty members and others facilitated by Mike Murakami, a well-connected member of the Japanese Canadian community. Table 4.1 below summarizes the collections.

Table 4.1. List and Description of Japanese Canadian
Archival Materials Collections

Collection	Description and Provenance	Status
F. G. Shears Collection	Consists of materials gathered by F. G. Shears in his capacity as the director of the Vancouver branch of the Custodian of Enemy Property Office. The office was established with the purpose of seizing and liquidating the properties of Japanese Canadians who were dispossessed and relocated during the World War II. When the war ended, the office also helped with the administration of Japanese claims for remuneration in accordance with the findings of the Bird Commission. The collection is composed of correspondence, reports, office documents, documents related to the Deep Bay Logging Company, newspaper clippings, and published items. **Provenance**: From the grandson of F. G. Shears via a faculty member.	Finding Aid available

Sharon Okuno Collection	Consists of photos taken at a National Council meeting of Japanese Canadians, an NAJC award of merit ceremony, and a redress celebration dinner. **Provenance**: Via Mike Murakami.	Finding aid available
Shirley Yamada Collection	Consists of photographs, slides, and negatives taken during Japanese Canadian redress campaign rallies in British Columbia, Ottawa, and Washington, DC, plus audio recordings of redress-related programs. **Provenance**: via Mike Murakami.	Finding aid available
Stan Hiraki Collection	Consists of typed minutes of meetings of the Toronto chapter of the NAJC and the Toronto Japanese Canadian Citizens Association (TJCCA) and thirty-five cassette tapes with recordings of various NAJC/TJCCA meetings concerning Japanese Canadian redress. **Provenance**: Via Mike Murakami.	Finding aid available
Wes Fujiwara Collection	Consists of recordings taped by Dr. Wes Fujiwara of redress-related meetings, including telephone conferences; NAJC meetings held in Vancouver, Toronto, and Winnipeg; redress debates; the Ottawa Rally; and meetings with Ann Scotton (executive director of the former Japanese-Canadian Redress Secretariat for the Government of Canada). Textual records are currently in the possession of his daughter, who lives in Victoria, BC, and they will be transferred to the University of Toronto at some future date. **Provenance**: Via Mike Murakami.	Finding aid available

Hide Shimizu Collection	Consists of documents (birth certificates, diplomas), family documents (sales of property, marriage certificates), numerous photo albums, Order of Canada award clippings and related documents and photographs, Order of the Rising Sun, and "Registered by Custodian" certificate. **Provenance**: Via Mike Murakami.	Finding aid available
NAJC Toronto Chapter Collection	The highlights of this collection include Harry Yonekura's files on redress, the applications for redress compensation that were processed by the NAJC, redress movement photographs, and posters used during the Ottawa Rally. In addition, board meeting and Annual General Meeting minutes are important for tracing the history and evolving nature of the NAJC— the organization that negotiated the redress settlement, whose current efforts are directed not only toward strengthening the Japanese Canadian identity but also toward advocating for human rights. **Provenance**: Via Mike Murakami.	Preliminary Inventory
Terry Watada Collection	Terry Watada is a poet, writer, playwright, musician, and composer. His publications include a novel, books of poetry, a history of the Buddhist churches in Toronto, and plays. He published a graphic novel in 2014. The collection consists of records created, accumulated, and used by Watada during his career. He used the internment of Japanese Canadians as an inspiration for his collection of short stories *Daruma Days*. He was very involved with the redress movement in the 1980s. **Provenance:** Via a faculty member.	Preliminary inventory

Tsuji Collection	Tsuji Communications, Inc., founded by Susan Tsuji (died 2002) and Roy Tsuji (died 2013), was a local production company and distributor/agent for the Nihon Hoso Kyokai (NHK) television network in Japan. The objectives of the company were to promote Japanese culture to Japanese Canadians and Canadians in general. Programs shot and produced by the Tsujis in Canada, such as *Hello Japan*, consist of interviews, musical performances, and local shoots of community clubs, organizations, and public events. Part of the video footage in the Tsuji Collection contains coverage of the Japanese Canadian redress movement. Mia Tsuji, the daughter of the founders of Tsuji Communications, initially reached out to the Multicultural History Society of Ontario hoping that it would accept the donation of twenty years of footage. Due to a lack of capacity and infrastructure with which to house the massive video collection, the University of Toronto Media Commons Media Archives was suggested as a home for this significant donation. **Provenance**: Via the Multicultural History Society of Ontario.	Preliminary Inventory

Academic Value

The historical significance of the Japanese Canadian internment and redress movement is undeniable. The movement succeeded in persuading the Canadian government to recognize the injustices it had inflicted on its own citizens, to issue an official apology, and to implement measures to prevent such atrocities from ever occurring again.

The academic value of these archival materials can be measured primarily by their relevance in supporting the University of Toronto's established minor in the Asian Canadian studies program, a multidisciplinary program that "provides students with an opportunity to better understand the historical, sociocultural, economic, and political forces that shape our knowledge about people of Asian heritage in Canada, and in relationship to Asia and the diaspora."[68] In addition to the University of Toronto's academic program, the materials are accessible to researchers who are not affiliated with the University of Toronto. Currently a

Ryerson University research team led by Professor Pam Sugiman is consulting materials from the F. G. Shears Collection for work they are doing for Landscapes of Injustice,[69] a multiorganizational research project that focuses on the dispossession aspects of the uprooting of Japanese Canadians during World War II.

Materials such as the audiocassettes taped by Wesley Fujiwara during the numerous redress meetings have been used as primary sources for the publication of significant works on redress, including Roy Miki's *Redress: Inside the Japanese Canadian Call for Justice* (2004), which that is highly referenced in this chapter.

History of Collecting and Preserving

The collecting of Japanese Canadian archival materials is fairly new to the University of Toronto Libraries, and the mandate continues to evolve according to the particularities that these new collections present. Recognizing the existence of the Nikkei National Museum and Cultural Centre, whose primary mission is to honor, share, and preserve Japanese Canadian history, as well as the Library and Archives of Canada, both carriers of national mandates, we had no intention to overstep any boundaries and collect materials that would be more appropriately housed by them. The main determining factor of our acceptance of the donations of redress materials was the strong Toronto focus, as many people who had been uprooted built their postwar lives in Ontario. As mentioned earlier, Toronto became a center for redress activism, and many leading figures of the movement were Toronto residents, including Wesley Fujiwara, Stan Hiraki, and Shirley Yamada. Therefore, keeping the materials that tell their stories where they originated seemed appropriate and responsive to the donors' wishes of preserving the materials locally. Given the University of Toronto's stature as the largest research institution in Canada, we embrace the responsibility of providing a home to historically significant primary sources that will support the research and teaching of academic programs in history, Canadian studies, human rights, and other areas of the humanities and social sciences.

Approach to Digitization and Provision of Access

One of the major challenges in handling archival donations is managing the donor's expectations of how materials will be processed, stored, preserved, and given access. The expectation of many is that all materials will be digitized and made accessible online. Although there are no concrete plans for digitization of the Japanese Canadian archival materials at this point, the library is open to responding to special requests provided that there is the capacity to allocate personnel time to conduct some digitization-related tasks. As a recent example, a request was received from an individual in British Columbia who is currently working on a documentary entitled *Nikkei Stories*. Hide Shimizu, the teacher who was in charge of overseeing all the Japanese Canadian camp schools during the internment period, and whose materials have been officially transferred to our collections, is one of the twenty people who will be featured in this documentary. As the requestor was not able to physically come to the library to access the collections, one of the librarians at the Fisher Library worked closely with her in identifying photographs from the Hide Shimizu Collection that portrayed Hide Shimizu's life as a child and her contributions to redress. Images were scanned and estimates of the cost of the digitization were given to the requestor.

For the time being, on-demand digitization seems to be the reasonable approach, but there may be opportunities for more comprehensive projects of digitization of photographs and selected textual records in the future, provided we have sufficient resources in terms of budget and personnel. For instance, the notion of a participatory archive could be further explored, and methods such as crowdsourcing could be considered for projects in which members of the community could assist with the identification of subjects in the photographs. Moreover, we must not neglect to consider the limitations of working with the newest technological tools, as the potential participants are part of an aging population that may not be comfortable with the latest technological trends.

Until opportunities for digitization projects are realized, access to archival materials will be available for those who are able to visit the library in person. The Thomas Fisher Rare Book Library allows the use of its collections by all scholars and researchers, whether or not they are affiliated with the University of Toronto. Video recordings and audiocassettes are held at the Media Commons Media Archives, as it provides the most suitable environment for media materials. Audio and video equipment are also available onsite.

Finding aids have been created for a number of the collections, but others are waiting to be processed. There are plans for the creation of a resource guide that will consolidate the information on Japanese Canadian archival collections and allow the public to consult their contents prior to their onsite visits.

Conclusion

The uprooting, displacement, and dispossession of Japanese Canadians constituted a serious violation of human and citizenship rights. The War Measures Act allowed the government to disguise its actions as measures of national security in order to push forward a political agenda defined by racist attitudes and economic opportunism. Thanks to the people's desire for justice, dedication, and perseverance, the redress movement succeeded, and it symbolized a major victory not only for Japanese Canadians but for Canada as a nation.

The several individual collections that were brought together via different channels are interconnected under the common theme of redress. The University of Toronto is committed to preserving and providing access to the Japanese

Canadian materials in support of research and teaching both at the university and by the scholarly community worldwide. The collecting of redress-related materials has created opportunities for strengthening the ties with the Japanese Canadian community, as well as fostering collaboration with other archival and academic institutions. The University of Toronto has had discussions with the Nikkei National Museum about devising strategies that will to avoid the duplication of efforts, as well as how to better inform our potential donors of our collection mandates and our capacity to store, preserve, and provide access to materials, so that they can take those matters into consideration when making decisions about where the home for their valuable materials should be. Last, but not least, we hope that providing access to our holdings will contribute to the success of other collaborative research projects such as Landscapes of Injustice.

Notes

*Several collections have been added since the submission of this paper. Please visit the following page for the most up-to-date information: https://east.library.utoronto.ca/resource/japanese/special-collections

[1] Roy Miki and Cassandra Kobayashi, *Justice in Our Time: The Japanese Canadian Redress Settlement* (Vancouver: Talonbooks, 1991), 16–17.

[2] Ken Adachi, *The Enemy That Never Was: A History of the Japanese Canadians* (Toronto: McClelland and Stewart, 1991), 203.

[3] Ann G. Sunahara, *The Politics of Racism: The Uprooting of Japanese Canadians during the Second World War* (Toronto: Lorimer, 1981), 7.

[4] Ibid., 8.

[5] Adachi, *Enemy*, 203–4.

[6] Ibid., 225.

[7] Ibid., 205–7.

[8] Roy Miki, *Redress: Inside the Japanese Canadian Call for Justice* (Vancouver: Raincoast Books, 2004), 88.

[9] Miki and Kobayashi, *Justice*, 88.

[10] Adachi, *Enemy*, 220.

[11] Miki, *Redress*, 88.

[12] Richard Reeves, *Infamy: The Shocking Story of the Japanese American Internment in World War II* (New York: Henry Holt, 2015), 66.

[13] Ibid., 75.

[14] Sunahara, *Politics*, 92.

[15] Miki and Kobayashi, *Justice*, 43.

[16] Sunahara, *Politics*, 89.

[17] Adachi, *Enemy*, 223.

[18] Yon Shimizu, *The Exiles: An Archival History of the World War II Japanese Road Camps in British Columbia and Ontario* (Wallaceburg, ON: Shimizu Consulting and Publishing, 1993), 59.

[19] Miki and Kobayashi, *Justice*, 37.

[20] Shimizu, *Exiles*, 60.

[21] Miki and Kobayashi, *Justice*, 37.

[22] Sunahara, *Politics*, 57–64.

[23] Miki and Kobayashi, *Justice*, 37.

[24] Shimizu, *Exiles*, 60.

[25] Sunahara, *Politics*, 69.

[26] Adachi, *Enemy*, 263.

[27] Frank Moritsugu, *Teaching in Canadian Exile: A History of the Schools for Japanese-Canadian Children in British Columbia Detention Camps during the Second World War* (Toronto: Ghost-Town Teachers Historical Society, 2001), 3–4.

[28] Moritsugu, *Teaching*, 35.

[29] Ibid., 8.

[30] Miki and Kobayashi, *Justice*, 60.

[31] Miki, *Redress*, 89.

[32] Miki and Kobayashi, *Justice*, 56.

[33] Miki, *Redress*, 113.

[34] Miki and Kobayashi, *Justice*, 58.

[35] Miki, *Redress*, 114.

[36] Ibid., 125.

[37] Ibid., 126.

[38] Ibid., 131.

[39] Miki and Kobayashi, *Justice*, 60.

[40] Momoye Sugiman, ed., *Japanese Canadian Redress: The Toronto Story* (Toronto: HpF Press, 2000), 84.

[41] Ibid., 92.

[42] Miki and Kobayashi, *Justice*, 64–65.

[43] United States, *Personal Justice Denied: Report of the Commission on Wartime Relocation and Internment of Civilians* (Washington, D.C.: The Commission, 1983).

[44] Miki and Kobayashi, *Justice*, 66–68

[45] Ibid., 105

[46] Ibid., 107.

[47] Miki, *Redress*, 155.

[48] Sugiman, *Toronto Story*, 123.

[49] Miki, *Redress*, 158.

[50] Sugiman, *Toronto Story*, 108.

[51] Miki, *Redress*, 194.

[52] Ibid., 172–73.

[53] Ibid., 184–85.

[54] Sugiman, *Toronto Story*, 134.

[55] Miki, *Redress*, 202–3.

[56] Ibid., 210–11.

[57] Sugiman, *Toronto Story*, 164–65.

[58] Ibid., 167–70.

[59] Miki, *Redress*, 213–14.

[60] National Association of Japanese Canadians, *Democracy Betrayed: The Case for Redress, November 21, 1984: [a Submission to the Government of Canada on the Violation of Rights and Freedoms of Japanese Canadians during and After World War II]* (Winnipeg: National Association of Japanese Canadians, 1984)

[61] Miki, *Redress*, 237–38.

[62] *Economic Losses of Japanese Canadians after 1941: A Study* (Winnipeg: National Association of Japanese Canadians, 1986), 1.

[63] Miki, *Redress*, 282–92.

[64] Sugiman, *Toronto*, 241-48.

[65] Miki and Kobayashi, *Justice*, 123–24.

[66] Miki, *Redress*, 304–5.

[67] Ibid., 307.

[68] "Minor in Asian Canadian Studies," Accessed June 9, 2015, http://www.uc.utoronto.ca/acs.

[69] "Landscapes of Injustice," accessed June 9, 2015, http://www.landscapesofinjustice.com.

5

Making the Sidney D. Gamble Photographs Digital Collection

Luo Zhou, Duke University

Sidney D. Gamble was a trained sociologist and an amateur photographer. He took nearly five thousand photographs during four trips to China between 1908 and 1932, covering a wide range of elements of Chinese society and providing a visual archive for an important period in Chinese history. Duke University Libraries received these nitrate negatives in 2006 as a donation from the Gamble family. This chapter summarizes the process of making the digital collection of Sidney Gamble photographs, addresses the many challenges involved in creating geographic headings, and discusses projects that aim to increase the visibility and accessibility of these photographs and to promote them to a wider audience in the world.

Introduction

In 1908, eighteen-year-old Sidney Gamble (1890–1968) arrived in China for the first time with his parents. The family visited Hangzhou, and the trip impressed Gamble so much that he came back to China three more times between 1917 and 1932, traveling throughout the country to collect data for socioeconomic surveys and to photograph urban and rural life, public events, architecture, religious statuary, and the countryside. As a sociologist and renowned China scholar, as well as an avid amateur photographer, Gamble used some of the pictures to illustrate his monographs, but most of his photographs were never published and therefore remain largely unknown.

About fifteen years after Sidney Gamble's death in 1968, his daughter, Catherine Curran, found a trove of nitrate negatives in a closet in the family's home in New York. Stored in beautiful rosewood boxes, the negatives were sheathed in individual paper sleeves and annotated with typed and handwritten captions (fig. 5.1). In order to properly preserve the negatives, Ms. Curran hired an archivist, who transferred them into archival sleeves and transcribed the captions onto typed labels. In 1986, Ms. Curran established the Sidney D. Gamble Foundation for China Studies to preserve the photographs and provide access to them. Duke University Libraries invited her to place her father's photographs in its Archive of Documentary Arts, and an agreement to bring the Gamble collection to Duke was signed in March 2006.

Figure 5.1. Gamble's nitrate negatives with handwritten captions

In October of that year, Duke University Libraries contracted with Chicago Albumen Works in Massachusetts to digitize the highly flammable nitrate negatives, a process that continued through the spring of 2007. The vendor also digitized the typed image labels to transform them into raw text, which became the foundation of the image captions and geographic headings in the Sidney D. Gamble Photographs digital collection. In early 2008, the geographic names on the labels were updated to Library of Congress subject headings and province names were added to the metadata, as well as standardized descriptions to support searching and browsing. The complete collection was published in fall 2008 and is accessible online at https://repository.duke.edu/dc/gamble. The collection marks the first comprehensive public presentation of this large body of work and includes photographs of China, Korea, Japan, Hawaii, and Russia.

Sidney Gamble's Four Trips to China

When Gamble visited Hangzhou in 1908, the Qing dynasty (1644–1912) was rapidly collapsing, and both the Empress dowager and the Guangxu Emperor died that winter. The final Qing emperor, Xuantong, was forced to abdicate in 1912, leaving China in the hands of inexperienced revolutionists headed by Sun Yatsen. The young Republic of China witnessed Yuan Shikai's failed attempt to revive the monarchy and in 1916 entered an era of competing warlords. Sidney Gamble arrived in China for the second time in May 1917, accompanied by Robert Ferris Fitch (who would become president of Hangchow Christian College in 1922) and Presbyterian missionary J. Hillcoat Arthur (Gamble 2004).[1] The three men traveled up the Yangtze River from Jiangsu Province deep into Sichuan Province. It was quite an adventure navigating the river's rapids in Sichuan, and Gamble took many photographs of his experiences. Figure 5.2, which shows him perched in a wheelbarrow wearing a pith helmet and holding his camera, is a fine representation of a western scholar doing fieldwork in Asia in the early twentieth century.

Figure 5.2. Sidney Gamble in a wheelbarrow
traveling from Xindu to Chengdu, 1917.

In the spring of 1918, Gamble visited relief camps in Tianjin, where a great flood had left millions of Chinese homeless the previous year (fig. 5.3). He joined the international staff of the Young Men's Christian Association (YMCA) in Beijing and became a member of the Princeton University Center in China in 1917. He visited Hebei and began to conduct fieldwork for a social survey of Beijing with an American missionary, John Stewart Burgess,[2] while teaching elementary economics and the principles of philanthropic and institutional work at Yenching University (Gamble 2004).

Figure 5.3. Flooded area being pumped by hand, Tianjin, 1918

In 1917, China entered World War I on the side of the Allies. Although China did not see any military action, it provided laborers who worked in Allied mines and factories. Gamble witnessed Republican China's celebration of the victory in the Forbidden City in 1918. Figure 5.4 documents an impressive military parade in front of the Hall of Supreme Harmony, the ceremonial center of imperial China. However, the Treaty of Versailles ignored China's plea to end concessions and foreign control of the country, and on May 4, 1919, students began to demonstrate against it. The May Fourth Movement, as it was called, quickly became a broader cultural movement focused on revitalizing and unifying China so that it could combat warlordism, exploitation, and foreign imperialism. With his camera, Gamble captured students from Peking University giving public speeches in front of the YMCA building (fig. 5.5).

Figure 5.4. Hall of Supreme Harmony, Thanksgiving Day review
with men and soldiers, Beijing, November 28, 1918.

Figure 5.5. Peking University students speaking and interacting
with police in front of the YMCA, Beijing, June 3, 1919.

In the winter of 1919, Sidney Gamble returned to California with negatives of some twenty-five hundred photographs taken during his second sojourn in China. In 1921, he published his first book, *Peking: A Social Survey*. In March 1924, he went back to Beijing to resume his post as secretary of the International Committee of the YMCA. From 1924 to 1927, he made several trips to Miaofeng Shan in the suburbs of Beijing, taking photographs and filming pilgrims visiting the mountain's famous goddess temple. (His original documentary footage was digitized and is available at https://repository.duke.edu/dc/gamble/RL10074-DBCAM-0001) He attended the funeral of Dr. Sun Yat-sen in 1925 and began to conduct research on prices, wages, and the standard of living in Beijing. He returned home in 1927.

In the summer of 1931, Gamble returned to China for the last time. That fall he served as research secretary of the National Association for the Mass Education Movement (MEM) and carried out surveys of village life in northern China. The MEM set up an experiment in Ding Xian, a county some two hundred miles south of Beijing, which aimed to create a new countryside through innovations ranging from planting better crops to staging village dramas and providing village health workers. Figure 5.6 depicts a farmer from Ding Xian with two big, beautiful pumpkins on a table. Gamble departed China for good in February 1932. Back in the United States, he published *How Chinese Families Live in Peiping* in 1933, followed by *Ting Hsien, a North China Rural Community* in 1954.

Figure 5.6. Model squash, Ding Xian, 1931.

The Creation of Image Captions and Geographic Headings

The typed image labels created based on Gamble's own handwritten and typed captions were digitized along with the fragile nitrate negatives and were transformed into raw text using optional character recognition (OCR), which became the foundation for the image captions and geographic headings in the Sidney D. Gamble Photographs digital collection. Figure 5.7 is an example of a digitized label.

```
210      Peking
1168     Kettlee Pia Lo
```

Figure 5.7. Ketteler Memorial Gate, Peking.

Gamble filed his negatives in the order of their roll and exposure numbers. In figure 5.7, 210 is the roll number and 1168 is the exposure number, so this photograph is the 1,168th image in the 210th roll (https://repository.duke.edu/dc/gamble/gamble_210A_1168). Peking is the location, and "Kettlee Pia Lo" is the title of the image. While "Pia Lo" must be "Pai Lou," "Kettlee" is a bit puzzling. Gamble may have misspelled the word or perhaps his handwriting was so unclear that the first archivist typed the wrong word when transferring it to the archival sleeve. The image is a typical *pailou* or *paifang*, a traditional Chinese architectural gateway. The archival-level scan of the negative provides a resolution of 3144 × 3947, which makes it possible to see a lot of details of the image. The tablet in the middle reads "克林德碑", which tells us that "Kettlee" should be "Ketteler" (a reference to Clemens von Ketteler, 1853–1900), a German diplomat who died in the Boxer Rebellion. The Qing government had been forced to build a *paifang*, called the Ketteler Memorial, which was dismantled in 1918 after Germany signed an armistice with the Allies. Therefore the title of this image is Ketteler Pai Lou. Beijing, the Pinyin spelling of the city, is used for Peking in our database.

In the spring of 2008, we extracted out of the raw text of the digitized image labels a list of all place-names and arranged them alphabetically. We removed duplicate names and had in the end a list of roughly a thousand entries on which to work. My work was to provide the Pinyin and Chinese characters for these place-names and to verify their physical location. I started by identifying similar names and deciding whether they were the same or not. This is relatively easy for names that are "almost" the same, for example, Ichang and Ichong should be Ichang (宜昌), the port city on Yangtze River in Hubei (湖北) Province. Pei Nin Ting, Pei Niu Ting, and Pei Niu Deng all refer to the same place, later identified as Beiniuding (背牛顶), a tourist attraction near Qinhuangdao (秦皇岛) in Hebei (河北) Province. After this step, the list was reduced to about five hundred relatively disparate geographic names. One difficulty in the process of decoding

Figure 5.8. Ketteler Pai Lou, Beijing, 1918

these geographic names was that the digitized images and the typed image labels resided in separate locations on the server. They were not yet linked at this time, so I was not able to compare the photographs with the captions and locations.

These placenames can be roughly grouped into three large categories. the first are those well known and popular among foreigners in China in the early twentieth century. Gamble's spelling of these places is standard Wade-Giles and easy to identify, such as Hangchow (Hangzhou 杭州) and the Lama Temple (Yonghegong 雍和宫) in Beijing. Geographic headings for these places were created rather quickly in 2008. The second is a small group of photographs that includes places in Russia, Japan, and Korea and unclear places such as "On the Sea." Some labels are even blank with no information at all. Photographs of Russia are mostly rural scenes with no clear landmarks, and Gamble wrote "Russia" as the location for these images, so their geographic heading is only the country name. The few cities in Japan and Korea are clearly captioned by Gamble, so their geographic headings were also created quickly. The names of well-known temples and other buildings in Japan and Korea were later identified by experts on the two countries. The last and the most challenging group includes images of places remote or less well known or those that have since changed their names. Gamble's romanization of these names is not always standard Wade-Giles and is often inconsistent. Location information for this last group of images was not properly identified until a year or two later, in 2009 or 2010, after more research was done on Gamble's trips and work in China. A few have been identified recently, more than six years after the database was created.

Challenges in Creating Image Captions and Geographic Headings

A regular process of creating captions and geographic headings for a photograph starts by looking at each image and the associated information to create the metadata before it is digitized. Because of the fragile nature of the nitrate negatives in this collection, digitization happened first, and captions and geographic headings were created afterward without access to the images. When the digital collection (https://repository.duke.edu/dc/gamble) was published in the fall of 2008, the photographs and their captions could finally be compared side by side. Research has been carried out since then, and there have been several important updates.

21A
109 Rowers, Fu Chou

Figure 5.9. Rowers in Fuling, 1917

Gamble filed his negatives with roll and exposure numbers in the order of his visits to different places. By simply arranging the photos by their roll numbers, I was able to understand his trips in detail and quickly discovered mistakes made earlier. Gamble used two cameras (he called them camera A and camera B), and the negatives have roll numbers ranging from 2A to 95A and 1B to 77B. He later used mainly camera A and used camera B occasionally, so we have roll numbers from 96 to 663, which actually are 96A to 663A. Gamble arrived at Shanghai in May 1917 and then traveled up the Yangtze River with two friends into Sichuan (四川) Province. Images in rolls from 2A to 95A and from 1B to 36B cover the places he visited on this trip, with the majority of them in Sichuan Province. The image in figure 5.9 has the placename of Fu Chou in roll 21A. Although the spelling is different, Fu Chou sounds very similar to FooChow (Fuzhou 福州), a city in Fujian (福建) Province, which was used as the location for this photograph. Now that I understood that this had to be a place in Sichuan, I went through potential places and realized that Fu Chou refers to Fuzhou (涪州), which sounds exactly like Fuzhou (福州) but has a different Chinese character. Fuzhou (涪州) later changed its name to Fuling (涪陵), a better-known name today. The database uses its current name as the geographic heading, while the typed label tells the user that Gamble used Fu Chou to describe it.

Figures 5.10 and 5.11 are images from rolls B25 and B22, so they are also places in Sichuan. There are three different places mentioned in the two photographs: Li Fan, Mao Chow, and Tsa Ka Lo. From B22 to B25, Gamble traveled from Li Fan to Tsa Ka Lo to Mao Chow. Considering the limited means of transportation and the challenging road conditions at that time in Sichuan Province, these places should be relatively close to each other.

Mao Chow was relatively easy to recognize as Maozhou (茂州), today's Mao County (Mao Xian茂县). Looking at Mao County on a Google map, there are two counties nearby: Wenchuan County (Wenchuan Xian汶川县) and Li County (Li Xian 理县). A famous Chinese photographer, Zhuang Xueben (庄学本)[3], visited this area in 1934. A map included in a published book (Zhuang 2007) illustrating his trip has Li Fan (理番) not far from Mao Xian. According to the *Dictionary of Chinese Geographical Names from Ancient Times to Present*,[4] Li County got its current name in 1945, and prior to that it was called Lifan County (Lifan Xian 理番县). Li County is in today's Aba Tibetan and Qiang Autonomous Prefecture (阿坝藏族羌族自治州). The Chinese character 番 means "foreign tribe" and 理 means "to manage." People living in this region are mainly Tibetans and Qiangs plus some Hui and Han Chinese. The Qianlong Emperor appointed rotating officials to rule this region as a means of incorporating minority groups in frontier regions of the Qing Empire. The character番 was removed from the county name during the Republican era because of its undesirable implications. The same entry

Figure 5.10. Two Men at a table, 1917.

Figure 5.11. Spinning on walk, 1917.

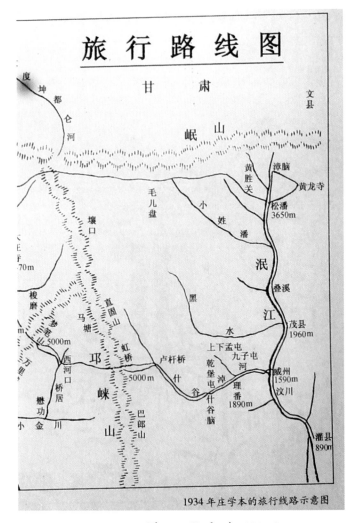

Figure 5.12. Zhuang Xueben's 1934 trip

in the dictionary also mentions Zagunao Town (Zagunao Zhen 杂谷脑镇), where the county government sits. The word Zagunao (杂古脑) comes from Tibetan, meaning "land of good fortune." Han Chinese heard it and spelled it Zagunao. It is not hard to match Zagunao with Tsa Ka Lo, Gamble's romanization of the place-name. While it was difficult to guess by itself, these three places are identifiable once they are put together as nearby places to which Gamble travelled.

The challenge in identifying Fuling, Mao County, and Li County also derives from the fact that all three places changed their names in the early Republican period. When Gamble arrived in 1917, they already had their new names but they were either still known as Fuzhou, Maozhou, and Lifan or the locals were still using the old names and Gamble picked them up. The administrative boundaries of these three places also changed. While Mao and Li counties belonged to the Sixteenth Administrative Prefecture of Sichuan (四川省第十六行政督察区) in the Republican period, they now belong to the Aba Tibetan and Qiang Autonomous Prefecture of Sichuan, which got its name in 1987. Fuzhou became Fuling County in 1913; Fuling City in 1995, administered by Chongqing on behalf of the province; and Fuling District of Chongqing Municipality in 1998. The database uses the current name of these places and their current administrative status. So figure 5.9 has Fuling, Chongqing, as its geographic location while figures 5.10 and 5.11 have Li Xian, Sichuan, and Mao Xian, Sichuan, respectively.

Jehol (Rehe 热河) is another example of name change. It is the name of a province that used to include part of today's Hebei (河北) Province, Liaoning (辽宁) Province, and the Inner Mongolia Autonomous Region (内蒙古自治区). It stopped being a province in 1955, and the name Rehe is no longer used. There are 94 photographs labeled as Jehol by Gamble from roll 410 to roll 425, and 24 of them in rolls 414, 415, 416, and 417 are images of the Tomb of Empress Dowager Cixi, in today's Zunhua (遵化) City in Hebei Province. Eleven images in rolls 413 and 418 have Malanyu Town (马兰峪镇) as the location, which is a town in Zunhua City. The remaining 59 photographs are images of rural scenes with no geographic identification. Photographs in rolls earlier than 410 are images of Qinhuangdao City (秦皇岛市) and Beidaihe District (北戴河区) in Qinhuangdao City, and photographs in rolls after 425 are images of Chengde (承德) City; all these places are in Hebei Province. It is very likely that those 59 rural images are villages and fields in the same province. But I decided to keep Rehe until further research supports my assumption.

So Village presented a different challenge. The name appears on photographs in rolls 44A to 51A and 17B to 19B. It is in Sichuan Province, and more specifically it is in the Mao County, Wenchuan County, and Li County area as photographs in rolls before and after those numbers were taken in that area. "Village" can be the translation of *cun* (村), *zhuang* (庄), or *zhai* (寨). So is likely the last name of prominent people living in this village. For example, we see village names like Li Cun (李村) or Zhou Zhuang (周庄), and their names can be translated as Li Village and Zhou Village. My initial guess for So Village was Suo Cun (索村) or Su Cun (苏村), but neither name was found in that area. Figures 5.13 and 5.14 are two photographs of So Village. Figure 5.14 shows a distinctive tower structure, and 5.13 shows an interesting guardian statue atop a gateway. The actual name and location of the village remained a mystery until a researcher in Sichuan called my attention to a blog post from China in 2015.

Figure 5.13. Town guardian crown, 1917.

Figure 5.14. Leaning tower, 1917.

According to the blogger, So Village is the Village of Suo Chieftain (Suo Tusi 索土司), called Wasi Tusi Guanzhai(瓦寺土司官寨). With this clue, I went through some local history resources and confirmed the blogger's findings. The village is in Wenchuan County, and the local residents are mainly Rgyalrong Tibetans who moved there from Tibet a long time ago. Rgyalrong Tibetans believe that they are the descendants of Dapengniao (大鹏鸟), a giant bird, and therefore they use Dapengniao as their totem. In figure 5.15, at the top of the gateway, there is a statue of a curved being with a bird's head and a human body holding a snake in its hands. The image matches the description of the village entrance in a local gazetteer.[5]

The first Wasi Tusi (瓦寺土司) was appointed by the Yingzong (英宗) Emperor in 1449 during the Ming dynasty. Tibetans don't have last names. The twentieth Wasi Tusi was given the last name Suonuomu (索诺木) by the Qianlong Emperor; later that last name was shortened to Suo (索). Gamble took a photograph of Suo Tusi and his son when he traveled to this village. Figure 5.16 is a photograph of Suo Tusi named Suo Daigeng (索代庚) and his son named Suo Guanyun (索观沄). Suo Daigeng was the twenty-third Wasi Tusi, and his son was thirteen years old in 1917 when Gamble traveled to their village. Interestingly, father and son are wearing typical Han clothing.

Figure 5.15. Detail of figure 5.13, the town guardian crown, 1917.

Figure 5.16. Suo and his son, 1917.

Captions and geographic headings in the digital collection continue to be updated as new research findings come out. Geographic headings are also challenging, as places change their names and administrative boundaries. In this digital collection, current placenames and administrative boundaries are used to describe a place. Ideally the database should present all forms of a placename, for example, Mao Chow (Gamble's spelling), Maozhou (Pinyin spelling of the same name), and Mao Xian (current name). Mao Xian is used as the name of the place, and Mao Chow appears in the scanned label displayed under the photograph, so as an image it is not searchable. Maozhou won't be shown at all unless it appears in the title of the photograph. The digital collection needs to develop ways to present multiple layers of information and make all keywords searchable so that researchers who may be familiar with only one placename can find the associated photographs and gain useful historical background knowledge by learning other names for the same place.

Translation of Geographic Headings and Image Titles into Chinese

The geographic headings in the Gamble photographs digital collection were transcribed into Pinyin and translated into simplified Chinese characters as soon as the place was identified. The translation of the photograph titles didn't start until 2012 and took about a year to finish.

One challenge in translation is the abbreviations Gamble used, apparently because of the limited space on the cover of the red wooden box where the negatives were stored. One example is "MEM worker." The geographic heading for this photograph is Ding County, where Gamble spent a lot time during his last trip to China, participating in the Mass Education Movement led by James Yen (晏阳初).[6] So MEM stands for National Association for the Mass Education Movement. Another Gamble's caption reads "Amer Bd Girls School, Middle School Room." "Amer Bd" turns out to be American Board of Commissioners for Foreign Missions (ABCFM).

Another challenge comes from personal names. Many of the portraits are of missionaries who lived in China for a long time and took a Chinese-like name well known in China. Gamble's friend and traveling companion Robert Fitch was the son of George Fitch, a Protestant missionary in China. George Fitch stayed in China for more than fifty years and had a Chinese name, Fei Qihong (费启鸿). Robert Fitch was born in Shanghai and later served as president of Hangchow Christian College; his Chinese name was Fei Peide (费佩德). Robert Morrison (1782–1834) was a Scottish evangelist and the first Protestant missionary in China. His Chinese name was Ma Lixun (马礼逊). Using their Chinese names will help researchers to associate the images in this photograph collection with existing Chinese-language materials about these westerners and to avoid the potential disconnect caused by transliteration of their names.

For images of Japan and Korea, titles and placenames were translated into Japanese and Korean. The translators were also able to identify important temples and other buildings, which added to the metadata and offered enriched keywords that researchers can use to locate specific photographs.

Adding New Materials: Lantern Slides

The outsourced digitization in 2006 and 2007 included two kinds of materials: the highly flammable nitrate negatives and the typed image labels on the sleeves that hold the negatives. The collection also has about 580 lantern slides, which were not processed individually until 2013. Each slide was compared to existing black-and-white images in the database, and 430 slides were matched to black-and-white photos in the database. All lantern slides were digitized and added to the digital

Figure 5.17. Devil dance at a lama temple in Beijing.

collection in 2014 (see https://repository.duke.edu/dc/gamble?f%5Bformat_facet_sim%5D%5B%5D=lantern+slides).

Lantern slides are often hand-colored glass slides that were commonly used in the first half of the twentieth century to project photographs or illustrations onto walls for better visualization. Gamble used these color slides in his public lectures introducing China to American audiences. The colors in these images are strikingly vivid, suggesting that they were crafted or the work was supervised by someone familiar with the scene or the culture. One can imagine the reaction of the audience when Gamble projected them onto the wall in his talk about mysterious China in the Far East. Whether it was a remote hillside village in a minority region in Sichuan or the famous Temple of Heaven in Beijing, the color versions are as lively as if taken by a recent visitor. Figure 5.17 is a comparison of black-and-white and the color slides of the same devil dance performer at Younghegong (雍和宫). The devil dance is an annual ritual to ward off bad spirits and disasters during the celebration of the Tibetan New Year at this lama temple. The color slide brings life to an image almost a century old.

Connection with the Audience

Trained in sociology and equipped with western technology, Gamble was a keen observer of the modernization of China unfolding not only in institutional changes (schools, prisons, hospitals) or new transportation technologies but also in people in all stages of life in all strata of society. The large number of images of Chinese life in the collection is also a record of his social survey work in Beijing,[7] the earliest of its kind ever done in China, and a reflection of his curiosity about and sympathy for Chinese people and their culture. It is quite natural that these photographs should attract academic researchers and the general public.

The digital collection has several features that help connect to users. Photographs are discoverable through Google searches and Duke University Libraries' discovery tool. Images with high resolution are freely accessible worldwide. Different social media tools, such as Facebook, Twitter, and Pinterest, are available for each photograph so users can share them with their friends. The comment feature under each photograph makes it easy for users to leave their feedback, and they sometimes point out our mistakes or provide more information about the photograph. In figure 5.18,[8] Gamble's original caption is "Steps." One viewer wrote, "These are the stone steps up to the Imperial Vault of Heaven." There are six photographs in roll 304, including one image of the Hall of Prayer for Good Harvests (祈年殿), which is not far from the Imperial Vault of Heaven. The two buildings belong to the Temple of Heaven. So the title of this image was updated to "Steps of Imperial Vault of Heaven, Temple of Heaven" and translated as 天坛皇穹宇的台阶.

Connection with the Audience: The Exhibits

One way to connect a digitized collection with a potential audience is through a physical exhibition. While a digital collection can reach an audience outside the boundary of a library building, and the translation of image titles and location information into Chinese, Japanese, and Korea makes it possible to reach those who don't read English in East Asia, there are many users who won't find them. A digital image can be buried and hard to discover among the vast sea of digital objects on the World Wide Web, and other people might not have access to the internet or are blocked by strong firewall. So, while a physical exhibit is costly and time consuming in preparation, it has the potential to reach a completely different audience. Looking at a photographic print hanging on a wall is a different experience compared to viewing an image on a screen. From 2012 to 2014, librarians worked with faculty and students at Duke University and curated a

Figure 5.18. Steps of Imperial Vault of Heaven,
Temple of Heaven, 1918–19.

traveling exhibition of the Sidney Gamble photographs in China (see http://sites.
duke.edu/sidneygamble/).

Beginning on June 16, 2013, at the Capital Library in Beijing, the traveling exhibition introduced Gamble's photograph collection to a Chinese audience at seven libraries and museums in Beijing and Shanghai. To Chinese visitors to the exhibit who didn't know about these wonderful photographs, this exhibit presented a rich collection of images of China and Chinese people from a different era when dramatic social and cultural reforms took place and new urban lifestyles and urban spaces emerged. They found that these images provided an interesting contrast with China today, which has also been undergoing profound and rapid social and cultural changes in the past few decades. The traveling exhibit ended at the Fudan University museum in the late fall of 2014.

The physical exhibit has brought more traffic to the digital collection. The library keeps statistics about the use of its digital collections by IP address. The total number of visits to the digital collection were 7,678 in 2012, 13,333 in 2013, and 13,237 in 2014. It is among our top ten collections in terms of traffic, and it is near the very top in terms of metrics that suggest engagement (such as duration of visit, returning users, and pages viewed or visited). The average visit duration across all the libraries' digital collections was four minutes and thirty-one seconds in 2013, while the average visit to the Gamble collection was fifteen minutes and forty-one seconds), so users are staying on the Gamble site more than three times longer than our average user. Also they viewed more than thirty pages per visit compared to about seven pages per visit for our average user. In sum, Gamble is one of the library's most heavily used digital collections by multiple measures.

Conclusion

Sidney Gamble published seven books on China and always used his photographs to supplement his narratives. He used color lantern slides in his lectures around the country. Those images are unforgettable and profoundly effective in their resonance and range. The Sidney D. Gamble Photographs digital collection is a comprehensive presentation of all his photographs and slides with metadata in English, Chinese, Japanese, and Korean. Published in 2008, the collection had the second-largest number of queries of all the libraries' collections that year. Over the past seven years, we have updated the tools, metadata, and platform, as well as curating eight exhibits featuring this collection. Duke University Libraries' Sidney D. Gamble Photographs Collection was migrated to a new platform (see https://repository.duke.edu/dc/gamble) in summer 2019. This provides enhanced features for presenting the images. The metadata across all digital collections have been structured so that it will lend itself to a much more comprehensive experience in which the users can effectively and efficiently share the materials. We are continuing to make this important collection accessible to more users in the world.

Notes

[1] Robert Ferris Fitch 费佩德 (1873–1954), born in Shanghai, was the president of Hangchow Christian College from 1922 to 1931. James Hillcoat Arthur 安而吉 (1885–1943) was a Presbyterian missionary based in Shanghai and the Hangzhou area.

[2] John Stewart Burgess 步济时 (1883–1949), was a missionary affiliated with the YMCA and a sociologist. He was head of the Sociology Department of Yenching University in 1924–26 and 1928–30.

[3] Zhuang Xueben 庄学本 (1909-1984), born in Shanghai, was an important early ethnographic photographer who extensively traveled and documented China's southern and western areas including Sichuan, Gansu, Qinghai and Yunnan. His first book,

published in 1937 by Shanghai Liangyou Tu Shu Gong Si, documented his trip to Sichuan and Qinghai in 1934. A reprint of the book includes a map of his trip.

Zhuang, Xueben /. 庄学本. Qiang Rong Kao Cha Ji : She Ying Da Shi Zhuang Xueben 20 Shi Ji 30 Nian Dai De Xi Bu Ren Wen Tan Fang / 羌戎考察记 : 摄影大师庄学本20世纪30年代的西部人文探访. Eds. Naihui Ma, Zhaowu Wang, and Wenjun Zhuang. Chengdu Shi: Sichuan min zu chu ban she; 成都市 : 四川民族出版社, 2007.

[4] Zang, Lishu and 臧励龢. 2015. 中国古今地名大辞典 / Zhongguo Gu Jin Di Ming Da Ci Dian Shanghai : Shanghai shu dian chu ban she, 2015; 上海 : 上海书店出版社, 2015

[5] 然后有一石砌门楼，门楼前上方有木刻大鹏鸟图腾，鸟嘴人身，足为鸟爪，手持大蛇一条 (There was a stone gateway, above which a wood statue had human body and bird head, holding a big snake)"

Zhongguo ren min zheng zhi xie shang hui yi. 1995. Wasi tu si shi mo. Wenchuan Xian: Zhongguo ren min zheng zhi xie shang hui yi Sichuan Sheng Wenchuan Xian wei yuan hui wen shi zi liao wei yuan hui. p.3.

[6] James Ye 晏阳初 (1890–1990) organized the National Association of the Mass Education Movement mostly famously at Ding Xian from 1926 to 1937 for rural reconstruction.

[7] Sidney Gamble did a social survey of the life of the ordinary residents in Beijing from 1918 to1919. The data on Beijing's population -incomes and occupation and its social services were published in his book Peking, A Social Survey in 1921 in New York.

[8] The photograph can be viewed at https://repository.duke.edu/dc/gamble/gamble_304A_1739.

Bibliography

Gamble, Sidney D. *Beijing De She Hui Diao Cha (= Bei Jing De She Hui Diao Cha* 北京的社會調查 *= Bei Jing De She Hui Diao Cha).* Edited by Yubing Chen and Xi Yuan. Beijing: Zhongguo shu dian 北京 : 中国书店, 2010.

———. Gamble, Sidney D. *Peking: A Social Survey Conducted under the Auspices of the Princeton University Center in China and the Peking Young Men's Christian Association.* Edited by the Princeton University Center in China and the Young Men's Christian Association (Beijing). New York: George H. Doran, [ca. 1921].

———. *Sidney Gamble's China Revisited: Photographs by Sidney D. Gamble from 1917 to 1931.* Edited by Nancy Jervis and Jonathan D. Spence. New York:China Institute,2004.

———. Gamble, Sidney D. *Ting Hsien, a North China Rural Community.* New York: International Secretariat, Institute of Pacific Relations, 1954.

Gamble, Sidney David, Ho-ch'en Wang, and Jen-ho Liang. How Chinese Families Live in Peiping; a Study of the Income and Expenditure of 283 Chinese Families Receiving from $8 to $550 Silver Per Month New York, London, Funk & Wagnalls Company, 1933.

Maowen Qiangzu Zizhixian Zhi 茂汶羌族自治县志. Edited by Sichuan sheng Aba Zangzu Qiangzu Zizhizhou Maowen Qiangzu Zizhixian di fang zhi bian zuan wei yuan hui bian 四川省阿坝藏族羌族自治州茂汶羌族自治县地方志编纂委员会编 and Sichuan Sheng Aba Zangzu Qiangzu Zizhizhou Maowen Qiangzu Zizhixian di fang zhi bian zuan wei yuan hui. Chengdu Shi: Sichuan ci shu chu ban she 成都市 : 四川辞书出版社, 1997.

Shen, Hong 沈弘. *Xi Hu Bai Xiang: Meiguo Chuan Jiao Shi Ganbo Minguo Chu Nian Pai She De Hangzhou Lao Zhao Pian* 西湖百象 : 美国传教士甘博民国初年拍摄的杭州老照片. Jinan: Shandong ren min chu ban she 济南 : 山东人民出版社, 2010.

Sichuan Sheng Wenchuan Xian wei yuan hui. Wen shi zi liao wei yuan hui. Wasi tu si shi mo 瓦寺土司始末. Wenchuan Xian: Zhongguo ren min zheng zhi xie shang hui yi Sichuan Sheng Wenchuan Xian wei yuan hui wen shi zi liao wei yuan hui; 汶川县: 中国人民政治协商会议四川省汶川县委员会文史资料委员会, 1995.

Wang, Mingke 王明珂. *Qiang Zai Han Zang Zhi Jian: Yi Ge Huaxia Bian Yuan De Li Shi Ren Lei Xue Yan Jiu* 羌在漢藏之間 : 一個華夏邊緣的歷史人類學研究. Taibei Shi: Lian jing chu ban shi ye gu fen you xian gong si 台北市 : 聯經出版事業股份有限公司, 2003.

Xing, Wenjun. *Social Gospel, Social Economics, and the YMCA: Sidney D. Gamble and Princeton-in-Peking.* PhD. diss. (Univeristy of Massachusetts Amherst, 1992)

Zhuang, Xueben 庄学本. *Qiang Rong Kao Cha Ji: She Ying Da Shi Zhuang Xueben 20 Shi Ji 30 Nian Dai De Xi Bu Ren Wen Tan Fang* 羌戎考察记 : 摄影大师庄学本20世纪30年代的西部人文探访. Edited by Naihui Ma, Zhaowu Wang, and Wenjun Zhuang. Chengdu Shi: Sichuan min zu chu ban she; 成都市 : 四川民族出版社, 2007.

6

The Chalfant/Britton Collection at Columbia's C.V. Starr East Asian Library

Ria Koopmans-de Bruijn, Columbia University

Introduction

In his foreword to a recent Online Computer Library Center (OCLC) report *Making Archival and Special Collections More Accessible*, James Michalko, vice-president of the OCLC Research Library Partnership, characterized archives (and special collections) as presenting "a similar schizophrenic management challenge across the community. They are treasures. They are burdens. They are valued. They are costly. They are important. *They are hidden.*"[1]

Archival collections can be a gold mine of rare information for scholars, and libraries do well to diligently collect such resources. However, as most librarians know, an archive is, generally speaking, not ready for public use at the moment it arrives at a library. A lot of work needs to happen in terms of sorting, inventorying, organizing, rehousing, and cataloging. Frequently conservation and preservation work is also needed before it is ready for the public. Until all the processing work is complete, these collections remain hidden. The Chalfant/Britton Collection is one such hidden archival collection in Columbia University's C.V. Starr East Asian Library that was in need of all the above treatment.

Here I discuss the (re)discovery of this highly valuable archival material, placing it in the larger context of the study of early Chinese inscriptions, particularly those on so-called oracle bones. I discuss the collection's background

Figures 6.1a and 6.1b. From chaos to relative order. Chalfant Britton
unprocessed files. Photographs by author. Courtesy of the
C.V. Starr East Asian Library, Columbia University.

and its presence in our library, as well as recent efforts to start processing the material in such a way that scholars will finally be able to make full use of the rich information it contains. I intend to share with you the path from initial chaos to, as of this writing, a modicum of order, although the work is by no means done.

Background

Columbia University's C.V. Starr East Asian Library owns a substantial amount of nonbook special collection materials, ranging from maps and prints to archives and artifacts. Among the artifacts is our well-known collection of Chinese inscribed divination relics, popularly known as oracle bones. Oracle bones can be described as inscribed bones (mainly bovid scapulae, or shoulder blades) and turtle shells (mainly plastrons, or undershells) that were used as divination tools during the Shang dynasty (c. 1600–1046 BCE), particularly the later part of that period (c. 1200–1046 BCE). These bones were buried for centuries and were only rediscovered relatively recently. Although we speak of the "discovery" of the oracle bones, anecdotal information suggests that the bone fragments in question had been known locally well before this time. According to some accounts, they were referred to as dragon bones and were marketed for medicinal purposes. In fact, one of the stories told about the discovery of the oracle bones (several different stories circulate) directly relates to this use and talks about a scholar named Wang, who, as part of his medication for malaria, is prescribed these bones but notes the inscriptions on them and—apparently forgetting his illness—begins to study the inscriptions instead.[2] It was in the last year of the nineteenth century that the markings on the bones were first recognized for what they were, and scholars started following up by finding out where these bones came from and whether more were to be found. This eventually resulted in intensive excavations, yielding a great many finds of bone fragments and causing wide interest in collecting and studying the inscriptions by both scholars and amateurs, Chinese and foreign. In fact, so great was the demand that a lively production of fakes and manipulated real bone fragments evolved. Most early collectors held more spurious bones than authentic ones, as was proven much later.

To this day the bone inscriptions are considered the oldest extant records of written Chinese. The bones were used in pyromancy practices for a variety of purposes, from weather forecasts to determining auspicious times to start wars or conduct weddings to recording historical records and much more. As far as we can tell these practices were only applied in the palace for royal purposes. One could almost speak of a very early form of government documents. Very broadly speaking, questions were carved on the front of the bones and indents were carved on the back, after which the indents were exposed to heat, causing the bones to crack. These cracks were then interpreted as answers to the questions, which in turn were engraved on the bones. Although the history of Chinese oracle bones is a fascinating topic in its own right, and even though the persons whose work will be discussed here spent much of their time and effort on the study of those particular inscriptions, the oracle bones themselves are not the primary subject.

History

While Columbia's oracle bone collection is well known, what is less known, if known at all, is that among Starr Library's archival holdings is a collection of the papers of the Rev. Frank H. Chalfant and Roswell S. Britton, henceforth referred to as the Chalfant/Britton Collection. In particular, Frank Chalfant was deeply engaged in collecting and studying the oracle bones ever since they were first discovered near Anyang, China, in 1899, so these papers have great relevance to our collection. Although Columbia scholars during the 1950s and 1960s were aware of the existence of these papers,[3] that awareness later faded, as they remained unprocessed in our backlog until very recently.

According to the library's annual report for 1950–51, the bulk of the collection was first received by the library in that fiscal year, with the receipt of additional Britton papers recorded for the 1952–53 fiscal year. In the "Our Growing Collections" section of the February 1952 issue of *Columbia Library Columns,* Howard Linton, then head of the East Asiatic Library, reports:

> Mrs. Frank Chalfant and Mrs. Rockwell [*sic*] Britton recently presented to the East Asiatic Library the unique collection of early Chinese writings that had been formed by their respective husbands. The Chalfant-Britton collection—easily one of the most distinguished acquisitions in the history of the East Asiatic Library—was gathered and analyzed over many years by two of the most competent scholars in the field. Their deciphering and interpretation of Chinese inscriptions made thousands of years ago on oracle bones and bronzes have thrown light on dark places in early Chinese history. Now the original materials upon which their research was based have become part of the resources of Columbia University.[4]

The collection consists of manuscript material, correspondence, photographic material, and more, all related to Chinese inscriptions on oracle bones, as well as other materials. Although the collection has been in the library for these many decades, it had never been properly processed and described, making it essentially unknown and unusable—the essence of a "hidden collection."

While the intellectual content of the collection is, for the most part, intact, the housing of the material left a lot to be desired. To provide access to the papers in that condition potentially would have been detrimental to the collection. Manuscript pages were glued into crumbling and highly acidic volumes and letters and other papers were inserted in ill-fitting containers and highly acidic scrapbooks. Papers that were not adequately enclosed were crumbling, and if ever there was order in the collection it had long ago vanished. No proper description of the content of the collection existed. In short, the collection was in no condition to be made available to interested scholars.

Given that Chalfant's portion of the collection is almost exclusively related to oracle bones, as the library began planning the rehousing and digitization using the Reflectance Transformation Imaging (RTI) method of its oracle bone collection,[5] it became all the more relevant to process this archival collection at this time, so that it would become available for scholarly use alongside the oracle bone collection, even though it should be noted that Columbia's collection does not include any bones collected by Chalfant. Those are in other collections.[6] Much scholarship has taken place on oracle bone and other inscriptions since the days of Chalfant and Britton, but from a historical perspective the collection's contributions are still quite relevant and might yet yield interesting new insights. However, bringing this collection into a shape manageable for scholarly perusal promised to be quite a challenge.

The Players

Below I discuss the collection itself, and the progress made so far in the pursuit of processing and managing it, but first let me begin by telling you something about the primary persons connected with these papers. There are three, although the collection only carries the names of two of them.

Frank Herring Chalfant (1862–1914)

A clergyman's son, Chalfant was born in Mechanicsburg, Pennsylvania.[7] He received his AB degree from Lafayette College in 1881, then attended the Western Union Theological Seminary, and was subsequently ordained by the Presbytery of Pittsburgh in 1886. In 1887 he was appointed as a missionary, whereupon the Board of Foreign Missions of the Presbyterian Church sent him to China where he was stationed in Weihsien, Shantung (Weixian, Shandong). He remained there for twenty-five years, until 1912, when he returned to the United States an invalid after sustaining a spinal injury in 1911. While in China, Chalfant pursued epigraphy as a hobby, initially studying and interpreting inscriptions on coins, bronzes, stoneware, and the like. When the oracle bones were discovered near Anyang, Chalfant was among the first westerners to see these bone fragments. Given his preexisting interest in inscriptions, it is not surprising that he began avidly collecting and studying them. As early as 1906 he published the first book-length treatment in English on the subject, *Early Chinese Writing*.[8]

Chalfant continued his scholarly work on oracle bone inscriptions for the rest of his life. At the time of his death, he left behind a manuscript for a

Figure 6.2. Frank Herring Chalfant (1862–1914).
Image circa 1910. Original photographer
unknown; digital image by Columbia University
Reprography Department. Courtesy of the C.V.
Starr East Asian Library, Columbia University.

major publication on the subject, which he had given the simple title "Bone Inscriptions." The manuscript of typewritten pages and hand drawings was inserted in three enormous volumes of the kind in which pharmacists used to save their prescriptions. The book was meant to be a two-volume publication, with the main text and Chalfant's meticulously hand-drawn facsimiles in volume 1 and a syllabary making up volume 2. Due to Chalfant's untimely death, this work was never published as is, though selections from volume 1 were published much later, under Roswell Britton's editorship, in three small publications with the respective titles *The Couling-Chalfant Collection of Inscribed Oracle Bone* (1935), *Seven Collections of Inscribed Oracle Bone* (1938), and *The Hopkins Collection of Inscribed Oracle Bone* (1939).[9] The original manuscript volumes are now part of the Chalfant/Britton Collection.

Figure 6.3. Lionel Charles Hopkins (1854–1952).
Image circa 1910. Original photographer
unknown; digital image by Columbia University
Reprography Department. Courtesy of the C.V.
Starr East Asian Library, Columbia University

Lionel Charles Hopkins (1854–1952)

A second person of importance in this context was Lionel Charles Hopkins,[10] who served in a number of British consular positions in China between 1874 and 1910, eventually becoming British Consul in 1898 at Chefoo (Chih-fou; present-day Yantai), and then, in 1902, Consul General in Tientsin (Tianjin). He was noted for his study of the Chinese language, and he was a longtime friend and correspondent of Chalfant, although they never met in person! In fact, L. C. Hopkins was so important to Chalfant that the latter had wanted Hopkins to take over his manuscript and see it into print on his behalf in case of his untimely death. Witness the note attached inside the cover of his manuscript volume 2, which reads:

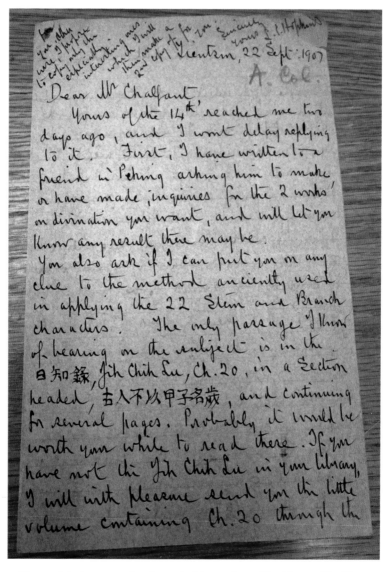

Figure 6.4. An example of a typical letter from Hopkins to Chalfant, dated 22 September, 1907. Photograph by author. Courtesy of the C.V. Starr East Asian Library, Columbia University.

In case of my inability to finish this work, all the MSS. And Syllabary are to be forwarded to L. C. Hopkins Esq, The Garth, Haslemere, Surrey, England, Mr. Hopkins to use his judgment as to the disposal of the papers. F. H. Chalfant, Weihsien, Nov. 21, 1911.

This, alas, never happened as a result of the outbreak of World War I, which prevented such a cross-Atlantic undertaking. The manuscript and other papers lingered, and moved around, first from Chalfant's home in Pittsburgh to the Field Museum in Chicago where Chalfant's friend, the Sinologist Berthold Laufer (1874–1934) was working. After Laufer's death, the papers were returned to Pittsburgh, whereupon Mrs. Chalfant and her son Edward entrusted them to Roswell Britton. Finally, in the early 1950s, Chalfant's widow joined Roswell Britton's widow in donating the manuscript and both men's papers to Columbia University.

Roswell Sessoms Britton (1897–1951)

Roswell Sessoms Britton was a missionary son born in Shanghai, China.[11] He studied at various American institutions, including Columbia University, in the School of Journalism, where he received his B.Litt. in 1923. That same year he won a Pulitzer Travelling Scholarship, which took him back to China. He helped establish the school of journalism at Yenching University in Beijing while at the same time starting formal study of the Chinese language, study he continued on his return to Columbia University in 1929. Eventually, in 1933, he received his PhD from Columbia as well based on his dissertation "The Chinese Periodical Press, 1800–1912." Although he was originally trained in journalistic history, Britton subsequently dedicated much of his time and effort to the study of China's antiquity, in particular the inscriptions of the Shang and Zhou periods (c. 1600–256 BCE). He also taught mathematics at New York University for many years. In the end, it was Britton who took charge of Chalfant's manuscript and saw parts of it into print under the three titles mentioned above.

The Collection

During the spring of 2015, a very basic inventory of the collection was created in order to get a rough idea of what is included, as well as what would be needed to prepare it for scholarly use. It was found that the collection included the following.

3 oversized manuscript volumes, originally created by Chalfant

170 Lionel Hopkins letters to Chalfant

16 envelopes filled with various papers by or related to Chalfant

74 scrapbooks assembled by Britton

50 notebooks assembled by Britton

10 envelopes filled with various Britton materials

5 article reprints collected by Britton and stored in an old Chinese book cover

3 unlabeled envelopes containing miscellaneous materials

A stack of loose-leaf materials

A large amount of photographs, as yet uncounted

Other ephemera

42 glass slides

Some photographs were taken to record and illustrate the collection's condition, and also some of the materials were reviewed with a conservator early on to get advice on the best way to rehouse what could be rehoused and get a preliminary estimate of conservation treatment needed for things that could not be simply rehoused. A small number of these items have been treated so far, but it was decided that the first priority should be to rehouse the material securely. More conservation and hopefully eventual digitization of parts or all of the collection will have to wait for a later time.

It was then determined that work on the collection would have to proceed in a number of phases: (1) identification and rehousing, (2) detailed recording of the contents, (3) creation of a catalog record and finding aid, and (4) publicity.

Phase 1: Identification and Rehousing

The Chalfant part of the collection, as already mentioned, includes the three oversized manuscript volumes, the letters from Hopkins to Chalfant with corresponding notes, and a small amount of random papers.

While the actual manuscript pages themselves seem to be in reasonable condition, the volumes they are glued into are in excessively poor condition—bindings are crumbling and broken, and the pages are extremely acidic and brittle. It was nonetheless decided not to rush the conservation treatment. Instead the volumes were carefully transferred into tissue-lined preservation boxes for safekeeping. In due course, we hope to detach the manuscript pages, and rehouse them in a way that we feel does justice to the manuscript as it was apparently envisioned by Chalfant while ensuring that the manuscript can be safely handled as needed. At that time we also hope to digitize the entire manuscript and make it publicly available.

The Hopkins letters number 170 and date from 1906 to Chalfant's death in 1914.[12] They are, by and large, in good condition and were already organized chronologically, many marked—presumably by Chalfant—with the date of receipt. Many are also marked with brief notes and underlines in red pencil. It is less clear whether this was done by Chalfant or later by Britton. Unfortunately, no envelopes were saved. The notes found in the same container as the letters were for the most part made by Chalfant and were meant for Hopkins's information.[13] They are written on extremely brittle paper, darkened to a deep shade of brown. As most notes are written in pencil, legibility has suffered substantially. Also, due to their poor storage and condition, bits and pieces have broken off the corners and tops of the paper. These notes will need to be conservation treated and enclosed before they can be safely handled. Once treated, digitization will hopefully help improve legibility so the notes can be interpreted in the context of the Hopkins correspondence.

Since the letters and notes were housed so precariously in a very ill-fitting open container, and because they seemed to be the oldest items in the collection, the rehousing project was started with that part (once the manuscript volumes had been taken care of). By the time each letter had been transferred into its own carefully marked folder, two archival boxes were filled, a substantial difference from the tiny harmonica folder they had lived in for so long.[14] And, although the original container was in poor condition, it had notes written on it in Chalfant's hand, so it was preserved as well.

The notes were in such dire condition that they had to be stored together unsorted until such time that a conservator can attend to them. Once the letters and notes were rehoused, a spreadsheet was created to record the collection. Virtually all the letters are exchanges regarding oracle bone inscriptions and their interpretation. No return letters from Chalfant to Hopkins are in this collection. It may be that those are contained in the Hopkins papers, which are held in the Cambridge University Library's Department of Manuscripts and University Archives. Unfortunately, an inquiry to that institution could not confirm whether any Chalfant letters are included since those papers also remain unprocessed.

In addition to the manuscript volumes and correspondence, the collection contains a small amount of papers belonging or relevant to Chalfant, which had been organized in sixteen large envelopes by Roswell Britton. One envelope, in fact, contained framed portrait photographs of Chalfant and Hopkins, a lucky find as no portraits of either gentleman had been found anywhere else.

The Britton portion of the collection consists of some ten large envelopes and other containers filled with loose papers and other ephemera, several small boxes of various sizes full of unsorted photographs, no less than forty-nine notebooks, and some sixty-five scrapbooks filled with photographs, notes, and the like loosely inserted between the extremely brittle pages.

Figure 6.5. A small sampling of the many scrapbooks assembled
by Rosswell Britton. Photograph by author. Courtesy of the
C.V. Starr East Asian Library, Columbia University.

Britton was a very meticulous person, and he had diligently applied numeric codes to everything he handled, attaching tiny labels to all the notebooks, scrapbooks, and envelopes. Unfortunately, over time many of those labels have come off, and others are broken in such a way that the number cannot be determined with certainty. To add to the confusion, many scrapbooks have multiple labels, sometimes with non-corresponding numbers and sometimes with words or (archaic) characters on them. The first step therefore had to be an attempt to chronologically organize these materials.

Thirty-two scrapbook labels are fully identifiable, nine have partial labels left, and twenty-four have no number label left at all. Likewise for the notebooks: twenty-two have identifiable labels and twenty-seven do not have labels. Eight of the unmarked volumes are clearly related to Britton's dissertation and other publications rather than to inscriptions. Ten of the envelopes of loose-leaf material have numeric codes as well, as does a set of reprints of articles by James M. Menzies, which together were enclosed in an old Chinese book enclosure, which in turn had a number code. The remaining loose-leaf material and other ephemera were unmarked, and their proper category and chronological order will have to be determined through close reading of the content. Once the numerical order of these materials was largely determined, they were transferred into archival boxes. A total of thirty-one archival boxes of various sizes were filled with these materials, and this number may grow as more of the material is sorted.

A small number of photographs had been housed in an open, broken box, and these were treated early on by the Conservation Department because they were not only brittle but completely curled up. Even now, after treatment, they have to be kept in tight enclosures because, despite intense conservation efforts, they could no longer be kept totally flat on their own. A further collection of many small photographs needed to be moved out of a broken index card box and two smaller boxes and into archival boxes. These, too, tend to curl and will need to be flattened and housed in protective envelopes.

Phase 2: Recording the Contents

Although phase 1 is not finished, it was important to consecutively start phase 2 as well, even while recognizing that much material is still likely to shift and subsequently the arrangement of the records will likely need to be adjusted in turn. Therefore, once each category of material was manageably housed, detailed spreadsheets were created to record the contents. This gives a better sense of what is included in the collection. The spreadsheets were created as an aid to proper description in the finding aid that will be created when the collection is fully processed and everything is permanently housed.

One spreadsheet covers the Hopkins correspondence and once finished can be considered finite since the letters will have been fully organized and permanently housed in chronological order. At present this spreadsheet includes the following categories of information.

- Archival box number
- Assigned letter number
- Number of sheets of paper and number of sides filled with writing
- Date sent (if known)

- Date received (if known)
- Place of origin (i.e., the place from which the letter was sent)
- Notes

The date received was frequently noted, presumably by Chalfant. The place of origin was recorded because Hopkins moved around from time to time, particularly after he left China for good. It will be determined at a later date whether this information is relevant and necessary, but that will require close reading of the content, and we have not yet reached that stage. The notes column includes the occasional notes that were added at the top of some letters in red pencil.

For the scrapbooks, notebooks, envelope content, and other items, a separate spreadsheet was created since the information to be collected on these materials differs substantially from that on the correspondence. This spreadsheet will list the content of the numerically coded material. This is by far the larger portion of the collection. The categories for this group include the following

- Original numeric code (if known)
- Archival box number
- Brief description (i.e., scrapbook, notebook, envelope, or loose leaf material)
- Notes (e.g., a rough indication of subject matter)
- Condition

This is a preliminary arrangement. The unmarked material will have to be sorted and carefully read to determine its chronological place in the collection before a more permanent list can be created and a final choice of relevant categories can be confirmed. At this stage it is not anticipated that a spreadsheet-level description of the photographs will be created.

Reviewing the three manuscript volumes page by page we come across some interesting issues. For instance, although it is clear that the volumes were originally put together by Chalfant, it also looks like Britton manipulated much of the material. Most images are clean copies rather than original drawings (only a few originals appear, mostly toward the end of volume 1, part 2). Britton also wrote notes on and around the plates and added his own page and plate numbers. The latter numbers correspond to the page and/or plate numbers in the three small publications he edited based on Chalfant's material. The drawing plates were pasted onto the album leaves. In the case of plates that were included in the publications edited by Britton. the drawing plates were pasted onto larger sheets of paper before being pasted on the album leaves. The question thus arises as to how much of the content and arrangement are Britton's rather than Chalfant's, and, as their handwriting does not differ much, who wrote what?

Various paginations are used.

- Page numbers in red pencil run continuously through a portion of volume 1, part 2 (album 2).

- Pages included in the publications edited by Britton include page numbers, as well as plate numbers, and pages not included have neither.

- All individual drawings are numbered.

Because Britton excluded certain parts of the manuscript from the three publications he edited, pagination stops corresponding between the red pencil and other page and plate numbers after page 37. For instance, Britton's page 38 corresponds to red pencil page 52 and so on.

Chalfant included not only oracle bones but also other inscribed objects among his drawings, such as dagger heads and amulets. Britton did not include any nonbone or nonshell illustrations in any of the three publications. He also for the most part excluded drawings of bones considered spurious.

The appendix to this chapter is a rough page-by-page inventory of the content of volume 1, parts 1 and 2. For the initial parts, the information is at times somewhat less detailed, but the condition of the volumes discourages revisiting those pages to enhance the information at this time. Volume 2 (album 3) is excluded from the inventory. That entire volume is made up of Chalfant's "Syllabary."

Phases 3 and 4: Finding Aid, Catalog Record, and Publicity

Although we now do have a much better sense of what the collection contains, the work is by no means finished. Among the tasks still before us, in addition to finishing the processing and description phases, is the eventual rehousing of Chalfant's manuscript; conservation treatment of parts of the collection; and, most importantly, the creation of a finding aid and public catalog record. However, in its current condition we are very close to being able to provide at least some access to parts of the collection to scholars who wish to use this material for research purposes, although it will still be some time before we can comfortably start to actively publicize the collection.

Conclusion

So what use is this collection to scholars? There is a variety of research that could profit from close perusal of it. For instance, although parts of Chalfant's original manuscript were brought into print by Britton, it would be interesting to see what the parts not included in those publications have to say and to make the full manuscript as it was originally put together by Chalfant available through digitization. Also those parts published later all came from the original volume

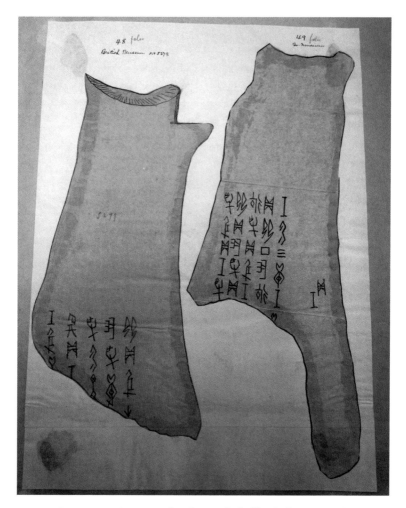

Figure 6.6. An example of one of Chalfant's few original
drawing pages. Photograph by author. Courtesy of the
C.V. Starr East Asian Library, Columbia University.

1, and the syllabary that was meant to form volume 2 never did see the light of
day. Although oracle bone scholarship may have moved on considerably since
Chalfant's days, interesting insights might well be gleaned from this volume as
well.

Another interesting project would be to locate the letters from Chalfant to
Hopkins, if they still exist, in order to be able to see the entire correspondence. From
what I have seen of Hopkins's letters thus far, their entire correspondence focused
exclusively on inscribed oracle bones, and fascinating insights might be gathered

from analyzing their reasoning in their respective interpretations. As mentioned, Hopkins's papers are held in the Department of Manuscripts and University Archives of the Cambridge University Library. Assuming that Chalfant's letters to Hopkins are indeed included among those papers, it would be an interesting challenge to see if we could eventually arrange a joined digitization project with that library in order to bring together the entire two-way correspondence.

And then there are Britton's scrapbooks, which contain abundant material related to his interactions with, and consultation work for, collectors and dealers of Chinese inscribed materials such as oracle bones, bronzes, and early pottery. This material, consisting of photographs, correspondence, and notes, can shed interesting lights on the collection of and trade in these objects in the first half of the twentieth century. The abundance of photographs might well also add to the current scholarship on inscribed artifacts.

As for Britton's eight notebooks that seem, at least in part, to relate to Britton's dissertation and other writings, though rather different from the bulk of the collection, they hold interest on their own and should, for instance, be of interest to scholars interested in China's early journalistic history, the subject of Britton's dissertation. Unfortunately, the notebooks are in very poor condition and will need conservation treatment before we can ascertain their exact content.

These are just a few possibilities for application of the collection to research. We will not be able to predict everything scholars might gain from the collection, nor would we want to restrict scholars in their creative application and interpretation of these resources. That is why it is so important to confirm what is included and let the world know of its existence so that the collection can finally serve the scholarly purpose for which it was meant.

Appendix: Chalfant MSS, page-by-page content list for volume 1, parts 1-2

Volume 1, part 1

- Bibliography (several loose pages)
- Preface (4 stuck pages)
- Introduction (25 pages, mostly stuck)

The following four collections are partially included in Britton's *The Couling-Chalfant Collection of Inscribed Oracle Bone* ("Britton page" refers to the pages in this publication).

Royal Scottish Museum

> Red pencil pages 1–37, Britton pages 1–37, plates 1–37; images 1–760
>
> Red pencil pages 38–44, images 761–914, not included in Britton (identified by Chalfant as RSM, but by Britton as Carnegie)

Carnegie Institute

> Red pencil pages 45–80, images 971–1408
>
> Red pencil pages 81–87, images 1409–1505, not included in Britton
>
> Note: a sheet of unrelated Britton material (a New York University final exam, Mathematics 13, Tues. May 26, 1936! Britton taught mathematics at the university for many years) is stuck between red pencil pages 47–48

British Museum

> Red pencil pages 88–152, images 1506–1989
>
> Red pencil pages 153–156, not included in Britton

Field Museum

> Red pencil pages 157–159, not included in Britton
>
> Red pencil pages 160–168, identified as British Museum rather than Field Museum; not included in Britton
>
> Red pencil pages 169–173 not included in Britton
>
> Red pencil page 174, Britton page 132
>
> Red pencil page 175–190, not included in Britton

Red pencil pages 191–252 cover the Liu T'ie Yun Collection ("Designated by the letter *L*"). This section starts with new numbering and is not included in Britton.

The following four collections are partially included in Britton's *Seven Collections of Inscribed Oracle Bone* ("Britton page" refers to the pages in this publication).

Royal Asiatic Society Shanghai Collection ("Designated by the letter *M*"). Image numbering is actually preceded by the letter *S* (i.e., not *M*)

> Red pencil pages 253–260, Britton pages 15–22, plates 5–12

Tientsin Collection ("Designated by the letter *T*"). Image numbering is preceded by the letter *T*.

> Red pencil pages 261–264, Britton pages 11–14, plates 1–4

Bergen Collection ("Designated by the letter *B*"). Image numbering is preceded by the letter *B*.

Red pencil pages 265–268, Britton pages 23–26, plates 13–16, images B1–B67

Red pencil page 269, images B81–B100, not included in Britton

Whitcher Collection, Princeton University ("Designated by the letter *W*"). Image numbers are actually preceded by the letter *P* (for Princeton), not *W*.

Red pencil pages 270–274, Britton pages 27–31, plates 17–21, images P1–P119

Red pencil pages 275–284, not in Britton

Red pencil page 285 starts the Hopkins Collection ("Designated by the letter *H*"), and runs, unfinished, to the end of the album, red pencil page 374. Part of this section was included in *The Hopkins Collection of Inscribed Oracle Bone* ("Britton page" refers to the pages in this publication). The new numbering starts with 1 but is not preceded by a letter. Not all images are of oracle bones, and some images of oracle bones not included in Britton are marked "false" or "suspect." This portion includes the following.

Red pencil pages 285–295, Britton pages 13–21, plates 1–9, images 1–127

Red pencil pages 296–324, images 128–366, not included in Britton

Red pencil pages 325–331, Britton pages 28–34, plates 16–22, images 367–418

Red pencil pages 332–333, images 419–447, not included in Britton

Red pencil pages 334–354, Britton pages 35–55, plates 23–43, images 448–560

Red pencil pages 355–357, images 561–571, not included in Britton

Red pencil pages 358–370, Britton pages 57–69, plates 45–57, images 572–670

Red pencil page 371, images 671–674, not included in Britton

Red pencil page 372, Britton page 71, plate 59, image 675

Red pencil pages 373–374, images 679–687, not included in Britton

End of volume 1, part 1.

Volume 1, part 2

This volume continues where volume 1, part 1, left off with the Hopkins Collection.

Red pencil pages 375–378, images 688–698, not included in Britton

Red pencil page 379, Britton page 74, plate 62, image 699

Red pencil pages 380–385, images 700–720, not included in Britton

Red pencil pages 386–387, Britton pages 77–78, plates 65–66, images 721–743

Red pencil pages 388–409, images 744–828, not included in Britton

End of the Hopkins Collection

There follows the remaining three collections covered in Britton's *Seven Collections of Inscribed Oracle Bone*.

Wilhelm Collection (new numbering, preceded by the letter W)

Red pencil pages 410–413, Britton pages 32–35, plates 22–25, images W1–W72

Sun Collection ("Sundry collection, designated by the letter S"). Image numbers are actually preceded by the letter X, not S.

No red pencil page number, Britton page 37, plate 27, images X1–X8, shows photographs of rubbings of these images

Red pencil page 414, Britton page 36, plate 26, images X1–X8, drawings of the same bones (the above pages are in the reverse order, as listed here, in the album)

Red pencil pages 415–418, Britton pages 38–41, plates 28–31, images X9–X31

Royal Asiatic Society, London (new numbering, preceded by the letter R)

Red pencil page 419, Britton page not indicated, plate 32 (top of page only), images R1–R6

Red pencil page 419, bottom of page: British Museum images 38–40, not included in Britton (the images look to be genuine, i.e., original Chalfant drawings)

Insert at red pencil page 423, large genuine-looking drawings of British Museum images 50–51

Red pencil page numbering stops here.

What follows next is a series of text pages interspersed with drawings of various objects. A note by Britton reads "Continuation of preface." However, it would seem instead to be continuing what is called the "Introduction" above, the first 25 pages of which can be found early in volume 1, part 1.

Text pages 26–28, followed by a page carrying the note "Figure 1, photo of jade pi" (no image included), followed by a drawing of a jade scepter (fig. 2)

Text pages 29–31, followed by 3 drawings and 1 photograph (British Museum) of bronze swords (figs. 3–6)

Text page 32, including figures 7–12, followed by 2 drawings of bronze axes (figs. 13–14)

Text page 33, followed by a drawing of bronze bells (fig. 15). Figures 16–20, "bells from Chinese cuts," mentioned but not included

Text page 34, followed by 2 drawings of "tun" (figs. 21–22)

Page carrying a note regarding figure 23, "Thundergong," but no image

Text page 35, followed by an unidentified image (fig. 24)

Text pages 36–40, followed by figures 25–27

Text pages 41–60

Page carrying a note, "Add concluding remarks to vol. I"

This concludes vol. I.

Volume 2

This portion starts with some notes in pencil, "copied by RSB" [Roswell S. Britton], and then continues with some pages, taken out of sequence, included in Britton's *The Hopkins Collection of Inscribed Oracle Bones*. Page and plate numbers refer to those in this publication.

- Page 22, plate 10
- Pages 23–27, plates 11–15
- Page 56, plate 44
- Page 70, plate 58
- Pages 72–73, plates 60–61
- Pages 75–76, plates 63–64

The remainder of this album is empty. Volume 2 continues in album 3, which contains Chalfant's syllabary.

Notes

[1] James Michalko, "Foreword," in *Making Archival and Special Collections More Accessible* (Dublin, OH: OCLC Research, 2015), 3 (my italics), accessed June 23, 2015, http://www.oclc.org/content/dam/research/publications/2015/oclcresearch-making-special-collections-accessible-2015.pdf.

[2] A version of this story can be found in Te-Kong Tong, "The Tortoise Shell Which Set Off a Mighty Chain Reaction," *Columbia Library Columns* 16, no. 3 (1967): 11–18.

[3] L. Carrington Goodrich refers to them in "Chinese Oracle Bones," *Columbia Library Columns* 8, no. 3 (1959): 11–14. Te-Kong Tong mentions them in "Tortoise Shell," 13.

[4] Howard Linton, "Our Growing Collections," *Columbia Library Columns* 1, no. 2 (1952): 24–25.

[5] As a computational photographic method that reveals surface information that would otherwise be unavailable, even under direct examination, RTI images are created from multiple digital photographs shot from a single stationary camera position. Images are viewed with RTI Viewing Software, which is open source and downloadable.

[6] Chalfant's own collection, which is now recognized as mostly spurious, found its way into a number of museums. The Carnegie Museum in Pittsburgh acquired 438 pieces in 1909, the Field Museum of Natural History in Chicago acquired a few pieces in 1913, and Princeton University owns another 117 pieces.

[7] The summary of Chalfant's life given here was culled from three obituaries: "Rev. Frank H. Chalfant of China" *The Missionary Review of the World* 37, no. 5 (1914): 397;

B. Laufer, "Frank H. Chalfant," *T'oung Pao,* 2nd ser., 15, no. 1 (1914): 165–66; and Roswell S. Britton, "Frank Herring Chalfant, 1862–1914," *Notes on Far Eastern Studies in America* 11 (1942): 13–22.

[8] Frank H. Chalfant, *Early Chinese Writing.* Memoirs of the Carnegie Museum, vol. 4, no. 1 (Pittsburgh: Carnegie Institute, 1906).

[9] Roswell S. Britton, ed., *The Couling-Chalfant Collection of Inscribed Oracle Bone* (Shanghai: The Commercial Press, 1935); F. Herring Chalfant and Roswell S. Britton, *Seven Collections of Inscribed Oracle Bone* (New York: Chalfant Publication Fund, 1938); Lionel Charles Hopkins, F. Herring Chalfant, and Roswell Britton, *The Hopkins Collection of Inscribed Oracle Bone* (New York: [Printed by the General Offset Co.], 1939).

[10] Information on Hopkins was hard to come by. This summary was drawn from Wikipedia contributors, "Lionel Charles Hopkins," *Wikipedia, the Free Encyclopedia,* accessed June 23, 2015, https://en.wikipedia.org/w/index.php?title=Lionel_Charles_Hopkins&oldid=635396928.

[11] L. Carrington Goodrich, "In Memoriam: Roswell Sessoms Britton (died February 2, 1951)," *Artibus Asiae* 14, nos. 1–2 (1951): 190–91.

[12] Subsequently another Hopkins letter was found among the random papers, but it was of a later date and addressed to Chalfant's son, so it is not counted here.

[13] Since these notes were found among Chalfant's papers, one wonders whether they were only draft copies, as they obviously were not sent to Hopkins.

[14] The archival boxes have not yet been permanently labeled. That will be left until the entire collection is permanently arranged and rehoused.

Bibliography

Britton, Roswell S., ed. *The Couling-Chalfant Collection of Inscribed Oracle Bone.* Shanghai: The Commercial Press, 1935.

Britton, Roswell S. "Frank Herring Chalfant, 1862–1914." *Notes on Far Eastern Studies in America* 11 (1942): 13–22.

Chalfant, Frank H. *Early Chinese Writing.* Memoirs of the Carnegie Museum, vol. 4, no. 1. Pittsburgh: Carnegie Institute, 1906.

Chalfant, F. Herring, and Roswell S. Britton. *Seven Collections of Inscribed Oracle Bone.* New York: [Printed by General offset Co., for the Chalfant Publication Fund], 1938.

Goodrich, L. Carrington. "Chinese Oracle Bones." *Columbia Library Columns* 8, no. 3 (1959).

Goodrich, L. Carrington. "In Memoriam: Roswell Sessoms Britton (died February 2, 1951)." *Artibus Asiae* 14, nos. 1–2 (1951): 190–91.

Hopkins, Lionel Charles, F. Herring Chalfant, and Roswell Britton. *The Hopkins Collection of Inscribed Oracle Bone.* New York: [Printed by General Offset Co.], 1939.

Laufer, B. "Frank H. Chalfant." *T'oung Pao,* 2nd ser., 15, no. 1 (1914): 165–66.

Linton, Howard. "Our Growing Collections." *Columbia Library Columns* 1, no. 2 (1952): 24–25.

Michalko, James. "Foreword." In *Making Archival and Special Collections More Accessible.* Dublin: OH: OCLC Research, 2015. Accessed June 23, 2015. http://www.oclc.org/content/dam/research/publications/2015/oclcresearch-making-special-collections-accessible-2015.pdf.

"Rev. Frank H. Chalfant of China" *The Missionary Review of the World* 37, no. 5 (1914): 397.

Tong, Te-Kong. "The Tortoise Shell Which Set Off a Mighty Chain Reaction." *Columbia Library Columns* 16, no. 3 (1967): 11–18.

Wikipedia contributors. "Lionel Charles Hopkins." *Wikipedia, the Free Encyclopedia.* Accessed June 23, 2015. https://en.wikipedia.org/w/index.php?title=Lionel_Charles_Hopkins&oldid=635396928.

7

Introduction to the Conant Collection at Columbia's C.V. Starr East Asian Library

Hee-sook Shin, Columbia University

Collection development is one of the major activities in academic libraries, and gifts play a very important role in the development of library collections, as seen in the C.V. Starr East Asian Library. In 2008, Theodore Richard Conant kindly contacted us and donated his unique collection to the C.V. Starr East Asian Library at Columbia University.

The owner of the collection, Conant, was born in 1926 in Cambridge, Massachusetts, the son of the former president of Harvard University, James Bryant Conant. He attended local schools in Cambridge and Vermont and later started his career in media, working as a radio studio assistant while in high school learning radar radiotelegraph and audio broadcasting technology. Before graduating from high school, he joined the US Coast Guard training program in order to enter the Merchant Marine as a radio officer. After that, he served as a radio officer in the Merchant Marine for three years around the end of World War II and remained in the Pacific area for a year to volunteer for Weather Flights. When the war came to an end, he returned to the United States and studied economics at Swarthmore College. He met Robert Flaherty, who was a pioneer of the documentary film and the director of *Nanook of the North*, while he was working at a broadcasting studio. Conant was greatly influenced by Flaherty and later became 'his assistant. He participated in the filming of *Louisiana Story* in 1948 as an assistant director. He was always interested in film and sound recording and continued to cultivate his interests by making his own film, *The Crime* (1951), with a classmate.

After graduating from Swarthmore in 1951, he worked briefly as a film technician in New York City until he was invited to participate in a film project funded by the United Nations (UN). He was dispatched to Korea in 1952 by the UN Korean Reconstruction Agency (UNKRA) where he participated as a recording engineer in Alfred Wagg's documentary film *Long Journey* (고집), which illustrates South Korean's' struggles during the Korean War.

At the end of the Korean War, Conant was recruited by Britain's BBC network to help record a UN and BBC radio program series on Korean reconstruction narrated by the Hollywood star Frederick March. Then he served as the acting head of the UNKRA Film Unit and worked as a filmmaker and sound-recording engineer at Syracuse University under a contract with the US Aid Mission to Korea until 1960.[1]

During the *Long Journey* film project, Conant met Hyŏng P'yo Yi (이형표), a Korean worker at UNKRA, who participated as an assistant producer and interpreter for the film. The film was never completed, but during an interview with the Korean Film Archives (KFA) in November 2009, Conant said that he later completed the film and included it in his collection. However, the collection at Columbia has only an incomplete version of the film.

Thereafter, Conant and Yi founded the Peninsula Studio (반도 영화사). They produced newsreels for NBC, CBS, and UN radio and TV documentary programs for the UN and US Army from 1952 to 1953. In addition, they worked together to produce documentary films such as *Korean Fantasy* (1955), *Korean Artist* (1955), and *Children in Crisis* (1955–56). Conant frequently collaborated with Korean artists such as Ki-ch'ang Kim (김기창) and Nae-hyŏn Pak (박래현) and produced films introducing Korean art to the world.[2] Oneof their films, *Korean Perspective*, was released by the Bureau of Public Information (공보처, BPI) when Yi was relocated from UNKRA to the BPI Film Department. Conant also made *With the Quakers in Korea* (1957), a documentary funded by UNKRA.[3]

Conant built good relationships with many Korean filmmakers, and his contributions to the field of Korean film included leasing film equipment and teaching recording techniques to Korean filmmakers, as well as providing books and audio recordings from the United States in the 1950s. Around 1956, he took part not only in film production but also in the installation of recording machines for BPI aided by UNKRA. When he was placed in charge of recording in BPI's Film Department in 1958, he taught Korean staff members about recording and took part in the installation of recording facilities more actively. His contributions have been confirmed by testimony from Hyŏng-p'yo Yi, Ik-sun Pak (박익순), and Sŏng-chŏl Yi (이성철), who was the head of the Film Department at BPI in 1950s.

Around 1957, Conant also was placed in charge of audiovisual education in the New Life Education Center (신생활 교육원), an agricultural school established in Suwŏn (수원) as part of the UNKRA reconstruction project. He taught audiovisual theory, slide production, and movie programming to students in the school.⁴

After returning from Korea, Conant worked at the Ford Foundation, assisting in the development of educational broadcasting, and then worked at the National Film Board of Canada in Montreal as a guest director until he joined the WGBH Educational Foundation in Boston. He also worked with Dr. Peter Goldmark and participated in the development of the first video disc in New York. In 1988, he was involved in the production of the Korean War documentary film *Korea: The Unknown War*, which was produced by the United Kingdom's Thames TV. Along with his documentary films, he was invited to several international film festivals, including the Berlin International Film Festival and the Montreal Film Festival.

Conant had always been interested in sound and film and his keen interest in Korea never faded. These interests tremendously enriched his life both professionally and personally, leading him to build his distinctive collection. A scholar from the KFA, Yŏng-min Kong (공영민), acknowledged that Conant is recognized as one of the most influential people who greatly contributed to the advancement of Korean film technology in the 1950s.⁵

As mentioned earlier, the Conant Collection was established in the C.V. Starr East Asian Library in 2008. To acquire the collection, Professor Charles Armstrong initiated the conversation and negotiated with Conant for the audio and film materials he made for UN during and after the Korean War in the 1950s. Armstrong contacted our former director, Amy Heinrich, to discuss the digitization and preservation of Conant's materials in 2007. Heinrich worked with both Armstrong and the library's Preservation Department to make the donation of the Conant Collection possible and was able to finalize an agreement signed by both Conant and the Columbia University Libraries in 2008.

Since Conant's personal collection contained a wide range of subject matter, a Korean librarian was sent to his home several times to assist with the selection process by sorting the materials related to Korea and shipping them to Columbia. Most of the materials focused on the Korean War and Korean art and were delivered to the library from 2008 to 2011. The collection now consists of 285 books, 21 periodicals, 123 film reels, 110 audio reels, 20 music reels, more than 1,300 black-and-white photos, and other printed materials such as scenarios, correspondence, pamphlets, and newspaper clippings.

After the materials arrived at the library, processing began with printed materials, including books and journals, followed by the film reels, photos, and other documents. So far most of the collection has been processed and finding aids have been created using spreadsheets, with the exception of the audio and music reels. The finding aids are directly linked to the Conant Collection website, http://library.columbia.edu/locations/eastasian/korean/rarespecial/conant_collection.html.

The most interesting and valuable part of the collection for scholars is the Conant film reels. There are 123 reels in their original metal containers, including documentary films (both finished and unfinished) and newsreels. Some were in very poor condition and others were even acidified. In 2010, Conant digitized some of his films, including *Children in Crisis*, and donated 12 titles to the library as digital video discs (DVDs). As examining the film reels would require professional knowledge, an intern, Erik Pil, a student at the Tisch School of Art at New York University, was hired to complete the task. He took an inventory, examined the film reels, and provided an inventory report in May 2011. While working on the film reels, Pil also replaced the original film containers with preservation plastic containers.

The Conant films are highly valuable because some are unique and have not been available in Korea. Examples include *I Am a Truck* (1954), produced by Ki Yŏng Kim (김기영); *Bad Boy*, by Sang Ok Sin (신상옥); and *Kojip* (고집), a UNKRA production recorded by Conant. *I Am a Truck*, which was shot on film left over from a news film, is a nineteen-minute documentary directed by Ki Yŏng Kim while he worked at the US Information Service. It features the story of a truck that was made in the United States, sent to Korea with the support of the UN, and scrapped after the war. The truck was subsequently disassembled and restored. Once the restoration had been completed, the truck swore that it would devote all its efforts to reconstructing postwar Korea. The director, Ki-yŏng Kim, made this film to encourage people to take action in recovering from the war and achieving economic security. The film is narrated in the truck's voice and consists of odd monologues by the truck and somewhat grotesque scenes that represent its unique style. The eleven-minute short film *Bad Boy* is a study film for editing by Sang-ok Sin, and it is identified by the words "P'yŏnjip hullyŏn yŏnghwa" (편집 훈련 영화) on top of the film reader. The label was confirmed to be in Sin's own handwriting by his wife, Ŭn-hŭi Choi (최은희), in 2010.[6]

Additionally, the Film Department of BPI Korea collaborated with Korean actors to produce educational films, and one of them, *Korean Perspective* (1953–54), directed by Yi and Conant, is included in the collection. *Children in Crisis* (1955), a short documentary film that shows war orphans, beggar children, protesting young men and students, and children's daily lives after the war; *Korean Artist* (1955) a film about the director and contemporary Korean painter Hyŏng P'yo Yi; and *Korean Fantasy* (1955), a survey of life in postwar Korea, are also included in the collection. Later *Korean Artist* was screened at the Manila Film Festival and *Children in Crisis* was invited and screened at the Berlin Film Festival.

Figure 7.1. The original film reels donated by
Conant before the inventory.

Figure 7.2. The film reels after the inventory. They are
now stored in an offsite location in New Jersey.

The collection also contains *With the Quakers in Korea* (1957), a documentary film supported by UNKRA about postwar restoration and war refugee relief programs of the Friends Service Unit, a Quaker Union of the United States and United Kingdom. It records services provided by the Friends Service Unit, including reeducating war widows and providing education, health, and housing assistance in Kunsan (군산). Conant met and worked with Yŏng-u Kim (김영우) when he was teaching audiovisual classes at the New Life Education Center. Yŏng-u Kim worked as a production assistant to produce an animated film, *Spring Fragrance* (1956), which is included in the Conant Collection. *Korea: Battle Ground for Liberty* (1959), produced by the US Air Force and starring Chi-mi Kim (김지미) and Mu-ryong Ch'oe (최무룡), and *Farewell General Coulter*, a narration of Coulter's life, are also included in the collection.

Of Conant's films, *Welcome to Motion Pictures* (1958), which described in great detail the history of the Film Production Center (영화제작소), and *Scenes from 4.19 (People Power in Korea)*, which documented the April 19 Korean Student Movement of 1960, are two of the most important sources.[7] Conant helped make several of the documentary films included in the collection when he was working at the BPI, and the films were used by Syngman Rhee's government to promote Korean news and culture abroad via Korean embassies. The collection also has newsreels from Rhee's government made for the Korean people and others created during the Myŏn Chang (장면) government, which succeeded the resignation of President Rhee. Several Korean directors, who worked with Conant on documentaries and feature films in the collection, did not use their real names, so the film collection is important as it reveals unknown aspects of the history of Korean film.[8]

As initially patrons had no way to use the film reels in the library, it sought a partner that could digitize the film reels. The KFA contacted the library and offered to cooperate as a partner on the digital project. Among the 123 film reels, some titles are on multiple reels. For example, there are 18 reels of *Korean Artist* and 11 of *Children in Crisis*, including different editions, soundtracks, and so on. Due to insufficient funds, the KFA sent a representative, Sŏ-wŏn Ch'oe (최서원), who examined and selected 13 film reels to be digitized in 2010. The library and its Preservation Department worked with the KFA on the first digital project, and the films were sent and digitized using an outside film laboratory, MediaPreserve, which completed the work in 2011. Again with support from the KFA and Korea University, 39 film reels were digitized in 2013 as the second digital project. As a result, 52 film reels out of 123 have been digitized. As mentioned earlier, most of the films feature Korea in the 1950s, and since the films are still under copyright they are only available at the C.V. Starr East Asian Library, the KFA, and Korea University.

Figure 7.3. DVDs converted from the original film reels.

Another prominent type of material in The Conant Collection is the 110 audio and 20 music reels, which consist of various kinds of music, including Korean traditional and modern music, music for film scores, and live performances and interviews. Most of the interviews were conducted during Conant's time as a disc jockey for the American Forces Korean Network (AFKN) radio. For example, there are interviews (in English) with Ik-t'ae An (안익태), the composer of the Korean national anthem; with Conant's cousin Gregory Henderson, a prominent Korea scholar affiliated with Harvard; and with US ambassadors and officials. There are also reels containing radio broadcasts from South Korea and, uniquely, broadcasts from Radio Pyongyang and Radio Peking that Conant picked up. One of the more interesting sound recordings is a lengthy live recording of April 19, 1960, about student movement taken from streets and the Bando Hotel in Seoul. This recording was made by an Associated Press reporter. Professor Armstrong digitized all the audio and music reels starting in 2007 and later sent the original reels with the digital versions of 146 CDs to the library in 2009. These materials are unique and are accessible only in the C.V. Starr East Asian Library.[9]

The third-most-prominent type of material in the collection is photographs. There are more than thirteen hundred black-and white-photos taken during the 1950s and early 1960. Most photos have no information attached and are undated. They include film stills, film crews and shooting, scenes of UNKRA activities, and Korean social life during the 1950s. There are also forty-four photos of President Rhee and fifty of the aforementioned April 19, 1960, Korean student demonstration. These photos are currently being digitized with support from the KFA, and soon digital versions will be available both there and at the library. There is a finding aid for the photographs available on the Conant Collection website. Figures 7.4 through 7.7 are some examples of the photographs.

Figure 7.4. Conant and other staff members readying
recording equipment for shooting.

Figure 7.5. Still from one of Conant's films, *Children in Crisis*.

Figure 7.6. Korea's first president, Syngman Rhee; General
John Coulter, agent-general of UNKRA; and the first lady,
Franziska Donner, inspecting a UNKRA housing project in Busan.

Figure 7.7. The student demonstration of 1960.

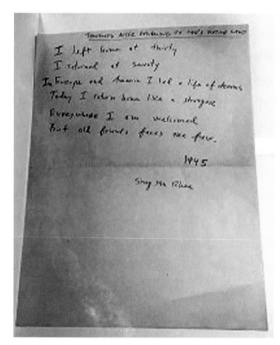

Figure. 7.8. Memo written by President Syngman Rhee.

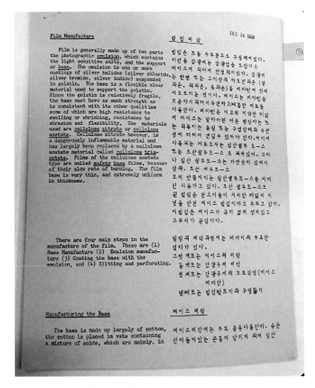

Figure 7.9. Conant's bilingual lecture notes for classes he taught in Korea.

Figure 7.10. Documents filed in a preservation box.

Figure 7.11. Parts of the Conant collection on a shelf in the Rare Book and
Special Collections Reading Room at C.V. Starr East Asian Library.

Some other interesting materials are radio scripts and playscripts. Examples
include a copy of "Two Million Kids," a twenty-one-page radio script by Conant
and Yi, and "The Long Walk," narrated by the film star Fredric March, which
commemorates the end of hostilities in Korea. *The Long Walk* was a special UN
radio feature broadcast to the world on July 27, 1954. There are many other
playscripts such as "Ours: The Story of a Village's 'Rebirth' through Cooperation,"
by Jong Hae Yang and Layton Mabrey; "Light above Heaven," by Conant and Yi;
"Our Shattered Showcase," by Mr. and Mrs. Conant; and the script for a military
film, *Be Ever Right Sacred Blood*, by Hyuptong Film Productions. Additionally,
Conant's lecture material from the classes he taught at Yonsei University, written
in both English and Korean, is also unique. The lecture material was initially
only available at Yonsei University, but it is now also available in the library at
Columbia. The Collection also includes additional materials, such as copies of the

personal correspondences between Conant and UNKRA, and discussion papers on Korea war films by various professors and experts

Included in the collection are other documents such as academic and newspaper articles about Conant's films; materials on the film *Korea: The Unknown War*; a number of presentation papers on North Korea; syllabi of classes Conant taught at Columbia, New York University, and other universities; materials on Korean art; Conant's English and Korean lecture notes; Syracuse project reports; BPI weekly meeting reports and inventory lists; documents on the installation of recording equipment at BPI; Conant's personal memos; and much more. Additionally, there is one very interesting document in the collection, a memo written by the first president of Korea, Syngman Rhee.

The collection's books, serials, and pamphlets have been cataloged and may be found in the Columbia Libraries Catalog (CLIO). These materials can be checked out any time during library hours. Since the library does not have equipment on which to play the film, audio, and music reels, these are stored at an offsite location in New Jersey and are not available to the public. Due to copyright issues, digital versions of the films on DVDs and CDs are only available in the Rarebook and Special Reading Room during the room's designated hours, which are posted on the library's website. As for the photos and other documents, they are also kept in the Rarebook and Special Reading Room. The finding aid for the Conant Collection is now available via CLIO (Columbia University Libraries Online Catalog), https://findingaids.library.columbia.edu/ead/nnc-ea/ldpd_8328755. These materials can be requested and are accessible to the public only in the room during its designated hours. The library has digitized the photos, which are now available. Hopefully, the library will be able to obtain more support with which to digitize the remaining collection and personal documents so that these materials can also be made accessible at any place and any time for free via the library website.

In conclusion, the Conant Collection is a unique and invaluable resource of audio and visual materials from 1950s and early 1960s Korea that cannot be found elsewhere. The collection consists not only of materials on the Korean War but also on the history of Korean film, social life, and living conditions during 1950s in multiple formats. Due to the fact that the collection was recently established in our library, it has not yet been fully explored or utilized by many scholars. Nevertheless, this collection will be of tremendous interest and great relevance to scholars who are engaged in research on modern Korean history, culture, and film.

Notes

[1] "Conant Biographical Note," Conant Collection, accessed June 17, 2015, http://library.columbia.edu/locations/eastasian/korean/rarespecial/conant_collection/biographical_note.html.

[2] Korean Film Archive (한국영상자료원), *Naengjŏn sidae Han'guk ŭi munhwa yŏnghwa* (냉전시대 한국의 문화영화) (Seoul: Korean Film Archive, 2011), 6.

[3] Ibid., 6, 34.

[4] Ibid., 34.

[5] Ibid., 33.

[6] Ibid., 5.

[7] Ibid., 35.

[8] Charles Armstrong, email message to author, June 17, 2015.

[9] Ibid.

Bibliography

"Conant Biographical Note." Conant Collection. Accessed June 17, 2015. http://library.columbia.edu/locations/eastasian/korean/rarespecial/conant_collection/biographical_note.html.

Korean Film Archive (한국영상자료원). *Naengjŏn sidae Han'guk ŭi munhwa yŏnghwa* (냉전시대 한국의 문화영화). Seoul: Korean Film Archive, 2011.

8

The Alfred Rodman Hussey Papers (1945–1948) at the University of Michigan Library

Keiko Yokota-Carter, University of Michigan

The Collection

The University of Michigan Library's Asia Library holds a unique archival collection, the Alfred Rodman Hussey Papers, 1945–1948, collected by Alfred Rodman Hussey (1902–64) during his work with the Government Section, Supreme Commander for the Allied Powers (SCAP), during the Allied occupation of Japan following World War II, and later in the Central Intelligence Agency. These documents were donated by the Hussey family after his death as stipulated in his will. On July 25, 1963, one year before he passed away, Hussey wrote to a colleague, Lt. Col. Milo E. Rowell, "Mine is going to Michigan."[1]

Hussey initially served as a member of the Planning Unit and then successively as chief, Internal Affairs Unit; chief, Governmental Powers Branch of the Governmental Powers Division; and special assistant to the chief, Government Section. He was a principal contributor to Douglas MacArthur's 1947 draft of the Japanese Constitution and had a significant role in the establishment of the new Labor Ministry. Hussey left Japan and returned to the United States in July 1948.[2]

The collection is historically significant for its government documents related to the drafts of Japan's new Constitution, including documents from the Far Eastern Commission (FEC), and the reform plans and related documents of new Japan based on the Constitution. It is also unique for its image collection, which includes a photo album of the Constitution ceremonies and the slides produced by the Kenpo Fukyu Iinkai (憲法普及委員会, Constitution Popularization Society) in which Hussey was involved.

The scope of the collection from the University of Michigan Library catalog.

Collection contains: correspondence, memoranda, orders, reports, official and unofficial policy papers, draft legislation, drafts of writings, clippings, and printed matter relating to Hussey's work with the Government Section, Supreme Commander for the Allied Powers, during the Allied occupation of Japan following World War II and to the efforts of the Allies to reorganize Japanese government and society; personal papers and correspondence of Hussey relating to his interests in civil rights and in the Central Intelligence Agency, as well as his various writings; oversize maps and charts; and audiocassette and magnetic tapes.[3]

Hussey's high position involved him in major missions during the occupation of Japan and allowed him to collect all kinds of major documents from the SCAP. He was aware of the significance of these documents and already intended to keep them for the future.

Preservation and Conservation Efforts

The Asia Library received Alfred Hussey's collection after his death in 1964. The original documents were organized in folders classified by subject, and the entire collection was kept in a dedicated cabinet in the library. In May 1977, the collection was microfilmed, except for duplicates, and a checklist was made.

A letter by a former librarian of the Asia Library, Naomi Fukuda, dated June 20, 1977, indicates that a set of microfilms with the checklist then sold for two hundred dollars. Sets were purchased by the Library of Congress, eleven US university libraries (University of California at Berkeley, University of Colorado, Harvard University Yenching Library, Stanford University Hoover Institution, University of Illinois, University of Iowa, University of Maryland, Princeton University, University of Washington, University of Chicago, and the University of Hawaii), two Canadian university libraries (University of British Columbia and University of Toronto), two Japanese university libraries (Tokyo Keizai Daigaku University and the Tsukuba University Department of Political Science), and one company, the Nissho-Iwai American Corporation. A set was also donated to the National Diet Library.[4]

The documents remained in their cases until 2014, when a new preservation effort was undertaken by the Asia Library, the Special Collections Library, and the University of Michigan Library's Department of Preservation and Conservation.

All the documents were rehoused in ten acid-free record boxes and secured in offsite storage as part of the Special Collections Library.

The preservation project was initiated by the Asia Library and organized by Ikumi Crocoll, a graduate student in the School of Information majoring in preservation. Crocoll worked under the supervision of the Archives Unit head and the Transportation History Collection curator at the Special Collections Library. The materials were carefully examined and rehoused in acid-free files and boxes. Bibliographic metadata were created, and the finding aid was made available online so that users all over the world could search and request documents online and obtain digitized copies made by the Special Collections Library according to its guidelines.

Later, in September 2014, the checklist for the microfilm set was digitized, and in May 2015 it became openly available in Hathi Trust in the worldwide public domain.

The online finding aid prepared by the Special Collections Library describes the collection down to the folder level, while the microfilm set checklist shows individual documents within the folders. For example, the online finding aid first shows the summarized title for a group of folders and then lists the folder names.

Organization of the Occupation (series):

1-A. Formation, Personnel, and Organization of the Government Section (1945–1948)

The microfilm checklist shows individual items, with dates, under each file.

1-A Formation, Personnel, and Organization of the Government Section (1945–1948)1. Memorandum re delineation of inter-divisional responsibilities 22.10.461a. Handwritten note re inter-divisional responsibilities. 2. Personnel roster of Governmental Power Division from 10.10.45-30.6.48 (2)

This checklist is full-text searchable in Hathi Trust, making it easier to find topics covered in the entire collection.

Presently, the Hussey Papers are housed in secure remote storage facility under the Special Collections Library's guidelines and custodial supervision while the curatorial responsibility still belongs to the Asia Library. The public can use these documents by searching the microfilm checklist and the online finding aid and visiting the Special Collections Library or requesting digitized documents online. The Asia Library and the Center for Japanese Studies provide travel grants for visiting researchers. This level accessibility is sufficient for academic research.

Collection Highlights

Constitution File

Historically the most significant documents in the Hussey Papers are those in the so-called Constitution file. This file includes the most important documents related to the process of drafting the Japanese Constitution, such as "Three basic points stated by Supreme Commander to be 'musts' in constitutional revision."[5] The original copies of these documents are held at the University of Michigan, while other copies are at the National Diet Library and at the archives of other SCAP members at other institutions: the Milo E. Rowell Papers at the Hoover Institution Library and Archives, the Charles L. Kades Papers at Amherst College, and the records at the Library and Archives of the MacArthur Memorial.

Usually three or four carbon copies were made when the documents were typed. These copies were used by twenty-two members of the Constitution Steering Committee. Not all members, however, created archive collections later in their lives. Only Rowell, Hussey, and Kades actively did so. Beate Sirota Gordon passed away in 2012 and her collection will be archived at Mills College.[6]

The "Constitution file" at the National Diet Library

The National Diet Library created the digital archives in 2003, including for the files donated by Dr. Robert E. Ward of the University of Michigan in 1980. In December 1980, Dr. Ward, Hussey's colleague, became the director of the Japan–United States Friendship Commission and visited the National Diet Library. He donated a file of documents given to him by Lt. Col. Milo E. Rowell. The file consists of documents related to drafting the Japanese Constitution collected by Hussey himself from February 1, 1946, to March, 6, 1946. Three sets of the same documents were produced. The first was for Gen. Douglas MacArthur, supreme commander for the SCAP in Japan. The second was for Maj. Gen. Courtney Whitney, and the third was for Cmdr. Alfred R. Hussey. Dr. Ward gave this third set, Hussey's file, to the National Diet Library. There is no record of how this document was separated from Michigan's Hussey Collection, entered the possession of Milo E. Rowell, and was then given to Dr. Ward.[7] At the National Diet Library photographic images of these documents were made available in the worldwide public domain in May 2003 as part of library's digital resources collection.[8]

The National Diet Library "Alfred Hussey papers–Constitution File No. 1,"

The National Diet Library created the digital archive "The Birth of the Constitution of Japan," including the "Alfred Hussey papers–Constitution File," http://www.ndl.go.jp/constitution/library/06/hussey.html.

Archive Collections of Other Members of the SCAP Constitution Steering Committee

Charles L. Kades Papers, Gordon W. Prange Collection at the University of Maryland at College Park, http://lib.guides.umd.edu/content. php?pid=223158&sid=1851840.

Charles L. Kades Papers, 1913–1997 (Bulk: 1945–1996), Amherst College. This collection includes the constitution files in addition to the other records covering Kades's career. See http://asteria.fivecolleges.edu/findaids/amherst/ma214_main.html.

Milo E. Rowell Papers, Hoover Institution Archives at Stanford University, http://www.oac.cdlib.org/findaid/ark:/13030/kt487034gj/.

Rowell Papers (ラウェル (Rowell, Milo E.) 文書), General Library, University of Tokyo, http://www.lib.u-tokyo.ac.jp/koho/guide/coll/Rowell.html.

Dale M. Hellengers Papers, Harry S. Truman Presidential Library and Museum, https://www.trumanlibrary.org/hstpaper/hellegrs.html. The collection includes interviews with Milo E. Rowell and other SCAP staff.

Beate Sirota Gordon Papers, Mills College.

Beate Sirota Gordon, the only woman on the Steering Committee, was involved in drafting the civil rights section of the Constitution and worked as an interpreter between American and Japanese representatives. She played a significant role as a member of the committee by translating documents from Japanese to English and collecting constitutions from various libraries in Tokyo to prepare for drafting the new one. Her archive is in the process of being acquired by her alma mater, Mills College.[9]

Hussey's Work on the New Constitution

The major mission of the SCAP, headed by the United States, was to transform Japan from a militaristic imperial power to a democratic power allied with the United States in the Pacific, where communist powers were expanding after World War II. Documents related to Japan's new Constitution and reform plans based on it occupy the majority of the Hussey Papers. The collection includes 3,650 document titles according to the index; most are paper materials such as typed or handwritten manuscripts, copies of documents, illustrations, and maps. The collection contains numerous memos and government correspondence among Japan, SCAP, the United States, and the FEC. It also includes research documents on Japanese political, social, and educational systems. In addition to these text materials, what is unique about. Hussey Papers is its image collection of a photographs and slides.

Political Background

In order to better understand Hussey's strong feeling toward this particular work, let us examine the political background behind the drafting of the new Constitution.

International politics put great pressure on the SCAP (and thus the US government) to hasten the process of creating a Constitution that would preserve the imperial system. General MacArthur saw that the imperial system would play a role in uniting Japan and keeping Japanese people from becoming sympathetic to communism, which was already gaining power in the region and becoming a great threat in world politics with the Soviet Union and growing communist power in China. Geopolitically, the stability of Japan as a noncommunist ally was crucial to US power in the Pacific and the Far East.[10]

In January 1946, just before the formation of the FEC in February, Australia demanded that Emperor Hirohito be tried as a war criminal. Twelve countries were to be members of the FEC: the United States as chair, the United Kingdom, China under the Nationalist (Chiang Kai-shek) government, the Soviet Union, France, India, the Netherlands, Canada, Australia, New Zealand, and the Philippines. Among these, the United Kingdom, China, the Soviet Union, and Australia were highly determined to prosecute Hirohito as having been responsible for the war. Once the FEC was formed, all major protocols of the occupation of Japan would need the approval of it . MacArthur decided that the SCAP would establish "de facto" conditions by drafting a Constitution that guaranteed the continuation of the imperial system.

The Steering Committee charged with drafting the Constitution was formed on February 4, 1946. The draft was finished in nine days and submitted on February 13, 1946, just after the FEC was formed in Washington, DC. Although the other members of the FEC were offended by the SCAP draft, now that it had been submitted to the Japanese government they had no choice but to start negotiations on the basis of this de facto draft, which maintained the emperor, albeit as the symbol of the state without political power. After much negotiation among the Japanese government, the SCAP, and the FEC, the Constitution was approved with Article 1 stating that "the Emperor shall be the symbol of the State and of the unity of the people, deriving his position from the will of the people with whom resides sovereign power."[11] Without doubt it became an essential task for Hussey, as the special assistant to the chief of the Government Section, to enhance the foundation of state unity by educating the Japanese people on the new position of the emperor and their own new role as a sovereign power in addition to the establishment of a new Labor Ministry, which would prevent communism from gaining ground among the Japanese people.

Society for the Popularization of the Constitution

On November 3, 1946, the new Constitution was promulgated and the work of promoting new concepts began. On January 17, 1947, Hussey attended a meeting of the Constitution Popularization Society (Kenpo Fukyu Iinkai, 憲法普及委員会), held at the official residence of Prime Minister Hitoshi Ashida. The memorandum containing the record of this meeting was cowritten with Ruth A. Ellerman.[12] This memorandum shows that Hussey felt strongly about promoting new concepts. It stated that he "called the attention of the Society to the importance of telling the people of Japan not only what was in the Constitution but what it meant to them, how they could and should use it and what their responsibilities were in developing a democratic Japan under it."[13] Ellerman also attended this meeting with Hussey and, as recorded in the same memorandum, "commented upon the fact that in the work of the Society the women of Japan posed a special problem, that that Society should devote time and effort toward educating the women of Japan in their social and political responsibilities under the new Constitution." Hussey clearly mentioned that "the advice and assistance of Government Section were offered in the furtherance of the work of the Society."

On February 5, 1947, Hussey wrote in his "Memorandum for the Chief, Government Section, Subject: Program for Publicizing the new Japanese Constitution" that "all programs and plans [for] a coordinated effort will be made to emphasize: first, the Bill of Rights; secondly, in conjunction with local elections, local autonomy and the responsibilities of the citizens; thirdly, the importance of the Diet and the citizens' relationship to the Diet. The independence of the judiciary will be briefly touched on."[14] He was sensitive to the status of the emperor, saying that "no mention will be made of the changed position of the Emperor since it is deemed wise not to emphasize that question. Perhaps the most important aspect of the entire program will be the development of and constant emphasis upon the theme that the new Constitution is but the vehicle whereby the people of Japan can and must determine their future destiny."[15]

Hussey, in collaboration with the Civil Information Education Section, worked very closely with Dr. Hitoshi Ashida, an "influential member of the Liberal Party," who was appointed president of the Constitution Popularization Society and Mr. R. Sakakibara, chief of the General Affairs Section of the Constitution Popularization Society, on producing promotional materials. Sakakibara, for example, reported resource needs such as "200 tons of coal to cover the deficit of paper used for the pamphlets of the new constitution."[16] He asked Hussey to "allocate [an] additional 70,000 lbs. of paper to the Dai Nippon Printing Company and 230,000 lbs. to the Kyoto Printing Company."[17] The distribution plan for the pamphlets shows that a total of 19, 443,000 pamphlets were to be distributed in Japan. Of these, "over 500,000 copies are reserved to be given to returning soldiers and civilians from the Soviet Union."[18] Hussey asked the Ministry of Finance to guarantee "an increase of seven million yen in the subsidy of the New Constitution Propagation Society (Kenpo Fukyu Kai)."[19]

Various activities were planned under this budget estimate: pamphlets, motion pictures, educational and documentary films (two motion pictures were being planned), slides, posters, paper plays (*kamishibai*, 紙芝居) for children, training lectures and meetings, and publications such as booklets. Various contests were held by newspaper agencies. Religious, cultural, and theater groups were also encouraged to plan events, and orchestras and choirs were encouraged to compose music to promote the new Constitution.[20]

Ten thousand yen were allocated for creating slide materials.[21] One box from a two-box slide set is preserved in the Hussey Papers collection.[22] (More than one slide set would have been produced.).

There are also many hand-drawn draft illustrations for posters explaining the changes in concepts from the old Constitution to the new one (e.g., documents 53-C-14-3, 53-C-14-4, and 53-C-14-7). These posters were used in the press conference at which Hussey presented the new Constitution on the March 3, 1946, and Japanese newspapers included them in their articles.[23] At the press conference Hussey introduced Article 1 and emphasized that "the ultimate authority, the source of all political power in Japan is the people."[24]

Slides and a Photo Album

The slides were produced by the Constitution Popularization Society and the Japan Gento Slide Company/Nihon Gento Kabushiki Kaisha (日本幻燈株式会社). The screen presentation of slides and filmstrips was already a popular method for disseminating information and public education in Japan.[25] In 1948 the Civil Information and Education Section of the SCAP (CIE) launched a nationwide campaign to promote the new ideas. The set of slides in which Hussey was involved would have been part of this campaign.

The slides are not held at the National Diet Library or in any Japanese university library collection. Neither have they been found in the antiquarian market in Japan as of today. Waseda University Engeki Hakubutsukan (早稲田大学演劇博物館, Tsubouchi Memorial Theater Museum) has one of the largest collections in Japan, with over three thousand slides, but it does not hold this Constitution promotion slide set. According to Dr. Hana Washitani, a researcher at this museum who specializes in the history of slides and filmstrips in Japan, the slides produced around this time period were often lost and not archived well. The slide set consisted of two boxes, but only box 2 is preserved at the University of Michigan Library. Box 1 has not been found anywhere. Therefore this slide set, kept by Hussey, is extremely valuable.[26]

Hussey seemed enthusiastic about producing and preserving visual materials. A photo album in the collection contains photos of the ceremony of the promulgation on November 3, 1946, and others of the ceremony of enforcement of the new Constitution held on May 3, 1947. These ceremonies were meticulously planned by the SCAP and Japanese government. Drafts and final versions of event documents, such as the Imperial Rescript (in both Japanese and English),[27] the ceremony schedules, and the seating chart for the House of Peers ceremony,[28] are held in the Hussey Papers.

Preservation and Access of Visual Material

In order to preserve and promote these unique historical image resources, Mari Suzuki, the Asia Library's Japanese materials librarian, initiated a digitization project with the Digital Preservation Office and made the slides available as an "Online Exhibition."

This image digitization project, offering the content in a different format in addition to the original paper resource, has been beneficial in preserving the original materials and promoting the use of historical primary sources in research, in education, and among the public. It fulfills the "three main processes" of collection management described by R. Robert Waller.[29]

1. Development of the collection by means of adding or removing items

2. Use of the collection, which includes activities such as processing, cataloging, restoring, and researching.

3. Preservation of the collection with the aim of maintaining its value at an optimum level.

In addition to the online exhibition of the visual materials, other methods of access to this resource—such as digitization of the manuscript—are still under investigation. The most significant part of the Alfred R. Hussey collection, the "Constitution files," are already available in the public domain through the National Diet Library home page. The Hussey Papers also include reports and records of many aspects of Japanese society and valuable information regarding the formation of "New Japan." However, these records also include "sensitive" information such as a record of the imperial household budget and many reports and pieces of information that were once classified "Top Secret" by the General Headquarters of the SCAP. None of the documents produced by the SCAP has been digitized. The legal and political issues surrounding public disclosure of these documents are to be carefully examined.

Research Using the Hussey Papers

The collection has mostly been used by legal, political science, and history researchers in Japanese studies who are studying the creation of the Japanese Constitution and the reform of Japan. There was a research boom after the microfilm became available in 1977, which resulted in many research publications in the 1980s and 1990s.

Examples include the following.

Inumaru, Hideo (犬丸秀雄)(yaku kaisetsu)(訳解説). "'Hasshi bunsho' to kenpo seitei katei: soshireibu no Nihonkoku kenpo kankei bunsho" (「ハッシ-文書」と憲法制定過程: 総司令部の日本国憲法関係文書). *Hogaku semina* (法学セミナ) 318 (August 1981): 152–84. Inumaru researched the process of the formation of Japan's Constitution.

Pharr, Susan J. "Politics of Women's Rights," in *Democratizing Japan: Allied Occupation*. Honolulu: University of Hawai'i Press, 1987. Dr. Pharr, an American political scientist, used the Hussey Papers to reveal the process of drafting "women's rights" and the contributions of Beate Sirota Gordon, the only woman in the committee.

Hellegers, Dale M. *We, the Japanese People: World War II and the Origins of the Japanese Constitution*. Stanford: Stanford University Press, 2002. The data produced during Hellegers' research—transcripts of interviews conducted by Hellegers and others of SCAP personnel involved in drafting the Constitution and managing the occupation, printed materials, typed and handwritten notes, and sound recordings—are held in the archives of the Harry S. Truman Presidential Library and Museum (https://www.trumanlibrary.org/hstpaper/hellegrs.htm).

Sasagawa, Ryotaro (笹川陸太郎). "Kenpo shiryoshitsu zo no 'Hussey bunsho' to 'Constitution File No. 1' (zen hen)" (憲政資料室蔵の'ハッシー文書'と'Constitution File No. 1'（前編）). *Ishinomaki Senshu Daigaku Keieigaku kenkyu* (石巻専修大学経営学研究) 16, no. 2 (March 2005): 179–93.

Hirayama, Asaji. "Pacifism in the Constitution of Japan and the Strategies of National Security." *Journal of International and Advanced Japanese Studies* 7 (March 2015): 1–25. Professor Hirayama is using the Constitution file in the Hussey Papers to examine present-day national security issues.

Recently the Japanese government has been attempting to amend the Constitution in order to enforce Japan's military power amid changes in the international power balance. As this new research indicates, The Hussey Papers remain important and valuable for examining the future of world politics.

Notes

[1] Document 93-D-10-1, Alfred Rodman Hussey Papers, 1944–1998 (bulk 1945–1948) (hereafter Hussey Papers), n.d. box 7.

[2] Manuscript Division, Library of Congress, "Alfred Rodman Hussey Papers: A Finding Aid to the Collection in the Library of Congress," 2010.

[3] Catalog Record for the Alfred Rodman Hussey Papers, Library Search, 2018.

[4] Fukuda, Naomi, 1947–1950. Library (University of Michigan) Records, Bentley Historical Library, University of Michigan, n.d., box 14.

[5] Document 23-B-3-1, Hussey Papers, n.d., box 3.

[6] Gordon.

[7] National Diet Library (国立国会図書館) 2013

[8] National Diet Library (国立国会図書館) 2003

[9] Gordon

[10] Hirayama 2015

[11] Shioda 2008

[12] Document 53-A-7-1

[13] Ibid.

[14] Document 53-D-6-1 1947

[15] Document 53-D-6-2

[16] Document 53-B-2-1 1947

[17] Document 53-B-3-1

[18] Document 53-B-9-2

[19] Document 53-B-11-1

[20] Document 53-B-10

[21] Ibid.

[22] Nihon Gento Kabushiki Kaisha (日本幻灯株式会社) 1947?

[23] Documents 52-F-1 to 52-F-9 1947

[24] Document 52-E-2-1 1947

[25] Washitani 2014

[26] Washitani 2015

[27] Document 31-A-7-1 1946 (Document 31-A-5-1 1946)

[28] Document 31-A-10-1 1946

[29] Waller 2003

Bibliography

Catalog Record for the Alfred Rodman Hussey Papers. Mirlyn Library Catalog, University of Michigan, 2014.

Document 23-B-3-1. Alfred Rodman Hussey Papers, 1944–1998 (bulk 1945–1948), n.d., box 3.

Document 31-A-10-1. Alfred Rodman Hussey Papers, 1944–1998 (bulk 1945–1948), 1946, box 4.

Document 31-A-5-1. Alfred Rodman Hussey Papers, 1944–1998 (bulk 1945–1948), 1946, box 4.

Document 31-A-7-1. Alfred Rodman Hussey Papers, 1944–1998 (bulk 1945–1948), 1946, box 4.

Document 52-E-2-1. Alfred Rodman Hussey Papers, 1944–1998 (bulk 1945–1948), 1947, box 4.

Document 53-A-7-1. Alfred Rodman Hussey Papers, 1944–1998 (bulk 1945–1948), n.d., box 4.

Document 53-B-10. Alfred Rodman Hussey Papers, 1944–1998 (bulk 1945–1948), n.d., box 4.

Document 53-B-11-1. Alfred Rodman Hussey Papers, 1944–1998 (bulk 1945–1948), n.d., box 4.

Document 53-B-2-1. Alfred Rodman Hussey Papers, 1944–1998 (bulk 1945–1948), 1947, box 4.

Document 53-B-3-1. Alfred Rodman Hussey Papers, 1944–1998 (bulk 1945–1948), n.d., box 4.

Document 53-B-9-2. Alfred Rodman Hussey Papers, 1944–1998 (bulk 1945–1948), n.d., box 4.

Document 53-D-6-1. Alfred Rodman Hussey Papers, 1944–1998 (bulk 1945–1948), February 5, 1947, box 4.

Document 53-D-6-2. Alfred Rodman Hussey Papers, 1944–1998 (bulk 1945–1948), n.d., box 4.

Document 93-D-10-1. Alfred Rodman Hussey Papers, 1944–1998 (bulk 1945–1948), n.d., box 7.

Documents 52-F-1 to 52-F-9. Alfred Rodman Hussey Papers, 1944–1998 (bulk 1945–1948), 1947, box 4.

Fukuda, Naomi. 1947–1950.Library (University of Michigan) Records. Bentley Historical Library, University of Michigan, n.d., box 14.

Beate Sirota Gordon Papers. Mills College Library, Special Collection.

Hirayama, Asaji (平山朝治). "Pacifism in the Constitution of Japan and Strategies of National Security" 日本国憲法の平和主義と安全保障戦略. *Journal of International and Advanced Japanese Studies* (2015): 1–25.

Ishimaru, Hideo 犬丸秀雄 (yaku kaisetsu 訳解説). "'Hasshi bunsho' to kenpo seitei katei: Soshireibu no Nihonkoku kenpo kankei bunsho" (「ハッシ-文書」と憲法制定過程: 総司令部の日本国憲法関係文書). *Hogaku semina* (法学セミナ) 318 (August 1981): 152–84.

Manuscript Division, Library of Congress. "Alfred Rodman Hussey Papers: A Finding Aid to the Collection in the Library of Congress." 2010.

National Diet Library (国立国会図書館). "Alfred Hussey Papers, Constitution File No. 1" (ハッシー文書　憲法ファイル)." リーサチ・ナビ. October 1, 2013. http://rnavi.ndl.go.jp/kensei/entry/Hussey.php.

———. 日本国憲法誕生 [Birth of the Constitution of Japan]. 2003. http://www.ndl.go.jp/constitution/index.html.

Shioda, Jun (塩田純). *Nihonkoku kenpo tanjo: Shirarezaru butaiura* (日本国憲法誕生: 知られざる舞台裏). Nihon Housou Shuppan Kyoukai (日本放送出版協会), 2008.

Waller, R. Robert. "Cultural Property Risk Analysis Model." *Gothenburg Studies in Conservation* 13 (2003): 150.

Washitani, Hana (鷲谷花). "Email correspondence," May 30, 2015.

———. "The Revival of 'Gentou' (Magic Lantern, Filmstrips, Slides) in Showa Period Japan: Focusing on Its Developments in the Media of Post-war Social Movements." *Iconics* (Japan Society of Image Arts and Sciences) 11 (2014): 27–46.

9

The Earliest Recordings of Korean Music (1896)

Robert C. Provine, University of Maryland

Introduction

On Friday, the twenty-fourth of July, 1896, a group of at least three Korean men visited the house of Alice Cunningham Fletcher (1838–1923) at 214 First Street, SE, in Washington, DC.[1] There Miss Fletcher made six Edison wax cylinder recordings of Korean songs, sung either solo or in duet by the Korean men. These 1896 recordings of amateur singers were made eleven years before the next known recordings of Korean music, which were made in Japan and published in 1907.[2] In a presentation to the National Gugak Center (Kungnip kugagwŏn 國立國樂院) in 1998,[3] I introduced these 1896 recordings to Korea, and they have subsequently gathered a fair amount of attention there, including reissue on CD (2007 and 2009).[4] There was also a Korean Broadcasting System (KBS) Special documentary in July 2010.[5] Since the location of 214 First Street SE is now occupied by the Madison Building of the Library of Congress, and the six cylinders were stored for many decades in the adjacent Jefferson Building, it is clear that the cylinders had traveled only a few yards since their recording in 1896 until the recent move of the library's entire cylinder collection to its Packard Campus facility in Culpeper, Virginia.

On the surface, nearly everything about this recording event appears highly unlikely. In 1896 probably the only Koreans in Washington, DC, were a handful of diplomats assigned to the Korean Legation,[6] and all of them were well-educated gentlemen with a Confucian upbringing. That a group of such Korean gentry might enter the house of a single lady and sing a group of songs, including children's songs, into a machine the likes of which they had never imagined challenges belief. Despite what might appear in hindsight to have been extraordinary circumstances, Miss Fletcher herself, to judge from materials in her surviving papers at the National Anthropological Archives,[7] took little or no interest in Korea or Korean music either at that time or any other.

It turns out that the recordings resulted from a remarkable set of coincidental circumstances, from an extraordinary collection of interesting and influential people, from exceptional historical events in Korea and the United States, and from serendipity; to paraphrase Stephen Jay Gould's famous metaphoric description of the Burgess shale, one could rewind the tape of life to about 1880 and replay it millions of times without these cylinder recordings, or anything like them, appearing by 1900.[8]

The six cylinder recordings form one part of a wider, ongoing research project that might be described as Korean music in the late-nineteenth-century United States. The other pieces of the larger investigation are two museum collections that include Korean musical instruments and the matter of a group of Korean musicians sent to the World Columbian Exposition of 1893 in Chicago.[9] All the parts of this puzzle are linked, to greater or lesser degree, to the story told in this chapter.

To explore the people and events that led to circumstances that set the stage for the overall research project, we would need to visit a number of impressive people and their activities through a variety of contexts: first of all, people and circumstances in Washington in the 1890s; second, historical events and people in Korea in the late nineteenth century; third, the World Columbian Exposition of 1893; fourth, collections of musical instruments; and, finally, a tangential connection to the University of Maryland, where I taught until my recent retirement. In this chapter, I propose to look at only the first two and the last (briefly), with only a meager mention of the other two items, which have been examined by others.[10]

This is still incomplete research, although the overall picture is already quite clear. If age allows me to finish the research, there will be more layers of detail in the data but little anticipated change to the basic narrative. So far I have little that is really new to offer in terms of information, in the sense that the data lie in various places in the obscure public record, but rather I attempt to link, in a fresh way, the known information to the specific subject of Korean music in the United States.

Part I: The Washington, DC, Scene

Alice Cunningham Fletcher (1838–1923), the person who made the cylinder recordings, is justly renowned today as one of the great pioneers of anthropology and ethnomusicology in the United States; in particular, she is noted now on the ethnomusicological side for her early use of sound recording in the study of American Indian music, and there are several book-length studies of her career.[11] As a woman, she could not hold a university professorship or join all academic societies, but her influence was such that she was an admired and frequently consulted colleague for numerous important men in anthropology. In fact, one of them, Professor Frederic Putnam (1839–1915) at Harvard (the second professor of anthropology in the United States), arranged for Fletcher to receive a lifelong fellowship, the Thaw Fellowship, starting in 1891. Her most important professional work, given the effort, mental energy, and determined partisanship she gave it for a decade, was land allocation to the Omaha, Winnebago, and Nez Percé tribes in the late nineteenth century.[12] Her respect and love for American Indians was exceptional and much to be admired; indeed, she "adopted" an Omaha chief's son, Francis La Flesche (1857–1932), who shared her house in Washington, along with a third interesting person, E. Jane Gay (1830–1919), who left a detailed description and photographs of Fletcher's fieldwork with the Nez Percé between 1889 and 1892.[13]

Fletcher, along with a good number of other highly accomplished women, was forbidden admission to the Washington Anthropological Society on grounds of gender, despite the genuine esteem in which they were otherwise held by the men. Strong women that they were, they founded the separate Women's Anthropological Society of America (WASA) in 1885, led by Matilda Coxe Evans Stevenson (1849–1915), and the society held regular meetings with formal readings and discussions of scholarly papers until times changed—eventually women were invited to attend paper readings at the Washington Anthropological Society and were admitted to full membership from 1899.[14] Within five years, Fletcher had become not just a member, but President of that formerly male-only Society.[15]

Fletcher obtained her "graphophone," as an Edison cylinder-recording machine was then called, in 1891, when she was already fifty-three years old; the device had been available commercially for only a few years.[16] There are 244 cylinders in the surviving collection of Fletcher cylinders now preserved by the Library of Congress; apart from the six Korean cylinders and a single cylinder of "European classical music," all the cylinders are of American Indian music.[17] Although it is not necessarily the case that all cylinders in Fletcher's collection were recorded by Fletcher herself, many certainly were. Other collectors, in fact, made far more recordings than did Fletcher. Her companion Francis La Flesche, for example, recorded a remarkable set of 254 cylinders documenting Osage rituals,[18] and the formidable Frances Densmore (1867–1957), a great admirer of Fletcher, recorded more than 2,000 cylinders and wrote numerous books documenting and transcribing the music of various American Indian tribes.[19]

The entry in Fletcher's tiny diary for July 24, 1896, is unfortunately rather uninformative, as well as nearly illegible in her inimitable handwriting.[20] She records only that she intends to write to five people, a list that includes Professor Daniel Brinton (1837–99), the first professor of anthropology in the United States (at the University of Pennsylvania) and the aforementioned Professor Frederic Putnam, the second such professor (at Harvard University) and Fletcher's benefactor via the Thaw Fellowship. Indeed, the archives at Harvard include a letter to Putnam written by Fletcher at 8:30 that very morning.[21] There is no mention either on this diary page or in the letter to Putnam about recording Korean music. Fletcher normally used her diary to list tasks she intended to do rather than as a record of things that actually occurred, and the recording session may not have been planned ahead of time.

There is, however, a tantalizing hint of information in a later diary entry, that for August 6. After noting that the temperature that day was "Hot 97°," she writes that she intends to send a copy of her friend and colleague Stewart Culin's 1895 book *Korean Games* to Miss Smith.[22] This was surely Anna Tolman Smith, about whom more will be said below.[23] Fletcher and Culin both worked at the Bureau of Ethnology, and they presented papers together at the Washington Anthropological Society.

While making the Korean cylinder recordings, Fletcher scribbled a few notes about them on small scraps of paper,[24] recopying some of them, and, while these contain no ethnography whatsoever, they are still informative in some ways. There are romanizations of the names of the three men: Jong Sik Ahn, He Chel Ye, and Son Rong. From evidence to be presented below (and well shown in the KBS documentary film), we now know that the first two were An Chŏngsik 安禎植 and Yi Hŭich'ŏl 李喜轍, although Son Rong's identification remains a matter of speculation. The notes identify, in English only, the tracks recorded on the cylinders and the performer(s) for each.

The papers in Fletcher's archive include a number of musical transcriptions drawn from the Korean cylinders. One song, "Song of the Moon" (Tara, tara, palgŭn tara 달아 달아 밝은 달아), is there in several versions, from draft to fair copy, scrawled on scraps of staff paper and the blank backside of some transcriptions of Native American music by the composer and much reviled transcriber of Indian music John Comfort Fillmore (1843-1898), with whom Fletcher had a voluminous correspondence.[25] To understand the significance and purpose of Fletcher's transcriptions, we need to look to another impressive woman of the time, who is probably the most important person in this entire story.

That person is Anna Tolman Smith (1840–1917), who, like Fletcher, was a member of the WASA. Smith worked at the US Bureau of Education (forerunner of the current Department of Education) and was outspoken about numerous important issues of the day, including coeducation, the role of religious education (her view was that religion and science should be mixed in the classroom), race psychology, and the principles that should govern the content of public education in the United States (a topic still much debated today). She was an established expert in foreign educational practices, and in particular she wrote in 1912 a substantial article that introduced to the United States the Montessori system of education.[26]

In February 1896, the year of the Korean recordings, Fletcher was president of the WASA and Smith was the director of its Section of Psychology.[27] Smith had the idea of presenting a paper to the WASA in 1896 or 1897 about Korean nursery rhymes, and in late 1897 this paper found its way into print in the *Journal of American Folk-lore*.[28] The article quickly reveals that some Korean students had given her information, indicating also that recordings and the transcriptions in the article had been made by Alice Fletcher.[29]

Miss Smith, no doubt with considerable assistance from someone familiar with Korea and the Korean language (a probable identification is given in part III), offers a "phonetic rendering" of part of one of the recorded songs, along with a translation of a longer portion of the song.[30] My own draft of the full Korean song text, along with a rough English translation, is as follows.[31]

달아 달아 밝은 달아 이태백이 놀던 달아
저기 저기 저 달속에 계수나무 생겼으니
옥도끼로 찍어내고 금도끼로 다듬어 내어
초가삼간 집을 짓고 우리 부모 모셔다가
천년만년 살고지고

아가아가 울덜마라 우리아기 잘도 잔다
개야개야 짖질마라 우리금동 아기 잘도 잔다
은동아기 잘도 잔다
개야개야 짖질마라 우리아기 잘도 잔다
잘도 잔다 짖지마라

Moon, moon, bright moon; the moon where Yi T'aebaek [Li Po] played.
There, there, in that moon there is a cinnamon tree.
With a jade axe, cut the tree down; with a gold axe, trim it.
Make a straw house of three rooms, serve our parents.
Thousand years, ten thousand years live.

Baby, baby, don't cry; our baby is sleeping well.
Dog, dog, don't bark; our golden baby is sleeping well.
Silver baby is sleeping well.
Dog, dog, don't bark; our baby is sleeping well.
Sleeping well, don't bark.

Such were the immediate circumstances surrounding the 1896 recordings, and perhaps the veil of disbelief is lifting from the event: young students are willing to do things that older people find awkward, a particular scholarly purpose was being served by the recordings, and a strong personality (Smith) was pushing the students to cooperate with her purposes. As mentioned earlier, Alice Fletcher is a deservedly important figure in the history of ethnomusicology and anthropology, and it is natural that we would wish such a person to have been a prime mover in the story of the earliest recordings of Korean music (as indeed she is portrayed in the KBS documentary); however, Anna Tolman Smith, as we shall increasingly see, is the primary hero in the story of the recordings, while Alice Fletcher played a much less significant and more technical role.

Part II: Historical Context in Korea and the United States

Late-nineteenth-century Korea, or more correctly the five-hundred-year-old kingdom of Chosŏn 朝鮮, was stagnant in many ways: its economy remained essentially agricultural (as it had been for many centuries); its social structure was largely defined by Confucianism and a repressive class system; it was nearly closed to foreigners; and its governmental system, also derived from Confucian principles, was conservative and difficult to change. In many ways, the government was based on a Chinese model and, to a degree, was subservient to China.

Japan, by contrast, had opened its doors to the outside world with the Meiji Restoration of 1868 and was making rapid progress toward modernization and the importation of western thinking. Both Japan and China wished to control Korea, and in due course they both installed military forces inside the country, particularly within the capital city of Hansŏng 漢城, which is now called Seoul.

The Korean government, especially those officials under the influence of Queen Min 閔 and her family, in great part leaned conservatively toward China, while those few who favored progressive ideas, with some support from King Kojong 高宗, looked to Japan as a model. There arose a group of young, activist Korean intellectuals, known as the Enlightenment Party or Progressive Party (Kaehwadang 開化黨), who were determined to bring Korea out of its stagnation and to import modern ideas from outside Korean borders. This period of Korean history is one of the most heavily researched and diversely interpreted, having drawn the attention of both Korean and foreign scholars for more than a century, and both the primary and secondary literature is immense. I give here only a bare outline of events that bear an informative relevance to the cylinder recordings.[32]

In 1882, a mission was sent to Japan to learn, among other things, about Japanese agriculture and recent modern developments to see whether such ideas might be productively applied in Korea. Two members of that mission were Kim Okkyun 金玉均 (1851–94) and Pyŏn Su 邊燧 (1861–91), both important members of the Progressive Party.[33] Also in 1882, a Treaty of Amity and Commerce (also known as the Shufeldt Treaty) was signed with the United States, the first such treaty with a foreign power.

In the next year, 1883, a further mission was planned and approved by King Kojong, this time a Special Mission to the United States (and, as it turned out, to Europe as well). Important members of the mission, again selected from the Progressive Party, included an adoptive relative of the queen, Min Yŏngik 閔泳翊 (1860–1914), as minister plenipotentiary and Sŏ Kwangbŏm 徐光範 (1859–97) as secretary, along with Yu Kilchun 俞吉濬 (1856–1914) and the already mentioned Pyŏn Su as attachés.[34] All these were young men, aged twenty-three, twenty-four, twenty-seven, and twenty-two, respectively. Sŏ Kwangbŏm and Pyŏn Su are especially important to this story and will reappear below.

In July and August 1883, the Special Mission stopped in Japan, and there, on only four days' notice, they employed a twenty-eight-year-old American named Percival Lowell (1855–1916), who happened to be in Japan at the time, to serve as their foreign secretary and counselor. Percival Lowell was a member of a well-to-do Bostonian aristocratic family of considerable wealth and status. Lowell's younger brother Abbott Lawrence Lowell (1856–1943) was to become president of Harvard University from 1909 to 1933, and their sister Amy Lowell (1874–1925) is notable as an important lesbian poet who possessed an interest in Japan.[35] In the view of Minister Plenipotentiary Min Yŏngik, "Mr. Lowell is not only well acquainted with the customs of this country, but is a man of sagacity, of clear intellect, and without the assistance of such a person things can not be brought to a successful termination."[36]

Staying in the United States for about two months in late 1883, the mission visited San Francisco, Chicago, Washington, DC, New York, and Boston, among other places, and various newspapers, including the *New York Times*, took note.[37] The mission went to Washington, DC, for a few days, but in fact discovered that it would have to travel to New York to meet President Chester A. Arthur.[38] Later it returned to Washington for a longer stay. At the end of their visit, part of the group, including Min Yŏngik, Sŏ Kwangbŏm, and Pyŏn Su, proceeded via New York to Europe for a tour, accompanied by Ensign George C. Foulk (1856–93).[39] most of the others returned to Korea via San Francisco accompanied by Lowell. Yu Kilchun alone remained in the United States to study at Boston University, an interesting tangential story not to be told here.

Back in Korea at the end of 1883, the group of young Korean intellectuals set about trying to pull Korea out of its hermit condition and into a productive relationship with the rest of the world. Lowell remained in Korea for only two months, until late February 1884; he studied and came to respect the country, and he subsequently wrote the book *Chosön: The Land of the Morning Calm* (copyright and preface 1885, published 1886).[40] He also published articles on significant events and sights in Korea, as well as taking a number of interesting photographs (e.g., of the king and crown prince). After several trips to Japan and elsewhere, he settled permanently in the United States and pursued a childhood interest in astronomy, establishing the still active Lowell Observatory near Flagstaff, Arizona, where his Korea photographs remain in the archives.[41] He enjoyed a successful career as one of the preeminent astronomers of the age. He was one of the first to explore the idea of canals on Mars and postulated the existence of an advanced civilization there, writing books and articles to that effect.[42] The "dwarf planet" Pluto (now not deemed to be a major planet), was predicted by Lowell and later discovered, in 1930, by a young observer (Clyde Tombaugh) at the Lowell Observatory.[43]

The young Korean intellectuals found themselves struggling against enormous conservative political forces and were unable to persuade the government to bring itself out of its stagnation. Eventually, under the leadership of Kim Okkyun and with apparent support from Japan, the same people we have been discussing, plus a number of others and some hired assassins, carried out a coup d'état in December 1884 (known as the Kapsin chŏngbyŏn 甲申政變). Six high officials on the conservative side were assassinated at a banquet contrived for that purpose under the pretense of celebrating the opening of the first Korean post office. The queen's adoptive relative, Min Yŏngik, who originally had been sympathetic to the Progressives and had led the Special Mission of 1883 to the United States and Europe, was also seriously injured in that bungled assassination attempt. Sŏ Kwangbŏm was one of the main leaders of the coup, and Pyŏn Su, who had access to the king, was stationed in the palace with the king and queen while the fateful banquet took place.[44]

This attempt to force Korea out of its slumber was a disaster, and it failed in only three days. The Chinese reestablished control for some time, and a number of the conspirators, including Sŏ Kwangbŏm and Pyŏn Su, narrowly escaped to Japan; others remained in Seoul, where they were tortured and put to death. Lowell, for his part, contributed an acerbic piece to the *Atlantic Monthly*, describing the coup d'état carried out by men he had known closely during his time with the 1883 Special Mission to the United States.[45]

Part III: Back in the United States with a Fresh Perspective

Japan was strongly pressured to return the conspirators for punishment, but Sŏ Kwangbŏm and Pyŏn Su managed, independently, to escape to the United States. Sŏ became a US citizen in New Jersey and eventually moved to Washington, DC, where he held various jobs and formed strong friendships.[46] One of his jobs was at the Bureau of Education, where, inevitably, he would have met Anna Tolman Smith and probably answered questions about educational systems in Korea and

Japan. Indeed, he wrote an extended article on Korean education that includes a short section on music.[47] He, together with Pyŏn Su, served as a consultant for various purposes, such as identification of and commentary on Korean materials in Smithsonian museums, and he wrote articles on Korean children's stories.[48]

Korea in the early 1890s was in turmoil, and political power shifted rapidly back and forth between conservative and progressive elements. In 1894, despite his role in the coup d'état a decade earlier and having taken American citizenship, Sŏ Kwangbŏm was invited back to Korea and given a high government post.[49] But in February 1896, he was posted back to Washington to serve as head of the Korean Legation, as reported in the *Washington Post*.[50] He held that position only until September of the same year before being relieved by a new head of legation who came from an opposing faction that had come to power in Korea.

Although the 1896 cylinder recordings may seem to have vanished from this article, we are ready for their reappearance. They were made in the middle of Sŏ Kwangbŏm's brief tenure as Korean minister in Washington, and we can now observe also that Sŏ certainly knew Anna Tolman Smith and was interested in education and Korean children's stories. This is the point at which serendipity arrives on the scene. About that time seven Korean students studying in Japan decided they would rather study in the United States.[51] They managed to escape and got as far as Vancouver before running out of money. A *Washington Post* article of May 8, 1896 carries the story further.[52] Sŏ found the students a place at Howard University, and the *Post* tells us that they sang "real Korean melody" at a party (reenacted in the KBS documentary).

The seven escapees were members of a rather large group of Koreans who had been sent to study at Keio University in Japan, where a high-definition group photograph was taken in 1895; everyone in the photograph is clearly identified on the back, including An Chŏngsik (安禎植) and Yi Hŭichŏl (李喜轍).[53]

Although some details are missing, the general background of the 1896 cylinder recordings is now sufficiently clear: a group of young Korean male students arrived in Washington, DC in May 1896 and were under the care of Sŏ Kwangbŏm, head of the Korean Legation. This led through his existing contacts with Anna Tolman Smith to Alice Fletcher, who had the technology with which to record the six cylinders (a session also reenacted in the KBS documentary). Surely Sŏ is the one who helped Smith with her article on Korean nursery rhymes.

If it weren't for Sŏ Kwangbŏm, a progressive who had traveled abroad with the Special Mission to the United States in 1883, conspired in the coup d'état of 1884, become a much-respected figure in Washington, been chosen for a high governmental post back in Korea in 1894, and been appointed head of the Korean Legation in Washington in 1896, the Fletcher recordings would never have been made. Ordered to return to Korea after being relieved of his position at the legation in September 1896,[54] Sŏ knew what would happen if he did so, and therefore he stayed on in Washington on grounds of ill health. In August 1897, he took a vigorous bicycle ride in the streets of Washington, aggravating his chronic tuberculosis, and he died on Friday the thirteenth at the age of thirty-eight.[55] In October of that year, his associate Anna Tolman Smith published a touching and strongly felt tribute titled "The Mission of Pom K. Soh," which described his many achievements and tribulations.[56]

To digress briefly, the other escapee, with whom Sŏ appears to have had little contact during much of his time in America, was Pyŏn Su. By 1887, Pyŏn's English was good enough that he could enroll in the Maryland Agricultural College (now the University of Maryland). He graduated in June 1891, delivering the student address at his graduation ceremony, and he is now recognized as the first Korean to graduate from an American college. He obtained employment with the Department of Agriculture and wrote a substantial article on the agriculture of Japan, calling on his memory of the 1882 mission of inspection to Japan.[57] In October 1891, four months after his graduation at the age of thirty, Pyŏn Su was struck by a train at what was then called College Station and died of his injuries.[58] The University of Maryland is proud to have him as part of its history, and the Pyŏn Su Room at the Student Union is a permanent commemoration of his presence at Maryland.[59]

Conclusions and More Relics of Korean Music in the United States

The cylinders recorded on July 24, 1896, are apparently the earliest sound recordings of Korean music or speech. It is barely conceivable that earlier recordings were made of the Korean musicians who performed at the World Columbian Exposition in Chicago in 1893, for the 101 surviving cylinders recorded by Benjamin Ives Gilman (1852–1933) at the exposition were recorded in September 1893.[60] The Korean musicians were only present for a short time in early May of 1893, however, just after the opening of the exposition, and Gilman was not present at that time (and his detailed catalog of his 101 cylinders does not list anything from Korea). The musical instruments used by the Korean musicians formed part of the Korean exhibition at the exposition and appear to have been purchased by Edward Sylvester Morse (1838–1925), who had been the teacher at Boston University of Yu Kilchun, one of the members of the 1883 Special Mission to the United States; much of the Morse collection went to the Peabody Essex Museum in Salem, Massachusetts, where ten Korean musical instruments from the exposition remain today, along with nine others obtained at other times.[61]

In summary, the 1896 recordings of Korean music made by Alice Fletcher preserve the amateur singing of three Korean male students, and she also made what are among the earliest transcriptions of Korean music into western staff notation.[62] While several people associated with her took a strong interest in Korea, Fletcher left no indication that she herself had any such interest, and she would appear to have made the recordings and transcriptions as a favor to her friend and colleague Anna Tolman Smith. The real heroes in this story are Sŏ Kwangbŏm and Smith (in contrast to the impression left by the KBS documentary).

The first recordings of Korean music would never have occurred were it not for a unique set of circumstances created unintentionally by a collection of extraordinary people, all intending to do, and many still famous for, quite different things. I suspect that in the end the recordings themselves will prove to be of little historical or musical value,[63] but what the story of their creation tells us about the intentions and characters of some very important historical figures may lead to some insights into their motivations.

Notes

I wish to acknowledge the kind assistance of numerous institutions and individuals as I conducted the research leading to this chapter: Academy of Korean Studies; Professor Lee Wan Bom (Yi Wanbŏm 李完範); Mr. Jung Changkwan (Chŏng Ch'anggwan 정창관); the National Anthropological Archives in Washington, DC; Dr. Pang Sunjoo (Pang Sŏnju 方善柱); the American Philosophical Society; Harvard Archives, Peabody Museum of Ethnology; Library of Congress (Judith Gray); and the Korean Broadcasting System (KBS), Lee Hokyoung (Yi Hogyŏng 이호경).

[1] The house may be seen at http://lcweb2.loc.gov/pnp/habshaer/dc/dc0300/dc0332/photos/026879pv.jpg.

[2] There is currently an active international search for surviving copies (ideally master discs) of these recordings. An initial reissue of eight of the 78 rpm discs surviving in Korea is *Han'guk ŭi ch'ŏt ŭmban 1907* 한국의 첫 음반 1907 [Korea's first sound recordings, 1907], Han'guk yusŏnggi ŭmban pogwŏn sirijŭ 한국 유성기음반 복원 시리즈 1 [Korean 78 rpm recordings reissue series] (Seoul: Tongguk taehakkyo Han'guk ŭmban ak'aibŭ 동국대학교 한국음반아카이브, 2007), DGACD-001.

[3] It was formerly called (in English) the National Classical Music Institute and, later, National Center for Korean Traditional Performing Arts. The Korean name has not changed since it was adopted in 1951.

[4] *Hanminjok ch'oech'o ŭi ŭmwŏn* 한민족 최초의 음원 [Korean first recording], Chŏng Ch'anggwan kugak nogŭmjip 정창관국악녹음집 [Jung Changkwan's Gugak Recording Collection] 10, 정창관 CKJCD-010 (2007) and CKJCD-010-A (2009).

[5] KBS Special 스페셜, *Palgul ch'ujŏk 114 nyŏnjŏn Han'gugin ŭi moksori* 발굴추적 114년전 한국인의 목소리 [Discovering Korean voices after 114 years], first broadcast July 18, 2010, on KBS TV 1.

[6] The legation was headquartered in a building on Logan Circle recently reacquired by the Korean government.

[7] The papers are described in "Guide to the Collections of the National Anthropological Archives (#F1)," http://www.anthropology.si.edu/naa/guide/_f1.htm. Details may be found in Joy Elizabeth Rohde, "Register to the Papers of Alice Cunningham Fletcher and Francis La Flesche" (April 2000), http://www.anthropology.si.edu/naa/fa/fletcher_la_flesche.htm.

[8] Stephen Jay Gould, *Wonderful Life: The Burgess Shale and the Nature of History* (New York: Norton, 1989), 48, 50.

[9] The interest in Korea was great enough to merit an exhibition in 2013. National Gugak Center (Kungnip kugagwŏn 국립국악원) and National Museum of Korea (Kungnip chungang pangmulgwan 국립중앙박물관), *120 nyŏn man ŭi kwihwan Migugŭro kan Chosŏn akki* 120년 만의 귀환 미국으로 간 조선 악기 [Musical instruments of Chosŏn in America] (Seoul: Kungnip Kugagwŏn, 2013). See also Yi Minsik 이민식, *Kŭndaesa ŭi han changmyŏn K'ollŏmbia segye pangnamhoe wa Han'guk* 근대사의 한 장면 콜럼비아 세계박람회와 한국 [A scene of modern Korean History: Chicago Columbian World's Exposition and Korea exhibits) (Seoul: Paeksan charyowŏn 백산자료원, 2006), esp. 154–69.

[10] See note 9.

[11] On Fletcher's historical significance, see, for example, the obituary by Walter Hough in *American Anthropologist*, new ser., 25 (1923): 254–58; Joan Mark, *A Stranger in Her Native Land: Alice Fletcher and the American Indians* (Lincoln: University of Nebraska Press, 1988); and Rebecca Hancock Welch, "Alice Cunningham Fletcher, Anthropologist and Indian Rights Reformer" (PhD diss., George Washington University, 1980).

[12] Nicole Tonkovich, *The Allotment Plot: Alice C. Fletcher, E. Jane Gay, and Nez Perce Survivance* (Lincoln: University of Nebraska Press, 2012).

[13] E. Jane Gay, *With the Nez Perces: Alice Fletcher in the Field, 1889–1892*, ed. Frederick E. Hoxie and Joan T. Mark (Lincoln: University of Nebraska Press, 1981). Many of Jane Gay's papers and photographs are preserved in the "Women Working, 1800–1930" collection at Harvard; see http://ocp.hul.harvard.edu/ww/gay.html.

[14] *Organization and Historical Sketch of the Women's Anthropological Society of America* (Washington, DC: By the Society, 1889), partly reproduced in Anita Newcomb McGee, "The Women's Anthropological Society of America," *Science* 13, no. 321 (1889): 240–42. The best description of WASA remains an undergraduate thesis: Joan Cindy Amatniek, "The Women's Anthropological Society of America: A Dual Role: Scientific Society and Woman's Club," AB honors thesis, Harvard University, 1979. On the Washington Anthropological Society, see Daniel S. Lamb, "The Story of the Washington Anthropological Society," *American Anthropologist*, new ser., 8, no. 3 (1906): 564–79.

[15] Lamb, "Story of the Washington Anthropological Society," 578.

[16] On the history of cylinder recording, see Alexander Rehding, "Wax Cylinder Revolutions," *Musical Quarterly* 88 (2005): 123–60; and Emily Thompson, "Machines, Music, and the Quest for Fidelity: Marketing the Edison Phonograph in America, 1877–1925," *Musical Quarterly* 79, no. 1 (1995): 131–71.

[17] Library of Congress, *The Federal Cylinder Project: A Guide to Field Cylinder Collections in Federal Agencies*, vol. 1: *Introduction and Inventory*, by Erika Brady, Maria La Vigna,

Dorothy Sara Lee, and Thomas Vennum (Washington, DC: Library of Congress, American Folklife Center, 1984), 62–66. Volumes of the Federal Cylinder Project are difficult to find, but some are freely available on HathiTrust at http://catalog.hathitrust. org/Record/000438261.

[18] Library of Congress, *The Federal Cylinder Project*, vol. 1, 79.

[19] For brief biographies of Densmore, see http://siarchives.si.edu/research/ sciservwomendensmore.html; and http://libguides.mnhs.org/densmore. For recordings, see Library of Congress, *Federal Cylinder Project*, vol. 1, 42–58.

[20] The diary is preserved in Fletcher's papers in the National Anthropological Archive, box 12A.

[21] Putnam Papers, Harvard University Archives, in "1891–1900 General Correspondence," HUG 1717.xx, box 9.

[22] Stuart Culin, *Korean Games, with Notes on the Corresponding Games of China and Japan* (Philadelphia: University of Pennsylvania Press, 1895).

[23] I am very grateful to Judith Gray at the Library of Congress, the expert in all matters to do with Fletcher, for help in deciphering Fletcher's handwriting.

[24] Fletcher was extremely ecological long before it became fashionable, and she reused any blank side of a piece or scrap of paper, writing in her very small (and often illegible) script. These notes on the recordings are kept with the cylinders at the Library of Congress rather than in the National Anthropological Archive.

[25] On Fillmore, some opposing views are presented in James C. McNutt, "John Comfort Fillmore: A Student of Indian Music Reconsidered," *American Music* 2, no. 1 (Spring 1984): 61–70; and Hewitt Pantaleoni, "A Reconsideration of Fillmore Reconsidered," *American Music* 3, no. 2 (Summer 1985): 217–28. See also James C. McNutt, "Reply to Pantaleoni," *American Music* 3, no. 2 (Summer 1985): 229–31. Many letters from Fillmore are included in Fletcher's papers at the National Anthropological Archive. There does not appear to be a Fillmore archive.

[26] Anna Tolman Smith, The Montessori System of Education: An Examination of Characteristic Features Set Forth in 'Il metodo della pedagogica scientifica,' United States Bureau of Education Bulletin, no. 17 (Washington, DC: Government Printing Office, 1912), 3–30. For more information on Smith, see Robert C. Provine, "Unsung Hero: Anna Tolman Smith and the Earliest Recordings of Korean Music," in *Han'guk ŭmakhak ŭi chip'yŏng* 한국음악학의 지평 [Musicology in Korea], ed. Hwang Chunyŏn kyosu chŏngnyŏn t'oeim kinyŏm nonjip kanhaeng wiwŏnhoe 황준연교수정년퇴임 기념논집간행위원회 [Editorial Committee for the Commemorative volume for Professor Hwang Chunyŏn's retirement] (Seoul: Minsogwŏn 민속원, 2014), 13–30.

[27] This information is recorded in *Science*, new ser., 3, no. 62 (1896): 376.

[28] Anna Tolman Smith, "Some Nursery Rhymes of Korea," *Journal of American Folk-lore* 10, no. 38 (1897): 181–86.

[29] Ibid., 181, 184n.

[30] Ibid, 182.

[31] There have been other attempts to transcribe this text, such as those in the liner notes of the published CD of the recordings (see note 4), in the 2010 KBS documentary (see note 5), and in Yoo Pil-jae (Yu P'ilchae 俞弼在), "Miguk ŭihoe tosŏgwan sojang minyo nogŭm charyo wa 19 segimal kugŏ ŭi moŭm mit moŭm chohwa" 미국 의회도서관 소장 민요 녹음 자료와 19세기말 국어의 모음 및 모음조화 [On the late-nineteenth-century Korean of the recordings of Korean songs in the US Library of Congress), *Chindan hakpo* 震檀學報 122 (2014): 175–96. As some readers will be aware, there are still numerous variants of "Tara tara palgŭm tara" 달아 달아 밝은 달아 circulating in Korea.

[32] A very useful English-language study of the period, drawn from both Korean and western sources, is Young Ick Lew, *Early Korean Encounters with the United States and Japan: Six Essays on Late Nineteenth-Century Korea* (Seoul: Royal Asiatic Society, Korea Branch, 2008).

[33] See, for example, Harold F. Cook, *Korea's 1884 Incident: Its Background and Kim Ok-kyun's Elusive Dream* (Seoul: Royal Asiatic Society, Korea Branch, 1972), 39–49.

[34] There are numerous writings about this 1883 mission, including Gary D. Walter, "The Korean Special Mission to the United States in 1883," *Journal of Korean Studies* 1, no. 1 (1969): 89–142; and the much earlier Harold J. Noble, "The Korean Mission to the United States in 1883: The First Embassy Sent by Korea to an Occidental Nation," *Transactions of the Korea Branch of the Royal Asiatic Society*, 18 (1929): 1–21.

[35] As it happens, I lived in Lowell House at Harvard for three years as an undergraduate.

[36] Letter from Min Yŏngik, July 16, 1883, in National Archives, *Notes from the Korean Legation in the United States to the Department of State, 1883–1906* [microform], September 18, 1883–April 24, 1906, National Archives microfilm publications, M; microcopy no. 166. Judging from the flowery English and handwriting, one would guess that this statement was written on Min's behalf by Lowell himself.

[37] See, for example, "The Embassy from Corea," *New York Times*, September 18, 1883.

[38] See, for example, "Oriental Salaams and Dress," *New York Times*, September 19, 1883.

[39] "Personal Intelligence," *New York Times*, November 7, 1883. On Foulk, see http://www.samuelhawley.com/foulk.html. They must have been the first Koreans to fully circumnavigate the earth.

[40] Percival Lowell, *Chosön: The Land of the Morning Calm* (Boston: Ticknor, 1886).

[41] Direct link to the photographs is http://www2.lowell.edu/Research/library/pub/main.php?selection=historic_photo&sphrase=Korea.

[42] The first was the astronomer Giovanni Schiaparelli (1835–1910), who drew diagrams of *canali* (meaning "channels," not canals) on Mars during the great opposition of 1877.

[43] The observatory's own description is at https://lowell.edu/in-depth/pluto/the-discovery-of-pluto.

[44] A building still stands today at the post office location as a small museum. See http://koreastamp.epost.go.kr/sp/eg/speg0304.jsp.

[45] Percival Lowell, "A Korean Coup d'État," *Atlantic Monthly* 58, no. 349 (November 1886): 599–618. Lowell wrote the piece as though he were present and watching events in Seoul, which he was not.

[46] A basic source on this period in Sŏ Kwangbŏm's life is Pang Sunjoo (Pang Sŏnju 方善柱), "Pom Kwang Soh: The Life of an Exile in the United States (1859–1897)," Data and Research Series, no. K-2 (Hyattsville, MD: Ameriasian Data Research Services, 1985?).

[47] Pom K. Soh (Sŏ Kwangbŏm), "Education in Korea," in *U.S. Commissioner of Education Report for 1890–91* (Washington, DC: Government Printing Office, 1892), vol. 1, 341–63.

[48] "Korean Stories," *The Path* 8, no. 4–5 (1893): 103–105 and 150–151. Walter Hough, "The Bernadou, Allen, and Jouy Korean Collections in the U.S. National Museum," *Annual Report of the Board of Regents of the Smithsonian Institution...: Report of the U.S. National Museum* (Washington, DC: Government Printing Office, 1892), 432.

[49] An article on Sŏ by an author using a pseudonym concludes by noting Sŏ's departure for Korea. Haddo Gordon, "A Young Korean Rebel," *Lippincott's* 55 (1895): 662–68. The same author (with name reversed) wrote also about the Progressive Party: Gordon Haddo, "The Rise and Fall of the Progressive Party of Korea," *The Chautauquan* 16, no. 1 (October, 1892): 46–49.

[50] *Washington Post*, February 16, 1896, 1.

[51] Possibly there were six or eight; the sources disagree on the number. For further information on these students and other early Korean visitors to the United States, see Pang Sŏnju 方善柱, *Chaemi Hanin ŭi tongnip undong* 在美韓人의 獨立運動 [The Role in the Korean Independence Movement of Koreans in the United States], Kyohyang ch'ongsŏ 교양총서, no. 2 (Ch'unch'ŏn 춘천시: Hallim University Press 한림대학교 출판부, 1989), esp. 303–30.

[52] "Seven Korean Students at Howard: Ran Away from Home to Be Educated in United States," *Washington Post,* May 8, 1896, 2.

[53] This photograph was located by the KBS documentary's director, Yi Hogyŏng 이호경, who kindly provided me with a copy. The photograph appears briefly at the very end of the documentary. One of the singing students, Yi Hŭich'ŏl, returned to Korea in 1901, and the documentary shows his grave.

[54] "Yi Pom Gin, New Corean Envoy," *New York Times,* July 25, 1896, 4. See also Pang Sŏnju 方善柱, "Sŏ Kwangbŏm kwa Yi Pŏmjin" 徐光範과 李範晉 [Sŏ Kwangbŏm and Yi Pŏmjin], in *Ch'oe Yŏnghŭi sŏnsaeng hwagap kinyŏm Han'guk sahak nonch'ong* 崔永禧先生 華甲紀念 韓國史學論叢 [Essays on Korean history commemorating the sixtieth birthday of Ch'oe Yŏnghŭi] (Seoul: T'amgudang 探求堂, 1987), 431–57.

[55] "Pom Kwang Soh Dead," *New York Times,* August 14, 1897, 7. See also, "Pom Kwang Soh Dead," *Washington Post,* August 14, 1897, 1.

[56] A. Tolman Smith, "The Mission of Pom K. Soh," *The Independent,* October 14, 1897, 1–2. This article indicates that there were six students, not seven, and it contains a fair number of errors that may well have arisen from the fact that Sŏ was her only and rather prejudiced informant.

[57] Penn Su [Pyŏn Su], "Agriculture in Japan," *Monthly Reports of the Division of Statistics of the Department of Agriculture* 8, nos. 81–90 (1891): 563–83.

[58] "Died While in Exile," *Washington Post,* October 24, 1891, 1.

[59] A useful short article on Pyŏn Su is Lee Kwang-rin, "Pyŏn Su (Penn Su), the First Korean Student in an American College," *Journal of Social Sciences and Humanities* (Seoul) 58 (1983): 1–25.

[60] Library of Congress, *Federal Cylinder Project: A Guide to Field Cylinder Collections in Federal Agencies*, Volume 8, ed. Dorothy Sara Lee (Washington DC: Library of Congress, American Folklife Center,1984), 1–34.

[61] For a brief description, see Robert C. Provine, "Nineteenth-Century Korean Musical Instruments in the United States," *Kugak nuri* 국악누리 129 (January–February 2013): 18–19. See also National Gugak Center and National Museum of Korea, *120 nyŏn man ŭi kwihwan Migugŭro kan Chosŏn akki,* 45–89.

[62] The transcriptions of Korean music, including "Arirang" 아리랑, published by Homer B. Hulbert in his "Korean Vocal Music," *Korean Repository* 3, no. 2 (February 1896): 45–53, are slightly earlier than the Fletcher ones.

[63] One interesting use to which the recordings have been put is a phonological examination of pronunciations. See note 31.

Bibliography

Writings

Amatniek, Joan Cindy. "The Women's Anthropological Society of America: A Dual Role: Scientific Society and Woman's Club." AB honors thesis, Harvard University, 1979.

Anonymous. "Guide to the Collections of the National Anthropological Archives (#F1)." http://www.anthropology.si.edu/naa/guide/_f1.htm.

Cook, Harold F. *Korea's 1884 Incident: Its Background and Kim Ok-kyun's Elusive Dream.* Seoul: Royal Asiatic Society, Korea Branch, 1972.

Culin, Stuart. *Korean Games, with Notes on the Corresponding Games of China and Japan.* Philadelphia: University of Pennsylvania Press, 1895.

Gay, E. Jane. *With the Nez Perces: Alice Fletcher in the Field, 1889–1892.* Edited by Frederick E. Hoxie and Joan T. Mark. Lincoln: University of Nebraska Press, 1981.

Gordon, Haddo. "A Young Korean Rebel." *Lippincott's* 55 (1895): 662–68. See also Haddo, Gordon.

Gould, Stephen Jay. *Wonderful Life: The Burgess Shale and the Nature of History.* New York: Norton, 1989.

Haddo, Gordon. "The Rise and Fall of the Progressive Party of Korea," *The Chautauquan* 16, no. 1 (October 1892): 46–49. See also Gordon, Haddo.

Hawley, Samuel. "George Foulk." http://www.samuelhawley.com/foulk.html.

Hough, Walter. "Alice Cunningham Fletcher." *American Anthropologist*, new ser., 25 (1923): 254–58.

———. "The Bernadou, Allen, and Jouy Korean Collections in the U.S. National Museum." In *Annual Report of the Board of Regents of the Smithsonian Institution . . .: Report of the U.S. National Museum*, 429–88. Washington, DC: Government Printing Office, 1892.

Hulbert, Homer B. "Korean Vocal Music." *Korean Repository* 3, no. 2 (February 1896): 45–53.

Lamb, Daniel S. "The Story of the Washington Anthropological Society." *American Anthropologist*, new ser., 8, no. 3 (1906): 564–79.

Lee Kwang-rin. "Pyŏn Su (Penn Su), the First Korean Student in an American College." *Journal of Social Sciences and Humanities* (Seoul) 58 (1983): 1–25.

Lew, Young Ick. *Early Korean Encounters with the United States and Japan: Six Essays on Late Nineteenth-Century Korea*. Seoul: Royal Asiatic Society, Korea Branch, 2008.

Library of Congress. *The Federal Cylinder Project: A Guide to Field Cylinder Collections in Federal Agencies*, Vol. 1: *Introduction and Inventory*, by Erika Brady, Maria La Vigna, Dorothy Sara Lee, and Thomas Vennum, 62–66. Washington, DC: Library of Congress, American Folklife Center, 1984.

———. *The Federal Cylinder Project: A Guide to Field Cylinder Collections in Federal Agencies*, Vol. 8: *Early Anthologies*, ed. Dorothy Sara Lee. 1-34. Washington DC: Library of Congress, American Folklife Center, 1984).

Lowell, Percival. "A Korean Coup d'État." *Atlantic Monthly* 58, no. 349 (November 1886): 599–618.

———. *Chosön: The Land of the Morning Calm*. Boston: Ticknor, 1886.

Lowell Observatory. "The Discovery of Pluto." https://lowell.edu/in-depth/pluto/the-discovery-of-pluto/.

Mark, Joan. *A Stranger in Her Native Land: Alice Fletcher and the American Indians*. Lincoln: University of Nebraska Press, 1988.

[McGee, Anita Newcomb]. *Organization and Historical Sketch of the Women's Anthropological Society of America*. Washington, DC: By the Society, 1889.

———. "The Women's Anthropological Society of America." *Science* 13, no. 321 (1889): 240–42.

McNutt, James C. "John Comfort Fillmore: A Student of Indian Music Reconsidered." *American Music* 2, no. 1 (Spring 1984): 61–70.

———. "Reply to Pantaleoni." *American Music* 3, no. 2 (Summer 1985): 229–31.

Minnesota History Center, Gale Family Library. "Frances Densmore: Recording and Preserving Native American Music." http://libguides.mnhs.org/densmore.

National Archives. *Notes from the Korean Legation in the United States to the Department of State, 1883–1906* [microform], September 18, 1883–April 24, 1906. National Archives microfilm publications, M; microcopy no. 166.

National Gugak Center (Kungnip Kugagwŏn 국립국악원) and National Museum of Korea (Kungnip chungang pangmulgwan 국립중앙박물관). *120 nyŏn man ŭi kwihwan Migugŭro kan Chosŏn akki* 120년 만의 귀환 미국으로 간 조선 악기 [Musical instruments of Chosŏn in America]. Seoul: Kungnip Kugagwŏn, 2013.

Noble, Harold J. "The Korean Mission to the United States in 1883: The First Embassy Sent by Korea to an Occidental Nation." *Transactions of the Korea Branch of the Royal Asiatic Society* 18 (1929): 1–21.

Pang Sŏnju 方善柱. *Chaemi Hanin ŭi tongnip undong* 在美韓人의 獨立運動 [The Role in the Korean Independence Movement of Koreans in the United States]. Kyohyang chʻongsŏ 교양총서, no. 2. Chʻunchŏn 춘천시: Hallim University Press 한림대학교 출판부, 1989.

———. "Sŏ Kwangbŏm kwa Yi Pŏmjin" 徐光範과 李範晉 [Sŏ Kwangbŏm and Yi Pŏmjin]. In *Chʻoe Yŏnghŭi sŏnsaeng hwagap kinyŏm Hanʼguk sahak nonchʻong* 崔永禧先生華甲紀念 韓國史學論叢 [Essays on Korean history commemorating the sixtieth birthday of Chʻoe Yŏnghŭi], 431–57. Seoul: Tʻamgudang 探求堂, 1987.

Pang Sunjoo [Pang Sŏnju 方善柱]. "Pom Kwang Soh: The Life of an Exile in the United States (1859–1897)." Data and Research Series, no. K-2. Hyattsville, MD: Ameriasian Data Research Services, 1985?

Pantaleoni, Hewitt. "A Reconsideration of Fillmore Reconsidered." *American Music* 3, no. 2 (Summer 1985): 217–28.

Penn Su (Pyŏn Su 邊燧). "Agriculture in Japan." *Monthly Reports of the Division of Statistics of the Department of Agriculture* 8, nos. 81–90 (1891): 563–83.

Provine, Robert C. "Nineteenth-Century Korean Musical Instruments in the United States." *Kugak nuri* 국악누리 129 (January–February 2013): 18–19.

———. "Unsung Hero: Anna Tolman Smith and the Earliest Recordings of Korean Music." In *Hanʼguk ŭmakhak ŭi chipʻyŏng* 한국음악학의 지평

[Musicology in Korea], edited by Hwang Chunyŏn kyosu chŏngnyŏn t'oeim kinyŏm nonjip kanhaeng wiwŏnhoe 황준연교수정년퇴임 기념논집간행위원회 [Editorial Committee for the commemorative volume for Professor Hwang Chunyŏn's retirement], 13–30. Seoul: Minsogwŏn 민속원, 2014.

Rehding, Alexander. "Wax Cylinder Revolutions." *Musical Quarterly* 88 (2005): 123–60.

Rohde, Joy Elizabeth. "Register to the Papers of Alice Cunningham Fletcher and Francis La Flesche," April 2000. http://www.anthropology.si.edu/naa/fa/fletcher_la_flesche.htm.

Smith, Anna Tolman. "The Mission of Pom K. Soh." *The Independent*, October 14 1897, 1–2.

———. *The Montessori System of Education: An Examination of Characteristic Features Set Forth in 'Il metodo della pedagogica scientifica.'* United States Bureau of Education Bulletin, no. 17 (Washington, DC: Government Printing Office, 1912): 3–30.

———. "Some Nursery Rhymes of Korea." *Journal of American Folk-lore* 10, no. 38 (1897): 181–86.

Smithsonian Institution Archives. "Frances Densmore (1867–1957)." http://siarchives.si.edu/research/sciservwomendensmore.html.

Soh, Pom K. (Sŏ Kwangbŏm 徐光範). "Education in Korea." in *U.S. Commissioner of Education Report for 1890–91*, vol. 1, 341–63. Washington, DC: Government Printing Office, 1892.

———. "Korean Stories." *The Path* 8, nos. 4–5 (1893): 103–5, 150–51.

Thompson, Emily. "Machines, Music, and the Quest for Fidelity: Marketing the Edison Phonograph in America, 1877–1925." *Musical Quarterly* 79, no. 1 (1995): 131–71.

Tonkovich, Nicole. *The Allotment Plot: Alice C. Fletcher, E. Jane Gay, and Nez Perce Survivance.* Lincoln: University of Nebraska Press, 2012.

Walter, Gary D. "The Korean Special Mission to the United States in 1883." *Journal of Korean Studies* 1, no. 1 (1969): 89–142.

Welch, Rebecca Hancock. "Alice Cunningham Fletcher, Anthropologist and Indian Rights Reformer." PhD diss., George Washington University, 1980.

Yi Minsik 이민식. *Kŭndaesa ŭi han changmyŏn K'ollŏmbia segye pangnamhoe wa Han'guk* 근대사의 한 장면 콜럼비아 세계박람회와 한국 [A scene of modern Korean history: Chicago Columbian World's Exposition and Korea exhibits]. Seoul: Paeksan charyowŏn 백산자료원, 2006.

Yu P'ilchae 兪弼在 (Yoo Pil-jae). "Miguk ŭihoe tosŏgwan sojang minyo nogŭm charyo wa 19 segimal kugŏ ŭi moŭm mit moŭm chohwa" 미국 의회도서관 소장 민요 녹음 자료와 19세기말 국어의 모음 및 모음조화 [On the late-nineteenth-century Korean of the recordings of Korean songs in the US Library of Congress]. *Chindan hakpo* 震檀學報 122 (2014): 175–96.

Recordings and Media

Han'guk ŭi *chŏt* ŭmban 1907 한국의 첫 음반 1907 [Korea's first sound recordings, 1907]. Han'guk yusŏnggi ŭmban pogwŏn sirijŭ 한국 유성기음반 복원 시리즈 1 [Korean 78 rpm recordings reissue series]. Seoul: Tongguk taehakkyo Han'guk ŭmban ak'aibŭ 동국대학교 한국음반아카이브, 2007). DGACD-001.

Hanminjok ch'oech'o ŭi ŭmwŏn 한민족 최초의 음원 [Korean first recording]. Chŏng Ch'anggwan kugak nogŭmjip 정창관국악녹음집 [Jung Changkwan's Gugak recording collection] 10. 정창관 CKJCD-010 (2007) and CKJCD-010-A (2009).

KBS Special 스페셜. *Palgul ch'ujŏk 114 nyŏnjŏn Han'gugin ŭi moksori* 발굴추적 114년전 한국인의 목소리 [Discovering Korean voices after 114 years]. First broadcast July 18, 2010, on KBS TV 1.

10

The Kan'ichi Asakawa Epistolary Network Project and Its Case Studies

Haruko Nakamura, Yale University

Introduction

This chapter explores the historical importance of the Kan'ichi Asakawa Papers held in Manuscripts and Archives, Yale University Library, by mapping the relationships between Asakawa and his associates with the use of digital technology. Kan'ichi Asakawa 朝河貫一 (1873–1948) was the one of the pioneering figures of East Asian studies in the United States. He was a distinguished historian who taught at Yale for thirty-five years and was the university's first professor of Japanese history. Building the premier Japanese collection (representative of the full sweep of the recorded history of the Japanese archipelago), he was the first curator of Yale's East Asia Collection, a post he held for forty-two years. Asakawa is also known for his involvement in public affairs, most notably in efforts to promote peace and narrow the gap of understanding between the peoples of Japan, the United States, and the world. The Kan'ichi Asakawa Epistolary Network Project aims to create a tool by which a map of Asakawa's relationships may be visualized. As a growing number of research projects have revealed various dimensions of Asakawa's life, this project may provide another way to probe his complex life and work. More important, this project will be a proof of concept for collaborative constructions of digitized resources concerning Asakawa and other important figures of twentieth-century Meiji Japan.[1]

Asakawa's Biography

The son of a former samurai from northern Japan raised during the Meiji period, Asakawa in adulthood was a cosmopolitan who wielded international influence. He was born on December 20, 1873, in Nihonmatsu, Fukushima. Japan at the time was experiencing a series of changes propelled by the Meiji Restoration, and Fukushima was on the losing side of the reforms enacted, which influenced him in his later travels to the United States. From an early age, Asakawa's talents were apparent, and he received a rigorous education from his father. After he graduated from Tokyo Senmon Gakkō (now Waseda University) in 1895, he continued his education in the United States. He received his BA degree from Dartmouth College in 1899 and his PhD in history from Yale University in 1902. After his graduation, he taught at Dartmouth from 1902 to 1906 and then took a position at Yale, teaching Japanese history (1906–42, professor emeritus 1942–48) and serving as the first curator of the East Asia Library (1907–48).

Although his scholarship did not gain wide recognition in Japan until recently, Asakawa's work has been much admired by many historians, especially in the United States. He was a pioneer in the fields of the institutional history of Japan and the comparative history of Japanese and European feudalism. On the strength of his earliest work, *The Early Institutional Life of Japan: A Study in the Reform of 645 A.D.* (1903), Asakawa was invited to teach at Yale. In *The Documents of Iriki* (1929), he examined the extensive archives of the Iriki clan in Kagoshima, which had been kept from the Kamakura through the Edo periods. Based mainly on the translation and examination of twenty-two documents from the twelfth century, *The Land and Society in Medieval Japan* (1965) is a study of the manor (*shō*) of Ushigahara in the district of Ono, Echizen Province, which belonged to the Daigoji of Kyoto. Asakawa examined the origins and development of feudalism in Japan and compared it to the system in place in Europe. Although Asakawa was not able to train his successors, his scholarship has influenced several important historians of Japan in the United States, including John Hall, Edwin O. Reischauer, and George B. Samson.[2] Asakawa also had close associations with and scholarly influence on quite a number of European historians, especially Marc Bloch, the founder of Annales School.

Besides his scholarly output and teaching, Asakawa was devoted to building one of the premier Japanese collections as the first curator of the East Asian Collection at Yale. Although, as one of the oldest Japanese collections in the United States, the East Asia Library collection's earliest acquisitions predate Asakawa's appointment (the first documented East Asian–language books were acquired in the 1840s,[3] and even before this Yale faculty traveled to the Far East and returned with materials), the systematic development of Yale's Japanese collection began with Asakawa. He used all his abilities and connections to build a collection of

Japanese materials that would raise the standard of scholarship in the United States. Asakawa accomplished this through a series of initiatives, beginning with a 1906–7 trip to Japan to acquire 8,120 titles in 21,520 volumes for Yale and 3,160 titles in 45,000 volumes of similar materials for the Library of Congress. During a second trip in 1917–19, Asakawa was active in mobilizing Japanese Yale graduates of the Meiji period, leading up to the creation of the Yale Association of Japan (YAJ). Asakawa's vision of an "oriental" museum at Yale became a reality. He proposed to the YAJ the creation of a collection of cultural materials representative of Japan's history and raised funds from forty-seven members totaling 11,300 yen. These impressive Japanese collections became the foundation of the Japanese research collections at Yale University.

Asakawa also utilized his vast network and knowledge of the United States and Japan in his involvement in public affairs. He published extensively in both scholarly and popular journals, wielding his influence to shape American views of Japan just as the Japanese nation was growing more powerful and eventually would become a major participant in World War II. His *The Russo-Japanese Conflict: Its Causes and Issues* (1904) sought to deepen Americans' understanding of Japan. This book was intended to explain both Japan's history and East Asian international relations. He also sought to clarify the Japanese stance in the Russo-Japanese War (1904–05). The publication became a best seller, and he was invited to give numerous speeches and participate in debates.[4] He eventually gained a reputation as an expert on Japan throughout the United States. The history of Japan's gradual rise to power after winning the Russo-Japanese War is beyond the scope of this chapter, but in gaining the concession of the Southern Manchurian Railroad, Japan sought reciprocal commerce with China and Chinese independence. However, Japanese commercial cartels influenced the interpretation of the Japanese concession so as to benefit Japanese interests, and the expansion of the railway brought Japanese troops into China. The West, particularly England, the United States, and Germany, started to become suspicious of Japan. Voicing a spectrum of opinions, both for and against Japan, in his *Nihon no Kaki* (Japan's Crisis, 1909), Asakawa warned that Japanese policies risked an erosion of support for Japan in the United States. His voluminous correspondence shows that he shared these views with many influential intellectuals.

Asakawa continued to devote himself to diplomacy. In close communication with Dr. Langdon Warner, a Japanese art scholar at Harvard University, Asakawa drafted an appeal to the emperor of Japan in an attempt to prevent the outbreak of World War II. The draft was brought by Warner to President Franklin Roosevelt for his signature before it was sent. Unfortunately, the letter did not reach the emperor before the fatal attack on Pearl Harbor was carried out. As war was breaking out, President Charles Seymour of Yale University sent a letter to Asakawa dated December 8, 1941.

> I can understand how painful these days must be for you and I write merely to tell you of my understanding and to assure you of my intense desire to do all that I can to make them a little easier. You can count upon the appreciative affection of your friends. All that lies in the power of the university will be done to keep your external life normal; anything that any one of us can do to ease the spiritual load you carry or shall want to do. Yale can never repay with any adequacy your service to her and to scholarship.[5]

As President Seymour promised, Yale provided Asakawa with complete protection during the war years, even though others, such as the Japanese specialist Ryūsaku Tsunoda 角田柳作 at Columbia University, were interned.[6] After his retirement as a professor of history, Asakawa spent much of his time organizing the books he had acquired for the library. He died in West Wardsboro, Vermont, on August 11, 1948. Every year many Japanese travel to the United States to visit Asakawa's grave in the Grove Street Cemetery, located at the center of Yale campus where he spent most of his life.

Scholarship on Asakawa: Traditional Uses of His Correspondence and Beyond

Many works have been published on Asakawa from a variety of perspectives using his correspondence, which is scattered among various collections. Although it has been criticized for a lack of proper citations, the first major biography of Asakawa was done by Yoshio Abe in 1983.[7] A good portion of the extant scholarship has focused on Asakawa as a prominent scholar of Japanese history in works by Jinno Takashi, Ebisawa Tadashi, Kondo Shigekazu[8] Yamauchi Haruko, Mineshima Hideo, and others.[9] Also, a number of Asakawa's scholarly works in English have been translated into Japanese by Yabuki Susumu, including *The Documents of Iriki* (2005) and *Land and Society in Medieval Japan* (2015), as well as other works of Asakawa's on comparative feudal systems. Asakawa as an advocate of peace has been plumbed extensively by scholars such as Yamaoka Michio and Kaneko Hideo, focusing on Asakawa's and Langdon Warner's efforts to prevent World War II.[10] Studies on Asakawa's family life, his Christian faith, and his romances with several women have been produced by such scholars as Ishikawa Eizō and Masui Yukimi.[11] In recent years, interest was heightened in Asakawa's accomplishments as the first curator of East Asia Library at Yale University by Ellen Hammond's work, and Kikuchi Hiroki's research on Asakawa's efforts to obtain important works through various Japanese scholarly networks by means of the practice of copying (写学).[12] This work has highlighted his creativity, as well as mining his rich correspondence archive. Matsutani Yumiko also recently published a close analysis of the subject categorizations of the collections formed by Asakawa (those assembled both for

Yale and for the Library of Congress).[13] Many other works connecting his scholarly and personal relationships have been written by William J. Tucker, Tsunashima Ryōsen 綱島梁川, George E Morrison, and others.[14] In addition, an extremely valuable reference work has been recently published that contains a detailed index of Asakawa-related archival collections held by Yale University, Waseda University, and the Fukushima Prefectural Library.[15 and 16]

Kan'ichi Asakawa: Visualizing His Networks

Correspondence in the Asakawa collection has significant academic value and has been heavily used in scholarly works on Asakawa. Beyond his tremendous scholarly and curatorial achievements and contributions to the world affairs, Asakawa's life is rich in interest because of his connections with prominent scholars, distinguished public figures, and associates in his various projects worldwide. Most of these relationships came about because of his move to the United States for the purposes of study. When he came to work and live in New Haven, he had many opportunities to meet intellectuals and international figures from all over the world. Going through his long letters to associates, family, lovers, and public figures, one can get a good sense of how his mind worked and how his scholarship, curatorial work, personal life, and efforts on the world stage meshed. Furthermore, mapping the connections between Asakawa and his associates panoramically may provide new understandings not only of Asakawa but of important figures who played significant roles in academic and political circles during the first half of the twentieth century.

While all the scholarly works mentioned above show a variety of connections by topic or based on individual relationships in the correspondence, those studies manually examined networks between Asakawa and individuals. With the rise of digital humanities, there are new opportunities for scholars to explore and manipulate analog data embedded in Asakawa's archive. There are several definitions of digital humanity. However, it can be generally defined as various scholarly activities to use "digital tools and methods in the pursuit of humanistic questions."[17] An exciting possibility is the creation of a network map of those of his relationships that would be difficult to see by simply reading the letters one by one.[18] Although detailed indexes and finding aids have been published to help future researchers, digitally creating networks of correspondence will add another layer of visibility and searchability by mapping his connections and providing a *"digital historical representation."*[19]

The project also aims to create added value to an academic resource by providing an experimental interface that can be used to connect the digitized collection with other archival collections related to Asakawa, as well as to crowdsource metadata information (such as provenance) and even transcriptions of the letters themselves in cases where they are hard to read. These additions will enhance access to the resources. By visually delineating the relationships between Asakawa and a number of contemporaneous intellectuals and public figures around the globe, the project will provide a trajectory toward new possibilities of scholarly practice in the realm of digital humanities.

Advancement of Epistolary Networking Technologies

Although they are fairly new, a few epistolary networking and associated projects have been launched. One of largest and most active undertakings is Oxford University's Republic of Letters, 1550–1750. "Using digital methods," this project aims to "reassemble and interpret the correspondence networks of the early modern period."[20] Through multiple project phases, a massive card catalog, the Index of Literary Correspondence in the Bodleian Library at Oxford University, was scanned and digitally indexed, which became the nucleus dataset in the database. Visualizing epistolary circles has been pioneered by the Mapping the Republic of Letters project at Stanford University, which attempts to ruminate on questions of intensity and evolution, as well as developing visual representations of relationships over time by using an interactive visualization tool. Circulation of Knowledge and Learned Practices in the Seventeenth-Century Dutch Republic is another cutting-edge project based on the text mining of an epistolary corpus. The project, based at the Huygens Institute, draws on some twenty thousand letters by seventeenth-century scholars of the Dutch Republic and can be analyzed with a tool that provides "visualizations of geographical, time-based, social network and co-citation inquiries."[21] By processing aggregated metadata (accumulating various bibliographic contents helpful for enhancing metadata of resources through crowdsourcing), these developments ended up creating a central platform for community building for scholars with common research interests.

This technique has already been successfully deployed to study Japanese literary figures by Hoyt Long (University of Chicago) as part of the Chicago Text Lab projects. This project facilitates the understanding of "how developments in communications technology at the turn of the last century impacted practices of writing, patterns of social association, and ideas of communication." Through the project, Professor Hoyt has discovered "emerging fantasies and beliefs about the meaning of connection in a postal age, particularly as they relate to changing attitudes toward handwriting, voice, memory, and brevity."[22] Projects such as this have demonstrated the importance of using digital technology to bring Japanese texts into conversation with a world of scholars.

An Introduction to the Kan'ichi Asakawa Papers at Yale

The Kan'ichi Asakawa papers held in Manuscripts and Archives at the Yale University Library were used as a basis for the epistolary project. This particular collection contains diaries and correspondence that document the provenance of items collected, as well as related materials that have been added posthumously, some of which have attracted scant attention from scholars thus far. There are about sixty-seven boxes in the collection consisting of correspondence, diaries, writings, lecture notes, photographs, and miscellanea on Asakawa's personal life and professional career. The Asakawa collection began as a gift from the estate of Kan'ichi Asakawa in 1946–48 and was expanded by Mary Rouse in 1984.[23] The collection grew with additions donated by Yoshio Abe, a scholar of Asakawa, in 1984; by the historian Jerome Pollitt in 1990;[24] and by transfers from the East Asian Collection Curatorial archive in 2000–2001, 2004, and 2009. The correspondence section of the collection contains more than 800 letters, mainly in English and Japanese, in boxes 1–4 of the Kan'ichi Asakawa Papers. Those letters have also been captured on four rolls of microfilm, which were digitized with the images recaptured into separate frames. A volume of selected letters was also edited, with some translations, and published in 1990. In that volume are included Asakawa's letters not only from the Yale collection but also from other repositories, including 2,546 from the Fukushima Prefectural Library.

The Asakawa epistolary site was created initially using the list of Asakawa's letters held at Yale, the Fukushima Prefectural Library, and other repositories. It was begun by Yamauchi Haruko 山内晴子 from Waseda University.[25] In addition to painstakingly inputting all the date, recipient, and sender information from each archive, Yamauchi extrapolated the dates of undated letters from internal evidence, and the names of the recipients and authors were added where necessary. Some individuals are identified in the notes, and clarifications are offered on the subjects dealt with in the letters. The edited volume of selected letters was used to confirm this information.[26] In addition, Asakawa kept detailed records of appointments in unbound diaries, which also offer insights into Asakawa's networks. Yamauchi added information from Asakawa's diary to the Excel list.

Peter Leonard, the director of the Digital Humanities Lab at the Yale University Library, then guided this project from the initial stages to the programming of the user interfaces.[27] Asakawa's correspondence was first divided by senders and recipients and put into two Excel files. Using the edited volume of the selected letters, an authority file was created in order to normalize names manually as well as by means of an electronic software tool (Open Refine). Romanization of Japanese names and a rough categorization of individuals were also added. Another enhancement of the database included adding fields for information about senders and recipients, identifying the language(s) in which the letters were written, and giving the location of senders and recipients using Geocoder software. The microfilm version of the correspondence collection was then scanned, each entry was captured, and images of individual letters were cropped and linked to the metadata with Gephi software.[28]

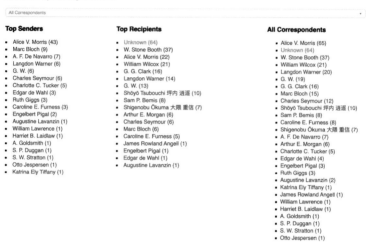

Asakawa Epistolary Network

All Correspondents

Top Senders
- Alice V. Morris (43)
- Marc Bloch (9)
- A. F. De Navarro (7)
- Langdon Warner (6)
- G. W. (6)
- Charles Seymour (6)
- Charlotte C. Tucker (5)
- Edgar de Wahl (3)
- Ruth Giggs (3)
- Caroline E. Furness (3)
- Engelbert Pigal (2)
- Augustine Lavanzin (1)
- William Lawrence (1)
- Harriet B. Laidlaw (1)
- A. Goldsmith (1)
- S. P. Duggan (1)
- S. W. Stratton (1)
- Otto Jespersen (1)
- Katrina Ely Tiffany (1)

Top Recipients
- Unknown (64)
- W. Stone Booth (37)
- Alice V. Morris (22)
- William Wilcox (21)
- G. G. Clark (16)
- Langdon Warner (14)
- G. W. (13)
- Shōyō Tsubouchi 坪内 逍遙 (10)
- Sam P. Bemis (8)
- Shigenobu Ōkuma 大隈 重信 (7)
- Arthur E. Morgan (6)
- Charles Seymour (6)
- Marc Bloch (6)
- Caroline E. Furness (5)
- James Rowland Angell (1)
- Engelbert Pigal (1)
- Edgar de Wahl (1)
- Augustine Lavanzin (1)

All Correspondents
- Alice V. Morris (65)
- Unknown (64)
- W. Stone Booth (37)
- William Wilcox (21)
- Langdon Warner (20)
- G. W. (19)
- G. G. Clark (16)
- Marc Bloch (15)
- Charles Seymour (12)
- Shōyō Tsubouchi 坪内 逍遙 (10)
- Sam P. Bemis (8)
- Caroline E. Furness (8)
- Shigenobu Ōkuma 大隈 重信 (7)
- A. F. De Navarro (7)
- Arthur E. Morgan (6)
- Charlotte C. Tucker (5)
- Edgar de Wahl (4)
- Engelbert Pigal (3)
- Ruth Giggs (3)
- Augustine Lavanzin (2)
- Katrina Ely Tiffany (1)
- James Rowland Angell (1)
- William Lawrence (1)
- Harriet B. Laidlaw (1)
- A. Goldsmith (1)
- S. P. Duggan (1)
- S. W. Stratton (1)
- Otto Jespersen (1)

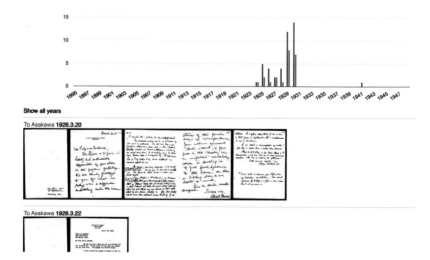

Figures 10.1 and 10.2. The Asakawa epistolary site as of January 2016. As these figures show, when a user clicks the hyperlinks of individual names (10.1), a chronological graph of correspondences appears. If a user clicks a bar representing a particular year in the graph (10.2), all the scanned letters exchanged for that year appear.

Challenges of Creation

There are substantial problems associated with the nature of the letters themselves. Just as with an edited volume of letters, the process of creating a visual representation of an epistolary network(s) runs up against challenges, such as numerous letters in which the dates were omitted by their authors and unsigned letters, as well as variant copies. Copies of letters can make for clutter in the dataset for the purposes of network analysis. In the case of the Asakawa collection of letters, the documents were mostly retained copies that Asakawa kept for his records. Thus, when the project became larger and began incorporating letters held in different archives, the process of eliminating duplicates became necessary, requiring a procedure for establishing the variant closest to what was sent. Furthermore, there is always the danger that a retained copy could represent a letter that was not actually sent to the recipient. The high proportion of letters that lack evidence for the recipient for whom they were intended has the potential to greatly distort findings.

One of the main criticisms of digital humanities projects is that low quality or insufficient data can distort conclusions and produce unfounded or even misleading analyses. When insufficient or flawed data are included in a dataset, digital humanities projects can be problematic. Normalizing names with initials and nicknames, as well as finding pronunciations and Romanizing Japanese names, has the potential to contribute to such issues. For example, collation of Japanese names added with romanization or hiragana became an absolute necessity for any sort of data analysis, given complex variations of Japanese names with multiple possibilities of readings with Chinese characters, archaic versions of characters, nicknames, and *ateji*.[29] Names of famous historical figures should not be difficult to identify, but the names of obscure individuals who do not appear in standard reference sources have to be inferred based on commonalities and recurring patterns of historical names. In the end, every stage of the process requires in-depth and substantial subject knowledge and close examination of the letters themselves.

Case Studies of Using the Database: Asakawa, Alice V. Morris, and the International Auxiliary Language Association

What can we glean from visualizing the network? Since this particular project is still in its early stages, it is difficult to give a complete answer at this time. However, some characteristics have emerged during the process. The most obvious finding was the sheer number of different recipients and authors among Asakawa's acquaintances. By visualizing patterns of the aggregated data of senders and recipients, the characteristics of the Yale collection compared to the Fukushima collection are clear. Among a total of more than eight hundred letters in the Yale collection, exchanges with the second-largest number of letters were between

Asakawa and W. S. Booth, William Wilcox[30], and Langdon Warner. But the largest number of letters (a total of seventy-two) with a single correspondent was the group of letters between Asakawa and Alice V. Morris.[31]

Little research has been done on either the relationship between Asakawa and Alice Morris or Asakawa's involvement with International Auxiliary Language Association (IALA) activities, the subject of most of the letters he exchanged with Morris. Transcripts and translations of several letters between Asakawa and Morris were published in the *Selected Letters of Asakawa*[32], but they were not the subject of analysis themselves.[33] Alice Morris's life and the history of the IALA have been detailed by Julia S. Falk in her collective biography *Women, Languages, and Linguistics*.[34] Asakawa's name is mentioned there only once, and close readings of their correspondence were not included in the book.

In fact, no studies have yet attempted to analyze the voluminous correspondence between Asakawa and Morris, nor to combine the history of the IALA with archival materials found in the Kan'ichi Asakawa Papers. A preliminary analysis of this correspondence suggests that Asakawa exercised considerable influence on Alice Morris and thus on the activities and policies of the IALA. A detailed study of Asakawa's impact on the IALA could provide a more nuanced and complete view of the organization's rise and fall, as well as new understandings of the international auxiliary language movement from the 1920s through the 1940s. Furthermore, Asakawa's involvement in the IALA sheds new light on the man himself because of the amount of time and energy he devoted to the movement between 1924 and 1940.[35]

Case Studies of Using the Database: Classroom Use and Inviting International Collaboration

In addition to tracking networks, the database can be linked to sites with other features to be used as a pedagogical tool for students in a classroom setting and for collaborators who are working in locations around the world. Because of the nature of Asakawa's cosmopolitan life, the correspondence in the Asakawa papers includes materials in multiple languages: English, Japanese, French, and Latin, as well as some auxiliary languages such as Esperanto and Occidental. Correspondence in Japanese cursive handwriting is difficult to read not only for foreign researchers who study Japanese but even for Japanese natives who lack training. In fact, the Japanese handwriting style was greatly impacted by drastic changes in printing technologies during the Meiji period when Asakawa was young. The evolving style variants were extremely diverse and consequently are difficult for modern readers to decipher. Such challenges are not unique to Japanese-language documents— old handwritten letters in European languages can be equally challenging to scholars—but modern Japanese researchers of Asakawa, the majority of potential users of the collection, will also face these difficulties, which could be alleviated through the transcription and translation functions of the project.

Some web-based projects have recently been developed to break such language barriers in order to advance scholarship collaboratively and internationally. For example, the site *Komonjo* (http://komonjo.princeton.edu), developed by Professor Thomas Conlan at Princeton University, introduces a number of medieval Japanese historical documents with English summaries, translations, and transcriptions intended to help readers interested in paleography compare the actual images of those documents. The Digital Vercelli (http://vbd.humnet.unipi.it/beta/#104v) was developed as a software application to enhance the reading experience of these multiple layers of texts. Currently, the software displays side by side, in two separate frames, an image of the manuscript and one of the transcribed text in order to allow viewers to compare the two different editions. The site also contains a variety of interactive features. Some of these include TextLink, which highlights lines of manuscript and the corresponding text; Hotspot, which lets users click on specific notes with the related information appearing in a pop-up window; and Magnifier, which significantly enlarges manuscript images for viewing details. This site is continuing to develop features that will include other accompaniments to the texts, such as commentary, critical editions, and translations. Other sites such as the University of Kyoto's *Minna de Honkoku* also provide tools for communities of people to transcribe, translate, and transliterate, as well as add comments to scanned original texts. Furthermore, Yale University's *Ten Thousand Room Projects* provides a platform for anyone to create their projects. It lets users upload their digitized documents and add various translations and commentaries.[36]

Based on these examples, and as figures 10.3 and 10.4 show, we have been developing a similar platform that enables the transcription process to be crowdsourced and translations of handwritten letters in various languages to be added through the Asakawa epistolary site. Because of the difficulties presented by handwritten materials, as well as issues of serving users who speak different languages, the site will be a virtual clearinghouse for researchers hoping to surmount the language barrier in their own work. Furthermore, the site will be a great tool for students of the Japanese language who wish to learn about the paleography of the Meiji period and for Japanese students learning western languages. Shakespeare's World (http://www.shakespearesworld.org/#/) is a great model for this sort of endeavor, as it uses crowdsourcing to expand shared knowledge and can be used as a teaching tool for the mastery of knowledge and skills. The site provides an excellent interface through which users can transcribe handwritten documents by Shakespeare's contemporaries in order to better understand his life and times. It includes detailed tutorials and tools with which to transcribe handwritten texts. The site also encourages users to explore the documents and possibly discover

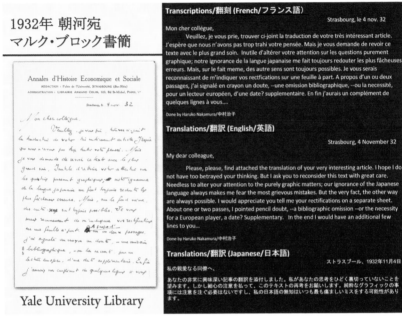

Figure 10.3. Marc Bloch's letter to Asakawa in 1932 with transcriptions (in French) and translations in English and Japanese.

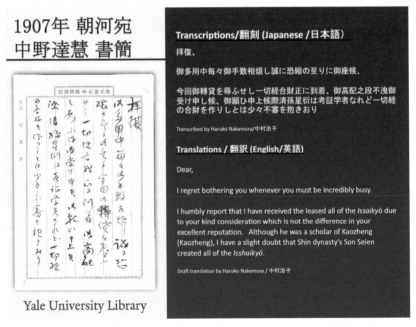

Figure 10.4. A letter from Nakano Tatsue to Asakawa in 1907 with transcriptions (in Japanese) and translations in English.

Figure 10.5. Transcribe@Yale invites users to transcribe historical texts such as this postcard in the Kan'ichi Asakawa Collection housed at Yale University.

words that are less commonly used and whose meanings haven't yet been recorded in authoritative sources. Furthermore, several paleography workshops and classes have been provided using the site. The idea of utilizing this epistolary corpus in a classroom setting is supported by Professor Daniel Botsman, who teaches Yale and Japan (a course on Yale and its history with Japan.) as well as other Japanese history courses. For this purpose, a database (Figure 10.5) was developed for transcribing letters of Asakawa. However, due to copyright restrictions of Kan'ichi Asakawa Paper, there are currently two levels of login required. First, in order to view those documents, one will need to enter with the login and passwords issued to Yale University affiliates. Then, to be able to enter transcriptions, the database will be prompted to create an account that is not linked to one's Yale login. In the future he plans to utilize this epistolary site to assign students to work on transcribing and translating the letters and uploading these transcriptions and translations on the site in hopes of making it a better tool for students to learn about various topics related to Asakawa and other world intellectuals during Asakawa's lifespan.

The current stage of this project has involved digitizing all the correspondence between Asakawa and others in high-quality images in order to allow for close paleographic analysis using the interface. Once the digitization is complete, the database will be further developed in order to share these high-quality images with the users of the database. The other major consideration for this sort of project are all the issues related to the continuously changing concepts and perceptions of copyright, property rights, fair use, and privacy. Since most of

Asakawa's corpus was created nearly a century ago and materials from the 1930s and 1940s are still in copyright, the program will be password protected, but it should be available to scholars under fair use. A recent case, that of Gale's Eighteenth Century Connect Online (ECCO) (https://www.gale.com/primary-sources/eighteenth-century-collections-online) set a new precedent by allowing access to texts in its database via Typewrite, a crowdsource transcription tool. In fact, the Asakawa epistolary project will involve much more complex interpretations of these rights issues, since it seeks to cross international borders. Thus any work on this aspect of the development of the project, working with the Yale university rights management office, can set a precedent for the development of future standards and guidelines for handling this sort of digital humanities project because of its reliance on international collaborators.

Conclusion

One of the many missions of any research library is to curate important yet unknown collections in order to provide wider awareness and easier access to researchers and even the public. Traditionally, correspondence collections have been scattered, making analysis difficult for researchers.

> The transformation of communications in the early modern period allowed ordinary scholars to scatter their letters across and beyond whole continents. The resulting integration of widely dispersed communities was fundamental to the intellectual fertility of the period. . . . While recent years have witnessed an efflorescence of online catalogues and digital editions of letters, these have tended to exist in the form of discrete silos around carefully defined collections and correspondents, making the large-scale exploration and analysis so essential to a full appreciation of early modern epistolary extremely difficult.[37]

Although this quote describes correspondence of the early modern period, those issues and challenges still remain in the scholarly investigations using correspondence today. Discovering those "discrete silos" can shed new perspectives on existing research. For example, in Asakawa's correspondence with Alice Morris and other individuals associated with the IALA, and in Asakawa's diary and manuscripts of his speeches, there exists a "silo" around the history of the IALA and the historiography of linguistics in the United States.

As the current project expands, the epistolary project will also become a great tool for crowdsourcing the extensive knowledge base of experts in a variety of subjects, including Japanese history, Japanese American history, the US-Japan relationship, and the US educational system, as well as the paleography of Japanese texts, English texts, and other European-language texts, including those in auxiliary languages like Occidental. Users of the site will be active contributors to the database, enhancing metadata information by providing such key information as dates, names of senders and recipients, transcriptions, and translations of letters, as well as other accompanying texts such as commentaries. This process of virtual community building for scholars will also function as a teaching tool in related subjects for students based on their participation in enhancing the site. Broadly, the project will create a central platform/repository of correspondence and archival resources for analyzing not only other Japanese intellectuals during the Meiji period but the circulation of knowledge among intellectuals and public figures throughout the world.

Future Possibilities for the Project

A significant number of possibilities and findings may proceed from this project. A larger correspondence collection of 2,546 letters are held in the Fukushima Prefectural Library and smaller numbers of Asakawa's letters are scattered in other repositories, such as the Waseda University Library. Adding the metadata of these collections into this platform and connecting senders and recipients is an ideal next step that will provide more content and a larger network to be visualized. Furthermore, Asakawa's letters exist in other collections such as the papers of Andrew Keogh and Edward Gaylord Bourne.[38] Epistolary data for Asakawa's letters also can be found in edited volumes of Sakatachi Yoshirō's correspondence, such as *Sakai Yashirō kankei shokanshū* (2013).[39]

There is also the possibility of the project expanding beyond the scope of the epistolary realm. As noted above, the Kan'ichi Asakawa Papers collection contains other forms of documents that represent Asakawa's networks. His diary is another promising resource for adding a different dimension to this project. By analyzing the figures that appear in this diary, the platform can provide another layer of connections with Asakawa. Yale University accepted an unusual number of Japanese graduates in the late nineteenth century. Although they are not in the Asakawa collection, some photo directories and albums of Japanese graduates are kept in the Manuscripts and Archives collection and will be contributing to prosopographic studies of Japanese figures in the Meiji period. By analyzing Asakawa's correspondence, we can identify the names of some who are mentioned, and these individuals can also be integrated as visual materials. With these potential expansions of the project, researchers and students will be able to form a more complete picture not only of Asakawa's life and work, but also of the many people he influenced and the rapidly changing times in which he lived.

Notes

[1] This chapter was first submitted in February 2016 and revised in September 2019, reflecting the project's situation at that time. The author would like to note that as a result neither recent scholarship on Asakawa or other digital scholarship on epistolary networks are reflected in this paper.

[2] Oshio Joji オシオ・ジョージ, "Asakawa Kan'ichi to eigo ni yoru Nihon no hōken seido no kenkyū" 朝河貫一と英語による日本の封建制度の研究 [Kan'ichi Asakawa and English language research into the Japanese feudal system], in *Yomigaeru Asakawa Kan'ichi: Fumetsu no rekishika idainaru paionia* 甦る朝河貫一：不滅の歴史家偉大なるパイオニア [Resurrecting Kan'ichi Asakawa: Eternal historian and great pioneer], ed. Asakawa Kan'ichi Kenkyūkai 朝河貫一研究会, (Tokyo: Kokusai Bunken Insatsusha, 1998), 184.

[3] The dates are 1849 for Chinese, 1851 for Japanese, and 1870s for a systematic collection of the Japanese materials. For detailed information about earlier acquisitions of Japanese books at Yale University, see William D. Fleming, "Japanese Students Abroad and the Building of America's First Japanese Library Collection, 1869–1878" *Journal of the American Oriental Society* 139.1 (2019): 115–141.

[4] Abe Yoshio 阿部善雄 and Kaneko Hideo 金子英生, *Saigo no"Nihonjin": Asakawa Kan'ichi no shōgai* 最後の「日本人」：朝河貫一の生涯 [The Last "Japanese": Kan'ichi Asakawa's Life] (Tokyo: Iwanami Shoten, 1983).

[5] Charles Seymour to Asakawa, December 8, 1941, Kan'ichi Asakawa Papers (MS 40), Manuscripts and Archives, Yale University Library (hereafter Asakawa Papers).

[6] Abe Yoshio 阿部善雄, and Kaneko Hideo 金子英生, *Saigo no "Nihonjin" : Asakawa Kan'ichi no shōgai* 最後の「日本人」：朝河貫一の生涯 (Tokyo: Iwanami Shoten, 1983), 34.

[7] Ibid.

[8] Ebisawa Tadashi 海老澤衷and et all. *Asakawa Kan'ichi to Jinbungaku no keisei* 朝河貫一と人文学の形成 [Kan'ichi Asakawa and the formation of the humanities]. 258–280. (Tokyo: Yoshikawa Kōbunkan, 2019). Ebisawa Tadashi 海老澤衷 and et all. *Asakawa Kan'ichi to Nichiō chūseishi kenkyū* 朝河貫一と日欧中世史研究 [Kan'ichi Asakawa and research on Japanese-European medieval history]. (Tokyo: Yoshikawa Kōbunkan, 2017).

[9] Yamauchi Haruko山内晴子, *Asakawa Kan'ichi ron: Sono gakumon keisei to jissen* 朝河貫一論: その学問形成と実践 [Kan'ichi Asakawa: The formation and practice of his scholarship], Waseda University monograph no. 2早稲田大学モノグラフ2 (Tokyo: Waseda Daigaku Shuppanbu, 2009). Mineshima Hideo 峰島旭雄 and Asakawa Kan'ichi Kenkyūkai朝河貫一研究会, *Asakawa Kan'ichi no sekai: Fumetsu no rekishika idainaru paionia* 朝河貫一の世界 : 不滅の歴史家偉大なるパイオニア [Campaign for submission of the letter to the President] (Tokyo: Waseda Daigaku Shuppanbu, 1993).

[10] Yamaoka Michio 山岡道男, ed., *Taiheiyō Mondai Chōsakai (1925–1961) to sono jidai* 太平洋問題調査会「1925–1961」とその時代 [Institute of Pacific Relations: "1925–1961" and its era] (Yokohama-shi: Shunpūsha, 2010). Kaneko Hideo 金子英生, "Daitōryō

shinsho konshin undō o megutte" 大統領親書懇親運動をめぐって [Campaign for submission of the letter to the President], in *Yomigaeru Asakawa Kan'ichi : Fumetsu no rekishika idainaru paionia* 甦る朝河貫一: 不滅の歴史家偉大なるパイオニア, ed. Asakawa Kan'ichi Kenkyūkai 朝河貫一研究会, (Tokyo: Kokusai Bunken Insatsusha, 1998), 193–204.

[11] Ishikawa Eizō 石川衛三, "Asakawa Kan'ichi no kōnen o kazatta jyosei: Sono aisetsunaru ai to shōshin no kiseki" 朝河貫一の後年を飾った女性: その哀切なる愛と傷心の軌跡 [The woman who enriched the later years of Kan'ichi Asakawa: The trajectory of that sorrowful love and heartbreak], *Chūōgakuin daigaku kyōyō ronshū* 中央学院大学教養研究 [Chuo-Gakuin University Review of Faculty of Liberal Arts] 6, no. 2 (September 1993): 3–35. Masui Yukimi 増井由紀美, "Asakawa Kan'ichi to Diana Watts no kankei" 朝河貫一とダイアナワッツの関係 [Asakawa Kan'ichi and Diana Watts: A modern scholar and a society woman], *Tsudajuku Daigaku Kiyō* 津田塾大学紀要 [Journal of Tsuda College] 41 (March 2009): 225–52.

[12] Ellen Hammond "A History of the East Asia Library at Yale," in *Collecting Asia: East Asian Libraries in North America, 1868–2008*, ed. Peter X. Zhou (Ann Arbor, MI: Association for Asian Studies, 2010), 3–20. Kikuchi Hiroki "Letting the Copy out of the Window: A History of Copying Texts in Japan," *East Asian Library Journal* 14, no. 1 (Spring 2010): 120–57.

[13] Matsutani Yumiko 松谷有美子, "Asakawa Kan'ichi ni yoru Iēru daigaku toshokan oyobi Beikoku gikai toshokan no tame no Nihon shiryō no shūshū" 朝河貫一によるイェール大学図書館および米国議会図書館のための日本資料の収集 [Japanese materials collected by Kan'ichi for Yale University Library and the Library of Congress], *Library and Information Science*, no. 74 (2014年): 1–35.

[14] See works by Kageyama Reiko 景山礼子 (pp. 3–14), Endō Kaizō 遠藤海蔵 (pp. 29–36), and Yamaoka Michio 山岡道男 (pp. 59–66) in *Yomigaeru Asakawa Kan'ichi: Fumetsu no rekishika idainaru paionia* 甦る朝河貫一: 不滅の歴史家偉大なるパイオニア , ed. Asakawa Kan'ichi Kenkyūkai 朝河貫一研究会, (Tokyo: Kokusai Bunken Insatsusha, 1998).

[15] Yamaoka Michio 山岡道男 et al., *Asakawa Kan'ichi shiryō : Waseda Daigaku, Fukushima Kenritsu Toshokan, Yēru Daigaku hoka shozō* 朝河貫一資料: 早稲田大学・福島県立図書館・イェール大学他所蔵 [Sources of Kan'ichi Asakawa: Collections in Waseda University, Fukushima Prefectural Library, Yale University, etc.] (Tokyo: Waseda Daigaku Ajia Taiheiyō Kenkyū Sentā. 2015). Jin'no Takeshi 甚野尚志, *Asakawa Kan'ichi shiryō mokuroku : Fukushima kenritsu toshokan shozoō* 朝河貫一資料目録: 福島県立図書館所蔵 [Catalog on Kan'ichi Asakawa: Fukushima Prefectural Library Collection]. (Fukushima: Fukushimaken Toshokan, 2019).

[16] More scholarship on Asakawa has emerged since the original writing of this chapter in 2015.

[17] Yale University Library Digital Humanities Lab, "What is Digital Humanities," Accessed September 10, 2019. https://dhlab.yale.edu/methods.html.

[18] The genesis of the project to visualize Asakawa's relationships came out of discussions in a class taught by Professor Daniel Botsman.

[19] Kate Theimer, "A Distinction Worth Exploring: 'Archives' and 'Digital Historical Representations,'" *Journal of Digital Humanity* 3, mo. 2 (Summer, 2014): 56–59.

[20] Cultures of Knowledge, "Networking the Republic of Letters, 1550–1750," accessed May 7, 2015, http://www.culturesofknowledge.org/.

[21] "Circulation of Knowledge and Learned Practices in the 17th-century Dutch Republic," accessed May 10, 2015, http://ckcc.huygens.knaw.nl/.

[22] See University of Chicago, "Hoyt Long, Ph.D." accessed February 10, 2016, https://ealc.uchicago.edu/faculty/long.

[23] Mary Mikami Rouse, the mother of Pete Rouse, the prominent American political consultant, taught at Yale's Institute for Oriental Languages.

[24] Jerome Pollitt was the Sterling Professor Emeritus of Classical Archeology and the History of Art., Yale University.

[25] The author would like to thank Professor Yamauchi for generously sharing the spreadsheets based on her voluminous and solid research on Asakawa.

[26] The list was published in the *Asakawa Kan'ichi Shiryō: Waseda Daigaku, Fukushima Kenritsu Toshokan, Ieru Daigaku hoka zō.*

[27] Another sincere acknowledgment is due to Peter Leonard and Catherine DeRose for their guidance and involvement of this project.

[28] Since the original writing of this chapter, other new technologies have emerged that may be used in addition to Gephi. Some examples are D3, Data-Driven Documents which deal with more substantial data for visualization, as well as Zooniverse, a powerful platform for crowdsourcing works.

[29] *Ateji* are words that have been assigned kanji characters that match phonetically but disregard the characters' semantic use.

[30] William Stone Booth (1864–1926) was an editor at the Houghton Mifflin publishing house and later at Macmillan. William B. Wilcox (1907–85) was an American historian thought at Yale University.

[31] This excludes four letters addressed to Dave but includes two addressed to Dave and Alice. Another nine letters from Asakawa to Alice and one to Dave Morris written between 1936 and 1940 are held at the Fukushima Prefectural Library. Twenty additional letters between Asakawa and other individuals were identified on the topics of the IALA or auxiliary language.

[32] Asakawa Kan'ichi朝河貫一 and Asakawa Kan'ichi Shokan Henshū Iinkai 朝河貫一書簡編集委員会編. *Asakawa Kan'ichi shokanshū* 朝河貫一書簡集 [Letters written by Dr. Kan'ichi Asakawa], Tokyo, Waseda Daigaku Shuppanbu, 1991.

[33] Ishikawa Eizō 石川 衛三, "<Honyaku> Asakawa Kan'ichi to IALA (Amerika Gasshūkoku, Kokusai Hogo Kyōkai: Nichi-bei kyōdō 'chiteki sagyō (purojekuto)' no ichidai jikken" <翻訳>朝河貫一とIALA (アメリカ合衆国・国際補助言語協会) : 日

米共同『知的作業 (プロジェクト)』の一大実験 [<Translation> Dr. Kan'ichi Asakawa and IALA (International Auxiliary Language Association): A major experiment of Japan-US joint "Intellectual Work (Project)"], *Chūōgakuin daigaku daigaku shizen ronsō* 中央学院大学人間・自然論叢 [The Bulletin of Chuo-Gakuin University : man and nature] 1 (December 1994): 165–256.

[34] Julia S. Falk, *Women, Language, and Linguistics: Three American Stories from the First Half of the Twentieth Century* (London: Routledge, 1999).

[35] The relationship between Asakawa and Alice V. Morris, as well as Asakawa's involvement in the development of the IALA, is detailed in Haruko Nakamura 中村治子. "Akasawa Kan'ichi to Kokusai Hojogo Kyokai: Asakawa to Arisu V Morisue to no kankei o jiku ni朝河貫一と国際補助語協会―朝河とアリス・Ｖ・モリスとの関係を軸に" [Kan'ichi Asakawa and the International Auxiliary Language Association - Focusing on the relationship between Asakawa and Alice V. Morris] In *Asakawa Kan'ichi to Jinbungaku No Keisei* 朝河貫一と人文学の形成, ed. Tadashi Ebisawa 海老澤衷and et all (Tokyo: Yoshikawa Kōbunkan, 2019), 258–280.

[36] Ten Thousand Room Projects, Accessed August 2, 2019. https://tenthousandrooms.yale.edu. Minna de Honkoku みんなで翻刻, Accessed August 15, 2019. https://honkoku.org.

[37] Cultures of Knowledge, "How Do You Solve A Problem Like Correspondence?," accessed May 25, 2015, http://www.culturesofknowledge.org/?page_id=28.

[38] Andrew Keogh was the Yale librarian from 1916 to 1938. Edward Gaylord Bourne (1860–1908) was an American historian and professor of medieval history and political science at Yale from 1885 to 1888. Bourne's papers are in Manuscripts and Archives, Yale University Library.

[39] Sakatani Yoshirō (1863-1941) was a bureaucrats and politicians who played an significant role in the finance of the Russo-Japanese War.

Bibliography

Abe, Yoshio阿部善雄 and Hideo Kaneko 金子英生. *Saigo no "Nihonjin : Asakawa Kan'ichi no shōgai* 最後の「日本人」: 朝河貫一の生涯 [The last "Japanese": Kan'ichi Asakawa's life]. Tokho: Iwanami Shoten, 1983.

Asakawa, Kan'ichi 朝河貫一 and Asakawa Kan'ichi Shokan Henshū Iinkai 朝河貫一書簡編集委員会編. *Asakawa Kan'ichi shokanshū* 朝河貫一書簡集 [Letters written by Dr. Kan'ichi Asakawa]. Tokyo, Waseda Daigaku Shuppanbu, 1991.

Asakawa, Kan'ichi. *Land and Society in Medieval Japan: Studies by Kan'ichi Asakawa*. Tokyo: Japan Society for the Promotion of Science, 1965.

Asakawa, Kan'ichi. *The Documents of Iriki, Illustrative of the Development of the Feudal Institutions of Japan. Translated and Edited by K. Asakawa*. New Haven, 1929.

Asakawa, Kan'ichi. *The Early Institutional Life of Japan; a Study in the Reform of 645 A.d., by K. Asakawa. with Introd. by Hyman Kublin.* New York, Paragon Book Reprint Corp, 1963.

Asakawa, Kan'ichi 朝河貫一. *Nihon No Kaki*日本の禍機 [Japan's Crisis]. Tōkyō: Jitsugyō no Nihonsha, 1909.

Asakawa Kan'ichi Kenkyūkai朝河貫一研究会, ed. *Yomigaeru Asakawa Kan'ichi: Fumetsu no rekishika idainaru paionia* 甦る朝河貫一： 不滅の歴史家偉大なるパイオニア [Resurrecting Kan'ichi Asakawa: Eternal historian and great pioneer]. Tokyo: Kokusai Bunken Insatsusha, 1998.

Asakawa, Kan'ichi and Williams, Frederick W. *The Russo-Japanese Conflict: Its Causes and Issues ... with an Introduction by F.W. Williams ... Illustrated.* A. Constable & Co: Westminster; Cambridge, Mass. printed, 1904.

Asakawa, Kan'ichi 朝河貫一 and Yabuki, Susumu矢吹進. *Chūsei Nihon No Tochi to Shakai* 中世日本の土地と社会 [Land and society in medieval Japan]. Tokyo: Kashiwashobō, 2015.

Asakawa, Kan'ichi 朝河貫一 and Yabuki, Susumu矢吹進. *Iriki Monjo* 入来文書 [The Documents of Iriki]. Tokyo: Kashiwa shobō, 2015.

Circulation of Knowledge and Learned Practices in the 17th-century Dutch Republic. Accessed February 10, 2016. http://ckcc.huygens.knaw.nl/.

Cultures of Knowledge. Networking the Republic of Letters, 1550–1750. Accessed May. 25, 2015. http://www.culturesofknowledge.org/.

Ebisawa, Tadashi 海老澤衷, Kondō. Shigekazu 近藤成一, and Jinno, Takashi 甚野尚, ed. *Asakawa Kan'ichi to Nichiō Chūseishi Kenkyū* 朝河貫一と日欧中世史研究 [Kan'ichi Asakawa and research on Japanese-European medieval history]. Tokyo: Yoshikawa Kōbunkan, 2017.

———. *Asakawa Kan'ichi to Jinbungaku No Keisei* 朝河貫一と人文学の形成 [Kan'ichi Asakawa and the formation of the humanities]. 258-280. Tokyo: Yoshikawa Kōbunkan, 2019.

Endō, Kaizō 遠藤海蔵. "Asakawa Kan'ichi to Tsunashima Ryōsen" 朝河貫一の綱島梁川 [Kan'ichi Asakawa and Tsunashima Ryōsen]. In *Yomigaeru Asakawa Kan'ichi: Fumetsu no rekishika idainaru paionia* 甦る朝河貫一： 不滅の歴史家偉大なるパイオニア, edited by Asakawa Kan'ichi Kenkyūkai 朝河貫一研究会, 29–36. Tokyo: Kokusai Bunken Insatsusha, 1998.

Falk, Julia S. *Women, Language, and Linguistics: Three American Stories from the First Half of the Twentieth Century.* London: Routledge, 1999.

Fleming, William D. "Japanese Students Abroad and the Building of America's First Japanese Library Collection, 1869–1878" *Journal of the American Oriental Society* 139.1 (2019): 115–141.

Gopsill, F. P. *International Languages: A Matter for Interlingua.* Sheffield: British Interlingua Society, 1990.

Hammond, Ellen. "A History of the East Asia Library at Yale." In *Collecting Asia: East Asian Libraries in North America, 1868–2008*, edited by Peter X. Zhou, 3–20. Ann Arbor, MI: Association for Asian Studies, 2010.

Interlingua Institute Records, 1921–2001. Manuscripts and Archives Division, New York Public Library.

International Auxiliary Language Association. *Outline of Program.* New York: IALA, 1924.

———. *Plan for Obtaining Agreement.* New York: IALA, 1936.

———. *Some Criteria for an International Language and Commentary.* New York: IALA, 1937.

Ishikawa, Eizō石川衛三. "Asakawa Kan'ichi no kōnen o kazatta jyosei: Sono aisetsunaru ai to shōshin no kiseki" 朝河貫一の後年を飾った女性: その哀切なる愛と傷心の軌跡 [The Woman Who Enriched the Later Years of Kan'ichi Asakawa: The Trajectory of that Sorrowful Love and Heartbreak]. *Chūōgakuin daigaku kyōyō ronshū* 中央学院大学教養研究 [Chuo-Gakuin University review of Faculty of Liberal Arts] 6, no. 2 (September 1993): 3–35.

———. "<Honyaku> Asakawa Kan'ichi to IALA (Amerika gasshūkoku, Kokusai Hogo Kyōkai: Nichi-bei kyōdō 'chiteki sagyo (purojekuto)' no ichidai jikken" <翻訳> 朝河貫一とIALA (アメリカ合衆国・国際補助言語協会) : 日米共同『知的作業 (プロジェクト)』の一大実験 [<Translation> Dr. Kan'ichi Asakawa and IALA (International Auxiliary Language Association) : A Major Experiment of Japan-US joint "intellectual Work (Project)"]. *Chūōgakuin daigaku daigaku shizen ronsō*中央学院大学人間・自然論叢 [The Bulletin of Chuo-Gakuin University : man and nature 1] (December 1994): 165–256.

Jin'no, Takeshi 甚野尚志, *Asakawa kan'ichi shiryō mokuroku : Fukushima kenritsu toshokan shozō* 朝河貫一資料目録: 福島県立図書館所蔵 [Catalog on Kan'ichi Asakawa: Fukushima Prefectural Library Collection]. Fukushima: Fukushimaken Toshokan, 2019.

Kageyama, Reiko 景山礼子. "Asakawa Kan'ichi no onjin, Uiriamu J Takka" 朝河貫一の恩人－ウイリアム・J・タッカー [The benefactor of Kan'ichi

Asakawa – William J. Tucker]. In *Yomigaeru Asakawa Kan'ichi: Fumetsu no rekishika idainaru paionia* 甦る朝河貫一: 不滅の歴史家偉大なるパイオニア, edited by Asakawa Kan'ichi Kenkyūkai 朝河貫一研究会, 3–15. Tokyo: Kokusai Bunken Insatsusha, 1998.

Kaneko, Hideo 金子英生. "Daitōryō shinsho konshin undō o megutte" 大統領親書懇親運動をめぐって [Campaign for submission of the letter to the President]. In *Yomigaeru Asakawa Kan'ichi: Fumetsu no rekishika idainaru paionia* 甦る朝河貫一: 不滅の歴史家偉大なるパイオニア, edited by Asakawa Kan'ichi Kenkyūkai 朝河貫一研究会, 193–204. Tokyo: Kokusai Bunken Insatsusha, 1998.

Kan'ichi Asakawa Papers (MS 40). Manuscripts and Archives, Yale University Library.

Kikuchi, Hiroki. "Letting the Copy out of the Window: A History of Copying Texts in Japan." *East Asian Library Journal* 14, no. 1 (Spring 2010): 120–57.

Masui, Yukimi, 増井由紀美. "Asakawa Kan'ichi to Diana Watts no kankei" 朝河貫一とダイアナワッツの関係 [Asakawa Kan'ichi and Diana Watts: A modern scholar and a society woman]. *Tsudajuku Daigaku Kiyō* 津田塾大学紀要 [Journal of Tsuda College] 41 (March 2009): 225–52.

Matsutani, Yumiko 松谷有美子. "Asakawa Kan'ichi ni yoru Iēru daigaku toshokan oyobi Beikoku gikai toshokan no tame no Nihon shiryō no shūshū" 朝河貫一によるイェール大学図書館および米国議会図書館のための日本資料の収集 [Japanese sources collected by Kan'ichi Asakawa for Yale University Library and Library of Congress]. *Library and Information Science*, no. 74 (2014年): 1–35.

Minejima, Asao 峰島旭雄. "Asakawa Kan'ichi to Tsunashima Ryōsen" 朝河貫一と綱島梁川 [Kan'ichi Asakawa and Tsuneshima Ryōsen]. in *Yomigaeru Asakawa Kan'ichi: Fumetsu no rekishika idainaru paionia* 甦る朝河貫一: 不滅の歴史家偉大なるパイオニア, edited by Asakawa Kan'ichi Kenkyūkai 朝河貫一研究会, 83–94. Tokyo: Kokusai Bunken Insatsusha, 1998.

Mineshima, Hideo 峰島旭雄, and Asakawa Kan'ichi Kenkyūkai朝河貫一研究会. *Asakawa Kan'ichi no sekai: Fumetsu no rekishika idainaru paionia* 朝河貫一の世界: 不滅の歴史家偉大なるパイオニア. Tokyo: Waseda Daigaku Shuppanbu, 1993.

Minna de honkoku みんなで翻刻, Accessed August 15, 2019. https://honkoku.org.

Nakamura, Haruko 中村治子. "Akasawa Kan'ichi to Kokusai Hojogo Kyokai: Asakawa to Arisu V Morisue to no Kankei o Jikuni" 朝河貫一と国際補助語協会―朝河とアリス・Ｖ・モリスとの関係を軸に [Kan'ichi Asakawa and the International Auxiliary Language Association - Focusing on the Relationship between Asakawa and Alice V. Morris] In *Asakawa Kan'ichi to Jinbungaku No Keisei* 朝河貫一と人文学の形成., edited by Ebisawa, Tadashi 海老澤衷and et all, 258-280. Tokyo: Yoshikawa Kōbunkan, 2019.

Oshio, Joji オシオ・ジョージ. "Asakawa Kan'ichi to eigo ni yoru Nihon no hōken seido no kenkyū" 朝河貫一と英語による日本の封建制度の研究 [Kan'ichi Asakawa and English language research into the Japanese feudal system]. In *Yomigaeru Asakawa Kan'ichi: Fumetsu no rekishika idainaru paionia* 甦る朝河貫一：不滅の歴史家偉大なるパイオニア, edited by Asakawa Kan'ichi Kenkyūkai 朝河貫一研究会, 181–192. Tokyo: Kokusai Bunken Insatsusha, 1998.

Sakatani, Yoshirō 阪谷芳郎 and Senshū Daigaku 専修大学 ed. *Sakatani Yoshirō kankei shokanshū* 阪谷芳郎関係書簡集 [Collection of letters related to Yoshio Sakatani]. Tokyo: Fuyō Shobō Shuppan, 2013.

Ten Thousand Room Projects, Accessed August 2, 2019. https://tenthousandrooms.yale.edu/.

University of Chicago, "Hoyt Long, Ph.D." Accessed February 10, 2016. https://ealc.uchicago.edu/faculty/long.

Yale University Library Digital Humanities Lab, Accessed September 10, 2019. https://dhlab.yale.edu/methods.html.

Yamaoka, Michio 山岡道男. "Asakawa Kan'ichi to George E Morrison" 朝河貫一とジョージ・Ｅ・モリソン [Kan'ichi Asakawa and George E. Morrison]. In *Yomigaeru Asakawa Kan'ichi: Fumetsu no rekishika idainaru paionia* 甦る朝河貫一：不滅の歴史家偉大なるパイオニア, edited by Asakawa Kan'ichi Kenkyūkai 朝河貫一研究会, 59–66. Tokyo: Kokusai Bunken Insatsusha, 1998.

———, ed. *Taiheiyō mondai chōsakai (1925–1961) to sono jidai* 太平洋問題調査会「1925〜1961」とその時代 [Institute of Pacific Relations: "1925–1961" and its era]. Yokohama-shi: Shunpūsha, 2010.

Yamaoka, Michio 山岡道男, Yukimi, Masui 増井由紀美, Igarashi, Takashi 五十嵐卓, Yamauchi, Haruko 山内晴子, and Satō, Yūki 佐藤雄基. *Asakawa Kan'ichi shiryō: Waseda Daigaku, Fukushima Kenritsu Toshokan, Yēru Daigaku hoka shozō* 朝河貫一資料：早稲田大学・福島県立図書館・イェール大学他所蔵 [Sources of Kan'ichi Asakawa: Collections in Waseda University, Fukushima Prefectural Library, Yale University, etc]. Tokyo:

Waseda Daigaku Ajia Taiheiyō Kenkyū Sentā 早稲田大学アジア太平洋研究センター, 2015.

Yamauchi, Haruko 山内晴子. *Asakawa Kan'ichi ron: Sono gakumon keisei to jissen* 朝河貫一論 : その学問形成と実践 [Kan'ichi Asakawa: The formation and practice of his scholarship]. Waseda University Monographs 早稲田大学モノグラフ, no. 2. Tokyo: 早稲田大学出版部, 2009.

11

By Accident and Design

Some Provenance Stories behind Interesting and Curious Japanese Materials in the Harvard-Yenching Library

Kuniko Yamada McVey, Harvard University

Introduction

The Japanese collection of the Harvard-Yenching Library goes back some 140 years, and, as is the case with other old library collections in North America, it contains numerous interesting and curious materials. With these materials come stories of how they came to be where they are. Their paths are typically connected with the intentions of individual collectors and often involve accident and drama. The unique character of today's research collections is at least as much a result of accidental acquisitions as it is of careful collection development policies.

These stories are often lost in standard cataloging practices and are hidden from subsequent readers. As a librarian, and in particular as steward of the collection, I am fascinated by these stories whenever I discover them and would like to shed some light on a few of these materials and the stories behind them. My hope is that they will thus become visible once again to those who would otherwise never see them and that new and original research ideas might result from this.

Individuals Important to the Collection

There were many who contributed to the creation of the Yenching Library's

Japanese Collection, and I would like to focus on several individuals whose lives and collections became a part of the library's history.

Anesaki Masaharu 姉崎正治 (1873–1949)
Hattori Unokichi 服部宇之吉 (1867–1939)
Langdon Warner (1881–1955)
Yanagi Muneyoshi 柳宗悦 (1889–1961)
Koizumi Shinzō 小泉信三 (1888–1966)
Ernest. G. Stillman (1884–1949)
Bruno Petzold (1873–1949)
Horikoshi Yoshihiro 堀越喜博 (1889–1946)
Charles E. Perry (1908–59)
Tsurumi Shunsuke 鶴見俊輔 (1922–2015)

Some of their stories are intertwined, others independent. These people, almost all contemporaries, had distinguished careers in different locations throughout the globe. While their paths were different, they share a common end in that their collections found their way into the Yenching Library.

The Beginning

A professorship of Japanese literature and life was established at Harvard in 1913 with funding from Japanese graduates of the university. Two Japanese scholars were invited from the Tokyo Imperial University to teach courses through the Department of Philosophy; they were Anesaki Masaharu (taught 1913–15) and Hattori Unokichi (taught 1915–16). During the course of their stays at Harvard they donated some books to the library, which became the foundation of the Japanese Collection today. Because these books had come to the Harvard library before the East Asian Library was established in 1928, no list of their donations exists. We occasionally encounter books on Chinese classics, philosophy, and Buddhism with the handwritten note "Gift of Prof. Anesaki, 1915," followed by the accession stamp, or a printed bookplate "Gift of U Hattori of Tokyo June 12, 1916." We are slowly constructing a list of these donations as we come upon them.

Books from Anesaki include *Kōtei katagi zenshū* 校訂気質全集 (Hakubunkan, 1912), Schopenhauer's *Ishi to genshiki to shite no sekai* 意志と現識としての世界 (Die Welt als Wille und Vorstellung) translated by Anesaki himself (Hakubunkan, 1910), and Kakei Katsuhiko 筧克彦's *Bukkyō tetsuri* 仏教哲理 (Yūhikaku, 1911). Hattori's donations include Nishimura Tenshū 西村天囚's *Nihon Sōgakushi* 日本宋学史 (Ryōkōdō shoten, 1909), Iwahashi Junsei 岩橋遵成's *Dai Nihon rinri shisō hattatsushi* 大日本倫理思想発達史 (Meguro shoten, 1915), Ōtsuki Fumihiko 大槻文彦's *Genkai* 言海 (Kobayashi Shinbe, 1904), and Haga Yaichi 芳賀矢一's *Kokubungakushi gairon* 国文学史概論 (Bunkaidō, 1913).

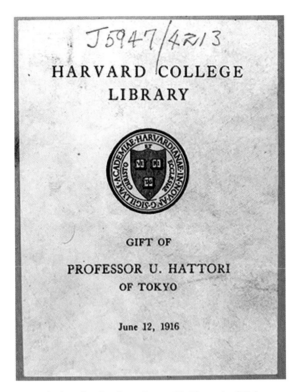

Bookplate "Gift of Professor U. Hattori of Tokyo,
June 12, 1916." Image taken by the author.

According to the *Harvard Crimson*, Harvard's student-run daily newspaper,
a 420-volume set of *Dai Nihon kōtei Daizōkyō* 大日本校訂大蔵経 (Kōkyō shoin,
1881–85) was also donated to the library by the Association Concordia of Tokyo
through Professor Anesaki on March 9, 1914. And, indeed, its accession stamp
reads "Feb 4, 1914. Gift of Association Concordia of Tokyo." This is an early edition
of the Chinese Buddhist canon and its Japanese commentaries, written entirely in
Chinese, and today the set is a part of the Chinese Collection of the Yenching
Library. Isomae Jun'ichi reports that Anesaki had also asked the Tokyo Imperial
University to send 180 glass plate photographs to Harvard in March 1914,[1] but
these have yet to be identified.

Langdon Warner (1881-1955)

Langdon Warner, art historian, explorer, archaeologist, and Asian art collector,
was an active player in building Harvard's Asian collection and advancing Asian
art research in general.

Warner graduated from Harvard College in 1903 and participated in the Pumpelly-Carnegie expedition to Russian Turkestan in 1904. On his return, he joined the staff of the Museum of Fine Arts (MFA) in Boston. Warner worked under Japanese art historian Okakura Kakuzō 岡倉覚三 (also known as Tenshin 天心, 1863–1913), who was invited to the MFA by William Sturgis Bigelow in 1904 and subsequently became the first head of the Asian Art Division in 1910. Okakura, who studied under Harvard-educated professor Ernest Fenollosa (1853–1908) at the Tokyo Imperial University, was an influential figure in Japan.[2] The MFA's outstanding collection of Japanese art is attributed to Okakura and Fenollosa.

The MFA sent Warner to Japan to study its art and language for the first time in 1906. He studied Buddhist sculpture of the Tenpyō period (eighth century) among others, situating himself in the ancient capital of Nara. There he interacted with a group of Okakura's students—Niiro Chūnosuke 新納忠之介 (sculptor), Rokkaku Shisui 六角紫水 (lacquerware specialist), and Yokoyama Taikan 横山大観 (painter). Warner was appointed an assistant curator of Chinese and Japanese art at the MFA in 1909.

Warner started to lecture on Chinese and Japanese Art at Harvard in 1912, where he would teach until 1950. He began working with Harvard's Fogg Art Museum in 1923 and there became a curator of Asian art. He traveled extensively throughout Japan, China, Mongolia, India, Siberia, and other parts of Asia and Europe for research and acquisition of artifacts not only for Harvard, but also for other art museums in the United States, as well as on other assignments. He traveled to China, Manchuria, and Mongolia for archaeological research on behalf of Charles Freer in 1913–14; a special U.S. consular assignment took him to Harbin in 1917–18; and he crossed Siberia several times in some unclear connection with isolated Czecho-Slovakian forces, to list but a few of his activities. Some of his actions while on his expeditions to China in 1923 and 1925 for the Fogg Art Museum remain controversial to this day.[3] Warner also founded the Rübel Asiatic Research Bureau. He played a critical role in establishing the Harvard-Yenching Institute in 1928, in particular by negotiating with the Charles Martin Hall estate to fund the institute's creation.[4] The Harvard-Yenching Library was created in the same year, fully funded by the Institute. The institute, located on campus but fiscally independent from Harvard, has been closely affiliated with Harvard scholars on Asia and the Asian research community since that time.

Warner left a huge amount of archival material at Harvard, reflecting his active and somewhat unconventional life. These materials include the following.

1. Travel diary, Kobe to Luchu, manuscript, November 2–14, 1909, held by the Houghton Library.

2. Photograph collection, 390 glass negatives of Japan, mostly taken by Warner in 1916–21. Many images are of Buddhist temple sites in and around Kyoto, including Kiyomizudera, Tōfukuji, Nanzenji, and Tōji, held by the Fine Arts Library.

3. Rubbings from China, 1800–1935. Many of these were made or collected by Warner during his time in China, 1923–25, and later donated. These 1,938 rubbings represent Chinese art and calligraphy from the Zhou through the Qing periods and include both images and text. Held and digitized by the Fine Arts Library.[5]

4. Papers of Langdon Warner, 1926–54, 21.75 linear feet in total, held by the Harvard University Archives. Notable in this large group are photos of Okinawa most likely taken by Yanagi Muneyoshi.

5. Langdon Warner correspondence, 1906–46. "Letters address the Fogg Museum and Museum of Fine Arts in Boston, financing employees at the Fogg Museum, acquisitions in Japan and Japanese rare books and artwork. Letters also concern Langdon's experiences in Japan, including being held up by bandits and his complaints of other men on the expedition, in particular Daniel Thompson. Langdon also discusses his trip to London: poem by Warner, the Moro; and telegrams."[6] Held by the Houghton Library.

Warner authored several books on Japanese arts: *The Craft of the Japanese Sculptor* (1936), *Japanese Gardens* (1947), *The Enduring Art of Japan* (1952), *Tempyo Bibliography* (1953), and *Japanese Sculpture of the Tempyo Period: Masterpieces of the Eighth Century* (1959).

Falconry and Archery Manuscripts

In 2014, further traces of Warner were found in the Japanese Collection of the Harvard-Yenching. His typed name slip was pasted on the lower part of the endpaper of each volume of a group of Edo period (1600–1867) falconry (*takagari* 鷹狩) and archery manuscripts and books, and at the top of each of those pages there appears the accession stamp "The Chinese-Japanese Library of The Harvard-Yenching Institute at Harvard University Dec 19 1955."

"He was an authority on such traditional sports as archery and falconry," wrote James Plumer in Warner's obituary,[7] but these volumes came to the library after Warner's death on June 9, 1955, and we do not know the particulars. The materials identified to date include ten manuscripts and one printed book (*hanpon* 版本) on falconry and five manuscripts and one book on archery.

Falconry Manuscripts / Practice

1. *Taka no sho.* 3 vols. 鷹書. 3冊.
2. *Taka kikigaki: 1-kan.* 鷹聞書 : 1巻.
3. *Taka hishō: 1-kan.* 鷹秘抄 : 1巻.
4. *Seiyō jikyū sesshō: 1-kan.* 青鷹似鳩拙抄 : 1巻.
5. *Taka kuden: 1-kan.* 鷹口傳 : 1巻. Digitized.[8]
6. *Taka ezu: 1-kan.* 鷹繪圖 : 1巻. Digitized.[9]
7. *Hiden takaha no jutsu: 1-kan.* 秘傳鷹羽之術 : 1巻.

Falconry Manuscripts / Literary

8. Fujiwara Sanekane 藤原実兼. *Taka Hyakushu.* 鷹百首.
9. Nijō Yoshimoto 二条良基. *Sagano monogatari: 1-kan.* 嵯峨野物語 : 1巻.
10. Nijō Yoshimoto 二条良基. *Hakuyōki : 1-kan.* 白鷹記 : 1巻.

Falconry Book[10]

11. *Nigiri kobushi: 1-kan.* 握拳 : 1巻. (Kariganeya Shōzaemon, 1709)

Archery Manuscripts

12. *Tachibana-ke hikime kuden hikan: 4-kan.* 橘家蟇目口傳祕卷 : 4巻.
13. *Inuoumono yazata no ki: 1-kan.* 犬追物矢沙汰記 : 1巻.
14. *Inuoumono yazata no uta: 1-kan.* 犬追物矢沙汰歌 : 1巻.
15. *Inuoumono babanawa ya no sata: 1-kan.* 犬追物馬場縄矢乃沙汰 : 1巻.
16. *Inuoumono no shiki: 1-kan.* 犬追物之式 : 1巻.

Archery Book

17. Takagi Masatomo 高木正朝. *Nihon kogi* 日本古義. 5 vols. (Tamiya Rankeidō, 1838)

Nine of the ten falconry manuscripts (nos. 1–6, 8–10) bear the same four library seals (*zōshoin* 蔵書印) showing the previous owners. They are *Shirakawa bunko* 白河文庫 Matsudaira Sadanobu 松平定信, *Rikkyōkan toshoin* 立教館図書印 (Kuwana domain school seal 桑名藩校蔵書印), *Zōen shūen sokuen tokuen* 蔵脩息遊 徳爲脩爲息爲徳爲 (Tayasu family seal 田安家), and *Kiitsudō toshoin* 克一堂図書印 *Tayasu Haruaki* 田安治察 (head of the Tayasu clan and brother of Matsudaira Sadanobu). All four seals belong to the same Tayasu family, which owned these manuscripts in the eighteenth century. All manuscripts are stitch-bound and covered with the same indigo-colored paper.

Matsudaira Sadanobu (1759–1829) was a grandson of the eighth shogun, Tokugawa Yoshimune 徳川吉宗 (r. 1716–45), who once again legalized falconry in 1716 after it had been banned by Tsunayoshi 綱吉, the so-called Dog Shogun,

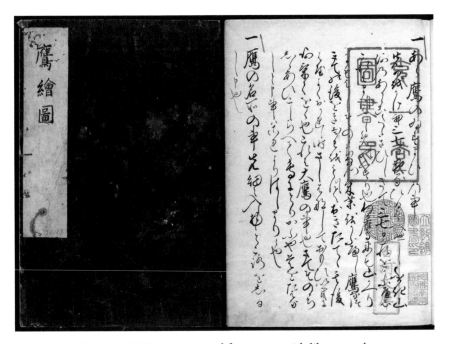

Figure 11.2: Front cover and front page with library seals
of original owners of 鷹繪圖 :1卷. [n.d.].
Persistent Link http://nrs.harvard.edu/urn-3:FHCL:8301535 (seq. 1 & 2)

in 1685. Sadanobu was the son of Munetake 宗武, who founded the Tayasu family,
and in 1778 he became the lord of the Shirakawa domain. He was appointed chief
senior councilor 老中 (1787–93) by the eleventh shogun, Ienari 家斉, after which
he carried out the Kansei Reforms. In 1794 he returned to the domain and became
involved in the domain school, or *rikkyōkan* 立教館. Sadanobu, an eminent
intellectual educated in the traditional Confucian style, is known to have collected,
read, and written books on a variety of subjects.

Four (nos. 2–5) of the falconry manuscripts in the Yenching collection
include in their colophons the original statements of two generations of copiers
(*hon'okugaki* 本奥書): "Copied on the 23rd day of the 2nd month in 1328" 嘉
暦3年2月23日書写, and "Copied by the Lord Jimyōin Motoharu on the 19th
day of the 6th month in 1519" 永正13年6月19日左金吾藤 [花押] 持明院基
春卿筆写,[11] but they include nothing regarding who copied the Tayasu family
manuscripts themselves. The art of falconry had been transmitted through the
generations within a few designated families such as the Jimyōin, and it is assumed
that the Tayasu family, which held high rank in the Tokugawa ruling class, sent
scribes to the Jimyōin family to copy them.

Five (nos. 12–16) of the archery manuscripts also include copiers' statements in their colophons, as follows: "Transmitting the [art of archery] from Ise Sadaharu to Matsuoka Heijirō in 1791, and from Torii Gohei to Tsubouchi Magobe in 1845" 寛政3年伊勢貞春より松岡平次郎へ, 弘化2年鳥居五兵衛より坪内孫兵衛へ 相伝. Unlike the falconry manuscripts, they do not bear any library seals.

These unique manuscripts came to the Yenching library thanks to Warner's curiosity and likely thanks also to his extensive network in Japan.

A Don Quixote Picture Book: *Ehon Donkihōte*

Serizawa Keisuke 芹澤銈介's illustrated *Don Quixote, Ehon Donkihōte* 繪本ど んきほうて (Hyūgaan, 1937) was donated to the library in 1939 by Carl Tilden Keller (1872–1955). Keller, a Harvard graduate of 1894 and vice-chairman and trustee of the Harvard-Yenching Institute, was a collector "especially known for collecting rare editions of Cervantes' Don Quixote."[12] These included translations of *Don Quixote* into all the major languages of the world, Japanese among them. Regarding his collection, Keller consulted the Japanese art critic Yanagi Muneyoshi (1889–1961), who in 1929 was a visiting scholar at Harvard, teaching a course on Japanese aesthetics. (He had come, as it happens, at the invitation of Langdon Warner). Yanagi was a leader of the Mingei 民芸 (Folk Craft) movement, which emphasized the beauty of handcrafted objects for daily use. Yanagi contacted his friend Jugaku Bunshō 寿岳文章, a well-known bibliophile and scholar of English literature. Jugaku provided more than a dozen shipments of books, but Keller wanted more; indeed, he asked Jugaku to identify an artist he might commission for the task. In late 1935, along with his friend the potter Kawai Kanjirō 河井寛次 郎, Jugaku asked the textile artist Serizawa Keisuke (1895–1984) to join in the *Don Quixote* project.[13] Serizawa re-created thirty-one scenes depicting Don Quixote as a samurai in a quasi-Japanese feudal time. The work was done in "Kappazuri" 合 羽摺 technique using paper stencils with multiple colors. Serizawa's paper stencils were donated by Keller to the Harvard Art Museums.. Only seventy-five copies of the work were produced, in accordion binding and enclosed in a *chitsu* 帙 case covered in Serizawa's indigo-dyed fabric.

The Serizawa *Don Quixote* is highly regarded for the quality of its art and craftsmanship, but its existence hinged on chance: Warner's invitation to Yanagi to come to Harvard in 1929, Yanagi's role in the arts and crafts community in Japan, and the friendship between Keller and Jugaku. Yanagi was in the right place at the right time for the *Ehon Donkihōte* to come into being.

Keio Gijuku University's Gifts: *Seiyō jijō* and Wood Blocks

For Harvard's tercentenary in 1936, Keio Gijuku University president Koizumi Shinzō was invited to come from Japan to attend the ceremony on September

16–18.[14] Professor Anesaki was awarded an honorary degree on that occasion, and several other Japanese universities were represented in the ceremony as well.[15] Koizumi brought several gifts to the university, including archaeological specimens, large ceramic vases, and the book *Seiyō jijō* 西洋事情 (Condition of the West), authored by Keio's founder Fukuzawa Yukichi, together with the wood blocks that had been used to print the book.

According to the accession stamp, *Seiyō jijō* and its wood blocks came to the Yenching Library on January 25, 1937. The two wood blocks are cased in a tailor-made wooden box, but there is no information about their provenance in the catalog records or on the materials themselves. When I learned that President Seike of Keio University would visit Harvard in March 2015, I mentioned these materials to a visiting scholar from Keio and asked if they had a connection to his institution. The scholar, a historian, immediately checked with his colleague at Keio and confirmed that they were gifts from the university in honor of Harvard's tercentenary. The copy of *Seiyō jijō* in the Harvard collection is from the first edition, published from 1867 to 1870 in three volumes, and bears the Fukuzawa family library seal on the first page of each volume.

Langdon Warner sent a personal letter of gratitude to President Koizumi on September 16, 1936. It includes this passage on the book and the wood blocks.

> As for the books which you have so generously presented, these will be acknowledged by the librarian of the University. But no one unfamiliar with Japan can perhaps appreciate the importance to us of a first edition of the works of your patriot and founder. The added interest of the actual woodblock used to print a page of this significant book will, however, be obvious to every American. The teachings of Fukuzawa Yukichi had a profound effect on the attitudes of our two nations toward each other, and America's debt to him is perhaps greater than we have ever realized.[16]

The Stillman Japanese Collection

Ernest Goodrich Stillman (1884–1949) graduated from Harvard College in 1908 and from the Columbia Medical School in 1913. He traveled to Japan with Archibald Coolidge in 1905.[17] The US diplomatic delegation led by William Howard Taft was traveling on the same ship.[18] Stillman was an avid collector of Japanese art and books, and he donated some five thousand items, including many Japanese books and other materials, to Harvard libraries and museums, some of which can be found in the Harvard-Yenching Library to this day. These include a gorgeous early-seventeenth-century *naraehon* 奈良絵本 entitled *Ogi shū* あふぎ 集, with full-color illustrations, produced by professional artists and calligraphers; a sketchbook of artist's seals made by Ernest Fenollosa (a Harvard graduate and

Figure 11.3: Earnest G. Stillman's Bookplate.
Image taken by author.

historian of Japanese art); large maps of Japan in color wood-block print, *Kanban jissoku Nihon chizu* 官版実測日本地図 (Kaiseisho, 1867?), which are based on the maps of the highly regarded cartographer Inō Tadataka 伊能忠敬; and fifteen Edo street maps in color wood-block print, *On Edo kiriezu* 御江戸切繪図, reprinted in 1863.

The Stillman materials in the Yenching collection are identified by his distinctive bookplate, featuring motifs of Mount Fuji and a shrine gate, and by their uniform copper-brown cloth bindings. These include color-illustrated books and design catalogs for kimonos, ceramics, vases, and lacquerware from the Edo and Meiji periods. These items were intended for practical use by designers and merchants, not scholars, and almost all the color illustrations consist of beautifully executed wood-block prints by Unsōdō, a renowned printer in Kyoto. The design books in the Stillman Collection include *Bijutsukai* 美術海 and *Shin Bijutsukai* 新美術海, and many were digitized and made publicly accessible in 2016. Stillman's photo albums of Japanese landscapes, people, craftworks, and other themes

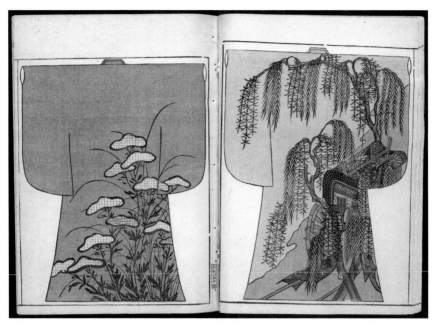

Figure 11.4: Kimono pattern catalog 模様雛形難波の梅
Moyo hinagata Naniwa no ume, 1886.
Persistent Link https://nrs.harvard.edu/urn-3:FHCL:26965334?n=18

designed to appeal to foreign tourists in the Meiji period are held in multiple libraries at Harvard; these, too, can be viewed virtually.[19] Many photos, originally meant as travelers' souvenirs, are individually cataloged as well. It is a wonderful accident that they came to Harvard and can now be made available to a larger set of users.

The Petzold Collection

Bruno Petzold was born in 1873 in Breslau, Silesia (today part of Poland). He studied economics, history, philosophy, religion, and art at the University of Leipzig and political economy at the University of Berlin Kaiser Wilhelm. After working as a journalist in Paris and London from 1902 to 1907, in 1908 he became an editor for the newspaper *Tageblatt für Nordchina* in Tianjin, China. His wife, Hanka Schjelderup, a Norwegian pianist and singer, was then offered a job as a professor of music at the Academy of Music in Tokyo, and Petzold was able to arrange a job as a Tokyo correspondent for the newspaper *Kölnische Zeitung.*

The family moved to Tokyo in 1909, and Petzold taught German and Latin at Dai-ichi Kōtō gakkō from 1917 to 1943. He took an interest in Buddhism around 1917, studying under Shimaji Daitō 島地大等 and Hanayama Shinshō 花山信勝,

Figure 11.5: Bruno Petzold's personal library Seal
「天台僧正徳勝ペツォールド蔵書印」
Image taken by the author.

and he received the Buddhist name Tokushō 徳勝 and the title *sōzu* 僧都 in the Tendai sect in 1923. He was elevated to *daisōzu* 大僧都 in 1928 and finally to *sōjō* 僧正, the second highest rank, in 1948.

A year after his death in 1949, the Yenching Library acquired some 6,000 volumes of Japanese books and some 450 scrolls from his collection, of which some 2,900 books and 370 manuscripts produced before 1868 are kept in the rare books room. Of the scrolls, 424 had lain largely untouched for decades but were recently cataloged following a survey led by Professor Annaka Naofumi of Tokyo's Risshō University in 2011.[20] They were digitized individually and made publicly accessible in 2012.[21]

Many of these are wood-block prints, paintings, calligraphy, and religious ephemera mounted on hanging scrolls. They depict not only Buddhism but folk religion from the late Edo through the early Showa periods. Seventeen scrolls were selected by the late Professor John Rosenfield and Mrs. Fumiko Cranston for display at the Yenching Library's seventy-fifth anniversary exhibition held

Figure 11.6: [釈迦八相] [Shaka hassō] [n.d.]
Persistent Link https://iiif.lib.harvard.edu/manifests/view/ids:44699096$1i

at the Houghton Library in the fall of 2003.[22] One of the seventeen scrolls is a lithograph titled *Shaka hassō* 釈迦八相 (Eight Aspects of the Buddha), in which Tendai monks are depicted like ancient Greek philosophers. It is believed to date from the late nineteenth century. Buddhism was on the defensive at that time for the Haibutsu kishaku 廃仏毀釈 movement was agitating to abolish Buddhism in favor of Shinto in 1870s. This is a good example of the rich socioreligious dimension of the Petzold collection, which has enhanced the breadth and depth of our Buddhism research materials immensely.

The Horikoshi Collection

The path from private collection to the Harvard library is particularly dramatic in the case of the eight thousand items assembled by Horikoshi Yoshihiro 堀越喜博 (1889–1946), who became director of a library and museum in the city of Tianjin, China, after twenty years of teaching in middle schools in Manchuria.

In September 1945, immediately after the end of the Second World War, Horikoshi met two Harvard affiliates, Donald H. Shively, a recent graduate, and Francis W. Cleaves, a scholar of China. It is not known how that meeting came about; what is known is that Horikoshi recognized that his collection of some right thousand items—including books, magazines, prints, paintings, and rubbings—could not be brought back to Japan in the aftermath of defeat, and so it was arranged through Shively and Cleaves that the materials would be donated to Harvard. Items from the Horikoshi collection are stamped with the accession date "March, 1946," often accompanied by another stamp, "Received thru Dr. F. W. Cleaves." Horikoshi's third daughter Shōno Ayaha, remembers helping pack the books: "I stamped my father's seal on each book, in hopes it would prevent their ending up as wrapping paper for roasted chestnuts."[23]

The history of these books was lost until 1982, when a visiting Japanese scholar investigated the collection and identified the Horikoshi family.[24] Donald Shively, who had met the family in Manchuria and arranged the donation in 1945 and in 1982 was directing Harvard's Japan Institute, sent a letter of gratitude to the Horikoshi family, the first link between the family and the collection since their separation in 1945.

The full story now came into view.

The Horikoshi family returned to Japan in April 1946, and Horikoshi Yoshihiro died in December of that year. Three generations of his family— daughter, granddaughter, and great-granddaughter—visited Harvard in March 2001 and viewed part of Horikoshi's collection. So who was this man?

As a student at Waseda Middle School in Tokyo, Horikoshi Yoshihiro enjoyed writing and sharing his work with a literary group that included Saijō Yaso西

条八十, who would later become a popular poet. Horikoshi studied literature under Hirata Tokuboku平田禿木 and Ueda Bin 上田敏, both highly regarded professors, while a student at the Third High School (Daisan kōtō gakkō) in Kyoto. In 1923, after teaching for several years in Tokyo following his graduation from the Tokyo Imperial University with a degree in Japanese literature, he moved to Manchuria, where he taught at middle schools in Fengtian, Anshan, and Tianjin. While in Manchuria he collected books and pieces of fine art and also took rubbings from historical sites. His students included Mieno Yasushi 三重野康, later the head of the Bank of Japan, and Abe Kōbō 安部公房, who would go on to become an important novelist. Horikoshi wrote and published *Manshū kanban ōrai* 満州看板往来 (Nihon kokusai kankōkyoku, 1940), a self-illustrated booklet documenting store signs and daily life in Manchuria.[25] He also authored *Kyodan kara katei e* 教壇から家庭へ, a book on education that was published in Fengtian in 1943 and later reprinted by his former students in Tokyo in 1983.

It has been almost seventy years since the individual items in the Horikoshi collection were received, cataloged, and physically integrated into Harvard-Yenching's collection; no list exists of the original collection. Yet, while browsing or searching the stacks, I have not infrequently encountered interesting and sometimes unique items that bear the Horikoshi seal, and this same experience was reported by a scholar of classical Japanese literature who methodically surveyed our rare books collection. The materials assembled by Horikoshi add wonderfully to the DNA of our Japanese holdings, particularly with regard to prewar literary journals and books. These include a complete run of *Konohana* 此の花 and its successor, *Fūzoku i zusetsu* 風俗図説 (published from October 1911 to August 1915). Edited and published by Asakura Musei 朝倉無声, these periodicals are devoted to Edo period society and culture and feature color wood-block prints in each issue. Horikoshi also had partial runs or individual issues of the Taisho period literary journals *Bunmei* 文明 and *Kagetsu* 花月 (both edited by Nagai Kafū 永井荷風) and the wartime literary journals *Bungei hanron* 文藝汎論 and *Kogito* コギト.

Horikoshi loved poetry, and his collection of poetry books—often first and/or limited editions signed by the poet—are a good sample of a lively period in Japanese literature. He owned a first edition of Toyama Masakazu 外山正一's *Shintai shishō* 新体詩抄 (Maruya Zenshichi, 1883), said to represent the starting point of modern Japanese poetry. His books from the 1920s include works by Horiguchi Daigaku 堀口大学 and Suzuki Shintarō 鈴木信太郎 (both of whom introduced the symbolists and contemporary French poets to Japan), as well as books by Susukida Kyūkin 薄田泣菫, Tominaga Tarō 富永太郎, and Ōte Takuji 大手拓二. These books were tastefully designed, frequently in an art nouveau–influenced style, and were sometimes bound in leather. Horikoshi was adventurous in his tastes, as evidenced by his possession of works by progressive poets of the 1930s and 1940s who sympathized with and participated in movements such as surrealism and Dada. Murano Shirō 村野四郎's *Taisō shishū* 体操詩集 (Aoi shobō, 1939) was designed by fellow poet Kitasono Katsue北園克衛 using his signature photomontage technique. Kitasono was connected to the European and American poetry scenes, was published in poetry journals on both continents, and corresponded with Ezra Pound. Other poets whose books were owned by Horikoshi spanned the gamut, from difficult modernist to lyric: Hishiyama Shūhei 菱山修平, Kitagawa Fuyuhiko 北川冬彦, Azuma Jun 東潤, Haruyama Yukio 春山行夫, Takenaka Iku 竹中郁, Hagiwara Kyōjirō 萩原恭二郎, Maruyama Kaoru 丸山薫, Yagi Jūkichi 八木重吉, Ozaki Kihachi 尾崎喜八, Jō Samon 城左門, and Yamanoguchi Baku 山之口獏.

Horikoshi collected poetry publications well into the war years, the titles of which typically include nationalist expressions such as *aikoku* 愛国 (patriotism) and *hōkoku* 報国 (contribution to the nation). Design and paper quality was declining. No longer are there found western influences or motifs in content or appearance. We find many collections of poems by soldiers at the front, such as *Yasen shishū* 野戦詩集 (Sangabō, 1941), and poems on Manchuria and China. There are exceptions to be found. The major poet Kitahara Hakushū 北原白秋's *Kaidō tōsei* 海道東征 (Seibunsha, 1943), consisting of patriotic poems and supplemented by Kazamaki Keijirō 風巻景次郎's annotations, was printed generously on high-quality Japanese paper, and the philosopher Kuki Shūzō 九鬼周造's *Pari shinkei* 巴里心景 (Kōchō shorin, 1942), a collection of sentimental poems about his days in Paris, was printed on quality paper, fashionably illustrated, and is graced by a postscript by Amano Tenyū 天野天佑.

Roughly 70 percent of the prewar translations of western literature in the Yenching Library are from the Horikoshi collection. Authors include Valéry, Gide, Cocteau, Radiguet, Flaubert, Stendhal, Balzac, Maupassant, Hardy, Jane Austin, Jack London, Gogol, Tolstoy, Dante, Nietzsche, Rilke, and Hesse. Our copy of *Sekai bungaku zenshū* 世界文学全集 (Shinchbung, 1927–30), a thirty-eight-volume set of world literature, also came from Horikoshi and reflects his broad and active interest in literature.

Horikoshi also collected books on art and design, as well as exhibition catalogs; these form an important part of our holdings in this area. Among his art books in our collection are *Suda Kunitarō sakuhin senshū* 須田國太郎作品選集 (Kōbundō, 1941), with the artist's dedication signature; Takehisa Yumeji 竹久夢二's *Yumeji shigashū* 夢二詩画集 (1941) and Hashimoto Okiie 橋本興家's *Nihon no shiro* 日本の城 (1944), both productions of the important Katō hanga kenkyūjo 加藤版画研究所, a wood-block print studio; and books produced by the traditional wood-block method, including Hokusai 北斎's *Santai gafu* 三体画

Figure 11.7: Travel brochures for Harbin in 1930s. Image taken by the author.

賦 (1816), *Kach1 gaden* 花鳥画伝 (1849), and Kawanabe Kyōsai's *Kyōsai donga* 暁斎鈍画 (1882) and *Kyōsai rakuga* 暁斎楽画 (1882).

Horikoshi was interested in contemporary art and design as well. *Gendai meika zuanshū* 現代名家図案集, edited by Ishii Hakutei 石井柏亭 (Oranda shobō, 1916), provides a good survey of contemporary artists, including Tsuda Seifū 津田青楓, Fujishima Takeji 藤島武二, Tomimoto Kenkichi 富本憲吉, and Sakamoto Shigejirō 坂本繁二郎, in well-executed color wood-block prints. Fujii Tatsukichi 藤井達吉's *Sōsaku senshoku zuan shū* 創作染織図案 (Bungadō, 1933) is a portfolio of fifty-one sheets of color wood-block prints, stored in a box whose cloth cover was also designed by the artist. Both works evidence contemporary trends. Yet Horikoshi also owned a copy of *Yamatoe monyō shunka shūtō* 倭繪文様春夏秋冬 (Uchida bijutsu shoshi, 1933), which contains exquisite color wood-block print reproductions of traditional Japanese design motifs. It is remarkable that Horikoshi collected such books, which were intended not for collectors but as pattern books for the trade. The high quality of their printing makes pattern books of this kind much sought after by museums today. Some sixty *ukiyo-e* prints, including several mounted on hanging scrolls, and several sheets of watercolor works by Tōgō Seiji 東郷青児 are also a part of his collection.

Horikoshi also collected materials related to Manchuria. These include *Senbu geppō* 宣撫月報, a propaganda journal issued by the public relations department of the Manchurian government; *Chōsa ihō* 調査彙報, a series issued by the research division of the central bank of Manchuria; *Heigen* 平原, a journal published by the tourism division of the Manchurian Railway Company; and *Kōa kokumin dōin taikai gahō* 興亜国民動員大会画報, issued by the quasi-official Kyōwakai 協和会 (the Concordia Association of Manchukuo, a political party subverted to become mean an instrument of the colonial occupation) to commemorate the tenth anniversary of the Manchurian empire. Other items include Mizuno Kaoru 水野馨's *Manshū chōrui genshoku daizukan* 満州鳥類原色大図鑑 (Purosesusha, 1940, Manchurian Birds in Color), in which all birds are identified with their Japanese, Latin, English, and Chinese names; and a group of tourist ephemera, including a city guide to Keijō (the Japanese colonial name for what is now Seoul in South Korea), a guide map of Kongōsan (Diamond Mountain in North Korea), a street map of the Manchurian city of Harbin, and destination guides issued by the Manchurian Railway Company. Ephemera of these sorts are not systematically collected by research libraries, yet they form important primary resources.

Some one thousand sheets of rubbings collected by Horikoshi were recently cataloged and digitized. These, along with twenty-six hundred other digitized rubbings held by Harvard's Fine Arts Library,[26] mostly donated by Langdon Warner, are searchable in Harvard's Digital Collections portal.

The Charles E. Perry Prints Collection

The library holds a few hundred sheets of color wood-block prints, or *nishiki-e* 錦絵, from the Edo and Meiji periods. About two-thirds (mostly Meiji productions) were donated in 2003 by Professor Elizabeth Perry, a Harvard specialist in modern China and director of the Harvard-Yenching Institute since 2008. Her father, Charles E. Perry (1908–59), a historian and missionary in China and Japan, had collected them. About half are *ukiyo-e* 浮世絵 prints depicting Kabuki actors, sumo wrestlers, and historical and scenic landscapes. The rest are *nishiki-e* prints produced in the late nineteenth century. Featuring contemporary war-related and political journalistic themes in bright, eye-catching colors, often with dramatic exaggerations, these were clearly meant for public consumption. They include images of the capture of the head of the rebel Saigō Takamori 西郷隆盛 (1827–77), a cabinet meeting discussing the possible annexation of the Korean Peninsula, the opening of the imperial parliament in 1890, the Naikoku hakurankai 内国博覧会 domestic exposition, an inspection of the military by the Meiji Emperor, and battle scenes from the Sino-Japanese (1894–95) and Russo-Japanese (1904–5) wars.

Six scenes from Aesop's Fables in three sheets by the highly acclaimed artist Kawanabe Kyōsai 河鍋暁斎 (1831–89) are also a part of the Perry Prints

Figure 11.8: Kawanabe Kyosai's wood block print 伊蘇普物語之内
Isoho monogatarai no uchi. Image taken by the author.

Collection.[27] Although Kyōsai's Aesop's Fables were well known, these six images were unknown even to Kyōsai specialists until 2014.

The following a brief biography of Charles E. Perry was provided by Professor Elizabeth Perry in 2011.

> Charles E. Perry moved to Shanghai in 1931 as an Episcopal missionary and a professor of history. He taught history at St. John's University and English at St. John's Middle School. In 1937 he married Carey Coles. She taught English literature as well as mathematics, first at St. Mary's Hall, an Episcopal girls' school in Shanghai, and then, after her marriage, at St. John's. He traveled to Manchukuo, of which he wrote his impressions in a travel diary and collected some materials.
>
> After Japan's Pearl Harbor attack in December 1941, he was taken as a POW [prisoner of war] to a concentration camp in Shanghai, where many died due to malnutrition and mistreatment. He was eventually released as part of a prisoner-exchange, and later returned to China with the U.S. Navy. After the war he resumed teaching at St. John's, where he was rejoined by his family. They subsequently left China in the spring of 1949 and moved to Japan in 1951, where Charles taught European History at Rikkyo University in Tokyo. In addition to Sino-Japanese relations, he

was also interested in the history of Japanese Christianity and in the Ainu, and he was active in the Christian community in Japan. For a number of years he edited *Japan Missions*, the journal of the Episcopal Church in Japan. In November, 1959 he was killed by a drunken Japanese student on the Rikkyo campus.[28]

Most of the *nishiki-e* wood-block prints given to the Yenching Library were collected by Professor Charles Perry when he was living in Japan from 1951 to 1959 and were primarily acquired from book dealers in the Kanda and Yushima neighborhoods of Tokyo.[29]

The Tsurumi Shunsuke Library

Tsurumi Shunsuke 鶴見俊輔 (1922–2015) was an influential intellectual and citizen-activist in Japan, cofounder of the magazine *Shisō no kagaku* 思想の科学 (1946–96, Science of Thought), and a widely published author on subjects ranging from philosophy to popular culture. The Harvard-Yenching Library holds forty-one volumes from the personal collection of his youth. What follows is the story of Tsurumi Shunsuke and how his books came to be in the Yenching collection.[30]

Tsurumi was born in 1922 and raised in Tokyo, the son of a prominent politician, Tsurumi Yūsuke 鶴見祐輔, and grandson of the influential statesman Gotō Shinpei 後藤新平. As a youth he was expelled from three different schools, and attempted suicide more than once. As a last resort, his father sent him to America in 1938. Tsurumi entered Harvard in 1939, where he studied philosophy, and he brought with him to America a small personal library. He loved Russian literature in particular. Peter Kropotkin's guide to Russian literature led him to Turgenev, Pushkin, and others. He read Mikhail Lermontov's *A Hero of Our Times* twice. Like many contemporary Japanese, he loved Tolstoy and Dostoevsky. On November 11, 1939, he finished reading Jules Renard's Journal. He read Nietzsche and Kierkegaard with enthusiasm. Tsurumi's excitement is apparent in the energetic red and blue pencil markings that fill these books.

Things changed with the Japanese attack on Pearl Harbor and the outbreak of the war. The *Harvard Crimson* interviewed Tsurumi and two other Japanese students and reported Tsurumi to be "somewhat philosophical" about events.[31] In March 1942, he was arrested by the Federal Bureau of Investigation (FBI) for self-identifying as an anarchist. He completed his honors thesis on the pragmatism of William James while an inmate at the Charles Street Jail in Boston.[32] Harvard granted him a degree, and he departed for Japan in June 1942 as part of a prisoner exchange. His books, which were seized by the FBI, eventually found their way into the Harvard-Yenching Library. The accession stamp dates their arrival as "June 30 1949" via the "War Dep't." Tsurumi never returned to the United States and lived in Kyoto until his death in July 2015.

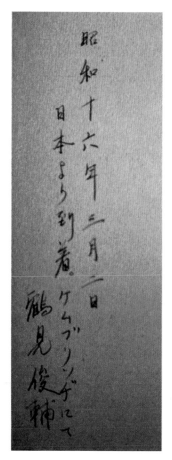

Figure 11.9: Tsurumi Shunsuke's note "Received from Japan on March 2, 1941, at Cambridge" on the book ドストエフスキイの生活 *Dosutoefusukii no seikats* (*Life of Dostoyevsky*), Tokyo, Sogensha, 1939. Image taken by the author.

I contacted Mr. Tsurumi about his collection at Harvard a few years ago. His response was kind, but he was philosophical about the fate of the books he had once read so intensely. These books, filled as they are with notes and markings, are mostly works by European authors in Japanese translation published between 1910 and 1940. They would not have been collected by academic libraries in the United States, yet they were a critical part of the intellectual landscape of Japan in the early twentieth century. The Yenching library is fortunate not only to hold the books themselves but also to preserve evidence of how these books were once read, in this case by the late Tsurumi Shunsuke.

Conclusion

I continue to be excited and surprised by the materials that turn up in the Japanese collection of the Yenching Library. The collection is rich and the stories equally so. Bookplates and accession stamps open doors to these stories, and yet they are all too often hidden and easily forgotten. I hope this essay will help to keep these scattered and fragmented institutional memories alive and connected and that they will become stepping stones to further understanding and the discovery of new and original ideas. Gradually some of the Japanese materials are being digitized for public access. It is my hope to share and preserve stories such as these, collectively and systematically, across all the collections of North America.

These stories also remind us that "unintended" and "accidental" acquisitions often become invaluable parts of a collection due to their uniqueness. The travel guides and brochures that Mr. Horikoshi used in Manchuria are much consulted by researchers today. A global comparison of falconry texts might now be possible, if it has not already been done. Who would have imagined that telephone directories and other such oft-discarded materials might become critical primary sources? It is part of the function of national libraries to collect all published and printed materials, but academic libraries make judgments about the value of materials in the present that all too often ignore the potential value of such materials for future researchers. In addition, it is a growing trend today that research libraries depend on vendor-supplied lists for collection development, which is done according to policy within a fixed scope. There is little room for surprises in such collections, and it seems more critical than ever that librarians have an active imagination in order to meet the research needs of the twenty-first century.

Notes

[1] Isomae, Jun'ichi and Hidetaka Fukazawa, *Kindai Nihon ni okeru chishikijin to shūkyō* 近代日本における知識人と宗教 (Tokyo: Tokyōdō shuppan, 2002), 265.

[2] Okakura was involved in founding both the Tokyo School of Fine Arts (東京美術学校 Tōkyō Bijutsu Gakkō) in 1887 and *Kokka* 国華, an important art magazine, in 1889.

[3] Justin M. Jacobs, "Langdon Warner at Dunhuang: What Really Happened?," *The Silk Road* 11 (2013): 1–11.

[4] Warner's active involvement in the negotiations is well documented in the Harvard-Yenching Institute Archives, Individual Papers, Warner, Langdon, Harvard University, Correspondence, 1924–1933, Harvard-Yenching Institute, Cambridge, MA, http://nrs.harvard.edu/urn-3:FHCL:8462990.

[5] Chinese Rubbings Collection, accessed March 16, 2017, http://vc.lib.harvard.edu/vc/deliver/home?_collection=rubbings.

[6] The quotation is from the collection's description in the finding aid.

[7] *Ars Orientalis* 2 (1957): 633–637.

[8] http://pds.lib.harvard.edu/pds/view/42898815. 鷹口傳 :1卷. [n.d.], accessed August 30, 2019.

[9] http://pds.lib.harvard.edu/pds/view/42898814. 鷹繪圖 :1卷. [n.d.], accessed August 30, 2019.

[10] Another early book on Falconry in the collection is Kawanabe Kyōsai 河鍋暁斎, *Ehon takakagami* 絵本鷹かがみ (Tōkyō-shi: Wa-Kan Tosho Shuppan Hakkōjo, Matsuyamadō shoten, 1879?), but this 3-volume set lacks Warner's stamp.

[11] Lord Jimyōin Motoharu (1453–1535) was a calligrapher for the imperial house who established the Jimyōin calligraphy school.

[12] Matthew Fraleigh, "El ingenioso samurai Don Kihōte del Japón: Serizawa Keisuke's 'A Don Quixote Picture Book,'" *Review of Japanese Culture and Society* (2006): 87–120.

[13] Jugaku wrote a firsthand account of the project. Jugaku Bunshō and Mika Yoshitake, "The Origins of a Don Quixote Picture Book," *Review of Japanese Culture and Society* 18 (2006): 121–31.

[14] Koizumi's account of this visit was published in Koizumi Shinzō 小泉信三, *Amerika kikō* アメリカ紀行 (Tokyo: Iwanami Shoten, 1938), 86–111.

[15] The Harvard Law School received a few hundred Japanese medieval documents, including *Goseibai shikimoku* 御成敗式目 (1225), the first code of conduct for the samurai warrior class. The gift was made by a wealthy Japanese and presented through the Tokyo Imperial University on this occasion. Some of these documents are digitized and viewable at the Harvard Law Library site, accessed March 16, 2017, http://www.law.harvard.edu/library/digital/japanese-scrolls.html.

[16] Letter from Langdon Warner to Koizumi Shinzō, September 16, 1936, quoted from a copy provided by Professor Shimizu Yūichiro, Keio University.

[17] Coolidge later became a professor of history and the first director of the Harvard University Library.

[18] Stillman's diary of his trip to Japan, from July to September 1905, is held at the Houghton Library, Harvard's rare books library, accessed August 30, 2019, Permalink http://id.lib.harvard.edu/alma/990100849210203941/catalog.

[19] Stillman's several photo albums are digitized including "Photographs of Kyoto, Japan" [1905?], accessed August 30, 2019, https://images.hollis.harvard.edu/permalink/f/100kie6/HVD_VIAolvgroup12189.

[20] ハーバード大学燕京図書館所蔵ブルーノ・ペツォールド旧蔵資料 (軸装・巻子装)目録 [Catalog of scrolls in the Bruno Petzold Collection preserved at the Harvard-Yenching Library], accessed August 30, 2019, http://id.lib.harvard.edu/alma/990129698010203941/catalog.

[21] The keyword "Petzold collection of Japanese scrolls digitization project" will retrieve all 424 images in Hollis. Accessed September 8, 2019, https://hollis.harvard.edu/primo-explore/search?query=lsr38,exact,Petzold%20collection%20of%20Japanese%20scrolls%20digitization%20project,AND&tab=everything&search_scope=everything&vid=HVD2&lang=en_US&mode=advanced&offset=0.

[22] The exhibition catalog includes an essay regarding the scrolls. John Rosenfield , and Fumiko E. Cranston, "The Bruno Petzold Collection of Buddhist and Shinto Scrolls," In *Treasures of the Yenching: Seventy-Fifth Anniversary of the Harvard-Yenching Library Exhibition Catalogue* (Cambridge, Mass. : Harvard-Yenching Library, Harvard University, 2003)

[23] Shōno Ayaha, interview with the author, 2005.

[24] This finding was reported in the Japanese daily paper *Asahi shinbun* on May 4, 1982.

[25] The library acquired a copy in 2010 through a Japanese bookseller.

[26] Chinese Rubbings Collection site offers all images of rubbings at Harvard. Accessed September 8, 2019, https://library.harvard.edu/collections/chinese-rubbings-collection.

[27] Koto Sadamura surveyed the prints and wrote the article 定村来人「ハーヴァード・イェンチン図書館蔵 河鍋暁斎＜伊蘇普物語之内＞新出六図」[Koto Sadamura "Kyōsai's Isoho-monogatari-no-uchi (from Aesop's Fables) in the collection of the Harvard-Yenching Library: Newly discovered six works." *Kyōsai: Kawanabe Kyōsai kenkyūshi* 12, no. 114 (October 2014): 167–73.

[28] The incident was reported in major Japanese newspapers, including *Asahi* and *Yomiuri* on November 27, 1959.

[29] Elizabeth Perry, personal communication, 2011.

[30] A short video on Tsurumi's library can be viewed at https://vimeo.com/22236320 (accessed June 28, 2015). A short essay I wrote about Tsurumi's books in the Harvard-Yenching Library was published in Japan. See マクヴェイ山田久仁子「一冊の書きこみ本から」 Kuniko Yamada McVey, "A Book with Hand-Written Notes," *Tosho* 748 (June 2011): 28–31.

[31] "Japanese Students Give Impressions of Startling Action of Fatherland," *Harvard Crimson*, December 8, 1942, accessed on June 28, 2015, http://www.thecrimson.com/article/1941/12/8/japanese-students-give-impressions-of-startling/.

[32] His thesis is now digitized and available for personal reference use. Accessed September 8, 2019, http://fds.lib.harvard.edu/fds/deliver/460770756/990039923140203941_HU_92_42_850_Tsurumi.pdf.

12

THE JAMES H. HAUSMAN ARCHIVE

Mikyung Kang, Harvard University

Introduction

There are several archival collections related to Korea at the Harvard-Yenching Library, Harvard University: the James H. Hausman Archive; Papers of George A. and Geraldine Fitch; Gregory Henderson Papers on Korea; Papers by Gillette, F. E. (Francis Edwin); and Blanche Stevens's letters, postcards, photographs of Korea. Among these archival collections, the James H. Hausman Archive has been the most popular among Korean studies scholars and students worldwide, and parts are often requested for interlibrary loans internationally.

The archive consists of four subcollections–the Hausman papers, the U.S. National Archives and Records Administration (NARA) materials collected by Professor Myung-Lim Park, the Allan R. Millett papers, and the Bertsch papers— all contained in a total of thirty-nine boxes. Each of the four subcollections was acquired individually at different times between 1997 and 2012, starting with the Hausman papers in 1997 as the first donation group.

Professor Carter Eckert, who was a key player in acquiring the archive from the beginning, plans to add more (if possible) in order to create one of the most prominent archival and primary source materials collections on the Korean War and Korean military history.[1]

This archive is unique because despite its military focus it is deeply related to US–Korean relations, and Korean politics as well, since the majority of the original contributors were all on the US side. This archive is important because it contains numerous materials on US policies toward Korea and clearly reflects the views of the US government and military during the Korean War and the Allied occupation of Korea.

Captain James H. Hausman

The archive is named after Captain James H. Hausman, who was a US Army military adviser to Korean Constabulary forces from 1946 to 1950. He spent thirty-six years in Korea beginning in 1946, with the exception of a five-year absence from 1950 to 1955. He had returned to the United States to serve as an expert on Korean military affairs in the US Department of Defense at the outbreak of the Korean War in 1950. After he returned to Korea in 1956, he served as the special adviser to the commander in chief of the United National Command for the next twenty-five years.

According to his appointment document, he was ordered to take up his new post in Ch'unch'ŏn (춘천), Korea, on August 12, 1946. Before his arrival in Tokyo in July 1946, he had never heard of "Korea," only of "Chosen" during his school days. He had only volunteered to go to Korea because there wasn't much work left for him to do in Tokyo. Therefore, after staying two weeks in Tokyo, he went to Korea. In his autobiography, he remembered the first time he saw Korea as his plane approached Kimpo Airport.[2]

Unlike other foreign military officers in Korea at that time, Hausman actively engaged with Koreans and started to learn the Korean culture and language so as to better understand the situation. Soon he became known as an expert on Korean military affairs. The US government relied on his input more and more heavily as time went on, even though his position in the military was not high enough to allow him to make direct decisions on important matters during the Allied occupation period.

John Toland refers to Hausman as "the father of the ROK [Republic of Korea] Army" and "advisor to ROK Chief of Staff Chung Il-kwon (정일권)" in his 1991 book *In Mortal Combat Korea*.[3] It is a well-known fact that Hausman was a key person in building the Korean military forces from scratch and maintained the respect of Korean military officers for a long time even after he left Korea.

Thus, this four-part archive was slowly developed starting with Hausman's personal papers, which were named as such in consideration of his important role in Korean military history.

The Hausman Papers

The James H. Hausman personal papers were donated to the Harvard's Korea Institute by the Hausman family in 1997 and transferred to the Harvard-Yenching Library in 2001. The materials were originally organized by students at the Korea Institute but had to be reorganized at the library (2010–11) because major parts

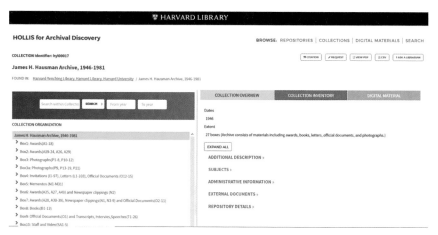

Figure 12.1. Display of the James H. Hausman Archive's searchable finding aid in HOLLIS for Archival Discovery.

of the detailed lists were missing from the finding aids. The revised finding aids were created at the library with the Korea Institute's support, and the finding aids' PDF files are now linked to the archive title record (http://id.lib.harvard. edu/alma/990090382890203941/catalog) in HOLLIS (http://hollis.harvard.edu) for public access. Also, the finding aids is currently keyword searchable through HOLLIS Archival Discovery—https://hollisarchives.lib.harvard.edu—as shown in Figure 12.1.

As for the donation process of the Hausman papers, Professor Carter Eckert played a major role in their acquisition. Professor Millett had met Captain James Hausman first through various research activities and interviews and introduced him to Professor Eckert. One of Professor Eckert's main research interests is Korean military history, so this was a great opportunity for him to conduct phone interviews with Hausman, which also led to the development of a personal friendship.

The Hausman papers include books, invitations and letters, mementos, newspaper clippings, official documents, awards, photographs and videos, speeches, transcripts, and interviews stored in ten boxes. They are organized mainly by format, and each PDF file contains a detailed list of the Hausman papers and indicates item locations, including box and folder information and accession numbers for each item.

Figure 12.2 shows the list of the Hausman papers' finding aids (in PDFs) that appears when a user clicks on the link that appears at the HOLLIS collection level cataloged record of the Hausman archive. When the user clicks on each line in the list, linked PDF files categorized by format appear in a new tab with detailed

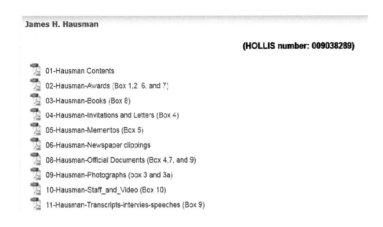

Figure 12.2. PDF finding aid of the Hausman papers through
the link in the HOLLIS collection level record.

information. In the lists, each item's date, title, description, box number, and
accession number are displayed so that the user can browse all items with the
detailed information and find the location of any necessary item using the finding
aids.

If the date is unknown, a question mark appears in the column for date
information in the list, as in table 12.1 below.

JAMES H. HAUSMAN ARCHIVE

Official Documents	Date	Item	Description	Box #
O1	-1990 -1987 -6/24/81	-Desk Calendar -May diary -Korea Herald	Feb-June used -5/15/87 meeting with Roh Tae Woo -"Perennial Advisor Leaves"	Box 9
O2	? 10/17/77 post-1981	Folder	KMAG Address Book -Sec. State Dead Rusk Eulogy for Gen. C.H. Bonesteel -Hausman resume, post-1981.	Box 7
O3	10/26/79	Folder	Schedule of Gen. Stilwell's visit to Korea on Eve of Pak Chung Hee's assassination.	Box 7
O4	5/11/81	Elva & Elmer Lowry	List of Principle Gov't Officers of ROK, 57th Edition, U.S. Embassy in Korea	Box 7
O5	YOSU FILE			Box 7
	6/19/50	CIA report	"Current Capabilities of the Northern Korean Regime"	Box 7
	?	Hausman	List of Task Forces in Yosu Operation, notes small number involved	Box 7
	?	US- G-2 Section	"History of Rebellion, 14th Constabulary Regiment," (6 pages)	Box 7
	?	US G-2 Section	"Short History of Yosu Campaign" (3 pages)	Box 7

Table 12.1. PDF Finding Aid of the Hausman papers
categorized by item format.

Since the finding aids are currently available in PDF form as well as in the newly-developed HOLLIS Archival Discovery system, which is keyword searchable.

In organizing the Hausman papers, the following format categories were used for finding aids: books, awards, invitations, letters, mementos, newspaper clippings, official documents, speeches, transcripts, interviews, photographs, and films. The papers were organized by graduate students in Korean studies at the Korea Institute after they were received from the Hausman family. The students organized and created the finding aids without much supervision in the initial stage, so after the papers were transferred to the Harvard-Yenching Library in 2001, there was quite a bit of missing and duplicated information. The library found that the finding aids had not been completed at the Korea Institute prior to the transfer. Therefore, with the institute's support, the library started to reorganize all the Hausman papers in early 2010 and completed the reorganization project in late 2011. To increase efficiency, the library retained the categorized formats that the Korea Institute had originally used. The materials were rehoused in new archival folders and containers during the reorganization process. These archival folders and containers were specifically made to maintain the archival collections in acid-free conditions, so that they could be preserved for long periods of time without suffering further damage. Accession numbers were assigned to all items for easy inventory later on. Unfortunately, the library found that a few photographs and documents were missing from the boxes, and they haven't been recovered since.

Among the contents of the Hausman papers, photographs and films have been the most popular due to their uniqueness—some were even taken by Hausman and his friends with his own camera. Among the four Hausman films that were originally stored as reel tapes, one shows the execution of Korean army officers during the purge of leftists and communists from the ROK army that commenced after the Yosu Rebellion in 1948. It is a rare film of its kind since Hausman made it himself using his own camera. In his autobiography, Hausman mentioned that one of the persons put to death was Lieutenant Chong-sŏk Kim (김종석). Hausman felt very sorry because Lieutenant Kim was not only a good friend but also an intelligent and bright young man who had the potential to become a top military officer if he had stayed alive.

There are about twelve hundred photographs in the Hausman papers. Some were taken by Hausman while some others were given to him in albums as commemorative gifts from the ROK Army or Korean military officers. Some depict informal occasions, while others portray formal events and activities. Currently, Professor Eckert is planning a research project to identify those military officers who appear in the photographs. Many may be still alive, but it might not be easy to identify them from these photos, which were taken in the 1940s and 1950s.

All the Hausman photographs and films in the archive were digitized after preservation treatment was done by conservation experts at Harvard. However, they are not accessible to the general public yet due to copyright issues and sensitive content. The digitized films are stored in both uncompressed file and DVD formats so that they can be used for online streaming when available. Also digitized photographs are stored on DVDs and kept in the Harvard Depository with other materials.

Figure 12.3: Hausman in Korean traditional costume (folder 17). Courtesy of the Harvard-Yenching Library. Stored in the box 3a of James H. Hausman Archive, 1946–1981.

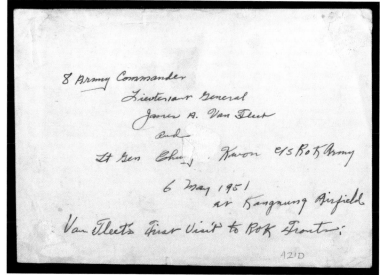

Figure 12.4: 8th Army Commander Lieutenant General James A. Van Fleet and Lt. Gen Chung Il Kwon ROK Army, May 6, 1951 at Kangnung airfield (folder 18) along with notes in the back side of the photo P18_0050. Courtesy of the Harvard-Yenching Library. Stored in the box 3a of James H. Hausman Archive, 1946–1981.

Figure 12.5: Pak Chung Hee (in uniform) and "Hutch"; Pak appears to be wearing two stars (folder 18). Courtesy of the Harvard-Yenching Library. Stored in the box 3a of James H. Hausman Archive, 1946–1981.

NARA Materials

The second subcollection in the Hausman archive is the NARA materials, which were collected by Professor Myung-Lim Park of Yonsei University while he was at the Harvard-Yenching Institute as a visiting scholar in 2000. His research trip for collecting NARA materials on the Korean War and the era from the 1940s to the 1960s in Korea was entirely funded by the Korea Institute. Professor Eckert planned to add the copies of NARA documents and captured materials to the James H. Hausman Archive, 1946–1981 from the beginning since they cover the same subject areas and periods as the Hausman papers.

Professor Myung-Lim Park is a faculty member at Yonsei University in the Area Studies Program of the Graduate School, and his research focus is modern

Korean politics and history. He has written several books on the Korean War and Korean politics, including *Han'guk chŏnjaeng ŭi palbal kwa kiwŏn* (한국전쟁의 발발과 기원, 1996), *Chabonjuŭi palchŏn kwa minjujuŭi* (자본주의의 발전과 민주주의, 1997), *Han'guk 1950* (한국1950, 2002), and *The Requiem for Peace* (2005).[5]

Since he is an expert on the Korean War and politics in Korea's modern history, Park's selection of NARA materials for the archive was meaningful and reliable and provides useful information for scholars of Korean modern history. Due to its detailed information in the finding aids and its easy access to the general public for browsing, there are many interlibrary loan requests, and external users visit the library to view this collection (even from the Washington, DC, area, which is near the location of NARA). All the NARA materials in the Hausman archive are stored in thirteen boxes, 11 through 23, and seven of them (11 through 17) contain copies of materials captured in North Korea by the US military during the Korean War. Boxes 18 through 23 contain official US government documents, reports, correspondence, and so forth on Korea-related issues covering mainly the years 1945–66. The majority of these official documents on Korea were selected and copied from the following original locations at NARA: R.G. (General Records of the Department of State), 59 (Bureau of Far Eastern Affairs Office of the Country Director for Korea), 94 (The Adjutant General's Office), 153 (Records of the Office of the Judge Advocate General, War Crimes Division historical reports of the war, 1952–54), 319 (Army Intelligence document file, Records of the Army staff), 338 (Records of US Army Commands, 1945–), and 407 (World War II Operations reports, 1940–48).

The Allan R. Millett Papers

Professor Allan R. Millett contributed his research materials, which were added to the Hausman archive little by little over a period of time roughly between 2006 and 2010, after he completed his scholarly books on Korean War history. He is a prominent historian of international wars, including the Korean War, and Korean military history.[6] He wrote several scholarly books on the Korean War, such as *The War for Korea, 1950–1951: They Came from the North* (2010), *The War for Korea, 1945–1950: A House Burning* (2005), *Their War for Korea: American, Asian, and European Combatants and Civilians, 1945–1953* (2002), as well as many essays, articles, encyclopedia entries, and commentaries on the Korean War.

It is fair to say that the Millett papers supplement the Hausman papers in terms of their coverage. They include correspondence, official documents, reports, and military records that cover subject areas and time periods similar to those of the Hausman papers. Also the Millett papers include interviews and letter correspondence with several military officers, including Hausman himself.

The Millett papers are stored in three boxes (24 through 26) and include letters, interviews, military and government documents, and books.

The Bertsch Papers

The Bertsch papers are the fourth and most recently added collection in the Hausman archive. Lieutenant Leonard Bertsch was a political adviser to Major General Archibald V. Arnold and General John R. Hodge, the military governor of Korea during the Allied occupation. Lieutenant Bertsch was stationed in Korea from 1946 to 1948, and his primary concern was the activities of Korean politicians during his stay. He knew most of the major Korean political leaders on the left and the right.[7]

The Bertsch family donated his personal papers to the Korea Institute in 2012, and the materials were transferred to the Harvard-Yenching Library promptly after receipt. Between 2012 and 2013, the materials were organized and finding aids with detailed lists were created. During the organization process, the materials were rehoused in thirteen archival boxes. The Bertsch papers consist of documents, correspondence, memorandums, minutes and notes, journals, magazines, books on Korea, and long-playing (vinyl) records of Korean music of the 1940s. The vinyl records were digitized by a specialist after preservation treatments, and digitized music recordings were stored on DVDs for easy access. These music recordings include Korean folk songs such as "Arirang" (아리랑), "Kŭm songaji t'aryŏng" (금송아지타령), "Toraji t'aryŏng" (도라지타령), and "Sin minyo" (新民謠). The songs were mostly recorded and produced, presumably in the 1940s, by production companies in Japan, such as Columbia, Okeh, and Eagle, but the singers and other musicians were all Koreans.

There are several sheets of Korean regional maps in English in boxes 9 and 10 of the Bertsch papers. These regional maps were all made in 1940s and mostly dated from 1944 to 1946. Major cities and provinces are covered in this map collection, and many map titles include regional names not only in Korean romanization but also in Japanese romanization. This map collection includes regions in both North and South Korea.

Access

The entire Hausman archive, including the Hausman papers, NARA materials, Millett papers, and Bertsch papers, have finding aids that show detailed lists of items in the archive in PDFs, and they are linked to HOLLIS record of the Hausman archive as shown in figure 12.6.

The Bertsch collection has its own collection-level record in OPACs in addition to the information appearing in the Hausman archive collection-level record, and

ARCHIVE / MANUSCRIPT
James H. Hausman Archive, 1946-1981
Hausman, James H., 1918-1996.
1946

** Harvard-Yenching Library, Harvard Library, Harvard University James H. Hausman Archive, 1946-1981 1946 27 boxes (Archive consists of materials including... **

! Harvard Yenching Library Offsite Special Collections (HD) >

☐ FINDING AID >

Send to

TEXT CALL #   EXPORT TO EXCEL   PERMALINK   E-MAIL   CITATION   EXPORT RIS   EXPORT BIBTEX   PRINT

RESERVES LIST

Details

Title	James H. Hausman Archive, 1946-1981
Author / Creator	Hausman, James H., 1918-1996. >
Finding aids	Electronic finding aid available https://id.lib.harvard.edu/ead/hyl00017/catalog
Description	28 boxes
History note	James H. Hausman (1918-1996) served with the U.S. armed forces in Korea from 1946-1981. Born in New Jersey, he was a veteran of World War II. He went to Korea in 1946, but returned to the United States to serve at the U.S. Dept. of Defense in 1950 at the outbreak of the Korean War as an expert on Korean military affairs. He returned to Korea in 1956 and served as the Special Advisor to the Commander-in-Chief to the United Nations Command for the next 25 years.
Summary	Archive consists of materials including awards, books, letters, official documents, and photographs.
Language	English
Subjects	Hausman, James H., 1918-1996 >
	Korean War, 1950-1953 -- Sources >
	United States -- Foreign relations -- Korea -- Sources >
	Korea -- Foreign relations -- United States -- Sources >
	Korea -- History -- 20th century -- Sources >
Contents	[Box 1-10]. Hausman papers -- [Box 11-23]. NARA materials collected by Prof. Park Myung-Lim -- [Box 24-26]. Allan R. Millett papers -- [Box 27-39]. Bertsch papers box 1-13

Figure 12.6. HOLLIS collection level record for
the James H. Hausman Archive, 1946–1981.

its finding aids link appears in both OPAC records—Hausman archive (HOLLIS # 990090382890203941) and Bertsch papers (HOLLIS # 990135887780203941).

All the boxes of the Hausman archive are currently stored in the Harvard Depository, which is located in Harvard University Library's archival media storage and retrieval facility. When any boxed items are requested by users individually, the requested boxes are delivered to the library by the next business day for users' viewing. The materials are available for users to view in the restricted rare book reading room for special collections, located on the third floor of the Harvard-Yenching Library, under the supervision of library staff members.

When requesting items for viewing, Harvard community users (including faculty, students, and staff) must use their Harvard Key to log in and then go to Aeon to complete requests. For those who are not currently affiliated with the university and do not have a Harvard Key, the system guides them first to Aeon to register and create an account. All special collections, including archival collections and rare books at the Harvard-Yenching Library, are accessible through HOLLIS (http://hollis.harvard.edu) for requests, but users need to take one more step to

Figure 12.7. Research Guide for Korean Studies: Personal papers on Korea.

complete their viewing requests through Aeon (http://aeon.hul.harvard.edu) for all special collection viewing requests.

Due to limited space in the rare book reading room, daily viewing may be limited to a certain number of boxed items. While viewing in the rare book reading room, users are not allowed to bring in any bags or pens; only pencils, notes, and laptops are allowed, as is common policy in many academic libraries.

In addition, the Hausman archive is only viewable by qualified scholars for research purposes only. These scholars must obtain written permission from the Korea Institute director and the librarian of the Harvard-Yenching Library before requesting items in HOLLIS. The Hausman archive is still restricted, and the library and institute require users to provide evidence of their status and specific reasons for their archive viewing in order to obtain written permission in advance.

Holdings in the Harvard-Yenching Library's archival collections that have been identified as Korea-related primary sources are listed on the Research Guide for Korean Studies website under the Archival Collection Finding Aids tab, and the finding aids of these archival collections are linked through the web page https://guides.library.harvard.edu/c.php?g=310159&p=2071094 (fig. 12.7).

On the research guide web page (fig. 12.7), HOLLIS records are linked through the HOLLIS record numbers listed beside each collection title while each finding aid is linked to the collection title.

In addition to the well-known Korean rare and old book collection at the Harvard-Yenching Library, which covers premodern periods in Korean history, these archival collections on modern Korea date mostly from the 1940s to the 1970s.

Conclusion

The James H. Hausman Archive is unique primary source on Korean military history from the Allied occupation period on and the Korean War. Even though its four distinct subcollections were donated one by one at different times, all of them fall into the same subject categories: Korean War and Korean military history of the 1940s. Also, in terms of each subcollection's original ownership, it was quite meaningful and logical to put them together for scholars researching the Korean War and Korean military history. Politics and foreign relations between Korea and the United States are also covered plentifully in this archive since these subject areas are closely related to Korean War and Allied occupation period issues. Both Captain Hausman and Lieutenant Bertsch worked as advisers in the US Army stationed in Korea and their papers show interesting views and perspectives by Americans toward Korea and Koreans in 1940s right after the colonial period.

Professor Carter Eckert hopes that the James H. Hausman Archive can be developed and expanded further in the future, and the library keeps adding similar content to this archive continuously. There may be some chances to receive additional materials from Professor Allan Millett in the future since he is still actively writing books on the Korean War and military history.

The finding aids of the archive are recently loaded into HOLLIS Archival Discovery, so that detailed information on the Hausman archive is now searchable through HOLLIS Archival Discovery. Browsing detailed information is still available through finding aids' PDF links from either collection-level HOLLIS records or the research guide for Korean studies website, but this archive will be better utilized if the library provides searchable mechanism for this archive in addition to the current browsable finding aids in PDFs.

Notes

[1] Mikyung Kang, interview with Professor Carter Eckert, May 20, 2015.

[2] James H. Hausman and Ir-hwa Chŏng 정일화, *Han'guk Taet'ongnyŏng ŭl umjigin Migun taewi: Hausŭman chŭngŏn* 한국대통령을 움직인 미군대위: 하우스만 증언 (Seoul: Han'guk Munwŏn, 1996), 105–7.

[3] John Toland, *In Mortal Combat Korea, 1950–1953* (New York: Morrow, 1991), 24, 286.

[4] Hausman and Chŏng, *Han'guk Taet'ongnyŏng ŭl umjigin Migun taewi*, 33.

[5] Wikipedia, s.v. "박명림," last modified September 26, 2013, https://ko.wikipedia.org/wiki/%EB%B0%95%EB%AA%85%EB%A6%BC/

[6] "Allan R. Millett, Ph.D.—Stephen E. Ambrose Professorship," University of New Orleans, accessed June 23, 2015, http://www.uno.edu/academicaffairs/endowed-chairs/allan-millett.aspx.

[7] Mark Gayn, *Japan Diary* (Rutland, VT: Tuttle, 1981), 351.

13

Revealing the Hidden

Uncataloged Japanese Manuscripts at the C.V. Starr East Asian Library, University of California, Berkeley

Toshie Marra, University of California, Berkeley

Introduction

In 1950, approximately one hundred thousand books, maps, rubbings, other graphics, and ephemera packed in 496 cases from Japan arrived at what was then called the East Asiatic Library at the University of California (UC), Berkeley.[1] These materials were previously part of Mitsui Bunko 三井文庫 (Mitsui Library), owned by the Mitsui family. Founded in the seventeenth century by a successful merchant, Mitsui Takatoshi 三井高利 (1622–94), the family had accumulated a large collection of their business records and other materials.[2] In 1903 Mitsui-ke Hensanshitsu 三井家編纂室 (Mitsui Family History Compilation Office) began collecting and organizing the records of the Mitsui family businesses, and eventually, in 1918, Mitsui Bunko was established in Togoshi, Tokyo.[3] After World War II, in 1951, the land and the building housing Mitsui Bunko were sold to the Japan's Department of Education, and the family's historical records were temporarily entrusted to Monbushō Shiryōkan 文部省史料館 (Ministry of Education Historical Archives), where they remained until 1965, when Mitsui Bunko was reestablished.[4] The general part of the library's collection, excluding family business materials, was acquired by UC Berkeley. For details of the Mitsui acquisition and a general description of the collection, there are several works already available for reference, so I will not repeat them here.[5] Instead, this chapter primarily focuses on the Japanese manuscripts collection within the Mitsui Collection. I next provide an overview of the collection and introduce some characteristic materials from it.

The Mitsui Manuscripts Collection: Processing History and Current Organization

The Mitsui Collection acquired by UC Berkeley is comprised of materials individually collected by members of the Mitsui family and Mitsui-ke Hensanshitsu, and also several fine collections compiled by other scholars. The East Asian Library made efforts, whenever possible, to preserve the integrity of the original organization for individual collections. With regard to handwritten manuscripts, however, the library took a different approach. These materials were culled from the individual collections and were made into a single separate collection. Then the manuscripts produced in China were separated and cataloged, leaving Japanese manuscripts untouched. Based on the most recent inventory of the Japanese manuscripts collection, which I began and was continued by Katsumata Motoi 勝又基 and his collaborators, it is believed that the collection comprises approximately 3,400 titles in more than 7,800 volumes. In addition, the collection also includes circa 4,200 single-sheet items.

Current arrangement of the collection is by the radical/stroke order of the title—the arrangement commonly used years ago even for public catalogs at UC Berkeley.[6] Since the collection includes a fairly large number of Chinese works, as well as those in Japanese written in *kanbun*, or Chinese script, the radical/stroke order by title might have proved practical as well in collocating the materials on related subjects whether they were written in Chinese or Japanese. I imagine that this mode of shelving was meant to be a temporary measure until the collection could be fully cataloged and rearranged in a subject-based classification system. Unfortunately, as of today the Japanese manuscripts collection remains mostly uncataloged, with the exception of an extremely limited number of items that have been cataloged online—approximately 1 percent of the whole collection.

This does not mean that the library did not make an effort to have the Japanese manuscripts collection cataloged during the seventy years that have passed since the materials arrived. On the contrary, as early as 1957 Elizabeth Huff, the first head of the East Asiatic Library, had already managed to arrange a special grant sponsored by the Department of State, the American Library Association, and the Special Libraries Association to have Ogura Chikao 小倉親雄, an assistant professor in the Department of Education at Kyoto University with librarian experience, assist her with processing the manuscripts collection for a one-year period.[7] According to a typewritten note dated 1959 and inserted in the library's shelf list cards file for this collection, Ogura examined 1,288 titles of manuscripts back then. In each manuscript he examined, he left a yellow slip with a handwritten note containing the title, author, a brief description, and any reference information. These yellow slips can still be found with each manuscript and can assist any user of the manuscript. On the basis of these notes, Huff decided whether to retain or remove the manuscripts; for example, simple copies of articles from journals were discarded if the library already had the original in printed form.[8]

The next major step was taken in 1983 under the directorship of Donald H. Shively, when four scholars from the National Institute of Japanese Literature and Kyoto University, namely, Hasegawa Tsuyoshi 長谷川強, Watanabe Morikuni 渡辺守邦, Ii Haruki 伊井春樹, and Hino Tatsuo 日野龍夫, were sent to the library with charge of surveying and organizing the Mitsui manuscripts collection.[9] Before their arrival, they were given a copy of the cards file in radical/stroke order with numbering from 1 through 2,819, which the library had developed by then, but they knew that the manuscripts were not arranged by these numbers on the shelves. Therefore, first they decided to conduct an inventory of the entire collection based on the cards file and to arrange the manuscripts in this order. In the process, they found many discrepancies between the cards file and the actual materials—sometimes materials corresponding to the cards were not found, and at other times no cards were found for the materials.[10] In the end, their inventory confirmed 2,724 titles in 7,400 volumes.[11] As a result of the survey, the inventory produced a brief title list with some descriptions when they were available.[12] Today this still serves as the primary access tool for the Japanese manuscripts collection.

For the most recent inventory, which I began in 2015, an Excel spreadsheet was first produced based on the brief title lists created by the scholars from Japan in the 1980s, which listed 2,913 entries in total.[13] Then I examined each manuscript in the shelving order, verified its description on the Excel spreadsheet, and made corrections accordingly. Correcting errors in title transcription, such as incorrect Chinese characters, is among the typical corrections that I have made in the Excel list. During this process, I soon realized that the title list included Chinese materials that had been cataloged as "not found" in the 1983 inventory, as well as reference entries. I removed from the Excel spreadsheet all entries for which no actual items were located, hoping to obtain an accurate count of the collection.

Manuscripts from the Edo Period

Although the Japanese manuscripts collection includes some materials from the Meiji (1868–1912) and later periods, the bulk of the collection is from the Edo period (1603–1867). Here it might be worth looking at manuscripts in Japan in general, with a particular focus on those from the Edo period. In Japanese the term *shahon* 写本 is generally used for handwritten manuscripts, in contrast with *hanpon* 版本, or printed books. For original manuscripts or holographs, different terms are often used, such as *genpon* 原本 or *jihitsu genpon* 自筆原本, but it would be difficult to verify an original manuscript.

In spite of the efflorescence of printing and commercial publishing from the seventeenth century onward, manuscript culture vigorously survived in Japan up to the nineteenth century. As of June 3, 2015, Nihon kotenseki sōgō mokuroku dētabēsu 日本古典籍総合目録データベース, the Union Catalogue of Early Japanese Books, maintained by the National Institute of Japanese Literature contains 537,048 bibliographic records of which about 40 percent are reported to be manuscripts.[14] With regard to the special functions of manuscripts in the Edo period, which complemented those of printed books, Peter Kornicki considered the following types of manuscripts: (1) Sūtra copying for devotional purposes; (2) manuscripts with calligraphic or artistic qualities such as those used as bridal gifts (*yomeiribon* 嫁入り本) or created for private collections; (3) manuscripts of the *hiden* 秘伝, or secret traditions for which the contents would be known only by a select circle of people, such as the various schools of flower arrangement, the tea ceremony, swordsmanship, and even medical practice; (4) certain literary genres, including fictionalized scandals, which were censored, and works of romantic fiction known as *ninjōbon* 人情本, some of which were initially written by amateurs; (5) manuscript copies of printed books that were made by individual readers because they were rare or unobtainable, as a hobby or a way to save on the costs of purchase, or as a way to obtain banned books; and (6) illicit manuscripts that were increasingly made publicly available, including *jitsuroku* 実録, or documentary stories, which usually contain an admixture of fictional elements and facts.[15] Especially regarding the illicit manuscripts, Kornicki noted that *Kinsho mokuroku* 禁書目録, a list of banned books published in 1771 by the Kyoto booksellers' guild, listed 122 titles of illicit manuscripts with the following note, which surely revealed the scale of the problem.

> Apart from those listed above there may be many other manuscript books including accounts of things heard (*kikigaki* 聞書) and miscellaneous records (*zatsuroku* 雑録), but there is not time to refer to them all. Even though they may not be included in the list above, it is strictly forbidden to handle any book that records recent events or deals with matters concerning the court aristocracy or samurai households, let alone matters concerning the court of the shōgun's household.[16]

It is noteworthy that among those types of manuscripts described by Kornicki, the UC Berkeley's Japanese manuscripts collection contains many that belong to the third and last categories, namely, those of the secret traditions, especially tea ceremony and flower arrangement, and illicit manuscripts. More detailed analysis on the subject coverage of the collection is discussed in the next section (Content Analysis).

Nagasawa Kikuya also analyzed manuscripts with research values and listed the following as the more valuable types of manuscripts.[17]

1. Manuscripts of unpublished works of valuable content
2. Manuscripts of printed books of valuable content whose copies are not extant or very rare
3. Manuscripts of a lineage of text totally different from those of the printed books or the common versions of manuscripts
4. Manuscripts copied before the printed books were published
5. Manuscripts corrected by scholars or famous persons, including those that were recopied, when the corrected texts were not published
6. Manuscripts with words and phrases different from those of the texts in the printed books, especially when the printed books have missing text
7. Precise copies of manuscripts based on old printed books or old manuscripts, especially those copied when the originals were in better condition than the currently existing books or facsimiles
8. Manuscripts copied long ago
9. Holographs, or manuscripts transcribed by famous people
10. Manuscripts with prefaces, postscripts, notes at the end (*okugaki* 奥書), or the owner seals of famous persons

Using these criteria to assess the value of manuscripts, UC Berkeley's Japanese manuscripts collection seems to include numerous examples of (1) manuscripts of unpublished works and (4) manuscripts copied before the printed books were published. There are some examples of (5) manuscripts corrected by scholars or famous persons, (7) precise copies of manuscripts, (9) holographs, and (10) manuscripts with prefaces, postscripts, *okugaki*, or the owner seals of famous persons. For the purpose of my inventory project, however, I did not examine individual manuscripts closely enough to determine whether or not they are (3) manuscripts of a lineage of text different from those of the printed books and the common versions of manuscripts, or (6) manuscripts with words and phrases different from those of the texts in the printed books. As for (8), manuscripts copied long ago, the term *koshahon* 古写本 generally refers to manuscripts produced by the mid-Edo period, but some scholars use the term more strictly to refer only to those produced before the Edo period.[18] The UC Berkeley's Japanese manuscripts collection includes only a few of such manuscripts produced before the Edo period.

Content Analysis

In this section, I attempt to describe the UC Berkeley's Japanese manuscripts collection from the perspectives of provenance and subject coverage.

Provenance

As mentioned above, the Mitsui Collection comprises materials individually collected by members of the Mitsui family and Mitsui-ke Hensanshitsu, as well as several fine collections compiled by other scholars. Although the Japanese manuscripts collection includes a small number of materials with no provenance information, the majority of the manuscripts bear the seals of previous owners or call number plates, and the library's shelf list cards also include the original call numbers used at Mitsui Bunko, from which I could trace the following individual collections included in the manuscripts collection.

The Sōshin Collection (1,494 titles in 5,320 volumes)

More than a half the titles in the Japanese manuscripts collection originally came from the Sōshin collection, which comprises as much as 71 percent of the entire collection.

The collector was Mitsui Takatatsu 三井高辰 (1845–1922) whose pen name was Sōshin 宗辰. He was the eighth hereditary head of Mitsui Shinmachi-ke 三井新町家 in Kyoto. His manuscript collection is particularly strong in Japanese literature and history, including local history and geography, as well as in the arts, especially the tea ceremony.

The Gakken Collection (799 titles in 1,265 volumes)

The Gakken collection is also well represented in the Japanese manuscripts collection (approximately 29 percent of title counts and 17 percent of volume counts). The collector, Dohi Keizō 土肥慶蔵 (1866–1931), was a professor of medicine with a specialization in dermatology and venereology at Tokyo Imperial University, and his collection was named after his pen name, Gakken 鴬軒. In 1931, the same year as Dohi's death, the Gakken collection was said to be sold to the Mitsui Bunko perhaps because of his marriage to Mitsui Tao 三井たお, a daughter of the sixth hereditary head of the Isarago 伊皿子 branch of the Mitsui family.[19] His collection is now scattered across four known locations: UC Berkeley, the National Diet Library (holding ca. 7,900 volumes of books primarily in Chinese poetry by Japanese authors from the Edo through early Meiji periods), the University of Tokyo Library (holding ca. 4,600 volumes in Chinese and Japanese medicine), and the Tokyo Medical and Dental University (holding ca. 1,340 volumes of books in medicine in western languages and 232 volumes in Japanese).[20] While the Gakken collection that came to UC Berkeley consists of circa 28,000 volumes of books on a wide range of subjects, including literature, history, art, philosophy/religion, geography, and science, his manuscript collection similarly has a wide range of subject coverage.[21]

The Basic Collection: (262 titles in 545 volumes)

It was thought that this collection must have served as the reference collection of Mitsui Bunko.[22] In fact, I encountered several manuscripts handwritten on special stationary with "Mitsui-ke Hensanshitsu 三井家編纂室" printed on center columns and embossed on covers. These manuscripts often included at the end of the material a handwritten note about the original manuscript from which the copy was made. From these notes it is clear that Mitsui Bunko had strong connections with some major libraries in Japan, such as the Imperial Library in Ueno and the Tokyo Imperial University Library, and that the tradition of making hand copies of rare manuscripts was still alive in the late Meiji (1868–1912) and even the Taishō periods (1912–26).[23] It should also be mentioned that some of these manuscripts contain the owner's seals of Mitsui Takakata 三井高堅 (1867–1945), an adopted son of Takatatsu, whose pen name was Sōken 宗堅. Takakata was known as a collector of maps, *sugoroku* playing boards, and other engravings, as well as Teihyōkaku 聴氷閣Chinese Rubbings Collection, which were also a part of the Mitsui acquisition.[24] Among the manuscripts originally in the Basic collection, or *kihon tosho* 基本図書, which holds about 10 percent of title counts and 7 percent of volume counts in the entire collection, such subjects as history, literature, Buddhism, politics, law, and customs are well represented.

The Motoori Collection (11 titles in 14 volumes)

The Motoori collection was the library of the well-known family of Kokugaku scholars founded by Motoori Norinaga 本居宣長 (1730–1801) and succeeded in Wakayama by Motoori Ōhira 本居大平 (1756–1833), his adopted son Motoori Uchitō 本居内遠 (1792–1855), and his grandson Motoori Toyokai 本居豊穎 (1834–1913), which must be distinguished from the collection kept by the Motoori family in Matsusaka. It is said that among Norinaga's early disciples was Mitsui Takakage 三井高陰 (1759–1839), a member of the Mitsui family (Matsusaka Kita-ke 松坂北家), who provided some financial support to Norinaga's scholarly career.[25] The Motoori collection was acquired by Mitsui Bunko in 1928 and had been stored there since 1937.[26] When the possibility that the UC Berkeley Library might acquire some parts of it from the Mitsui Bunko became known to the public in 1950, apparently a report addressing the treatment of Motoori Bunko was prepared by some Japanese scholars, which indicated that "among the materials included in Motoori Bunko, those found to be relatively less important should be wood-block printed books and typeset editions, but the following types of materials should be retained: (1) those containing handwritten annotations by

Motoori family members, (2) those containing handwritten annotations even by unknown persons, and (3) rare journals; based on the above-mentioned principles, those found relatively less important numbered 1,734 items."[27] Whether or not the recommendations in the report were precisely followed, the Motoori collection ultimately was divided between the Department of Literature at the University of Tokyo and the UC Berkeley East Asian Library. Most of the manuscripts seem to have been sold to the University of Tokyo while a majority of the materials UC Berkeley acquired were wood-block printed books from the Edo period and modern typeset publications.

The Japanese manuscripts collection includes a small number of manuscripts of unknown provenance and those unrelated to the Mitsui acquisition. For example, it is known that the manuscripts collection should include some items from the Murakami collection, another large collection that the library acquired in 1948, but unfortunately the manuscripts from the Murakami collection do not seem to have any mark or indication of origin.[28]

Another group of manuscripts of unknown provenance is anthologies of poems that are marked as "ei" 詠 or "shi" 詩 in the brief title list compiled by the scholars at the National Institute of Japanese Literature, but no special markings were found on the materials themselves. Some of these seem to require special attention, such as records of more than 400 poetry-composing occasions dating between 1511 and 1846 and collections of poems consisting of more than 3,300 *origami eisō* (folded leaves) by generations of poets from the aristocratic Sanjōnishi 三条西 family.[29] The latter are known to have a close relationship with another collection of Japanese poetry originally from the Sanjōnishi family, which was acquired in 1950 by the Waseda University Library.[30]

Subject Coverage

The brief title lists created by the scholars from the National Institute of Japanese Literature and Kyoto University in the 1980s provided classification information whenever possible. Although the task of assigning classification does not seem to have been performed consistently among the five scholars involved in this project, this information provides an important point of access. At this point, it is the only way to bring together materials dealing with certain subjects in this vast manuscripts collection. By using this classification information where it is available and assigning a classification where it is not to all 2,728 titles in 7,545 volumes included in the manuscripts collection, in table 13.1 I attempt a subject analysis of the collection.[31]

Because the variation of classification terms used in the brief title lists is so wide—as many as 290 terms were used—the first step I took for the purpose of subject analysis was to reassign a larger classification category to each of those

290 terms based on the list of classification terms used by the National Institute of Japanese Literature in compiling the Nihon kotenseki sōgō mokuroku dētabēsu.[32] Consequently, each manuscript title was placed in one of twenty different categories in Japanese: *sōki* 総記 (general works/bibliography), *gakumon, shisō* 学問・思想 (scholarship, philosophy/thought), *jingi* 神祇 (Shinto/deities), *Bukkyō* 仏教 (Buddhism), *shūkyō* 宗教 (religion), *gengo* 言語 (languages), *bungaku* 文学 (literature), *ongaku, engeki* 音楽・演劇 (music, theater), *rekishi* 歴史 (history), *chiri* 地理 (geography), *seiji, hōsei tsuketari kojitsu* 政治・法制 附故実 (politics, law, customs), *keizai* 経済 (economics), *fūzoku, seikatsu* 風俗・生活 (social life), *kyōiku* 教育 (education), *rigaku* 理学 (science), *igaku* 医学 (medicine), *sangyō* 産業 (industry), *geijutsu* 芸術 (fine arts), *shogei* 諸芸 (arts), and *bugaku, bujutsu* 武学・武術 (military arts).

The following are the classification categories in ranking order by title counts as well as by volume counts.

Table 13.1. Subject coverage distribution by title counts and volume counts

	Classification Categories	Titles	%	Volumes	%
1	歴史 History	948	34.8	3,358	44.5
2	文学 Literature	521	19.1	1,390	18.4
3	政治・法制 附故実 Politics, law, customs	272	10.0	623	8.3
4	諸芸 Arts	247	9.1	534	7.1
5	学問・思想 Scholarship, philosophy/ thought	161	5.9	400	5.3
6	地理 Geography	107	3.9	393	5.2
7	芸術 Fine arts	86	3.2	80	1.1
8	仏教 Buddhism	77	2.8	133	1.8
9	武学・武術 Military arts	59	2.2	108	1.4
10	神祇 Shinto/deities	51	1.9	115	1.5
11	教育 Education	49	1.8	67	0.9
12	産業 Industry	30	1.1	99	1.3
13	言語 Languages	29	1.1	85	1.1
14	総記 General works/bibliography	22	0.8	56	0.7
15	医学 Medicine	19	0.7	27	0.4
16	音楽・演劇 Music, theater	18	0.7	25	0.3
17	理学 Science	16	0.6	28	0.4
18	経済 Economics	11	0.4	19	0.3
19	宗教 Religion	3	0.1	3	0.0
20	風俗・生活 Social life	2	0.1	2	0.0
	Total	**2,728**	**100.0**	**7,545**	**100.0**

Classification Categories	Volumes	%	Titles	%
1 歴史 History	3,358	44.5	948	34.8
2 文学 Literature	1,390	18.4	521	19.1
3 政治・法制 附故実 Politics, law, customs	623	8.3	272	10.0
4 諸芸 Arts	534	7.1	247	9.1
5 学問・思想 Scholarship, philosophy/ thought	400	5.3	161	5.9
6 地理 Geography	393	5.2	107	3.9
7 仏教 Buddhism	133	1.8	77	2.8
8 神祇 Shinto/deities	115	1.5	51	1.9
9 武学・武術 Military arts	108	1.4	59	2.2
10 産業 Industry	99	1.3	30	1.1
11 言語 Language	85	1.1	29	1.1
12 芸術 Fine arts	80	1.1	86	3.2
13 教育 Education	67	0.9	49	1.8
14 総記 General works/bibliography	56	0.7	22	0.8
15 理学 Science	28	0.4	16	0.6
16 医学 Medicine	27	0.4	19	0.7
17 音楽・演劇 Music, theater	25	0.3	18	0.7
18 経済 Economics	19	0.3	11	0.4
19 宗教 Religion	3	0.0	3	0.1
20 風俗・生活 Social life	2	0.0	2	0.1
Total	**7,545**	**100.0**	**2,728**	**100.0**

According to both the title and the volume counts, the top six ranked categories are the same; the materials in history are by far the largest, followed by those in literature and politics, law, and customs. Among those 948 titles classified in history, representative subclassification terms include miscellaneous history (*zasshi* 雑史・*zakki* 雑記・*zatsuroku* 雑録), biographies (*denki* 伝記・*nikki* 日記), and records (*kiroku* 記録), which account for 37, 16, and 15 percent of the total respectively. *Miscellaneous history* is a vague term and seems to have been assigned to a variety of materials, including essays and *jitsuroku* (documentary stories), although essays and *jitsuroku* are generally classified as literature. Somewhat characteristic types of materials in the Japanese manuscripts collection are those in family history and genealogy (*kaden* 家伝・*keizu* 系図・*keifu* 系譜), which account for about 13 percent of all manuscripts classified as history. Another distinctive feature of this collection is the inclusion of multiple manuscripts with the same title, which allows comparison of the texts. For example, the collection includes four copies of *Sannō gaiki* 三王外記, *Namiaiki* 浪合記, and *Kuroda kafu* 黒田家譜 and three copies of *Kyūmei kōki* 休明光記 and *Sekigahara gunki* 関ケ原軍記, many of which were circulated only in manuscript form.

Among the 521 titles in literature, essays are the most representative, amounting to 31 percent of the total, followed by Japanese poetry, including *haikai* and *waka*, travel diaries, and *jitsuroku*, which account for 24, 11, and 10 percent respectively. As for those classified in the politics, law, and customs category, ceremonies/manners/customs of the imperial court and the samurai class (*yūsoku kojitsu* 有職故実), politics, various directories (*meiroku* 名録 · *meikan* 名鑑 · *bukan* 武鑑), and law are the most representative, amounting to 34, 25, 14, and 13 percent respectively, of a total of 272 titles. In the arts category, tea ceremony and flower arrangement are well represented, amounting to 44 and 28 percent, respectively, of a total of 247 titles. In the scholarship, philosophy/thought category, as much as 82 percent of the materials out of a total of 161 titles are on Chinese studies (*kanseki* 漢籍 · *kangaku* 漢学 · *jugaku* 儒学), many of which came from the Gakken collection. In geography, regional gazetteers on various places, including Ezo and Europe, are overwhelmingly represented, amounting to 79 percent of the total of 107 titles.

Characteristic Materials from the Japanese Manuscripts Collection

In this section, I introduce some characteristic materials from the Japanese manuscripts collection that I have seen during my ongoing inventory project.

Manuscripts of Unpublished Works

As I conducted the inventory of the manuscripts collection, I regularly consulted the Nihon kotenseki sōgō mokuroku dētabēsu and checked for any other copies held by libraries in Japan. I found many cases in which manuscripts were known to exist without printed counterparts. For example, *Torikaebaya monogatari* とりかへばや物語 (A Tale of Changing Roles), was circulated only in manuscripts from its creation in the late Heian period (794–1185) through the Edo period (1603–1867), and many manuscript copies survive in Japan. But our library's copy of this literary work, *Torikaebaya* とりかへばや has special features. There is a note at the end by Motoori Norinaga in someone else's hand about the manuscript copy that Motoori borrowed to make the copy, and there is also a printed advertisement for a publisher/distributor in Osaka glued on the inner back cover. This seems to suggest that this publisher/distributor made and possibly distributed this particular manuscript as a commercial product.[33]

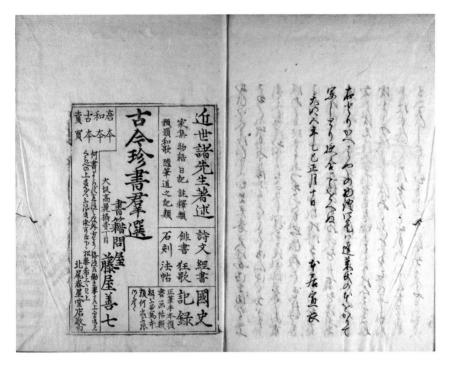

Figure 13.1. *Torikaebaya monogatari* with a note by Motoori Norinaga in someone else's hand and a printed advertisement by Fujiya Zenshichi.

Other examples of manuscripts of unpublished works include the following.

Kyōkun nakanu uguisu 教訓不鳴鶯, by Tōkaen Michimaro 桃花園三千麿
Koden tsūkai 古伝通解, by Nonoguchi Takamasa 野々口隆正
Zōtei Nankai hōfu 増訂南海包譜, edited by Yamanaka Nobufuru 山中信古

No copy of the same title has been found for the first item, whereas several manuscript copies have been located for the other two. At a glance, all these manuscripts look like they could be copies of printed versions in terms of the page layout, but the existence of printed publications has not been confirmed. Interestingly, *Zōtei Nankai hōfu* features many leaves of elaborate color illustrations of citrus.

Holographs

The collection includes several manuscripts of literary works and essays by well-known modern writers, seemingly holographs, including the following.

Genkō monogatari 元寇物語, by Fukuchi Ōchi 福地桜痴 (1841–1906)
Giwaku 疑惑, by Chikamatsu Shūkō 近松秋江 (1876–1944)
Haha 母, by Akutagawa Ryūnosuke 芥川龍之介 (1892–1927)
Kabukigeki no hozon ni tsuite 歌舞伎劇の保存に就いて, by Tsubouchi Shōyō 坪内逍遥 (1859–1935)
*Nara o tatsu mae*奈良を発つ前, by Mushanokōji Saneatsu 武者小路実篤 (1885–1976)
Sōka ni tsuite 挿花について, by Kōda Rohan 幸田露伴 (1867–1947)
Yoakemae 夜明前, by Osanai Kaoru 小山内薫 (1881–1928)

The works by Fukuchi Ōchi, Chikamatsu Shūkō, Akutagawa Ryūnosuke, Tsubouchi Shōyō, and Osanai Kaoru were eventually published, but it is still unknown whether those by Mushanokōji Saneatsu and Kōda Rohan were published. Regardless of whether they were published or not, manuscripts of original creation certainly offer a different impression than a published typeset edition, sometimes permitting readers to trace the author's polishing process of the text.

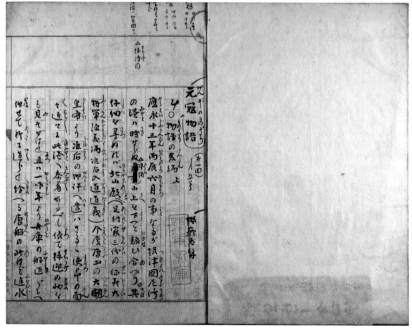

Figure 13.2. The beginning of *Genkō monogatari* by Fukuchi Ōchi.

Old Manuscripts

Most of the manuscripts held by the UC Berkeley East Asian Library are part of the Mitsui Collection, but old manuscripts of Buddhist scriptures are also included in the Ho-Chiang Collection of Early Buddhist Scriptures 賀蔣佛經善本文庫.[34] While the manuscripts in the Mitsui Collection are mostly from the Edo period, what follows are some earlier examples.

> *Jūichimen kannon shuhō kuketsu* 十一面観音修法口決, transcribed by Kūgen 空源 in 1305 with the date and transcriber's name of the original copy also recorded. It features *detchōsō* 粘葉装 binding and *oshikai* 押界 border lines.
>
> *Ise monogatari kikigaki* 伊勢物語聞書, dating probably from the sixteenth century.

Especially regarding the latter, as many different texts are known to exist for this old commentary on *Ise monogatari* (Tales of Ise), further research is required to determine the lineage of the text.

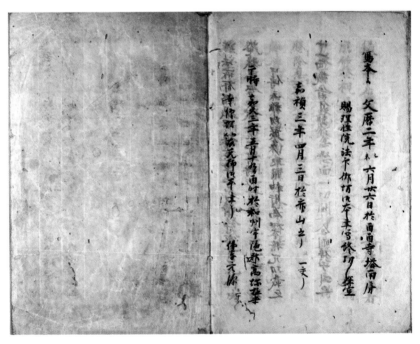

Figure 13.3. The end of *Jūichimen kannon shuhō kuketsu*.

Manuscripts with Illustrations

The Japanese manuscripts collection includes only one example of *Nara ehon* 奈良絵本 as a representative of manuscripts with illustrations, which is *Bunshō-zōshi* 文正草子. Other manuscripts with color illustrations include *Imaichi monogatari* 今市物語 and *Izumi nikki* 和泉日記, both of which are known to be held by only a few libraries in Japan. In the case of *Izumi nikki*, a travel diary written by Tsuchiya Ayako 土屋斐子 (b. 1759) during her stay in Sakai from 1807 to 1809 as the wife of the city commissioner Tsuchiya Tadanao 土屋廉直, our library holds two sets of manuscripts of this literary work, one with illustrations and the other without. The text has not been published in a typeset edition.

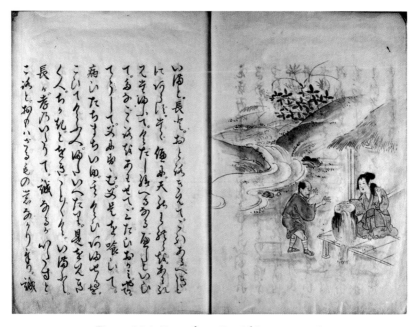

Figure 13.4. Pages from *Imaichi monogatari*.

As for maps and atlases, as long as the primary nature of the materials can be determined as such, these manuscripts are included in the library's map collection. On the contrary, when manuscripts feature maps and other illustrations less prominently, they are included in the manuscripts collection. *Teisei zōyaku Sairan igen* 訂正増訳采覧異言 by Yamamura Saisuke 山村才助 is one such example, consisting of fourteen volumes, of which the last volume is an atlas.

Figure 13.5. Page from *Izumi nikki* with reading notations by Ozawa Suien Keijirō 小澤醉園圭次郎 (1842–1932).

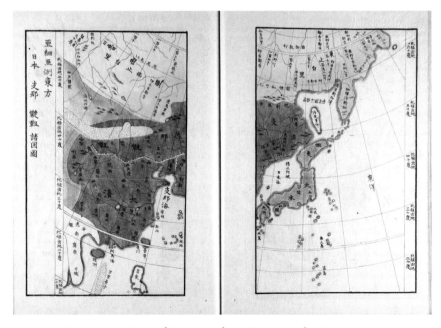

Figure 13.6. Map of East Asia from *Teisei zōyaku Sairan igen.*

Manuscript Leaves

As mentioned earlier, the Japanese manuscripts collection includes a collection of poetry by generations of poets of the aristocrat Sanjōnishi family written on more than 3,300 separate folded leaves, including the following.

Sanenori eisō 実教詠草 consisting of 61 leaves
Kintomi eisō 公福詠草 consisting of 860 leaves
Saneyoshi eisō 実称詠草 consisting of 1,307 leaves
Nobusue eisō 延季詠草 consisting of 587 leaves
Saneisa eisō 実勲詠草 consisting of 157 leaves
Suetomo eisō 季知詠草 consisting of 384 leaves

The manuscripts collection also contains a collection of poems presented at more than 400 poetry-composing occasions between 1511 and 1846, consisting of 323 bundles of leaves of different sizes, which is known as *Gyokai kankei shiryō* 御会関係資料.

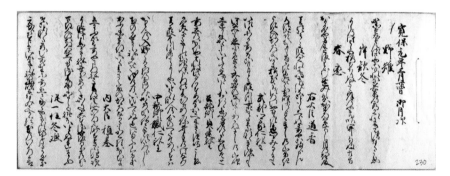

Figure 13.7. Page from *Gyokai kankei shiryō*.

Conclusion

As mentioned earlier, manuscripts make up a large portion of the entire corpus of textual materials produced in Japan during the Edo period, which is often characterized as having a flourishing publishing culture. Because of their originality, manuscripts offer tremendous opportunities for research, but also challenges, especially for a library outside Japan that usually does not have a librarian on staff who specializes in Japanese manuscripts. Although Japanese manuscripts are still largely understudied, recent trends in the digitization of special collections and the active development of digital humanities have made manuscripts more accessible for study. We hope that these trends will promote more global research and help researchers worldwide to use various materials of research value more effectively.

Notes

I would like to express my sincere gratitude to my colleagues Dr. Peter Zhou and Dr. Deborah Rudolph, as well as to my predecessors, Mr. Hisayuki Ishimatsu and Dr. Eiji Yutani, who kindly extended their support to me on several occasions during my investigation.

[1] Elizabeth Huff, "The Mitsui Library," *CU News* 5, no. 50 (1950): 1. Regarding the number of cases in the shipment, Roger Sherman used the number 485 with a note indicating a possible additional shipment. Roger Sherman, "The Acquisition of the Mitsui Collection by the East Asiatic Library, University of California, Berkeley" (MA thesis, University of California, Los Angeles, 1980), 75.

[2] Yashiro Kuniji 八代國治, Hayakawa Junzaburō 早川純三郎, and Inobe Shigeo 井野邊茂雄, eds., *Kokushi daijiten*國史大辭典 (Tokyo: Yoshikawa Kōbunkan, 1979–97), s.v. "Mitsui-ke shiryō" 三井家史料, by Kagawa Takayuki 賀川隆行, via JapanKnowledge, accessed July 31, 2021): https://japanknowledge.com/lib/display/?lid=30010zz456480

[3] Ibid., s. v. "Mitsui Bunko" 三井文庫, by Kagawa Takayuki 賀川隆行, via JapanKnowledge, accessed July 31, 2021: https://japanknowledge.com/lib/display/?lid=30010zz456650; Mitsui Bunko, "Mitsui Bunko no rekishi" 三井文庫の歴史, chap. in *Mitsui Bunko: enkaku to riyō no tebiki* 三井文庫: 沿革と利用の手引き (Tokyo: Mitsui Bunko, 1988), 3–20.

[4] Ibid.

[5] Sherman, "Acquisition of the Mitsui Collection"; Elizabeth Huff, "The Mitsui Romance," in *Teacher and Founding Curator of the East Asiatic Library: From Urbana to Berkeley by Way of Peking*, interview conducted by Rosemary Levenson (Berkeley: Regional Oral History Office, Bancroft Library, University of California, Berkeley, 1977), 172–87; Donald H. Shively, "The Mitsui Bunko and Murakami Bunko," *Waseda Daigaku Toshokan kiyō* 早稲田大学図書館紀要 35 (January 1992): 1–13.

[6] In a 1955 special report on the Far Eastern Collections in the East Asiatic Library of UC Berkeley, Elizabeth Huff mentioned three public catalogs used at the library since 1951: the Title-Author Catalogue arranged in the order of characters, the Author-Title Catalogue for works in European languages in the roman alphabet, and the Subject Catalogue. George M. Beckmann, "News of the Profession," *Far Eastern Quarterly* 14, no. 3 (May 1955): 443–46.

[7] Huff, "Mitsui Romance," 179; Ogura Chikao 小倉親雄, "'Kyū Mitsui Bunko-bon' e no tsuioku" 「旧三井文庫本」への追憶, *Chōsa kenkyū hōkoku* 調査研究報告No. 5 (March 1984): 264–65.

[8] Huff, "Mitsui Romance," 179.

[9] Ii Haruki 伊井春樹, "Bākure-kō zō kyū Mitsui Bunko-bon chōsa shimatsuki" バークレー校蔵旧三井文庫本調査始末記, *Chōsa kenkyū hōkoku* 調査研究報告 5 (March 1984): 266–72.

[10] Ibid.

[11] Watanabe Morikuni 渡辺守邦, "Kariforunia Daigaku Bākure-kō kyū Mitsui Bunko-bon chōsa no hōkoku" カリフォルニア大学バークレー校旧三井文庫本調査の報告, *Bungaku* 文学 54, no. 8 (1984): 113–21.

[12] Hasegawa Tsuyoshi 長谷川強 et al., "Kariforunia Daigaku Bākure-kō kyū Mitsui Bunko shahon mokuroku kō" カリフォルニア大学バークレー校旧三井文庫写本目録稿, *Chōsa kenkyū hōkoku* 調査研究報告 No. 5 (March 1984): 261–340. As more manuscripts were found in later years, a supplementary list was also published: Oka Masahiko 岡雅彦, "Kariforunia Daigaku Bākure-ko kyū Mitsui Bunko shahon mokuroku kō tsuika" カリフォルニア大学バークレー校旧三井文庫写本目録稿追加, *Chōsa kenkyū hōkoku* 調査研究報告 No. 8 (March 1987): 360–61.

[13] Ibid.

[14] The Nihon kotenseki sōgō mokuroku dētabēsu 日本古典籍総合目録データベース is available at the National Institute of Japanese Literature website, accessed July 31, 2021, http://base1.nijl.ac.jp/~tkoten/index.html. The information about the proportion of manuscripts within the database is based on the response to my email inquiry from the National Institute of Japanese Literature on July 1, 2015.

[15] Peter Kornicki, "Manuscripts in the Tokugawa Period," in *The Book in Japan: A Cultural History from the Beginnings to the Nineteenth Century* (Leiden: Brill, 1988), 99–111.

[16] Ibid., 105. A Japanese original of *Kinsho mokuroku* 禁書目録 is reproduced in Munemasa Isoo 宗政五十緒 and Wakabayashi Shōji 若林正治, eds., *Kinsei Kyōto shuppan shiryō* 近世京都出版資料 (Tokyo: Nihon Kosho Tsūshinsha, 1965), 84, 176–87.

[17] Nagasawa Kikuya 長沢規矩也, *Kosho no hanashi* 古書のはなし (Tokyo: Fuzanbō, 1994), 47–50.

[18] Inoue Muneo 井上宗雄 et al., eds., *Nihon kotenseki shoshigaku jiten* 日本古典籍書誌学辞典 (Tokyo: Iwanami Shoten, 1999), s.v. "Koshahon" 古写本, by Tsuji Katsumi 辻勝美.

[19] Asakura Haruhiko 朝倉治彦, ed., *Gakken Bunko zōsho mokuroku* 鶡軒文庫蔵書目録 (Tokyo: Yumani Shobō, 2008), vol. 2, 4–5.

[20] "Gakken Bunko" 鶡軒文庫, National Diet Library, accessed November 14, 2021, https://rnavi.ndl.go.jp/research_guide/entry/theme-honbun-304011.php; "Gakken Bunko" 鶡軒文庫, General Library, University of Tokyo, accessed November 14, 2021, https://www.lib.u-tokyo.ac.jp/ja/library/general/collectionall/gakken_new_2; Asakura, *Gakken Bunko zōsho mokuroku*, vol. 2, 5–6.

[21] Sherman, "Acquisition of the Mitsui Collection," 106.

[22] Ibid., 101.

[23] For another example, copying activities at the Historiographical Institute of the Imperial University is summarized in Hiroki Kikuchi, "Letting the Copy out of the Window: A History of Copying the Texts in Japan," *East Asian Library Journal* 14, no. 1 (2010): 120–57.

[24] Most items of Takakata's Japanese historical maps and sugoroku collections were digitized and are available at UC Berkeley Library Digital Collections website, accessed July 31, 2021: https://digital.lib.berkeley.edu; Teihyōkaku Chinese Rubbings Collection is

included in: Bokelai Jia Zhou da xue dong ya tu shu guan 伯克萊加州大學東亞圖書館, ed., *Bokelai Jia Zhou da xue dong ya tu shu guan cang bei tie*伯克萊加州大學東亞圖書館藏碑帖 (Shanghai: Shanghai gu ji chu ban she, 2008).

[25] Sherman, "Acquisition of the Mitsui Collection," 119–20.

[26] Ibid., 119.

[27] Nakada Yasunao中田易直, "Sengo no Mitsui Bunko to Monbushō Shiryōkan ni tsuite" 戦後の三井文庫と文部省史料館について, interview with Yoshii 由井, Mitsui Bunko, December 21, 2000, *Mitsui Bunko ronsō* 三井文庫論叢 no. 35 (2001): 29.

[28] The inclusion of manuscripts in the Murakami collection is mentioned in "University of California, Berkeley," in *A Guide to the Japanese Library Collections of Western North America* (Berkeley, CA: Western Regional Japanese Library Conference, 1989), 13.

[29] The former are analyzed in "Kariforunia Daigaku Bākure-kō kyū Mitsui Bunko zō gyokai kankei shiryō saimoku kō カリフォルニア大学バークレー校旧三井文庫蔵御会関係資料細目稿," *Chōsa kenkyū hōkoku* 調査研究報告 No. 9 (March 1988): 95–118.

[30] Inoue Muneo 井上宗雄 and Shibata Mitsuhiko 柴田光彦, "Waseda Daigaku Toshokan zō Sanjōnishi-ke kyūzō bungakusho mokuroku" 早稲田大学図書館蔵三条西家旧蔵文学書目録, *Kokubungaku kenkyū* 国文学研究 32 (October 1965): 110–18. Some materials in the collection have been digitized and are available in Kotenseki sōgō dētabēsu 古典籍総合データベース, Waseda University, accessed July 31, 2021: https://www.wul.waseda.ac.jp/kotenseki/index.html.

[31] Because the inventory project was not complete at the time of writing, these figures are based on estimates and do not include the total item counts for single-sheet items and poetry reading records. The title counts used for the purpose of subject analysis do not include any analytical entries.

[32] "Bunruigo ichiran" 分類語一覧, in Nihon kotenseki sōgō mokuroku dētabēsu 日本古典籍総合目録データベース, National Institute of Japanese Literature, accessed July 31, 2021: http://base1.nijl.ac.jp/~tkoten/howto.html#keylist.

[33] Nishimoto Ryōko 西本寮子, "'Torikaebaya' Hōrai-shibon keitō no denpon o meguru kōsatsu: Motoori Norinaga no okugaki o kiten to shite" 『とりかへばや』蓬莱氏本系統の伝本をめぐる考察: 本居宣長の奥書を起点として, *Kokubungaku kō*国文学攷 178 (June 2003): 13.

[34] Selections from the Ho-Chiang Collection of Early Buddhist Scriptures are listed in Okuda Isao 奥田勲, "Kariforunia Daigaku Higashi Ajia Toshokan zō kokyō korekushon mokuroku kō" カリフォルニア大学東アジア図書館蔵古經コレクション目録稿, *Seishin Joshi Daigaku ronsō* 聖心女子大学論叢 94 (January 2000): 112–70.

14

The Significance of the Korean Materials in the William Elliot Griffis Collection at Rutgers University

Young-mee Yu Cho and Sungmin Park, Rutgers University

Introduction

Situated among Northeast Asia's major powers—China, Russia, and Japan—Korea has been a strategic hub geopolitically, as well as culturally, throughout its millennia-old history. The relationship between the United States and Korea has been dynamically complex from the first encounter between the two countries in 1871 (*Shinmi Yangyo*), throughout the Japanese colonial occupation (1910–45) and the Korean War (1950–53), with its continuing legacies of the Cold War. As the leading public university in the state of New Jersey, Rutgers University is uniquely positioned to respond to the challenges of promoting a deeper understanding of Korean culture, language, and people. The Korean program in the Department of East Asian Languages and Cultures encourages research and sponsors lectures and workshops to enhance the understanding of Korea. One such endeavor resulted in a workshop on the William Elliot Griffis Collection (WEGC) in March 2008, and a bilingual compilation of the Griffis Korean materials is now available.

William Elliot Griffis (1843–1928) graduated from Rutgers University in 1869 and went to Japan to participate in the Japanese government's westernization project for three years (1871–74) by teaching natural sciences and helping organize

Figure 14.1. Photo of William Elliot Griffis circa 1869,
with his handwriting, in the William Elliot Griffis
Collection at Rutgers University.

education in Echizen (later named Fukui). Upon returning to the United States, he became one of the preeminent western authorities on American-Japanese relations, East Asian history and culture, and Korea through his numerous publications, including *The Mikado's Empire* (1876); *Japanese Fairy World* (1880); *Asiatic History: China, Corea, Japan* (1881); *Corea: The Hermit Nation* (1882); *Corea, Without and within: Chapters on Corean History, Manners, and Religion* (1885); *The Religions of Japan* (1895); *Japanese Nation in Evolution: Steps in the Progress of a Great People* (1907); *China's Story in Myth, Legend, Art, and Annals* (1911); *The Unmannerly Tiger and Other Korean Tales* (1911); *A Modern Pioneer in Korea: The Life Story of Henry G. Appenzeller* (1912); and *Korean Fairy Tales* (1922). Although Griffis did not travel to Korea until 1927, he collected on all subjects that concerned East Asia, including articles, pictures, and artifacts related to Korea between 1874 and his death in 1928.

The Special Collections and University Archives of Rutgers University Libraries holds the William Elliot Griffis Collection (WEGC), which was received as family gifts mostly after Griffis's death in 1928. In this chapter, we first present an overview of the WEGC and the Korean materials in the collection. Then, we provide a list of past Korean studies research on Griffis and chronicle the utilization of Korean materials. Next, we describe the arrangement and organization of the WEGC, focusing on Korean materials within the collection for the benefit of future studies. We list some limitations in access and retrieval of materials in the WEGC while laying out the potential significance of the journals and correspondence for Korean studies research. We conclude the chapter with a number of suggestions for improvement.

The William Elliot Griffis Collection

William Elliot Griffis's numerous publications on Japan and Korea, from *The Mikado's Empire* in 1876 through to *Korean Fairy Tales* in 1922, contributed to the formation and dissemination of western images of Japan and Korea in the late nineteenth and early twentieth centuries (S-T. Kim 2010: 126; S-M. Kim 2008: 40). Griffis was one of the first experts on Japan in the United States. After spending three and a half years there as a *yatoi* (foreign government adviser), he wrote *The Mikado's Empire*, which turned out to be the most popular book of its time about the nation of Japan, a country not very well known and considered quite mysterious in the late nineteenth century. Griffis also established himself as a Korea expert, and he wrote several books and newspaper and magazine articles about Korea.[1] One of his best sellers, *Corea: The Hermit Nation* (1882), was reprinted numerous times, going through nine editions in thirty years. It has functioned as an important entry into Korea for Americans and Europeans over the years and was translated into Korean in the 1970s.

K-S. Chŏng (2008) argues that in the nineteenth century the most important medium for manufacturing images of a nation was the printed book. Between 1876, when Japan forced the opening of Korea, and the 1882 treaty between Korea and the United States, the most important monographs on Korea were by Charles Dallet, John Ross, Ernest Opert, and Griffis. Dallet's book (1874) was published in French whereas the other books were published in English or translated into English shortly after their publication. Among these works, Griffis's books on Korea were not only the most complete in their coverage but also had a longer-lasting effect. K-S. Chŏng (2008) observes that interest in Korea by westerners often started with an interest in its neighbors, China and Japan. Books about Korea during this time were instrumental in forming contemporary images of Korea, and these images, once formed, were not easy to change. They often exerted great influence on the destiny and development of the country. The Japanese annexation of Korea in 1910 was a historical event determined by complex domestic and international factors, but one cannot deny the fact that international images of Korea were one of the contributing factors. Not all national images are value neutral, and many such images were rooted in the results of the orientalism that treated the Other as barbaric compared to western civilizations. Oft-cited metaphors that characterize Korea as the "Hermit Nation" and as the "Land of Morning Calm" are examples.

H-G. Sim (2008) also notes Griffis's influence by listing his encyclopedia entries in Box 112 G in the WEGC, where Griffis's contributions to encyclopedia entries between 1874 and 1903 were chronologically compiled. Most entries were for the *Universal Cyclopedia and Atlas and Annual Cyclopedia*. Between 1884 and 1902, Griffis was solely responsible for the entries on "Japan," "Corea," and "Korea."[2]

The WEGC is currently housed in the Special Collections and University Archives at the Alexander Library, the main library of Rutgers, the State University of New Jersey. The collection consists of Griffis's own work and the materials he collected. It is described as "over 120 cubic feet in size, including journals, manuscripts, printed materials, photographs, family papers, and scrapbooks, correspondence and ephemera" (Rutgers University Libraries). "He also collected a wealth of other articles, manuscripts, photographs and artifacts relating to Korea between 1874 and his death in 1928" (Gass and Perrone 2008). According to the Rutgers Libraries website, the WEGC has both non-Asian and Asian materials. While three-quarters of its East Asian materials are about Japan, a quarter are about Korea and China. The collection came to Rutgers University by means of bequests and family gifts between 1928 and 1982 in a series of acquisitions (*JTWE Guide*: 23; Rutgers University Libraries).[3] The following figures (Figure 14.2, 14.3, & 14.4) show some representative examples of the collection.[4]

Portions of the WEGC were published in microfilm as parts 2–5 of *Japan through Western Eyes: Manuscript Records of Traders, Travellers, Missionaries, and Diplomats, 1853–1941 (JTWE)*. The Korean materials within the WEGC, however, have not been cataloged in detail, nor has their significance in Korean studies been fully explored. The Korean materials in the collection provide a unique opportunity to Korean studies researchers as they include invaluable "in-process materials," including photographs. "In-process materials" in Gass and Perrone (2008) consist of three books in Korean and four boxes of Korean photographs, many of which are part of a series published for sale and whose photographers are unidentified. For these materials, Huigi Sim [Sim Hŭi-gi] of Yonsei University wrote an essay, "Rare Books and Pamphlets in the William Elliot Griffis Collection" in Korean, which was translated into English (2008). Both versions are available upon request at the Special Collections and University Archives at Rutgers University.

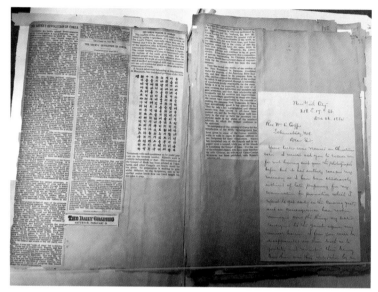

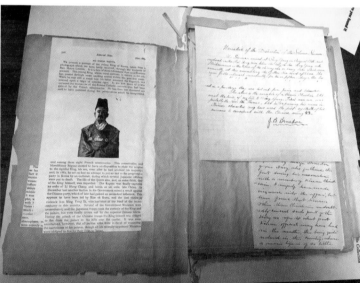

Figure 14.2. Korean materials from of the Scrapbooks series of the WEGC (Box 112K << Scrapbooks series << William Elliot Griffis Papers [Group I] << The Manuscript Collection << WEGC).

NOTE: A << B here denotes that A is a super category that contains B. For instance, "Box112K << Scrapbooks series << William Elliot Griffis Papers" means "Inside Box 112K, Scrapbook series are found, and inside the Scrapbook series, William Elliot Griffis Papers are included."

CITY OF SEOUL.

COREA

THE HERMIT NATION

I.—ANCIENT AND MEDIÆVAL HISTORY
II.—POLITICAL AND SOCIAL COREA
III.—MODERN AND RECENT HISTORY

BY

WILLIAM ELLIOT GRIFFIS
LATE OF THE IMPERIAL UNIVERSITY OF TOKIO, JAPAN
AUTHOR OF "THE MIKADO'S EMPIRE"

NEW YORK
CHARLES SCRIBNER'S SONS
1882

Figure 14.3. Griffis's *Corea: The Hermit Nation* and *The Unmannerly Tiger and Other Korean Tales* in the rare book collection of the WEGC.

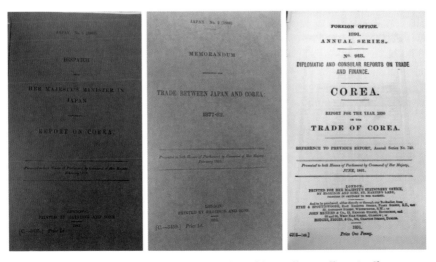

Figure 14.4. Korean pamphlets collected by William Elliot Griffis in the rare book collection of the WEGC.

Despite the historical value of the WEGC, until quite recently most research on Griffis conducted in Korea has been based on his books, overwhelmingly on *Corea: The Hermit Nation*.[5] We believe that the WEGC as a collection of primary sources will provide researchers with more accurate, systemic takes on Griffis's research. C-C. An (2011), for example, has pointed out the importance of the WEGC in understanding Griffis's changing views toward Japan and the independence of Korea.[6] The collection also would have great value in research that is not directly related to Griffis because it reflects many aspects of Korea in the late nineteenth and early twentieth centuries, and records of Korea of that time are rather limited (H-G. Sim 2008).[7]

Furthermore, the value of the WEGC lies in its coverage of multiple disciplines, including history, literature, art, and art history. This is because Griffis was a prolific writer with diverse interests in a wide spectrum of areas and also because he was an avid collector. Most of the research that has utilized the WEGC, though sparse, has been in the field of history. In literature, one letter from the Korea Letters subseries in the collection was featured on the front page of *Munhak sasang* (Kim, Yun-sik 2008), one of the most influential literary magazines in South Korea. The article by Yun-sik Kim, a preeminent literary critic, is about an important new discovery of letters written to Griffis by Ŭn-sik Pak (Eun Sic Park) and Kwang-su Yi (Kwang Soo Lie).

It is well known that Griffis was very interested in myths, legends, fairy tales, and folktales across different cultures. He wrote books on tales in Japan, China, the Netherlands, Belgium, and so on, and he also collected fairy tale materials. His books on Korean folktales, *The Unmannerly Tiger, and Other Korean Tales* (1911) and *Korean Fairy Tales* (1922) deserve attention. The WEGC has folktale and fairy tale materials in both its manuscript and rare book collections. According to Ross King of the University of British Columbia, the manuscripts relating to Korean folktale and fairy tale materials in the WEGC are "among the earliest collected in English" (pers. comm., May 28th, 2015). C-C. Kim (2008) also asserts the historical value of the two Korean "old novels" in the WEGC and the Griffis folktales.

P-M. Chŏng (2008) examines Griffis's views on Korean art and specifically calls for research on many of the illustrations found in Griffis's books on Korea. According to Chŏng, because the illustrations were the work of Ozawa Nankoku and later were done again by an anonymous American illustrator, there are numerous unrealistic depictions of Korea and Korean artifacts.

The highlight of the WEGC is photos of Korea. According to King, "The five photos from a Korean settlement in Primorsk, Russia in the 1880s [in the WEGC] are quite rare" (pers. comm., May 28th, 2015). King's article on the photographs of Koreans in Russia was published in *Photographs of Korea in the William Elliot Griffis Collection* (2019). He also mentions the value of the photos of a Korean hat

Figure 14.5. The front page of *Munhak sasang*, November 2008.

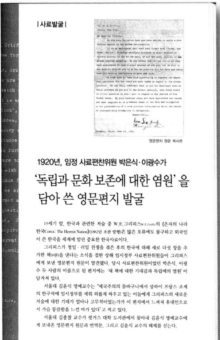

Figure 14.6. The article by Yun-sik Kim published in *Munhak sasang*, in November 2008 and the letter written by Ŭn-sik Pak (Eun Sic Park) discovered in the WEGC.

collection in light of Frank Hoffmann's recent posts on the Association for Korean Studies in Europe (AKSE) listserve, illustrating how underresearched Korean hats are. The historical significance of the Korean photos in the WEGC was examined for the first time in Yang, Pak, and Yu (2014). The photos include depictions of Korean landscapes, customs, historical ruins, lifestyles, and cities with various buildings in the late nineteenth and the early twentieth centuries. The study examined all the photos and classified 592 in seven categories: (1) four ceremonial occasions, (2) war, (3) lifestyle, (4) palaces and royal family, (5) cities and buildings, (6) religion, and (7) other. It was determined that a total of 358 photos in the collection are new discoveries that have never been seen in any publication until now. In particular, pictures of Queen Min's funeral, the construction of the Kyŏngin Railway from Seoul to Chemulp'o, technical schools, and the first three graduates of Ewha Womans University, as well as a panoramic view of Seoul and the capital's significant buildings, will facilitate in-depth historical research in this period.

Figure 14.7. Queen Min's funeral.

Figure 14.8. Construction of the Kyŏngin Railway from
Seoul to Chemulp'o, December 1898.

Figure 14.9. The first three graduates of Ewha Womans University, 1914.

The Utilization of the WEGC in Research on Korea

In contrast to published books, primary materials and manuscripts are often either not known to researchers or difficult to utilize because of geographic distance or lack of online access. In order to determine the utilization of the Korean materials in the WEGC, we compiled a comprehensive list of studies on Griffis, beginning with P-D. Yi (1918), which was published from prior to the formation of the WEGC to the present (Table 14.1).

Table 14.1. The use of the WEGC in research related to Korea.

Year	Author	Title	Use of WEGC	Mention of WEGC
1918	Yi, Pyŏng-do 이병도	"Toksŏ ugam" 讀書偶感	X	X
1960a	Burks and Cooperman	"Dr. William Elliot Griffis (1843–1928) and 'The Hermit Nation'"	O	O
1960b	Burks and Cooperman	"The William Elliot Griffis Collection"	O	O
1962	Hong, I-sŏp 洪以燮	"Kumiin ŭi Han'guk yŏsŏnggwan" 歐美人의 韓國 女性觀	X	X
1987	Sin, Hyŏng-sik 申瀅植	"Ilche ch'ogi Miguk sŏn'gyosa ŭi Han'gukkwan: Griffis ŭi *Corea, The Hermit Nation* ŭl chungsim ŭro" 日帝初期 美國 宣教師의 韓國觀: Griffis의 *Corea, The Hermit Nation* 을 中心으로	X	X
1997	Ch'oe Tŏk-su 최덕수	"Kaehanggi sŏyang i parabon Han'gugin Han'guk yŏksa" 개항기 서양이 바라본 한국인 한국 역사	X	X
1998	Yi, Tae-Jin [Yi, T'ae-jin]	Was Korea really a "Hermit Nation"?	X	X
1999	Yi, T'ae-jin 이태진	"Kŭndae Han'guk ŭn kwayŏn 'ŭndun'guk' iŏttŏn'ga?" 근대 한국은 과연 '은둔국'이었던가?	X	X

1999	Chŏng, Yŏn-t'ae 정연태	"19-segi huban 20-segi ch'o sŏyangin ŭi Han'gukkwan - sangdaejŏk chŏngch'esŏngnon, chŏngch'i sa-hoe pup'aeron, t'ayulchŏk kaehyŏk pulgap'iron" 19세기 후반 20세기 초 서양인의 한국관 - 상대적 정체성론, 정치사회 부패론, 타율적 개혁불가피론	X	X
2000	Chŏng, Sŏng-hwa 정성화	"W. Kŭrip'isŭ. Ŭnja ŭi nara Han'guk: Kŭrip'isŭ ŭi Han'gukkwan ŭl chung-gsim ŭro" W. 그리피스. 『은자의 나라 한국』: 그리피스의 한국관을 중심으로	X	O
2000	Cheong, Sung-hwa [Chŏng, Sŏng-hwa]	"William Elliot Griffis and emerging American images on Korea"	X	O
2002	Cho, Ŭn-yŏng 조은영	"Miguk ŭi Tongyang ilki" 미국의 동양읽기	X	X
2006	Kim, Su-t'ae 김수태	Williŏm Kŭrip'isŭ ŭi Ŭndun ŭi nara, Han'guk - Han'guk kodaesa sŏsul ŭl chungsim ŭro" 윌리엄 그리피스의 『은둔의 나라, 한국』 - 한국 고대사 서술을 중심으로	X	O
2008	Kim, Sang-min 김상민	"Kaehwa Ilchegi Han'guk kwallyŏn sŏyang munhŏn e nat'anan Han'guk insik yangt'ae yŏn'gu" 개화일제기 한국관련 서양문헌에 나타난 한국인식양태연구	X	X
2008	Kim, Chong-chŏl 김종철 [Kim, Jong-Cheol]	"Kŭrip'isŭ sujip Han'guk kojŏn sosŏl tu p'yŏn kwa Kŭrip'isŭ ŭi Han'guk sŏrhwajip" 그리피스 수집 한국 고전소설 두 편과 그리피스의 한국 설화집	O	O

2008	Chŏng, Kŭn-sik 정근식 [Jung, Keun-Sik]	"Kŭrip'isŭ ŭi *Ŭndun ŭi nara Han'guk* ŭi t'eksŭt'ŭ hyŏngsŏng kwajŏng" 그리피스의 '은둔의 나라 한국'의 텍스트 형성과정	O	O
2008	Sim, Hŭi-gi 심희기	"Williŏm Elliŏt'ŭ Kŭrip'isŭ (William Elliot Griffis) kŏlleksyŏn ŭi hŭigwi sŏjŏk kwa soch'aekcha" 윌리엄 엘리어트 그리피스 (William Elliot Griffis) 컬렉션의 희귀 서적과 소책자	O	O
2008	Sim, Huigi [Sim, Hŭi-gi]	"Rare Books and Pamphlets in the William Elliot Griffis Collection"	O	O
2008	Chŏng, Pyŏng-mo 정병모 [Chung, Byong Mo]	"Kŭrip'isŭ ŭi Han'guk misul e taehan insik" 그리피스의 한국미술에 대한 인식	X	X
2008	Yu, Yŏng-mi 유영미 [Cho, Young-mee Yu]	"Kŭrip'isŭ ŭi Han'gugŏ e taehan ihae" 그리피스의 한국어에 대한 이해 (William E. Griffis on the Korean Language)	X	X
2008	Kim, Yun-sik 김윤식	"*Ŭnja ŭi nara Han'guk* ŭi chŏja Kŭrip'isŭ ege ponaen Pak Ŭn-sik, Yi Kwang-su yŏnmyŏng ŭi p'yŏnji" <은자의 나라 한국>의 저자 그리피스에게 보낸 박은식·이광수 연명의 편지	O	O
2010	Kim, Su-t'ae 김수태	"Williŏm Kŭrip'isŭ ŭi Han'guk kŭndaesa insik" 윌리엄 그리피스의 한국 근대사 인식	X	O
2010	Yi, Yŏng-mi 이영미	"Han-Mi sugyo ijŏn sŏyangindŭl ŭi Han'guk yŏksa sŏsul" 朝-美 修交 이전 서양인들의 한국 역사 서술	X	X
2010	Yu, Hwang-t'ae 류황태	"Kŭrip'isŭ rŭl t'onghae pon Han-Il kwan'gye" 그리피스를 통해 본 한일관계	X	X

2010	O, Yun-sŏn 오윤선	"Tan'gun sinhwa Yŏngyŏkcha ŭi sigak ilgoch'al" 〈단군신화(檀君神話)〉 영역자(英譯者)의 시각(視角) 일고찰	X	X
2011	An, Chong-chŏl 안종철	"Williŏm Kŭrip'isŭ (William E. Griffis) ŭi Ilbon kwa Han'guk insik (1876-1910)" 윌리엄 그리피스 (William E. Griffis)의 일본과 한국인식 (1876-1910)	X	O
2011	Yook, Young-Soo	"Fin de Siècle Korea as Exhibited at the World's Columbian Exposition of 1893 in Chicago: Revisited"	X	X
2011	Kim, Hŭi-yŏng 金喜永	"Kaehwagi sŏyangindŭl ŭi Tonghak insik: Kidokkyo ŭi yŏnghyang kwa kwallyŏnhayŏ" 개화기 서양인들의 동학 인식: 기 독교의 영향과 관련하여	X	X
2012	O, Yun-sŏn 오윤선	"Kŭndae ch'ogi Han'guk sŏrhwa Yŏngyŏkchadŭl ŭi pŏnyŏk t'aedo yŏn'gu -Allen, Griffis, Hulbert, Carpenter rŭl chungsim ŭro" 근대초기 한국설화 영역자들 의 번역태도 연구 - Allen, Griffis, Hulbert, Carpenter를 중심으로	X	X
2013	Pennanen, Henna-Riikka	"Building a career in and out of East Asia: 19th century American experts S. W. Williams and W. E. Griffis"	X	X
2014	O, Yun-sŏn 오윤선	"19-segi mal 20-segi ch'o Yŏngmun Han'guk sŏrhwa ŭi charyojŏk kach'i yŏn'gu" 19세기말 20세기초 영문(英文) 한 국설화의 자료적 가치 연구	X	X
2014	Yi, Yŏng-mi 이영미	"Ilbon ŭi Han'guk chibae e taehan Kŭrip'isŭ ŭi t'aedo" 일본의 한국 지배에 대한 그리피 스의 태도	O	O

2014	Yang, Sang-hyŏn, Pak So-yŏn and Yu Yŏng-mi [Cho, Young-mee Yu] 梁尙鉉, 朴素姸, 劉永美	"Kŭrip'isŭ kŏlleksyŏn e sojangdoeŏ innŭn Han'guk kŭndae sajin charyo ŭi haksulchŏk kach'i e taehan koch'al" 그리피스 컬렉션에 소장되어 있는 한국 근대 사진자료의 학술적 가치에 대한 고찰	O	O
2015	Yi, Yŏng-mi 이영미	"Kŭrip'isŭ (1843-1928) ŭi Han'guk insik kwa Tong Asia 그리피스 (1843-1928)의 한국 인식과 동아시아"	O	O
2015	Lee, Yeong-Mi [Yi, Yŏng-mi]	"W. E. Griffis' Understanding of Korea, and East Asia"	O	O
2015	Cho, Kyŏng-dŏk, Chŏng Hye-gyŏng, and Yang Sang-hyŏn 조경덕, 정혜경, 양상현	"Kŭrip'isŭ kŏlleksyŏn sajin e taehan Kidokkyosajŏk koch'al" <그리피스 컬렉션> 사진에 대한 기독교사적 고찰	O	O
2015	Yi, Kyŏng-min, Yang Sang-hyŏn, and Mun Pyŏng-guk 이경민, 양상현, 문병국	"Kŭrip'isŭ kŏlleksyŏn e p'oham toen kŭndae Inch'ŏn kwa Hansŏng sajin yŏn'gu" 그리피스 컬렉션에 포함된 근대 인천과 한성 사진 연구	O	O
2015	Yi, Yŏng-mi 이영미	"Kŭrip'isŭ (W. E. Griffis, 1843~1928) ŭi munmyŏnggwan kwa Tong Asia insik" 그리피스 (W. E. Griffis, 1843-1928)의 문명관과 동아시아 인식	X	X
2015	Yi, Yŏng-mi 李映美	"Kŭrip'isŭ (W. E. Griffis, 1843~1928) ŭi Han'guk insik pyŏnhwa" 그리피스 (W. E. Griffis, 1843-1928)의 한국 인식 변화	X	X

2015	Pak, So-yŏn 박소연	"Kŭrip'isŭ k'ŏlleksyŏn e p'oham toen Han'guk kŭndae tosi, kŏnch'uk sajin charyo e kwanhan yŏn'gu" 그리피스 컬렉션에 포함된 한국 근대 도시 · 건축 사진 자료에 관한 연구	O	O
2016	Chang, Chae-yong 장재용	"Kŭndae sŏyangin ui chŏsul e nat'anan Han'guksa insik" 近代 西洋人의 著述에 나타난 韓國史 認識	O	X
2019	King, Ross	"'Photographs of Mind' and 'Photographs Taken on the Soil': William Elliot Griffis, Korean Language, Writing and Literature, and Koreans in Russia"	O	O
2019	Lee, Eunice	"William E. Griffis's Virtual Experience of Korea: A Threefold Conceptual Map of Griffis's 'Hermit Nation'"	O	O
2019	Park, Sungmin and Young-mee Yu Cho	"William Elliot Griffis and His Visit to Korea in 1927"	O	O
2021 (this volume)	Cho, Young-mee Yu and Sungmin Park	"The Significance of the Korean Materials in the William Elliot Griffis Collection at Rutgers University"	O	O

In the above table, X means no reference, and O refers to the use/mention of the WEGC.

Although Burks and Cooperman (1960a, b) introduced the WEGC to researchers in Korea, the collection was not mentioned again until S-H. Chŏng (2000). Since Korean scholars started visiting Rutgers University in 2006 with the specific goal of examining the WEGC, the existence of the collection has become better known. The 2008 workshop, Korean Materials of the William Elliot Griffis Collection involved twelve scholars in the fields of sociology, history, law, literature, art, architecture, linguistics, and library sciences. It is only since 2014 that the WEGC has begun to be utilized fully by researchers (e.g., by Y-M. Yi [2014, 2015] and Yang, Pak, and Yu [2014]).

The WEGC: Arrangement and Organization

The WEGC consists of three parts: (1) the manuscript collection, (2) the rare book collection, and (3) the unprocessed non-Asian materials. The manuscript collection consists of "Griffis's personal papers and material collected during his lifetime" while the rare book collection consists of "bound volumes and pamphlets that belonged to William Elliot Griffis or that have been acquired by purchase or gift." The rare book collection "focuses on Westerners in Japan and her neighbors during the Meiji and Taisho periods" (Gass and Perrone 2008: 2). Non-Asian materials are included in the collection, and Fernanda Perrone (Curator, William Elliot Griffis Collection, Special Collections and University Archives) has informed the authors that "most of the non-Asian materials are unprocessed and most of the Asian materials are processed, with a few exceptions. [The Rutgers Libraries] are working on processing both parts of the collection, but the Asian materials are a priority" (pers. comm., June 4th, 2015).

The books and pamphlets bequeathed by Griffis are part of both the WEGC and the rare book collection at the Rutgers Libraries. Within the rare book collection, they are grouped under the sublocation X-GRIF.

The manuscript collection is manually searchable by means of the "Finding Aid" while the rare book collection is electronically searchable by means of IRIS (the Rutgers University Libraries online public catalog, as of Aug. 2015). The unprocessed non-Asian materials will not be searchable until they are processed. Table 14.2 shows the overall organization of the WEGC.

Table 14.2. The organization of the WEGC

Category	Searching/Browsing Tools
The manuscript collection	manually searchable by means of the "Finding Aid"
The rare book collection	electronically searchable by means of IRIS (the Rutgers University Libraries online public catalog) (as of Aug. 2015)
The unprocessed non-Asian materials	N/A

The manuscript collection of the WEGC is divided into five groups, as shown in Table 14.3. While most of the Korean materials are found in Group I, the Korean photographs are in Group IV. To better understand what kinds of materials are to be found in each group, it is best to consult the "Finding Aid" for details.

Table 14.3. Organization of the manuscript collection[8]

Group Number	Group Name	Type of Materials
Group I	William Elliot Griffis Papers	Griffis's diaries, correspondence, writings, and collected articles
Group II	Margaret Clark Griffis Papers	The papers of Griffis's sister, Margaret
Group III	Griffis Family Papers	Journals and correspondence of Griffis's family members
Group IV	Group IV: Papers Collected by Griffis	The records of other yatoi collected by Griffis, including Korean photographs
Group V	Griffis Related Materials	Archival material from other sources related to Griffis

Figure 14.10 on the following page provides an overview of the organization of the collection in tandem with the *JTWE* microfilm series. The areas where Korean materials are found are shaded. We can see that most of the Korean materials belong to Group I, but the Korean photographs belong to the Photographs series in Group IV of the manuscript collection. They do not belong to unprocessed non-Asian materials, as some researchers have mistakenly stated (e.g., Yang, Pak, and Yu 2014: 13–14), probably because they are listed under "in-process materials" in Gass and Perrone (2008). They are currently stored not with the other WEGC materials but in the processing room.

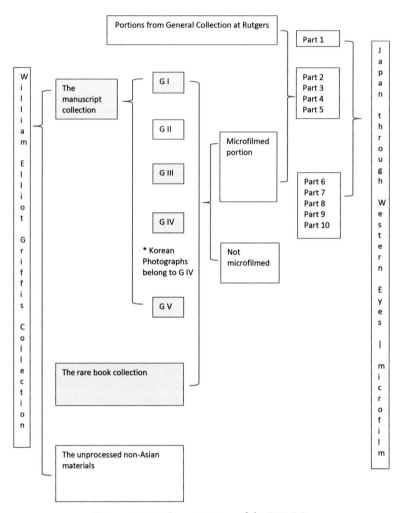

Figure 14.10. Organization of the WEGC

Limitations in Access and Retrieval

The Korean materials in the WEGC have been hidden from researchers for many reasons. One of the reasons is the lack of detailed information of Korean materials on the Rutgers Libraries website. The page that includes the WEGC on the website is mainly about Japanese materials while Korea is mentioned only once and briefly.

There are five useful guides to the Korean materials, as shown in Table 14.4. All except Gass and Perrone (2008) are guides to the WEGC in general. The browsing/searching guides listed in Table 14.4 are illustrated in Figure 14.11 through Figure 14.15.

Table 14.4. Key browsing/searching guides for Korean materials in the WEGC

Browsing/Searching Guide	Target of the Guide	Online Accessibility
"Finding Aid"	The manuscript collection of the WEGC	X (as of Aug. 2015)
"Korean Materials in the William Elliot Griffis Collection" (Gass and Perrone 2008) (as of Aug. 2015)	The Korean materials in the WEGC	X
Rutgers IRIS (online catalog) (as of Aug. 2015)	The rare book collection of the WEGC	O (as of Aug. 2015)
JTWE Guide	The microfilmed portions of the WEGC	O
"The William Griffis Collection" (Burks and Cooperman 1960b)	The WEGC in general	O

The limitations to using the guides in Figures 14.11 though 14.15 include: (1) the two most updated resources, the "Finding Aid" and Gass and Perrone (2008) are not available online, (2) IRIS (the Rutgers University online catalog) can only be used for the rare book collection of the WEGC, and (3) the online version of the *JTWE Guide* is not well known among researchers.

Moreover, confusion results from discrepancies across the core guides. First, the arrangement of the collection explained in Burks and Cooperman (1960b) is different from the current one since the WEGC went through comprehensive processing in the 1994–95 project. The first introduction of the Korean materials in the WEGC is done by Burks and Cooperman (1960a, b), which formed the basis of studies published around the year 2000. Second, there are some differences in the organization and arrangement of the materials from the WEGC between the "Finding Aid" and the *JTWE Guide*. The "Finding Aid" lists items in the order of the box numbers under the group numbers (I-V) of the manuscript collection of the WEGC, while the JTWE as described in *JTWE Guide* is not in the order of the box numbers. In addition, inconsistencies between box numbers in the "Finding Aid" and the JTWE Guide also cause confusion. For example, the items described as contained in Boxes 97, 124, and 125 in the *JTWE Guide* are in Boxes 106, 135, and 136 in the "Finding Aid." Third, the *JTWE Guide* is a guide to the microfilmed portions of the WEGC, which is only a fraction of the total, and it includes some works that are not found in the WEGC.

Figure 14.11. "Finding Aid."

Korean Materials in the William Elliot Griffis Collection

**Leah H. Gass,
Intern, Fall 2003
Revised Edition, Fernanda Perrone, 2008**

William Elliot Griffis, an accomplished teacher, author, scholar, and theologian, was one of the first thousand Americans to enter Meiji Japan. Born in 1843, he fought for the Union during the Civil War. Griffis graduated from Rutgers College in 1869, and shortly thereafter traveled to Japan to teach natural sciences and help organize education in provincial Echizen (later named Fukui), as part of the Japanese government's broad Westernization/modernization project. Griffis remained in Japan for some three years between 1871 and 1874. Upon returning to the United States, he became one of the foremost Western authorities on American-Japanese relations. His work The Mikado's Empire was the leading publication on Japan in the U.S. for several decades. Griffis was an avid reader and collector on all subjects that concerned the Far East, including Japan, China and Korea. Although Griffis did not travel to Korea until 1927, he was knowledgeable about the country's culture and politics. He published several books, including Corea: The Hermit Nation, Corea, Within and Without, A Modern Pioneer in Korea, Korean Fairy Tales, and The Unmannerly Tiger and Other Korean Tales, in addition to many newspaper and magazine articles on Korea. He also collected a wealth of other articles, manuscripts, photographs and artifacts relating to Korea between 1874 and his death in 1928.

Figure 14.12. "Korean Materials in the William Elliot Griffis Collection"
(Gass and Perrone 2008).

RUTGERS
University Libraries
Library Catalog
Basic Search
Advanced Search
Call Number Search
Reserves
E-ZBorrow
Interlibrary Lo
GO BACK
HELP
Advanced Search
words anywhere
author
title
subject
medical subject
form / genre
series
periodical title
AND
searchoper7
Search
Reset
match on:
Keywords
library:
SPCOL/UA: Special Collections/University Archives (College Avenue)
language:
ANY
format:
ANY
type-circulate?:
ANY
sub-location:
X-GRIF

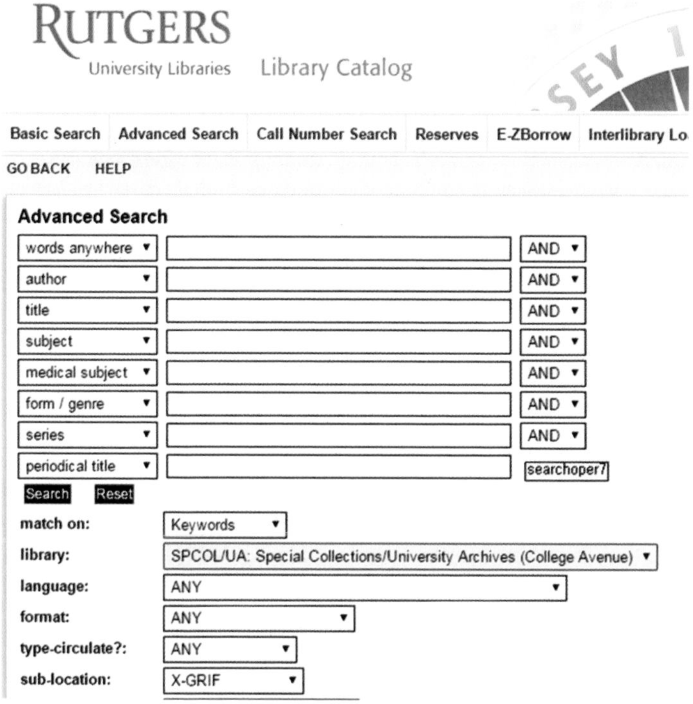

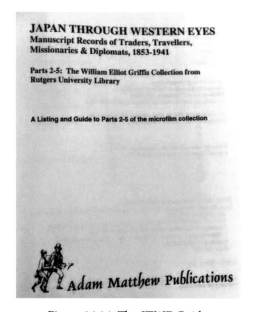

Figure 14.13. IRIS (the Rutgers online catalog).

JAPAN THROUGH WESTERN EYES
Manuscript Records of Traders, Travellers, Missionaries & Diplomats, 1853-1941
Parts 2-5: The William Elliot Griffis Collection from Rutgers University Library
A Listing and Guide to Parts 2-5 of the microfilm collection
Adam Matthew Publications

Figure 14.14. The *JTWE Guide.*

NOTES

The William Elliot Griffis Collection

ARDATH W. BURKS
JEROME COOPERMAN

THE William Elliot Griffis Collection in the Rutgers University Library, New Brunswick, New Jersey, embraces material on Japan, Korea, and China. It is contained in twenty-nine legal-size manuscript file cases: twenty relate to Japan; four to Korea; three to China; and one contains miscellaneous data. The collection is now in shelf order and the following is a summary of the arrangement of the Griffis papers.

Organization of the Collection

All of the Griffis material relating to the Far East has been classified as follows:

Japan, Internal

Language, literature, arts, mythology .... Boxes I-V
Feudal Japan, Imperial Family, Japanese family, women, education,
   religion, economics .... Box   VI
Politics, the military, cities .... Box   VII
Foreign employees (*yatoi*), missionaries .... Boxes VIII-X

Japan, External

Extrality, Sino-Japanese and Russo-Japanese wars, Japan-American
   relations, World War I, and the Washington Conference .... Box   XI

Figure 14.15. "The William Griffis Collection" (Burks and Cooperman, 1960b).

Currently the WEGC can be accessed in two ways: by visiting the library in person or through microfilm. Microfilmed portions of the Korean materials are hidden under the title "Japan through Western Eyes." There also are limitations in the access through microfilm. First, not all materials in the WEGC are accessible through microfilm. Second, the microfilm may be a convenient way to access materials without a visit, but, as it is intended for preservation, the retrieval is cumbersome. Third, the microfilm guide is accessible online through the publisher's web page but is not on the Rutgers Libraries website. At the Rutgers Libraries, the microfilm guide is not circulated. Without previous knowledge of the existence of the online version,[9] researchers have to visit the library in order to consult it. Fourth, the "Finding Aid" is the only way to find out which portions of the collection are microfilmed, which is important because researchers accessing the microfilm guide will want to know what they are missing. But the "Finding Aid" is not available online. Finally, the scope note and arrangement note of the microfilm guide are not specifically about the microfilmed portions but are about the entire collection.

In response to our request asking for the rationale and future plans for microfilming, Perrone replied as follows.

The microfilm was done under my predecessor, Ruth J. Simmons, who made the selection of parts to be microfilmed. I don't have all her old files, so I am not entirely sure about the sequence of events. The U.S. Department of Education Title II-C grant (1994–1995) included a plan to microfilm the collection. Approximately 30 reels of microfilm were produced. Because the project lost funding after one year, the microfilm set was not completed. In 1996, Ruth was approached by Adam Matthew Publications in England, and Rutgers Libraries made an agreement to microfilm and sell the collection commercially. The company copied the microfilm already made and microfilmed an additional approximately 50 reels. The selections were made by Ruth Simmons as per the agreement. The microfilm guide was prepared by William Pidduck, an editor at Adam Matthew Publications. Except for the Publisher's Note and the Reel Contents, the guide reproduces the main Griffis Collection "Finding Aid" as it was in 2000.

A few years ago, I met with a representative from Adam Matthew about digitizing Group III (Family Papers) and Group V (Griffis-Related) as part of their Japan through Western Eyes series. The company chose not to pursue it, probably because they felt there was not enough unique material for it to be profitable. We would like to microfilm the rest of the collection and digitize the microfilm, but funding is an issue. (Pers. comm., June 4th, 2015)

We can infer the original rationale for the selection of the microfilmed portion from the publisher's note on the *JTWE Guide*, which reads, "[It] provides valuable insights into the political, commercial and cultural history of Japan."[10]

The WEGC: Journal and Correspondence

In this section we focus on Boxes 59 and 60 of the "Correspondence series" (letters received by Griffis, many of which were from Henry G. Appenzeller and other colleagues with an interest in Korea) and on his journal entries from September 17th, 1926 to January 1st, 1928 in Box 36. Occasionally, Korean visitors to the WEGC have made "discoveries" (see, e.g., publication of the 1920 letter from Eun Sic Park [Pak, Ŭn-sik] and Kwang Soo Lie [Yi, Kwang-su] in *Munhak sasang* (Y-S Kim 2008), and Syngman Rhee's 1919 letter proposing the purchase of the Griffis's forthcoming book on Korean history presented in 2014 at the annual meeting of CEAL (Council on East Asian Library) by Hyoungbae Lee, Korean Studies Librarian at Princeton University). Through intertextual research on the Korean materials in the collection, we think the proper historical background will be provided to his Griffis's Korean correspondences. These letters deserve publication for future research, just as the journal entries during Griffis's trip to Korea in 1927 were made available in Park and Cho (2019). The Correspondence series of the WEGC are shown in Figures 14.16, 14.17, and 14.18.

In the Correspondence series, the letters received by Griffis (including some letters sent to others and forwarded to him) and the letters or drafts of letters written by Griffis (except letters sent to family members) are grouped together. Letters in the scrapbooks, which were made by Griffis himself, are not included here.

These letters are grouped as Korea, China, or Japan Letters by name and subject. However, it is not clear how these letters were classified.[11] There are three subseries in the Correspondence series: Japan Letters, Korea Letters, and China Letters. Currently letters in each subseries are arranged first in alphabetical order and then in chronological order (*JTWE Guide*).

The "Korea Letters" in Boxes 59 and 60 are valuable materials for Korean studies, and they total more than a thousand pages. As for their academic importance, H-G. Sim (2008) noted that Griffis used letters as a way to collect information for his writing. Furthermore, as to the Correspondence series in general, the microfilm guide states that "the correspondence is especially rich and lays bare the entire network of contacts that Griffis built up in Japan, Korea

Figure 14.16 Correspondence series of the WEGC: Boxes 45–60.

Figure 14.17. Correspondence series of the WEGC:
Box 59 (the first box of Korea Letters).

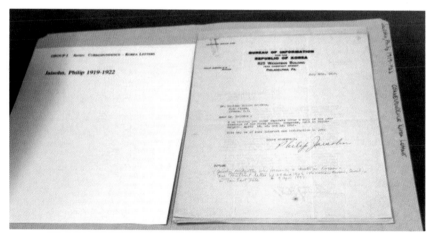

Figure 14.18. Correspondence series of the WEGC:
Jaisohn, Philip, 1919–1922 (Folder 37 of Box 59).

and China and his full range of interests."[12] K-S Chŏng (2008) has argued for the systematic categorization and analysis of the Griffis correspondence in relation to Christian missionaries such as Hulbert, McKenzie, Appenzeller, and McCune. Table 14.5 contains a list of senders found in the Korea Letters subseries in the Correspondence series of the WEGC.[13]

Table 14.5: List of senders in the Korea Letters
subseries of the Correspondence series
(Korea Letters ≪ Correspondence ≪ the Manuscript Collection ≪ WEGC)

Name	Year	Name	Year	Name	Year
Allen, Horace Newton	1888– 1890	Griffis, William Elliot	1920	M	1920– 1927
Allen, Horace Newton	1895– 1911	G	Undated and 1910	Niwa S.	1927
Appenzeller, Alice	1911– 1912	Harada Tasuku	1915	N	1894– 1912
Appenzeller, Alice	1918– 1921	Hulbert, Homer B.	1892– 1897	Owen, H.	1927
Appenzeller, Alice	1922– 1927	Hulbert, Homer B.	1900– 1906	Park Eun Sie[c]	1920
Appenzeller, Ellen	1912– 1913	Hulbert, Homer B.	1911– 1917	P	1911– 1921
Appenzeller, Henry	1912– 1926	H	1890– 1899	Rhee Syngman	1919
Appenzeller, Ida	1912– 1917	H	1911– 1920	R	1902– 1919
Appenzeller, Mary	1912– 1920	Ito, Prince	1908	R	1920– 1927
A	1894– 1916	I	1877– 1908	Saito M.	1920– 1927
B	1874– 1912	Jaisohn, Philip	1919– 1922	Scribner's, Charles Sons	1884– 1918
B	1919– 1924	Heber-Jones, George	1894– 1912	Shibata Z	1921

Cho H. Y.	1923	J	1894–1912	Sok Ye Koi	1896
Crowell, Thomas Y. & Co.	1911–1921	Kim P. Yongji?	1927	Sonoda Y.	1923
C	1874–1907	Komatz Midori	1893	S	1895–1926
C	1920–1929	Korea, Legation of	1901	T	1896–1904
D	1888–1920	Kraik, Earl	1916	Underwood, H.	1899–1909
E	1911, 1921	Kuir, Henry	1914-1917	Usami K.	1912
Fletcher, Dr. A. G.	1927	K	1912–1925	V	1903–1919
F	1890–1898	Loomis, Henry	1914–1917	Walters, Jeanette	1919
F	1900–1927	L	1877–1912	Watanabe N.	1910–1921
Gale, Jas S.	1900–1921	Morris, C. D.	1911–1916	W	1894–1904
Gifford, D. L.	1895	Morris, Louise	1902, 1910–1911	W	1921
Gillett, Philip L.	1902–1905	M	1894–1906	Yun Ye Che	1890–1892
Gilmore, George W.	1893–1919	M	1907–1919	Unidentified	

Figure 14.20 is a letter to Griffis from Ito Hirobumi dated May 6th, 1908, shortly before the annexation of Korea by Japan in 1910. It is his response to Griffis's request for photos and pamphlets about Korea. The photos sent by Ito are located in "Korean Photographs" in the WEGC, but the list of these photos is included in "Korea Letters."[14] With this finding, the source of some photographs, which were labeled "Murakami series" in Yang, Pak, and Yu (2014), was confirmed.

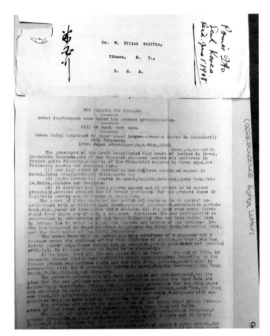

Figure 14.19. Letter from Prince Ito (Ito
Hirobumi, 1841–1909) September 20th, 1908.
(Folder 35, Box 59 ≪ Korea Letters ≪ Correspondence ≪
The Manuscript Collection ≪ WEGC.).

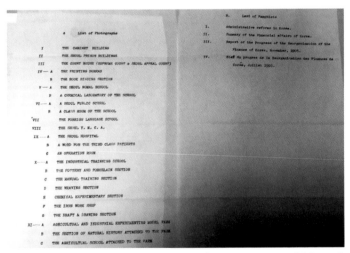

Figure 14.20. Letter from Prince Ito (Ito Hirobumi: 1841–1909) May 6th, 1908:
the list of photographs and pamphlets requested by Griffis to Prince Ito.
(Folder 35, Box 59 ≪ Korea Letters ≪ Correspondence ≪ The Manuscript
Collection ≪ WEGC.).

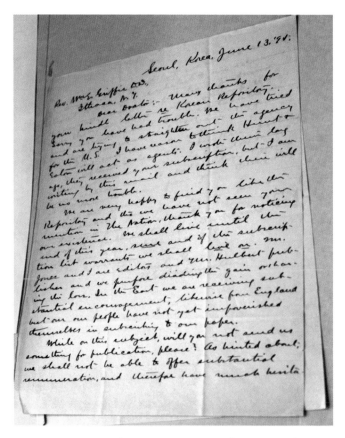

Figure 14.21. Letter from Henry Appenzeller, June 13th, 1895.
(Folder 7, Box 59 ≪ Korea Letters ≪ Correspondence
≪ The Manuscript Collection ≪ WEGC.).

Figure 14.22 is a letter from Philip Jaisohn (Sǒ Chae-p'il) sent on July 25th, 1921. In the letter Jaisohn asked Griffis to write an article on Korea for an upcoming international conference in Washington, DC, dealing with "the Far Eastern questions."

Figure 14.23 is a letter from Horace G. Underwood sent on July 14th, 1900. He writes, "Things in Korea are more disturbed than ever and politically no one in Korea can be trusted and we cannot tell what will happen." Yet, he continues, "in other ways however there has been advances: railroads are coming in, mainly however for the benefit of foreign investors."

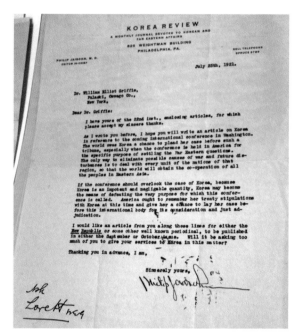

Figure 14.22. Letter from Philip Jaisohn (Sŏ Chae-p'il), July 25th, 1921.
(Folder 37, Box 59 ≪ Korea Letters ≪ Correspondence
≪ The Manuscript Collection ≪ WEGC.).

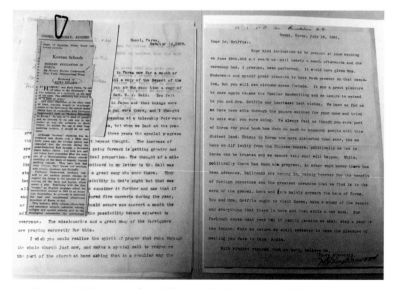

Figure 14.23. Letter from Horace G. Underwood, July 14th, 1900.
(Folder 13, Box 60 ≪ Korea Letters ≪ Correspondence
≪ The Manuscript Collection ≪ WEGC.).

Figure 14.24. Journals series in the WEGC: Journal no.1–31 (Box 7 to 37).

There are in total thirty-one journals in the WEGC (Figure 14.24). They are arranged in chronological order, and each journal is assigned a box number.[15] Among these volumes, Journal 30 (about 230 pages, assigned box number 36) could be valuable for research in Korean studies. Journal 30 is the second to the last journal book and covers the period from September 17th, 1926 to January 1st, 1928. The value of this particular volume lies in the fact that it recorded Griffis's first and the last visit to Korea. Although he wrote many books and articles about Korea and was considered an expert on the country for several decades, he did not visit Korea until 1927, one year before his death. In this context, researchers would be very interested in knowing what Griffis did during his visit. Gass and Perrone (2008: 3) commented, "While in Korea Griffis visited Seoul, made several speeches, met with various Eastern and Western colleagues, and toured areas of the country of general interest."

Griffis usually allotted one page for every two days, at least when he was in Korea. Each entry starts with the date, the day of the week, and the weather. According to the journal entry shown in Figure 14.25, he left Seoul on April 1st, 1927, for Songdo. He seems to have been impressed with the mills, modern plant machinery, and automobiles in Korea, which was still considered an "ancient kingdom."

Yang, Pak, and Yu (2014: 13) comment that Griffis, who had not seen or experienced Korea in person, collected Korea-related materials to compensate for

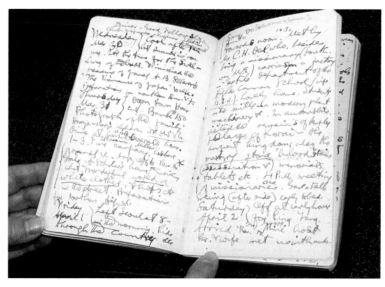

Figure 14.25. Journal entries, March 30th–April 2nd, 1927 in Journal no. 30. (Journal no. 30 ≪ Journals series ≪ The Manuscript Collection ≪ WEGC).

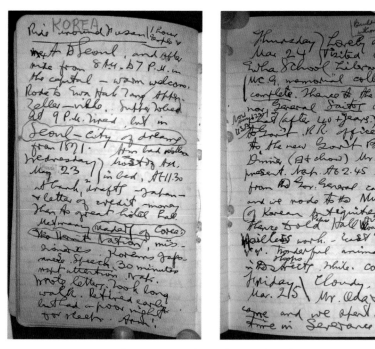

Figure 14.26. Journal entries, March 23rd–March 25th, 1927 in Journal no. 30 (Journal no. 30 ≪ Journals series ≪ The Manuscript Collection ≪ WEGC).

his lack of firsthand experience. According to the journal entry in Figure 14.26, he described Seoul as a "City of dreaming from 1871." He had been eager to see the country long before he wrote *Corea: The Hermit Nation* (1882).

Conclusion

In this chapter, we have described the organization of the WEGC and its current use and limitations. In order to facilitate future use, we suggest the following. First, the "Finding Aid," the first step in researching the WEGC, should be made publicly available online in order to make searches more convenient. Second, Gass and Perrone (2008) should be properly updated by including information about the microfilmed portions of the Korean materials. This document, even if incomplete, should also be made available online. Third, in the current WEGC introduction on the Rutgers University Libraries website, it would be helpful to provide information on Korean materials, as well as a link to those materials. Finally, it is important to redress discrepancies among the search and browsing guides to minimize the challenges of searching for materials.

In making a list of Griffis-related Korean studies materials, we have included only journal articles (and a few books) published in Korea, but in the future we intend to make a list of publications other than journal articles and gather information on works produced in countries other than the United States and Korea. We also recommend the publication of typed manuscripts of Korea Letters, the subseries of Correspondence series, and Journal no. 30 (with the original images and the corresponding typed texts, as well as Korean translations of the texts).

Notes

*Since the manuscript was completed, we have been engaged in the following Griffis-related projects: (1) publication of Korean Photographs in the William Elliot Griffis Collection (2019) and a paper in the book, "William Elliot Griffis and His Visit to Korea in 1927: From His Journal and Korea Letters"; (2) research on the Korean Materials in the Griffis Collection funded by a grant from the Overseas Korean Cultural Heritage Foundation (2018–19); (3) hosting a workshop, "The Griffis Collection: Exploring Ways to Use the Korean Materials for Korean Studies" (August 2019); (4) publication of a forthcoming book, The William Elliot Griffis Korea Letters (forthcoming in 2022, Rutgers University Press).

[1] Griffis has been established as the first American author to publish books and articles on Korean history (S-T. Kim 2010: 126).

[2] See H-G. Sim (2008: 6).

[3] Throughout this chapter "*JTWE*" refers to the microfilm series and "*JTWE Guide*" refers to *Japan through Western Eyes: Manuscript Records of Traders, Travellers, Missionaries,*

and Diplomats, 1853–1941, parts 2–5, *The William Elliot Griffis Collection from Rutgers University Library: A Listing and Guide to Parts 2–5 of the Microfilm Collection.*

[4] Scrapbooks in the Scrapbooks series in the WEGC contain various kinds of materials, including newspaper and journal clippings and ephemera, according to the unpublished "Finding Aid," prepared by Simmons, Piez, and Perrone and available at the WEGC at Rutgers Libraries. Letters are also found in the series. They "span the dates of 1859 to 1914 and chiefly concern Griffis' Asian interests" ("Finding Aid": 163)

[5] Research on Griffis has been quite limited both inside and outside Korea. A handful of publications in the West are about Griffis's views on Japan, and we find hardly any serious research on his views on Korea. Korean publications almost exclusively focus on his *Corea: The Hermit Nation.*

[6] C-C. An (2011) points out that Griffis received the Order of the Rising Sun, Fourth Class, in 1908 and the Order of the Rising Sun, Third Class, in 1926 from the Japanese emperor while he worked with Sŏ Chae-p'il and Rhee Syngman, the key figures involved in the Korean independence movement in the United States. As a New York City member of the League of the Friends of Korea organized by Sŏ, Griffis criticized the harsh Japanese colonial policies imposed after the March First Movement in Korea.

[7] Although Griffis wrote voluminously on Japan, Korea, and China during the late nineteenth and early twentieth centuries, what is as important from today's perspective as his publications is the historical value of the materials he collected in that particular time period (H-G. Sim 2008: 1).

[8] On the other hand, the *JTWE Guide* groups the WEGC first into "Japan/Far East materials" and "Griffis-Related and Griffis Research Materials." The guide also further divides the former into four groups. The following are the four groups of the "Japan/Far East materials."

> Group I (main group): WEGC materials (Griffis's own writing in print and manuscript), the greatest bulk of the collection
> Group II: Margaret Clark Griffis materials; diaries of Griffis's sister
> Group III: Papers pertaining to other members of the Griffis family (war journals kept by his brother; diaries and account books kept by his two wives; family correspondence)
> Group IV: Manuscript materials collected by Griffis, including the following.
> • Richard Henry Brunton manuscript
> • Memoirs and journals of James Ballagh and Samuel Robbins Brown
> • Manuscripts in English by Japanese literary figures
> • Scrapbooks on polar exploration by Captain Silas Bent (a member of the Perry Expedition to Japan of 1853–54)
> • Letters from Griffis to Harada Tasuku (president of Doshisha University) ("Arrangement note" of "JTWE Digital Guide," http://www.ampltd.co.uk/ digital_guides/japan_through_western_eyes/arrangement%20note.aspx, accessed on August 20th, 2019)

[9] "JTWE Digital Guide" (http://www.ampltd.co.uk/digital_guides/japan_through_western_eyes/publishers%20note.aspx, accessed on August 20th, 2019)

[10] See "Publisher's note" of the "JTWE Digital Guide," accessed on August 20th, 2019, http://www.ampltd.co.uk/digital_guides/japan_through_western_eyes/publishers%20note.aspx.

[11] The classification was done by Wendell Piez, one of the creators of the "Finding Aid" (Perrone, pers. comm.).

[12] According to "Publisher's note" of the "JTWE Digital Guide": "Part 3 covers the extensive correspondence files and Griffis's scrapbooks. The correspondence is especially rich and lays bare the entire network of contacts that Griffis built up in Japan, Korea and China and his full range of interests. Consisting primarily of letters to Griffis, it features letters by: Amenomori Nobushige, Ando Taro, James Ballagh, Edward Warren Clark, Deguchi Yonekichi, Harada Tasuku, Hayashi Uta, Imadate Tosui, Prince Ito, Prince Iwakura, Iyesato Tokugawa, Katsu Kaishu, Karl Kawakami, Viscount Kuroda Nagaatsu, Matsudaira Yatsutaka, J Low, Edward Morse, Nitobe Inazo, Fred Pearson, Matthew Perry, Baron Shibusawa, Shidehara Kijuro, Arthur Stanford, Takahashi Korekujo, Tanaka Akamaro, Charles Tyler, Uyeda Yoshitake, Guido Verbeck, Booker T Washington, Wing Yung, Wu Ning Nang, Martin Wyckoff, Yokoi Tokino and Yun Ye Cha. Primarily written in English, these letters show that Griffis maintained contact with many of his students. Many of them travelled to, or worked in, America, and many rose to eminent positions. These letters are a valuable record of their experiences." Accessed on August 20th, 2019, http://www.ampltd.co.uk/digital_guides/japan_through_western_eyes/publishers%20note.aspx.

[13] In some cases the names of senders are fully spelled out, while others use initials.

[14] The source of these photos was identified as the Murakami series by Sanghyun Yang (pers. comm., July 26th, 2015).

[15] According to "Detailed Listings, Part 2" of the "JTWE Digital Guide,": "Griffis's early journal work is occasional and sporadic; only in 1877 does he appear to have developed a consistent system for keeping and maintaining journals. The final sequence of nineteen journals [Ac. 2074, nos. 14–32], beginning with this date, was collated and dated by Katharine G. M. Johnson, whose brief notes appear in most volumes. Titles are given as they appear on volume spines. A number of volumes also have one or a few clippings pasted into the front." Accessed on August 20th, 2019, http://www.ampltd.co.uk/digital_guides/japan through western eyes/part%202.aspx.

References

Adams, Charles Kendall, and Rossiter Johnson. 1902. *Universal Cyclopaedia and Atlas*. New York: D. Appleton.

An, Chong-chŏl 안종철. 2011. "Williŏm Kŭrip'isŭ (William E. Griffis) ŭi Ilbon kwa Han'guk insik (1876–1910)" 윌리엄 그리피스 (William E. Griffis) 의 일본과 한국인식 (1876–1910). *Ilbon yŏn'gu* 일본연구 15: 439–61.

Burks, Ardath W., and Jerome Cooperman. 1960a. "Dr. William Elliot Griffis (1843–1928) and 'The Hermit Nation.'" *Asea yŏn'gu* 아세아연구 3, no. 1 (June): 169–77.

―――. 1960b. "The William Elliot Griffis Collection." *Journal of Asian Studies* 20: 61–69.

Cheong, Sung-hwa. 2000. "William Eilliot Griffis and Emerging American Images on Korea." *Review of Korean Studies* 3, no. 2 (December): 53–72.

Cho, Ŭn-yŏng 조은영. 2002. "Miguk ŭi Tongyang ilki" 미국의 동양읽기. *Misul sahak yŏn'gu* 미술사학연구 (September): 125–54.

Ch'oe, Tŏk-su 최덕수. 1997. "Kaehanggi sŏyang i parabon Han'gugin Han'guk yŏksa" 개항기 서양이 바라본 한국인 한국 역사. *Minjok munhwa yŏn'gu* 민족문화연구 30: 127–42.

Chŏng, Kŭn-sik 정근식. 2008. "Kŭrip'isŭ ŭi *Ŭndun ŭi nara Han'guk* ŭi t'eksŭt'ŭ hyŏngsŏng kwajŏng" 그리피스의 '은둔의 나라 한국'의 텍스트 형성과정. Presentation at the workshop Korean Materials of the William Elliot Griffis Collection, Rutgers University, March 14th, 2008.

Chŏng, Pyŏng-mo 정병모. 2008. "Kŭrip'isŭ ŭi Han'guk misul e taehan insik" 그리피스의 한국미술에 대한 인식. Presentation at the workshop Korean Materials of the William Elliot Griffis Collection, Rutgers University, March 14th, 2008.

Chŏng, Sŏng-hwa 정성화. 2000. "W. Kŭrip'isŭ. *Ŭnja ŭi nara Han'guk*: Kŭrip'isŭ ŭi Han'gukkwan ŭl chungsim ŭro" W. 그리피스. 『은자의 나라 한국』: 그리피스의 한국관을 중심으로. *Haeoe Han'gukhak p'yŏngnon* 해외한국학평론 1 (2000): 9–35.

Chŏng, Yŏn-t'ae 정연태. 1999. "19-segi huban 20-segi ch'o sŏyangin ŭi Han'gukkwan―sangdaejŏk chŏngch'esŏngnon, chŏngch'I sahoe pup'aeron, t'ayulchŏk kaehyŏk pulgap'iron" 19세기 후반 20세기 초 서양인의 한국관―상대적 정체성론, 정치사회 부패론, 타율적 개혁불가피론. *Yŏksa wa hyŏnsil* 역사와 현실 34: 159–206.

Dallet, Charles. 1874. *Histoire de l'Église de Corée, précédée d'une introduction sur l'histoire, les institutions, la langue, les moeurs, et coutumes coréennes.* Paris: V. Palmé.

Gass, Leah H., and Fernanda Perrone. 2008. "Korean Materials in the William Elliot Griffis Collection." Special Collections and University Archives, Rutgers University Libraries.

Griffis, William Elliot. 1876. *The Mikado's Empire.* New York: Harper.

———. 1880. *Japanese Fairy World: Stories from the Wonder-Lore of Japan.* Schenectady, NY: J. H. Barhyte.

———. 1881. *Asiatic History: China, Corea, Japan.* New York: Phillips and Hunt.

———. 1882. *Corea: The Hermit Nation.* New York: Scribner.

———. 1895. *The Religions of Japan: From the Dawn of History to the Era of Méiji.* New York: Charles Scribner's Sons.

———. 1907. *The Japanese Nation in Evolution: Steps in the Progress of a Great People.* New York: Thomas Y. Crowell.

———. 1911a. *China's Story in Myth, Legend, Art, and Annals.* Boston: Houghton Mifflin.

———. 1911b. *The Unmannerly Tiger, and Other Korean Tales.* New York: Thomas Y. Crowell.

———. 1912. *A Modern Pioneer in Korea: The Life Story of Henry G. Appenzeller.* New York: Fleming H. Revell.

———. 1922. *Korean Fairy Tales.* New York: Thomas Y. Crowell.

Griffis, William Elliot, and Hendrik Hamel. 1885. *Corea, without and within: Chapters on Corean History, Manners, and Religion.* Philadelphia: Presbyterian Board of Publication.

———. 1885. *Corea, Without and Within: Chapters on Corean History, Manners, and Religion.* Philadelphia: Presbyterian Board of Publication.

Hong, I-sŏp 洪以燮. 1962. "Kumiin ŭi Han'guk yŏsŏnggwan" 歐美人의 韓國 女性觀. *Asia yŏsŏng yŏn'gu* 아시아여성연구 1 (December): 17–31.

"JTWE Digital Guide" ["Digital Guide: Japan Through Western Eyes: Manuscript Records of Traders, Travellers, Missionaries and Diplomats, 1853–1941: Parts 2–5: The William Elliott Griffis Papers from Rutgers University Library"]. Adam Mathew Publications. Accessed on August 20th, 2019. http://www.ampltd.co.uk/digital_guides/japan_through_western_eyes/index.aspx.

Kim, Chong-chŏl 김종철. 2008. "Kŭrip'isŭ sujip Han'guk kojŏn sosŏl tu p'yŏn kwa Kŭrip'isuŭ ŭi Han'guk sŏrhwajip" 그리피스 수집 한국 고전소설 두 편과 그리피스의 한국 설화집. Presentation at the workshop Korean Materials of the William Elliot Griffis Collection, Rutgers University, March 14th, 2008.

Kim, Hŭi-yŏng 金喜永. 2011. "Kaehwagi sŏyangindŭl ŭi Tonghak insik: Kidokkyo ŭi yŏnghyang kwa kwallyŏnhayŏ" 개화기 서양인들의 동학 인식: 기독교의 영향과 관련하여. *Tonghak yŏn'gu* 동학연구 30 (June): 51–69.

Kim, Kyŏng-ae 김경애. 2014. "100-yŏnyŏn chŏn 'kŭndae Chosŏn mosŭp' pongin p'uldŏn sun'gan chŏnyul" 100여년 전 '근대 조선 모습' 봉인 풀던 순간 전율. *Han'gyŏrye* 한겨레 (December 21st, 2014). Accessed June 23rd, 2015. http://www.hani.co.kr/arti/culture/religion/670129.html.

Kim, Sang-min 김상민. 2008. "Kaehwa Ilchegi Han'guk kwallyŏn sŏyang munhŏn e nat'anan Han'guk insik yangt'ae yŏn'gu" 개화일제기 한국관련 서양문헌에 나타난 한국인식양태연구. PhD diss., Myŏngji Taehakkyo 명지대학교.

Kim, Su-t'ae 김수태. 2006. "Williŏm Kŭrip'isŭ ŭi Ŭndun *ŭi nara, Han'guk*—Han'guk kodaesa sŏsul ŭl chungsim ŭro" 윌리엄 그리피스의 『은둔의 나라, 한국』—한국 고대사 서술을 중심으로. Presentation at P'ŭrinsŭt'ŏn Han'gyŏrye munhwa kangjwa 프린스턴 한겨레문화강좌 45, June 16th, 2006.

———. 2010. "Williŏm Kŭrip'isŭ ŭi Han'guk kŭndaesa insik" 윌리엄 그리피스의 한국 근대사 인식. *Chindan hakpo* 진단학보 110 (December): 125–56.

Kim, Yun-sik 김윤식. 2008. *"Ŭnja ŭi nara Han'guk* ŭi chŏja Kŭrip'isŭ ege ponaen Pak Ŭn-sik, Yi Kwang-su yŏnmyŏng ŭi p'yŏnji" <은자의 나라 한국>의 저자 그리피스에게 보낸 박은식·이광수 연명의 편지. *Munhak sasang* 문학사상 (November): 21–27.

King, Ross. 2019. "'Photographs of Mind' and 'Photographs Taken on the Soil': William Elliot Griffis, Korean Language, Writing and Literature, and Koreans in Russia." *Photographs of Korea in the William Elliot Griffis Collection.* Eds. Sang Hyun Yang and Young-mee Yu. Seoul: Noonbit Publishing: 447–466.

Lee, Yeong-Mi. 2015. "W. E. Griffis' Understanding of Korea, and East Asia." PhD diss., Inha University.

O, Yun-sŏn 오윤선. 2010. "*Tan'gun sinhwa* Yŏngyŏkcha ŭi sigak ilgoch'al" < 단군신화 *(檀君神話)*> 영역자(英譯者)의 시각(視角) 일고찰. *Kukche ŏmun* 국제어문 48 (April): 67–100.

———. 2012. "Kŭndae ch'ogi Han'guk sŏrhwa Yŏngyŏkchadŭl ŭi pŏnyŏk t'aedo yŏn'gu—Allen, Griffis, Hulbert, Carpenter rŭl chungsim ŭro" 근대초기 한국설화 영역자들의 번역태도 연구—Allen, Griffis, Hulbert, Carpenter 를 중심으로. *Tonghwa wa pŏnyŏk* 동화와 번역 23: 205–31.

———. 2014. "19-segi mal 20-segi ch'o Yŏngmun Han'guk sŏrhwa ŭi charyojŏk kach'i yŏn'gu" 19세기말 20세기초 영문(英文) 한국설화의 자료적 가치 연구. *Urimunhak yŏn'gu* 우리문학연구 41 (January): 145–79.

Park, Sungmin and Young-mee Yu Cho. 2019. "William Elliot Griffis and His Visit to Korea in 1927." *Photographs of Korea in the William Elliot Griffis*

Collection. Eds. Sang Hyun Yang and Young-mee Yu. Seoul: Noonbit Publishing: 366–391.

Pennanen, Henna Riikka. 2013. "Building a Career in and out of East Asia: 19th Century American Experts S. W. Williams and W. E. Griffis." *Migukhak nonjip* 미국학논집 45, no. 1: 371–98.

Rutgers University Libraries. William Elliot Griffis Collection. Rutgers University Libraries. Accessed June 23rd, 2015. https://www.libraries.rutgers.edu/rul/libs/scua/griffis/griff.shtml.

Sim, Huigi. 2008. "Rare Books and Pamphlets in the William Elliot Griffis Collection." Presentation at the workshop Korean materials of the William Elliot Griffis Collection, Rutgers University, March 14th, 2008.

Sim, Hŭi-gi 심희기. 2008. "Williŏm Elliŏt' ŭ Kŭrip'isŭ (William Elliot Griffis) kŏlleksyŏn ŭi hŭigwi sŏjŏk kwa soch'aekcha." 윌리엄 엘리어트 그리피스 (William Elliot Griffis) 컬렉션의 희귀서적과 소책자. Presentation at "Workshop on the Korean Materials of the William Elliot Griffis Collection," Rutgers University, March 14th, 2008.

Sin, Hyŏng-sik 申瀅植. 1987. "Ilche ch'ogi Miguk sŏn'gyosa ŭi Han'gukkwan: Griffis ŭi *Corea, The Hermit Nation* ŭl chungsim ŭro" 日帝初期 美國 宣教師의 韓國觀: Griffis 의 *Corea, The Hermit Nation* 을 中心으로. *Chuje yŏn'gu*主題硏究 14: 25–38.

Yang, Sang-hyŏn, Pak So-yŏn, and Yu Yŏng-mi 梁尙鉉, 朴素姸, and 劉永美. 2014. "Kŭrip'isŭ kŏlleksyŏn e sojangdoeŏ innŭn Han'guk kŭndae sajin charyo ŭi haksulchŏk kach'i e taehan koch'al" 그리피스 컬렉션에 소장되어 있는 한국 근대 사진자료의 학술적 가치에 대한 고찰. *Han'guk kŭnhyŏndaesa yŏn'gu* 한국근현대사연구 71 (December): 7–50.

Yi, Pyŏng-do 이병도. 1918. "Toksŏ ugam" 讀書偶感. *Hakchigwang* 학지광 15 (March): 398–415.

Yi, Tae-Jin. 1998. "Was Korea Really a 'Hermit Nation'?" *Korea Journal* 38, no. 4: 5–35.

———. 1999. "Kŭndae Han'guk ŭn kwayŏn 'ŭndun'guk'iŏttŏn'ga?" 근대 한국은 과연 '은둔국'이었던가? *Han'guksaron* 한국사론 41, 42: 717–49.

Yi, Yŏng-mi 이영미. 2010. "Han-Mi sugyo ijŏn sŏyangindŭl ŭi Han'guk yŏksa sŏsul" 朝-美 修交 이전 서양인들의 한국 역사 서술. *Han'guksa yŏn'gu* 한국사연구 148 (March): 169–97.

———. 2014. "Ilbon ŭi Han'guk chibae e taehan Kŭrip'isŭ ŭi t'aedo" 일본의 한국 지배에 대한 그리피스의 태도. *Han'guksa yŏn'gu* 한국사연구 166 (September): 271–97.

———. 2015. "Kŭrip'isŭ (1843-1928) ŭi Han'guk insik kwa Tong Asia" 그리피스 (1843-1928) 의 한국 인식과 동아시아. PhD diss., Inha Taehakkyo 인하대학교.

Yook, Young Soo. 2011. "Fin de Siècle Korea as Exhibited at the World's Columbian Exposition of 1893 in Chicago Revisited." *Seoul Journal of Korean Studies* 24, no. 1 (June): 1–27.

Yu, Hwang-t'ae 류황태. 2010. "Kŭrip'isŭ rŭl t'onghae pon Han-Il kwan'gye" 그리피스를 통해 본 한일관계. *Migukhak nonjip* 미국학논집 42, no. 3: 107–31.

Yu, Yŏng-mi 유영미 (Cho, Young-mee Yu). 2008. "Kŭrip'isŭ ŭi Han'gugŏ e taehan ihae" 그리피스의 한국어에 대한 이해 [William E. Griffis on the Korean language]. Presentation at workshop Korean Materials of the William Elliot Griffis Collection, Rutgers University, March 14, 2008.

15

Fissures in the Terrain

Revisiting the Cold War in East Asia in the Hoover Archives

Hsiao-ting Lin, Hoover Institution, Stanford University

Arising from post–World War II tensions between the United States and Soviet Russia, the Cold War rivalry between the two nations lasted for much of the second half of the twentieth century, resulting in mutual suspicion, heightened apprehension, and a series of international incidents that brought the world's two superpowers to the brink of disaster. The Cold War came to an end in the early 1990s as a consequence of the Soviet dissolution, yet its legacies, politically, economically, institutionally, and culturally, can still be felt in world politics today.[1] In the past two decades, the trickle of historical source materials from the defunct Soviet Union and its former satellite states has allowed scholars to develop new theses and perspectives from the post–Cold War vantage point; as a result, a "new" Cold War history—to borrow a term from historian John Lewis Gaddis—came into being.[2]

It may be premature, however, to exclaim that a new Cold War history has indeed taken root in the study of the war's Asian theater. Fortunately, with new Chinese source materials having become available at the Hoover Institution Archives during the past decade, reinterpreting the Cold War in East Asia, with an emphasis on the roles played by Chiang Kai-shek and the Kuomintang (KMT), the Taiwan-based Chinese Nationalist government, has become both practicable and necessary. To speak of the Cold War in Asia is to position Asia's history in the complicated rivalry between the two superpowers. Yet, as Hoover's newly accessible archival materials indicate, during the Cold War, when an Asian country's internal systems were conditioned by the interests and decisions of the superpowers, its actions also may have been driven by its domestic concerns, such as nationalism, independence, and nation building. Thus the received wisdom that depicts Asia's Cold War as a dichotomy of confrontation between two major contending ideologies (communism and liberal capitalism), two political powers (the United States and the Soviet Union), and their client states deserves further scrutiny and reconsideration.

The purpose of this chapter is to sift through several personal papers at the Hoover Archives and raise fresh insights into the study of the Cold War in East Asia. Relatively little known and understudied, these "hidden" archival treasures disclose an unfamiliar political, military, and diplomatic landscape that in all likelihood will change the way we understood the region during the Cold War. These archival materials also provide scholars everywhere with glimpses into a previously unknown historical scenario in East Asia, enriching our understanding of the intricate Cold War politics in that part of the world.

Secret Japanese Military Advisers

The year 1949 was a dark one for the Chinese Nationalist government. Having gained little military advantage against the Chinese Communist forces led by Mao Zedong, and struggling politically as well, Chiang Kai-shek stepped down that January. But even in this semiretirement Chiang kept the reins of power largely intact as the head of the KMT. In the fall of 1949, for example, he instructed a trusted military subordinate in Tokyo to organize a "New Army," consisting of former Japanese imperial soldiers, as a completely trustworthy and loyal new force to serve his anticommunist cause.[3] No New Army was formed in the subsequent months in light of the worsening situation on the Chinese mainland. By February 1950, however, two months after the Nationalist regime had retreated to the island refuge of Taiwan, eighteen Japanese ex-officers arrived surreptitiously in Taipei from Yokohama via Hong Kong. Those officers, under the leadership of Tomita Naosuke, formerly chief of staff for the Japanese Imperial Twenty-Third Army who had taken a Chinese name Bai Hongliang, formed the group dubbed Baituan (Bai's group), which began its military education and training program in Chiang's residual forces. A Military Officers' Training Corps was established at an obscure spot near Yuanshan, Taipei, where the Japanese military advisers undertook their unofficial, secret program.[4]

Chiang Kai-shek was convinced that no nation in the world understood China and the communist problems it faced better than the Japanese, who after all had fought a bitter war with the Chinese for eight years. That rationale may have been behind Chiang's decision to employ former Japanese imperial officers to train his demoralized force in Taiwan. But Baituan may also have made it possible for the Generalissimo to use Japanese influence to neutralize General Sun Liren, his able but often recalcitrant commander in chief of the Nationalist ground forces, who was the all-time US favorite. In the late 1940s and the early 1950s, rumors began flying that, with support from Uncle Sam, Sun would eventually kick the Generalissimo out in a coup and lead "Free China" (a synonym for Taiwan).[5]

To many Americans, the presence of Baituan was incredible given that Japan had been Chiang Kai-shek's arch-rival and deadly enemy not long ago. In the spring of 1951, shortly after the US Military Assistance Advisory Group (MAAG) was officially instituted in Taipei, the existence of Baituan, whose numbers had grown from eighteen to seventy-six, became one of the most pressing issues the Americans aimed to settle with Chiang.[6] As the Americans became aware that a main goal of the Baituan training program was to demonstrate that US methods, both political and military, were unsuited to China and that the Nationalists could learn more from Japan than from the United States in the military field, Washington saw Baituan's ousting as imperative.[7]

Faced with strong US pressure, in July 1952 Chiang Kai-shek ordered Baituan to go even deeper underground. The training corps at Yuanshan was shut down, and its staff was reduced to about thirty. But the Japanese training program soon resumed in another place under the pretext of researching military theories and implementation. As the recently added increments to the Hoover Archives' Japanese manuscript collection reveal, Chiang continued to allow Baituan to play a crucial role. The Japanese military advisers were frequently invited to participate in planning the KMT's mainland counteroffensive and other secret military operations. Chiang even went so far as to share top-secret military intelligence with members of Baituan, notably those from the MAAG and the CIA, regarding Taiwan's national defense, guerrilla warfare, and raiding programs along China's southeast coast.[8]

Amazingly enough, the relocated Japanese military corps operated quietly for another seventeen years. Not until early 1969 were the last four Japanese advisers asked to end their training program and return to Japan. Estimates are that in the almost two decades of Baituan's existence in Taiwan, more than ten thousand of Chiang Kai-shek's high-ranking military officers had attended its training program. In the fall of 1972, when Japanese prime minister Kakuei Tanaka moved to normalize relations with Beijing and sever diplomatic ties with Taipei (as seen in the personal papers of Deng Zumou at the Hoover Archives), former members of Baituan were a crucial factor in bridging the collapsing political, military, and intelligence ties between Taipei and Tokyo. In a joint letter to Deng, Taiwan's last military attaché in Tokyo, Baituan members pledged to serve as a useful channel of communications based on their shared anticommunist ideology, as well as to be a pressure group to check Prime Minister Tanaka's new China policy.[9] Until the early 1980s, in the absence of diplomatic relations, the surviving Baituan members continued to play a useful role in fostering friendship between Chiang Ching-kuo and senior statesmen in Japan's political circles.

Secret German Military Advisers

The outbreak of the Korean War in June 1950 led to a game-changing contingency that prompted overnight rethinking by the Truman administration and its about-face on issues surrounding Taiwan. Washington's decision to interpose the Seventh Fleet in the Taiwan Strait became a critical linchpin on which Chiang Kai-shek and his hitherto abandoned Nationalist cohorts could build their hopes. In the following decades, Chiang relied heavily on the United States to defend and consolidate his island redoubt against a Communist invasion.[10] Under the facade of an ostensibly formidable US-Taiwan Cold War alliance, however, from time to time Chiang would turn to his erstwhile enemies in World War II for military advice. Relying members of Baituan from 1950 to 1969 enhanced Chiang's innate distrust of the US government and his instinct to undermine US influence as much as possible.

The covert use of Japanese ex-officers was by no means the only example of fissures in the US-Taiwan alliance during the Cold War. Beginning in the early 1960s, as the Hoover Archives' Yue-che Wang Papers disclose, without consent from Washington or joint consultation with the MAAG, Chiang Kai-shek hired former German officers as his personal advisers to train, lecture, and assess the US-equipped Taiwanese military forces. His reasons were both philosophical and practical; Chiang was fretful that the thinking of US warfare, hinging on its superior war materials and weaponry, would be unsuitable for his tiny island state. As Chiang saw it, German forces were noted for prevailing against overwhelming odds with limited supplies.[11] In the spring of 1961, Chiang expressed his concerns to a senior representative named Reinhard Gehlen, then head of West Germany's Federal Intelligence Service (Bundesnachrichtendienst), seeking Gehlen's help in finding a candidate to serve as his personal military adviser. Gehlen recommended Walther Wenck, who had served as an aide to Hans von Seeckt, Chiang Kai-shek's military consultant in his war against the Chinese Communists between 1933 and 1935. Wenck then, for health reasons, recommended that his erstwhile comrade-in-arms Oskar Munzel take the position.[12]

Oskar Munzel stepped on Taiwanese soil for the first time in November 1963 and stayed for six months as Chiang Kai-shek's special adviser. Munzel, a highly decorated generalmajor in the Wehrmacht during World War II and General der Kampftruppen of the Bundeswehr who commanded all German army combat troops after the war, impressed his Nationalist hosts from the beginning. The Generalissimo especially enjoyed conversations with the German general concerning every aspect of the military issues surrounding Taiwan.[13] To work with the new German advisers under Munzel, a shadow office was discreetly created within Taiwan's military establishments and under the radar of the MAAG. Between 1965 and 1975, Munzel and his two successors, Paul Jordan and Kurt Kauffmann, led an unofficial German military advisory group of about twenty-four to reform Taiwan's armored forces, inspect Taiwan's military training, bridge military and intelligence cooperation between Taipei and Bonn, and transform the mind-set of Chiang's military echelons. The group also created a program under which Chiang began sending his military officers to study and intern in German military academies. Between 1964 and 1973, twenty-five officers had enrolled in this program. Among them, seventeen were promoted to the rank of general and served in Taiwan's key military and national security positions in the decades that followed.[14]

Toward the end of 1966, as President Lyndon Johnson began talking about a possible shift in America's China policy, a fretful Chiang Kai-shek deepened his reliance on his group of German military advisers. The personal papers of Wang Yue-che elucidate that an experimental infantry force at the battalion level was covertly forged under the supervision of Oskar Munzel sometime in late 1966. Trained, equipped, and exercised in German fashion, the experimental battalion quickly gained Chiang's favor. With extra military and financial resources pouring in and in a state of combat readiness, the German-led infantry force caught the Americans' attention. For several weeks in the spring of 1969, MAAG officials frequented the battalion for inspections, suspecting, wrongly as it turned out, that Chiang was secretly preparing for a mainland counterattack.[15]

While its Japanese counterpart ended its secret advisory role in Taiwan in 1969, the German group was still at work well into the mid-1970s, four years after Taipei was expelled from the United Nations and Bonn had normalized its relations with the People's Republic of China. It was disbanded in December 1975, eight months after Chiang Kai-shek's death. Perhaps Chiang Ching-kuo, now the de facto leader of Taiwan, no longer deemed it vital to retain the Germans.[16] Between 1971 and 1975, however, the advisory group had functioned as a critical, albeit unofficial, channel of communications between Taiwan and West Germany at a time when Taiwan was suffering disastrous blows to its international status and becoming isolated.[17] Whether Chinese Nationalist leaders resorted to their existing connections with West German military establishments to procure urgently needed ammunition, including sensitive devices for developing nuclear weapons, when the Nixon White House was preparing to open US relations with Communist China, deserves future investigation.

Secret Rendezvous between Taipei and Moscow

Since the mid-1960s, the split between Moscow and Beijing had widened such that both sides were increasing their troop deployments along the Sino-Soviet and Sino-Mongolian borders. By the end of 1968, both sides had several hundred thousand troops on their mutual frontier. The Soviet invasion of Czechoslovakia in August of that same year and Moscow's enunciation of the Brezhnev Doctrine of "limited sovereignty," which justified Soviet armed intervention to prevent the overthrow of a communist government, sent a serious warning to Mao Zedong and his cohorts.[18] In Taipei, Chiang Kai-shek, carefully watching the Sino-Soviet relationship, predicted that Moscow would take military action against the Communist mainland after its invasion of Czechoslovakia. Chiang sought to explore a "Russia option" by dispatching a Russian-speaking cabinet official to Mexico to meet with local Soviet diplomats. By early September 1968, Chiang had learned through his Mexican channel that the Soviets were eager to overthrow Mao Zedong's rule on the mainland, and that a joint collaboration with Taiwan was apparently a serious option to the Kremlin.[19] The timing could not have been worse for the US-Taiwan alliance; almost simultaneously, Arthur Goldberg, US ambassador to the United Nations, urged in a commentary in the *Washington Post* that Washington adopt a "two-Chinas" formula to solve the China representation dilemma in the coming UN session. Goldberg's point deepened Chiang's concerns about the shift of stance on the part of the Johnson White House vis-à-vis China, serving to strengthen Taipei's ties with the Soviets, whom Chiang had long castigated as the source of all evil in Asia since 1949.[20]

Thus, in October 1968, when Victor Louis, the Moscow correspondent for the *London Evening Star* and clearly a KGB agent, requested an entry visa to visit Taiwan from Tokyo, Chiang Kai-shek gave him a green light. James Wei, a confidant of Chiang Ching-kuo whose personal papers are among the many treasures in the Hoover Archives, became Louis's point of contact. According to Wei's diaries, Louis's message was that the Nationalists and the Soviets should explore ways to cooperate so as to bring about the downfall of Mao Zedong.[21] Chiang Ching-kuo, who met with Louis on October 29, responded by stating that because the United States was trying to open relations with Beijing and would never allow Taipei to launch a counterattack against China, and because Mao Zedong's regime posed a serious threat to the Nationalist government on Taiwan, there was room for negotiations between Taipei and Moscow. But the Generalissimo's son also made known to Louis his father's difficulties in engaging with the Soviets. As a result, all the future bilateral communications were to be conducted in secret.[22]

In the spring of 1969, a deterioration in Soviet relations with Communist China resulted in military clashes over Zhenbao Island (Damansky) on the Ussuri River. The episode became a turning point that hastened the new Nixon

White House's reconfiguration of its grand triangular strategy toward Beijing and Moscow, as Henry Kissinger divulged years later.[23] The clash also sped up the pace of clandestine negotiations between the Nationalists and the Soviets. In early May 1969, Wei's personal journal reveals, Chiang Kai-shek's secret agents in West Germany reported that after the border clash members of the Soviet Politburo such as Alexander Shelepin and Petro Shelest began advocating an approach to Taiwan as a way to encircle and pressure Mao's China. A directive was duly formulated within the Politburo suggesting that a secret pact be forged between the Soviets and Chiang Kai-shek in order to launch a joint action against Mao Zedong, and that Moscow should encourage the Nationalists on Taiwan to join anti-Mao factions in the Chinese Communist Party to form a coalition government once Mao was overthrown.[24]

This piece of intelligence, whatever its authenticity, prompted the Chiangs, father and son, to work out five points of cooperation vis-à-vis Moscow, the basis of which was that Chiang Kai-shek would collaborate with the anti-Mao elements on the mainland to organize a "post-Mao" coalition government but only if the Nationalists dominated the coalition free of intervention from Moscow.[25] On May 14, bringing the terms of cooperation with him, James Wei flew to Vienna to meet in secret with Victor Louis. Although he was evasive about Chiang's message regarding Moscow-Taipei cooperation, Louis urged Taipei to begin a military intelligence exchange program with Moscow and submit a list of munitions Chiang wished to procure from the Soviets as first steps toward overthrowing Mao.[26]

In the weeks following the Vienna rendezvous, Louis pushed Taipei to devise a military plan to attack the Chinese mainland, going so far as to promise that the leaders in the Kremlin were ready to allow Chiang's troops to use some of Soviet Russia's military bases.[27] In August 1969, Soviet border patrols raided their Communist Chinese counterparts on the Kazakh-Xinjiang border, resulting in a minor skirmish. When the news reached Taipei, Chiang was convinced that it was time to consider restoring full diplomatic ties with Soviet Russia. In Chiang's eyes, destroying Communist China's nuclear facilities would mutually benefit both Taipei and Moscow.[28] When James Wei, again bearing Chiang's message about cooperation, arrived at Rome in early October for another secret discussion with Louis, the KGB spy failed to show up. Louis explained his absence in a coded telegram to Wei declaring that Rome was an unsafe place for such a highly sensitive meeting. The true reason, perhaps, was that the Kremlin did not want to cause additional trouble when tensions between Beijing and Moscow were easing thanks to a September meeting between premiers Alexei Kosygin and Zhou Enlai in Beijing.[29]

Clandestine communications between Taipei and Moscow continued for the next several years. In late October 1970, James Wei and Victor Louis met again in Vienna. Louis informed Wei that there was a split within the Soviet Politburo between the hawks, led by Leonid Brezhnev, who favored developing closer relations with Chiang Kai-shek as a way to checkmate Mao Zedong, and the doves, headed by Kosygin, who preferred to mend relations with Beijing and thus opposed the Taiwan option. Despite the murky political landscape in the Politburo, Victor Louis proposed a draft document of cooperation for Taipei, the underlying message of which was clear: because President Richard Nixon would never agree to Chiang's military recovery of the Chinese mainland, the Soviet Union would be the only power in the world willing to help Chiang fulfill that goal. Louis again pressed Taipei to present its matériel, logistic, and personnel requests to Moscow as soon as possible.[30]

In the early 1970s, as it became obvious that the Nixon administration was going out of its way to improve US-China relations at the expense of Taiwan, Chiang Kai-shek retained the Soviet option in reaction to the unfavorable international situation. Shortly after James Wei returned from Vienna, the Chiangs, father and son, decided to accept Louis's proposals without delay. They now agreed to ask Moscow for Soviet-made weapons and ammunition on the condition that the Soviets provide advisory assistance and training for the Taiwanese forces. In return for the Soviet military aid, Chiang's forces would target Communist Chinese military bases in Shanghai, Nanjing, Wuhan, and Guangzhou. Around mid-November 1970, Chiang instructed Wei to relay the above message to Louis via a secret contact in Bangkok.[31]

Suddenly, just as Chiang Kai-shek turned serious in his negotiations with the Soviets, Moscow lost interest. Unbeknownst to Taipei, the Russians and Chinese Communists had begun negotiations to settle the border dispute, with a treaty signed on December 18. That treaty lessened the prospect of war between the Soviet Union and China, making Moscow's approach to Taiwan for military cooperation less urgent.[32] The border settlement, however, did not have much effect on the hostile relations between the two communist nations. The Russians continued to engage in secret talks with Taiwan, through Louis and Wei, who had resumed contact, as well as through other channels in Mexico City and Tokyo. In a desperate attempt to increase Taiwan's ability to survive in a deteriorating international situation, the Chiangs continued their exploratory yet increasingly sporadic contact with the Russians, though not as earnestly as before. But nothing of substance came of it. In the spring of 1972, when Victor Louis requested an entry visa to revisit Taipei, the Chiangs turned him down, ending the poker game for good.[33]

Taiwan's Cold War in Asia

In the 1970s, as the Cold War gradually transformed into détente owing to the general easing of tensions between Washington and Moscow and Washington and Beijing, the status of Taiwan, along with the political legitimacy of the ruling KMT, was reduced to a minimum. Although they were still seeking an alliance with the United States, Taiwan's leaders also explored other foreign policy alternatives. The secret communication between Taipei and Moscow in the late 1960s and the early 1970s resulted in a brief political flap in the spring of 1972 when Chiang Kai-shek's foreign minister, answering a reporter's question about Nixon's historic trip to Beijing, said that Taipei might have its own "Warsaw talks" but with Moscow.[34] Although Chiang Ching-kuo, who at this juncture was substantially in charge of Taiwan's national affairs, determined that it had no alternative but to live with the new US approach toward the Chinese mainland, he was also resolute about seeking to reduce Taiwan's dependence on the United States. The Chiangs were aware that, as Taipei had been expelled from the United Nations and had lost almost all its important seats in international organizations, there was no way to prevent a diplomatic landslide or stop Taiwan's allies from switching diplomatic recognition to Beijing. But they were convinced that Taiwan's national security could best be preserved if anticommunism continued to be a predominant ideological force in East Asia, where Taiwan's military and intelligence cooperation with its neighbors was threatened by communism, no matter whether diplomatic links existed or not.

Wang Sheng, best known for his close friendship with Chiang Ching-kuo, which began in the late 1930s, was entrusted to undertake Taiwan's military and intelligence diplomacy in the 1970s. In 1939 Wang had joined the KMT and been sent to join the Three Principles of the People Youth Corps training course run by Chiang Ching-kuo. After the course, Wang was chosen to work for Chiang, which he did for the next fifty years, including assuming responsibility for the the care of Chiang's twin sons, the result of an extramarital affair. In the 1950s, Wang established the precursor to the General Political Warfare College, the elite training school for Nationalist army and party cadres. Second in command of the civil-military programs, welfare, and services section of Chiang Ching-kuo's cadre system, Wang's main task was laying the foundation for the China Youth Corps under Ching-kuo's leadership. He spent most of the 1950s and 1960s training army political cadres, helping the Chiangs reinforce their anticommunist ideology in every corner of Taiwan's military.[35]

Wang Sheng made his name as a prominent anticommunist in the Cold War's Asian theater when he was slated to export and transplant Taiwan's political warfare system to South Vietnam. In early 1961, at the request of Ngo Dinh Diem, the president of South Vietnam, Wang led seven KMT officers in inaugurating a series of anticommunist political and psychological training programs in

Saigon to strengthen anticommunist ideology and consciousness in the South Vietnamese forces.[36] The program, which subsequently became an official military advisory group, signified the beginning of what Chiang Kai-shek described as an interdependent anticommunist alliance between Taiwan and South Vietnam. In the spring of 1975, as Saigon was about to be captured by the North Vietnamese, Taiwan was the only country in the world that still had an unofficial military advisory group there to assist the hapless South Vietnamese government in its doomed defense against the North.[37]

In March 1970, following a military coup against Prince Norodom Sihanouk, an anticommunist regime was established in Cambodia under General Lon Nol. Delighted to see an anticommunist regime emerging in Indochina, Chiang Kai-shek assigned Wang Sheng the task of forging ties between Taipei and Phnom Penh. The Nixon administration, in the midst of its endeavor to expand relations with China, strongly objected to Taipei's attempt to establish diplomatic relations with Lon Nol lest the move provoke a Communist invasion of Cambodia and agitate nonaligned governments in Southeast Asia. Thus, a Taiwanese military mission, rather than an embassy, was installed in Phnom Penh to promote bilateral cooperation. Wang Sheng's papers reveal that Lon Nol was so determined to introduce Taiwan's political warfare system into his army that he wanted to do it regardless of whether his American patrons liked it or not. Beginning in September 1972, Wang's personnel began streaming into Cambodia to kick-start a psychological and political warfare training program at the expense of Taiwan's government budget. That cooperation soon expanded to several other fields, including intelligence gathering, mass mobilization, sabotage, raids, and infiltration.[38] But those training programs did little to prevent Lon Nol's regime from deteriorating, largely owing to external threats and internal power struggles. Wang Sheng conducted his last inspection trip to Cambodia in December 1974, only to witness the rapid worsening of morale and local economic and security conditions.[39] On the eve of the collapse of the Lon Nol regime in mid-April 1975, Taiwan was the last country to evacuate its mission from Phnom Penh.

The fall of Indochina to the Communists in the spring of 1975 increased Chiang Ching-kuo's urgency in implementing Taiwan's secret military and intelligence diplomacy. Between mid-1975 and the early 1980s, Wang Sheng made many clandestine visits to virtually every noncommunist state in Southeast Asia, including Thailand (1975 and 1982), Indonesia (1975), the Philippines (1979), and Malaysia (1982), where he met with top leaders and discussed military and intelligence cooperation. In Manila, President Ferdinand Marcos told Wang that he would not allow international politics to affect the close collaboration between the two countries, including, according to Wang's personal papers, Taiwan's arms exports to the Philippines, the training of Filipino soldiers, and a joint intelligence-gathering program aimed at the People's Republic of China.[40] In Kuala Lumpur, Prime Minister Mahathir Mohamad told Wang Sheng that he wanted Malaysia to learn from Taiwan's anticommunist ideology and experience and asked Taipei for assistance in pacifying Malayan communist forces. Other Malaysian military chiefs requested Wang's help in building Malaysia's electronic warfare and veterans service systems and asked Taiwan to play an advisory role in Malaysia's military training programs. Those collaborations, as Mahathir asserted, could be achieved even in the absence of formal diplomatic relations between Taipei and Kuala Lumpur.[41]

The personal papers of Wang Shang also reveal for the first time the mysterious role the Liu Shaokang Office—a small, unlabeled unit under the supervision of the KMT party's secretary-general charged with working out possible counteroffensives against the Communists in the early 1980s—had played. The normalization of relations between Washington and Beijing in January 1979, followed by Beijing's peace overtures toward Taiwan, prompted an anxious Chiang Ching-kuo to find a way out; the creation of the Liu Shaokang Office was one such resolution. When Wang Sheng was first charged with heading the office in early 1979, his purpose was merely to conduct a thorough study of the mainland situation and how Taiwan could cope with it. The office itself had no command authority, was ad hoc in nature, and needed to draw personnel from other offices on a loan basis.[42]

Within a relatively short period of time, the Liu Shaokang Office exceeded its original mandate. As the treasures in the Wang Sheng Collection indicate, the office did not deal simply with the Communist peace offer or threat but covered a wide range of issues, including overseas Chinese affairs, military intelligence, espionage and infiltration on the Chinese mainland, education and ideology on Taiwan, and party, government, military, and foreign affairs.[43] The office was thus transformed into a policy advisory body, a think tank, serving Chiang Ching-kuo and the upper KMT leadership. As such, it tapped the brightest minds in Taiwan to advise on virtually any policy question. The power of the office was such that it was dubbed the inner court of the KMT party headquarters, and Wang Sheng's position was seen as second only to that of President Chiang Ching-kuo. In March 1983, when the Reagan administration invited Wang to tour the United States, military-intelligence quarters in Washington DC and mass media outlets such as *Newsweek* also began describing him as Chiang's heir apparent. Five months later, in August 1983, when Chiang decided to send Wang to Paraguay as Taiwan's ambassador, it not only marked the end of the Liu Shaokang Office but also the end of Wang's special role in Taiwan's politics.[44]

Dual Developments: Democratization and Cross-Strait Relations in the Cold War's Last Stage

Along with the January 1979 worsening of diplomatic relations between Taipei and Washington, there was a resurgence of anti-KMT sentiments throughout Taiwan. The political opposition saw Taiwan's lack of diplomatic recognition as damaging the ruling party's claim to power. It argued that the Americans had walked out on the Nationalist government and that Taiwan was isolated, weak, and in danger of being turned over to Beijing because of KMT claims that it was the legitimate government of all China. The end result of the increased opposition pressure was the Kaohsiung demonstrations on Human Rights Day in December 1979.[45] According to reminiscences of US State Department staff posted to Taiwan under the newly created American Institute there, the KMT enticed the opposition into instigating a street riot and then crushed it under martial law. Also swept up in the government crackdown and tried in a military court was the leadership of the pro-independence Presbyterian Church of Taiwan.[46] From 1979 on, the worst aspects of the authoritarian government that had been in place since 1949 were exhibited to the fullest.

In February 1980, the family of one of the defendants in the 1979 Kaohsiung riots trial, Lin Yixiong, was slaughtered in his home. The KMT claimed to know nothing about it, even though Lin's house was under twenty-four-hour police surveillance. In July 1981, a Chinese American scholar and human rights advocate, Chen Wenchen, was found dead at the bottom of a five-story building while in police custody. The responsibility for his murder lay with one of the intelligence branches of the KMT government. All these events led to changes in the way the KMT governed Taiwan.[47] As the papers of Tian Chaoming in the Hoover Archives suggest, after about two decades of the *dangwai* (outside the KMT party) democracy movement, in which all members of the opposition who ran as candidates in KMT-sponsored elections had claimed the title, the anti-KMT movement gradually transformed itself into an organized and coordinated opposition political group. Tian, a Japanese-educated physician known for his efforts in promoting Taiwan's democracy, human rights, and political independence, was an eyewitness to the bloody incident of February 1947 when the KMT suppressed an antigovernment uprising in Taiwan. Tian thus became a lone dissident in the face of Nationalist authoritarian rule in the decades after 1949. When the opposition movement formed the Democratic Progressive Party on September 28, 1986, Tian was one of its pioneers.[48]

The upsurge of fierce anti-KMT sentiment and the party's brutal responses, including murder, prompted deep reflection on policy formulation and implementation within the ruling KMT itself, especially among the younger, American-educated elites who had advocated enlightened, or moderate, political procedures rather than strong-arm tactics.[49] Wei Yong, whose papers are among Hoover Archives' historical treasures, was a prominent example. A native of Hubei Province and an emigrant to Taiwan during the Chinese civil war, Wei earned his doctorate in political science from the University of Oregon in 1967 and, like numerous Taiwanese elites of his generation who had studied abroad, stayed to teach in the United States for several years. In 1974, Wei became the first non–US citizen to be awarded a National Fellowship at the Hoover Institution. At the invitation of then premier Chiang Ching-kuo, Wei returned to Taiwan the next year to serve as chairman of the Research, Development, and Evaluation Commission in the cabinet; he remained in that position for the following twelve years.

Presumably with Chiang Ching-kuo's consent or tacit permission, in 1980 Wei Yong put forward his innovative "multi-system nations" and "dual recognition" theories with a view to seeking a way out of Taiwan's increasingly difficult position vis-à-vis Beijing and to breaking the country's international isolation. The theme was that the different parts of a "divided nation" should be allowed proper international status before being unified.[50] Wei's theories triggered widespread debate and had an impact on Taiwan's foreign and cross-Strait policies in the final stage of the Cold War. The influence of the multi-system nations may have reached Deng Xiaoping, who advanced the "one country, two systems" formula in 1981 as the rubric under which China could unify with Taiwan.[51]

Thus, two very different figures, with different backgrounds and life paths, witnessed the dual track of Taiwan's internal and external development in the final years of the Cold War. Their personal papers, now in the Hoover Archives, reveal the painful process of Taiwan's democratization, as well as the transformation of the KMT's mainland policy from complete reclusiveness to a novel hypothesis that would lay the foundation for the subsequent massive interactions and exchanges across the Taiwan Strait in the post–Chiang Ching-kuo and post–Cold War era.

Concluding Remarks

What do the aforementioned personal papers in the Hoover Archives convey to a wider scholarly community? These archival treasures show numerous fissures in the Cold War's historical terrain and serve as rich source materials with which historians may challenge the previous interpretive frameworks in the study of the Cold War. They provide both evidence and an opportunity for scholars to reconsider the Cold War binary thinking in Asia that has simplified the intricate and intriguing political and military landscape in the region, overlooking the complicated intra-alliance between Taiwan and the United States.

Thanks to the Hoover Archives' treasures, we now know that during the Cold War Chiang Kai-shek acted against the will of his American patrons by secretly employing Japanese and German military advisers. We also know that top leaders in Taipei surreptitiously engaged in secret negotiations with their supposed sworn enemies in the Soviet Union for a possible joint action against Communist China years before President Richard Nixon's opening of relations with Beijing. We now know that in the 1970, the Chiangs, father and son, undertook a series of clandestine military and intelligence meetings with Taiwan's Asian neighbors as a way to break the country's increasingly unfavorable international position and national security. Those diplomatic endeavors were initiated regardless of whether or not official ties existed. Finally, the historical treasures in the Hoover Archives provide us with a glance into the contrast between Taiwan's democratization and political self-identification and the thawing of the cross-Strait relationship in the last decade of the Cold War. It is hoped that these hidden historical records can offer a first step toward comprehending the history of Cold War's East Asian theater, the repercussions and implications of which continue to be felt today.

Notes

[1] Carole K. Fink, *Cold War: An International History* (Boulder, CO: Westview, 2013), 1–4.

[2] John Lewis Gaddis, *We Now Know: Rethinking Cold War History* (Oxford: Oxford University Press, 1997), 238.

[3] Hsiao-ting Lin, "U.S.-Taiwan Military Diplomacy Revisited: Chiang Kai-shek, *Baituan*, and the 1954 Mutual Defense Pact," *Diplomatic History* 37, no. 5 (2013): 975–77.

[4] Barak Kushner, "Ghosts of the Japanese Imperial Army: The 'White Group' (Baituan) and Early Post-war Sino-Japanese Relations," *Past and Present*, supplement 8 (2013): 139–42.

[5] On the mysteries surrounding the coup against Chiang Kai-shek in the early 1950s, see, for example, Thomas J. Schoenbaum, *Waging Peace and War: Dean Rusk in the Truman, Kennedy, and Johnson Years* (New York: Simon and Schuster, 1988), 209; Ronald L. McGlothlen, *Controlling the Waves: Dean Acheson and US Foreign Policy in Asia* (New York: Norton, 1993), 104–27.

[6] Chiang Kai-shek diary entry for June 27, 1951, Chiang Kai-shek Diaries, Hoover Institution Archives, Stanford University (hereafter CKSD), Box 49.

[7] Lin, "U.S.-Taiwan Military Diplomacy," 977–78; Kushner, "Ghosts," 143–44.

[8] See Report on the activities of the KMT Mainland Affairs Division for the year 1952, April 30, 1953; Statistics on the Nationalist guerrillas on the mainland, May 2, 1953, both in the Japanese Modern History Manuscript Collection, Hoover Institution Archives, Stanford University, Box 96.

[9] See Joint letter from members of the former Baituan to Deng Zumou, December 1972, Deng Zumou Papers, Hoover Institution Archives, Stanford University, Box 1; Statement by the Japanese National Assembly toward the Republic of China, 1972 (n.d.), ibid.; materials relating to the Okamura Yasuji Comrade Association (n.d.), ibid.

[10] On the overall U.S.-Taiwan alliance during the Cold War, see John W. Garver, *The Sino-American Alliance: Nationalist China and American Cold War Strategy in Asia* (New York: M. E. Sharpe, 1997).

[11] See Wang Yue-che, "Chiang Wei-kuo's relations with the German Military Group" (1990), Wang Yue-che Papers, Hoover Institution Archives, Stanford University (hereafter Wang Yue-che Papers), Box 1.

[12] Transcript of an oral interview with Wang Yue-che, September 5, 2001 (Taipei), Wang Yue-che Papers, Box 2.

[13] Chiang Kai-shek diary entries for November 23, 1963, December 30, 1963, and April 1, 1964, CKSD, Box 70.

[14] Oskar Munzel, Erfahrungsbericht 1968, Wang Yue-che Papers, Box 1.

[15] Wang Yue-che, Review report on the German military advisory group, May 1976, Wang Yue-che Papers, Box 1.

[16] Transcript of an oral interview with Wang Yue-che, September 5, 2001 (Taipei), Wang Yue-che Papers, Box 2.

[17] Wang Yue-che, Review report on the German military advisory group, May 1976, Wang Yue-che Papers, Box 1.

[18] Mingjiang Li, *Mao's China and the Sino-Soviet Split: Ideological Dilemma* (London: Routledge, 2012), 135–52.

[19] Chiang Kai-shek diary entries for September 2, 7, and 12, 1968, CKSD, Box 74.

[20] Chiang Kai-shek diary entries for September 14 and 19, 1968, CKSD, Box 74.

[21] James Wei diary entries for October 23 and 24, 1968, James Wei Diaries, Hoover Institution Archives, Stanford University (hereafter JWD), Box 12.

[22] James Wei diary entry for October 26, 1968, JWD, Box 12.

[23] Henry Kissinger, *Diplomacy* (New York: Simon and Schuster, 1994), 722–24.

[24] James Wei diary entry for May 5, 1969, JWD, Box 11.

[25] Ibid.

[26] James Wei diary entry for May 15, 1969, JWD, Box 11.

[27] James Wei diary entry for September 20, 1969, JWD, Box 11; Chiang Kai-shek diary entries for July 23 and 28, 1969, CKSD, Box 75.

[28] Chiang Kai-shek diary entry for September 6, 1969, CKSD, Box 75.

[29] James Wei diary entry for October 16, 1969, JWD, Box 11; Chiang Kai-shek diary entry for November 25, 1969, CKSD, Box 75.

[30] James Wei diary entries for October 30 and 31, 1970, JWD, Box 12.

[31] Chiang Kai-shek diary entries for November 8 and 9, 1970, CKSD, Box 76; James Wei diary entry for November 13, 1970, JWD, Box 12.

[32] On the 1969 Sino-Soviet border conflict, see, for example, Yang Kuisong, "The Sino-Soviet Border Clash of 1969: From Zhenbao Island to Sino-American Rapprochement," *Cold War History* 1, no. 1 (2000): 21–52; Lyle J. Goldstein, "Return to Zhenbao Island: Who Started Shooting and Why It Matters." *China Quarterly*, no. 168 (2001): 985–97.

[33] Paul H. Tai, "The Russian Option," *Hoover Digest* 3 (2010): 186; Jay Taylor, *The Generalissimo: Chiang Kai-shek and the Struggle for Modern China* (Cambridge, MA: Harvard University Press, 2009), 578.

[34] Ralph N. Clough, *Island China* (Cambridge, MA: Harvard University Press, 1978), 168–72.

[35] Thomas A. Marks, *Counterrevolution in China: Wang Sheng and the Kuomintang* (London: Frank Cass, 1998), 37–39, 128–72.

[36] See The Vietnam Files, Wang Sheng Papers, Hoover Institution Archives, Stanford University (hereafter Wang Sheng Papers), Box 13.

[37] Chen Jian, *Foreign Policy of the New Taiwan: Pragmatic Diplomacy in Southeast Asia* (Cheltenham: Edward Elgar, 2002), 168–70.

[38] See The Visit to Cambodia File (1972), Wang Sheng Papers, Box 14.

[39] See The Visits to Cambodia and Thailand Files (1975), Wang Sheng Papers, Box 14.

[40] The Visit to the Philippines File, Wang Sheng Papers, Box 15.

[41] The Visits to Thailand and Malaysia Files, Wang Sheng Papers, Box 16.

[42] Marks, *Counterrevolution*, 256–62; Jay Taylor, *The Generalissimo's Son: Chiang Ching-kuo and the Revolutions in China and Taiwan* (Cambridge, MA: Harvard University Press, 2000), 374–75.

[43] Files regarding Chairman Chiang Ching-kuo's instructions, two vols., Wang Sheng Papers, Box 13.

[44] Marks, , 288–89.

[45] John F. Copper, *Taiwan: Nation-State or Province?* (Boulder, CO: Westview, 1999), 113–14; Richard C. Bush, *At Cross Purposes: U.S.-Taiwan Relations since 1942* (New York: M. E. Sharpe, 2004), 76–77.

[46] Nancy Bernkopf Tucker, ed., *China Confidential: American Diplomats and Sino-American Relations, 1945–1996* (New York: Columbia University Press, 2001), 422–23.

[47] Hung-mao Tien, *The Great Transition: Political and Social Change in the Republic of China* (Stanford, CA: Hoover Institution Press, 1989), 95–101.

[48] See correspondence between Tian Chaoming and members of his family in the 1980s in the Tian Chaoming Papers, Hoover Institution Archives, Stanford University, Boxes 2 and 3.

[49] For a detailed discussion, see Edwin A. Winckler, "Elite Political Struggle, 1945–1985," in *Contending Approaches to the Political Economy of Taiwan*, ed. Edwin A. Winckler and Susan Greenhalgh (New York: M. E. Sharpe, 1988), 151–74.

[50] See Wei Yong's writings on "multi-system nations" and "dual recognition" in the Wei Yong Papers, Hoover Institution Archives, Stanford University, Boxes 12 and 13.

[51] For more information about Wei Yong, see his website www.yungwei.url.tw (accessed May 7, 2014).

16

Primary Sources for the Study of the Sino-Japanese War (1937–1945) in the Library of Congress

Yuwu Song, Library of Congress

Constituting one of the most destructive components of World War II, the Sino-Japanese War (1937–45) started with the Marco Polo Bridge Incident of July 7, 1937 and ended with the surrender of Japan in the fall of 1945. This war marked the culmination of growing Japanese aggression toward China since the First Sino-Japanese War (1894–95). With an estimated 20 million Chinese dead and 480,000 Japanese soldiers killed, the eight-year conflict was one of the bloodiest in world history.

Over the years, the Library of Congress has collected a large amount of materials related to the Sino-Japanese War, including books, newspapers, periodicals, photos, moving pictures, sound recordings, manuscripts, archives, and maps. Although the library has a rich lode of information and materials about the Sino-Japanese War, they have not been fully explored. Because of the scattering of materials all over the library, it is hard for researchers to locate and identify the relevant items. This chapter is intended to provide research clues for locating original sources in various formats concerning the Sino-Japanese War in the collections at the Library of Congress so researchers will be better informed about the nature and content of those collections. It is hoped that scholars can make groundbreaking achievements in their respective academic fields by digging deep into these sources, especially primary sources, so as to rediscover the forgotten or lesser-known history under study.

The Asian Division

With the largest and most comprehensive collection of Asian-language materials outside Asia, the library's Asian Division contains books, periodicals, newspapers, manuscripts, and microfilms. The division has in its holdings 6,667 titles in Chinese published from 1931, when the Japanese army invaded China, to the end of the war in 1945. They cover almost all facets of history and life in wartime China: politics, the economy, the military, international relations, society, the home front, intelligence, mass media, and so on. A crucial part of the resources on the war derives from the materials seized by the American occupying forces under General Douglas MacArthur from 1945 to 1952, during which time around 300,000 volumes of Japanese-language research materials were added with the transfer of resources sent initially to the Washington Document Center (WDC), an operational entity established at the end of the war to take care of captured Japanese records. These materials contain extensive research reports prepared by the South Manchurian Railway Company and the East Asia Research Institute, Japan's most important research organs at that time. Many of these materials are pre–World War II studies on China and its surrounding regions that show Japanese civil and military activities leading up to the conflict between the two countries. Included in this collection are Japanese Army and Navy publications, censored materials from the former Japanese Ministry of Home Affairs, and other important collections vital to research on Japanese history before and during World War II.

The Asian Division also keeps newspapers and periodicals in the Chinese and Japanese languages. The *Central Daily,* published in China, shows how the war was being reported to the Chinese people while Japanese newspapers such as the *Asahi Shinbun, Mainichi Shinbun*, and *Yomiuri Shinbun* provide journalistic accounts of the war from the Japanese perspective. Some of the library's unique collections are presented in figures 16.1, 16.2, and 16.3.

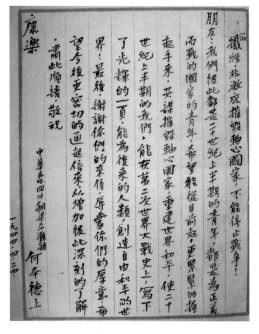

Figure 16.1. A letter from the collection of greetings from the Chinese people to the American people (Asian Division, Library of Congress).

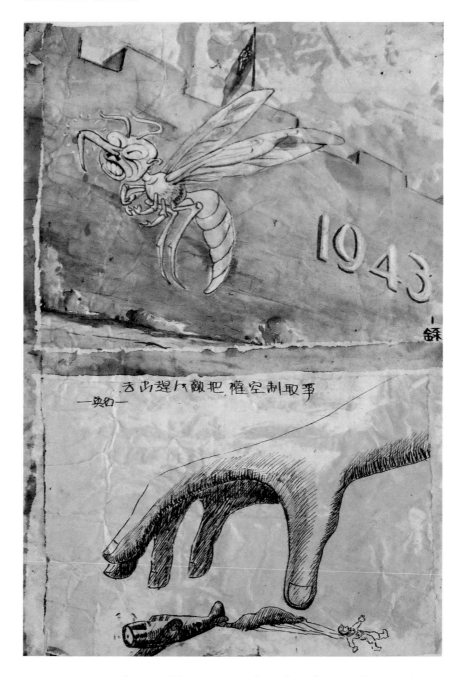

Figure 16.2. A selection of four paintings from the collection of water color paintings (Asian Division, Library of Congress).

整裝待發！

興敵机同歸於盡！

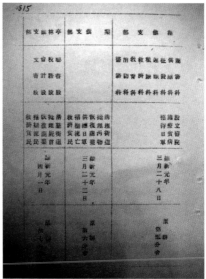

Figure 16.3. Records the Japanese Army's propaganda and relief efforts from the Records of the Propaganda and Relief Unit in Songjiang, China, 1938 (Asian Division, Library of Congress).

The Geography and Map Division

The Geography and Map Division, Manuscript Division, and Asian Division of the Library of Congress hold some valuable maps related to the Sino-Japanese War (1937–45). They include military, newspaper, propaganda, resource, and hand-drawn maps. There is no doubt that these cartographic materials can help historians to interpret history from a unique perspective. Particularly worth mentioning among the subject-specific maps are the Chinese military maps made during the war that show battles and the military maneuvers. Also interesting are captured maps, including Japanese military maps created as the Japanese Army advanced into China in 1937. A collection acquired by the library in the 1990s is the cartographic archives of Richard E. Harrison, one of the prominent American journalistic cartographers. His perspective and landform depictions of strategically important war zones caught the imagination of the world. One of his most famous maps is "One world, one war; a map showing the line-up and the strategic stakes in this first global war."

Other useful maps include the following:

- Postal Map of the Western Szechwan District by the General Bureau of Postal Service, Szechwan, China: General Bureau of Postal Service, April 1942.

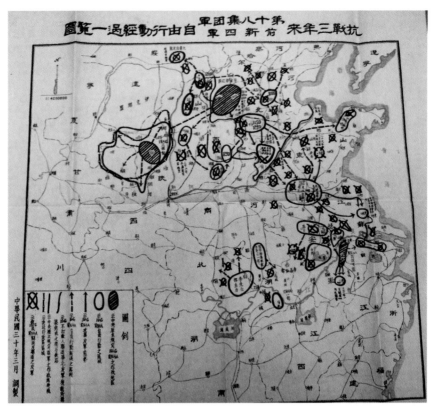

Figure 16.4. Map of Military Maneuvers of the Eighteenth Army Group and the
Former New Fourth Army since 1937, March 1941, Owen Lattimore Papers,
1907–1997, box 27, folder 10, Manuscript Division, Library of Congress.

- Mukden, United States. Army Map Services. Washington, DC:
  United States Army, 1944.
- China Special Strategic Map [Southeastern China], United States
  Army Map Services. Washington, DC: United States, Army, 1945.
- The Burma Road: Yunnan to Burma Highway, Office of Economic
  Warfare, Economic Potential Division; drawn in Cartographic
  Section, OEW, 1943.
- Major Battle Area in China since July 7, 1942, United States Office
  of Strategic Services, Research and Analysis Branch, 1942.
- China Fronts Compiled and Drawn in the Branch of Research and
  Analysis, OSS [Office of Strategic Services], Research and Analysis
  Branch, 1944.
- China Campaigns, Great Britain, War Office, General Staff.
  Geographical Section, 1944.

- Atlas of the Present Far East and Pacific War Zones Published/
  Created: Chungking, Chien kuo shu tien, Min-kuo 34 (1945).

In additional to maps in Geography and Map Division, other divisions in the Library of Congress hold a limited number of maps. For example, the Manuscript Division has a "Map of Military Maneuvers of the Eighteenth Army Group and the Former New Fourth Army since 1937, March 1941."

The Law Library

The Law Library has in its holding dozens of law publications of research value in Chinese and Japanese related to the Sino-Japanese conflict.[1]

The Main Reading Room and Microform Reading Room

In the Main Reading Room there is access to the 30 million books in the library's collection. The Online Catalog provides subject, name, and title headings. In addition, users can use a key word search. For example, a search using "Sino-Japanese War, 1937–1945" brought up more than 5,216 bibliographic titles as of the end of 2015. In addition to contemporary publications in English, there are little-known titles of unique research value in other western languages, for example, Wolf Schenke's *Travel on the Yellow Front; Observations of a German War Correspondent in China* (*Reise an der gelben Front; Beobachtungen eines deutschen Kriegsberichterstatters in China*).[2] Obviously, the author recorded his observations firsthand at the battle front, which seems to be vital for gaining an understanding of the war, especially from the perspective of a reporter from Germany, an ally of Japan at that time.

The Microform Reading Room has many items in its collection that concern the Sino-Japanese War of 1937–45. For instance, there are Records of the Joint Chiefs of Staff (1942–1945) and Confidential U.S. State Department Central Files for China: Foreign Affairs, 1940–1941, and Internal Affairs, 1930–1944. Other microform series include items on strategic issues and China. One collection of great import is Archives in the Japanese Ministry of Foreign Affairs, which contains more than 2 million pages (2,116 reels) of documents covering the period 1868–1945. It also contains documents of the International Military Tribunal and a long telegram series of outgoing and incoming messages between Foreign Service officers in the field and the minister in Tokyo. This collection supplements the collection based on the archives of the Japanese Army, Navy, and other government agencies entitled Selected Japanese Army and Navy Archives, Microfilm 5041.

There is a rarely seen letter written during World War II in the captured Japanese materials in the library's International Military Tribunal collections: the letter from Yoshizo Takamatsu (高松芳三) to former Japanese Prime Minister Fumimaro Konoe (近衞文麿) on January 16, 1945.

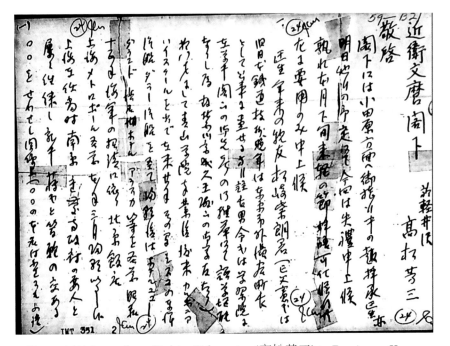

Figure 16.5. Letter from Yoshizo Takamatsu (高松芳三) to Fumimaro Konoe (近衛文麿) on January 16, 1945. IMT 351, Jan. 16, 1945. (IPS Doc. no. 496). 8 p. Reel WT 46, Microform Reading Room, Library of Congress.

Never having been recorded in official histories, the letter revealed that Chinese wartime leader Chiang Kai-shek once may have sent out peace feelers to Japan in early 1945. If the letter can be proven authentic and true, it will present great challenges for interpretation of World War II history as we know it.

The Manuscript Division

The Manuscript Division maintains twenty-five collections of the papers of prominent individuals during World War II, including wartime correspondence, diaries, memos, telegrams, speeches, articles, and newspaper clippings relevant to the study of the war. Significant among them are the Henry Luce Papers, 1898–1967 and the Clare Boothe Luce Papers, 1862–1988. So, too, are the important naval papers of such figures as admirals Harry E. Yarnell and William Leahy. One of the key collections is the Nelson Trusler Johnson Papers, 1887–1954. As the US Ambassador to China, Johnson had frequent communications with American and Chinese leaders such as Henry L. Stimson, Cordell Hull, Stanley K. Hornbeck, Chiang Kai-shek, Hu Shih, H. H. Kung, and T. V. Soong.

The Owen Lattimore Papers, 1907–1997 can be considered a good resource for the study of wartime China and its international relations. Lattimore, a sinologist

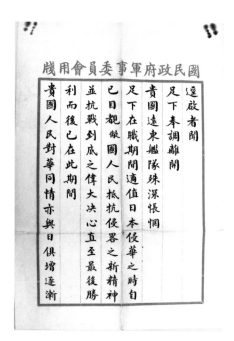

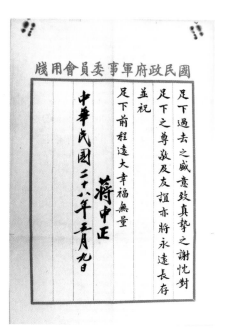

Figure 16.6. Letter from Chinese Nationalist leader Chiang Kai-shek to American admiral Harry Yarnell, May 9, 1939, Harry Ervin Yarnell Papers, 1875–1959, box 1, Manuscript Division, Library of Congress.

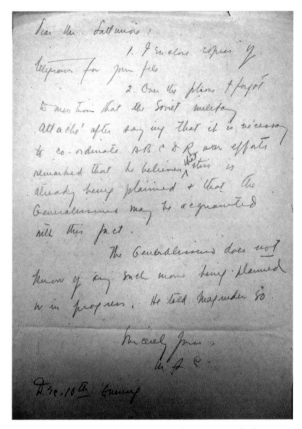

Figure 16.7. Letter from Mme. Chiang Kai-shek to Owen
Lattimore, December 10, 1941, Owen Lattimore Papers, 1907–
1997, box 27, Manuscript Division, Library of Congress.

and Asian scholar, was appointed in June 1941 by President Franklin D. Roosevelt
to be a US adviser to Chinese Nationalist leader Chiang Kai-shek, a post he held
for one and a half years. Before the end of the war, he also worked as the director
of Pacific operations in the US Office of War Information Overseas Operations
Branch. Useful among the sources are conversations and correspondence between
Lattimore and wartime leaders in China and the United States.

Dear Mr. Lattimore:

1. I enclosed copies of telegram for your file.

*2. Over the phone I forgot to mention that the Soviet military attaché
after saying that it is necessary to coordinate ABC & R war efforts
remarked that he believes that this is already being planned and that the
Generalissimo may be acquainted with this fact.*

The Generalissimo does not know of any such move being planned and in progress. He told Magruder so.

Sincerely yours,

MSC

Dec. 10th Evening

This letter indicates that China was the last one to learn about major decisions of the Allied nations and that China learned of such decisions in an informal setting and an informal way.

The letter that President Roosevelt's adviser Lauchlin Currie wrote to Owen Lattimore on August 21, 1941, states "The thing that is bogging me down and

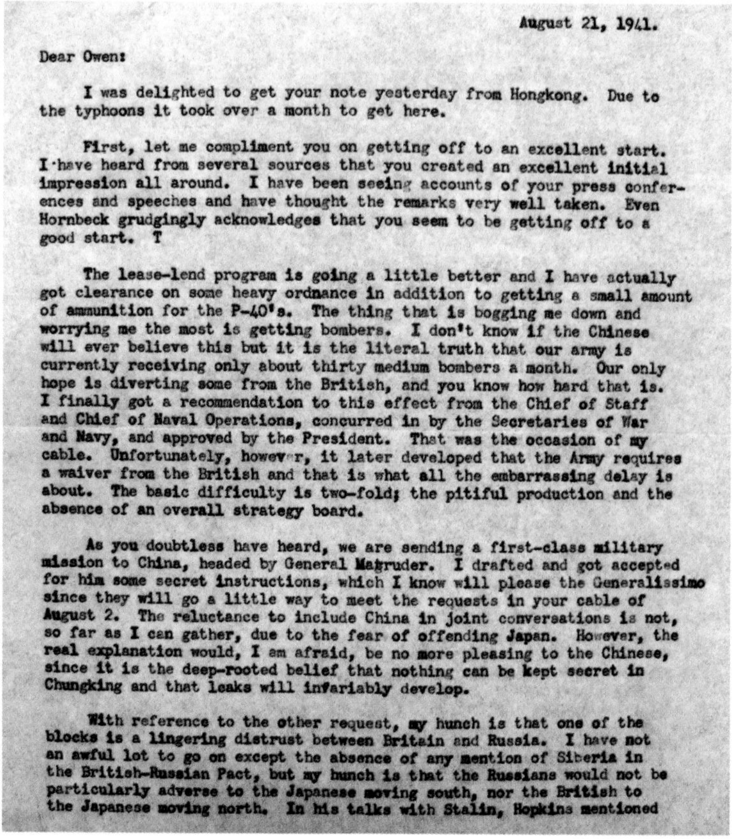

Figure 16.8. Letter from Lauchlin Currie to Owen Lattimore, August 21, 1941, Owen Lattimore Papers, 1907-1997, box 27, Manuscript Division, Library of Congress.

worrying me the most is getting bombers. I don't know if the Chinese will ever believe this but it is the literal truth that our army is currently receiving only about thirty medium bombers a month. . . ." The letter reveals the misunderstandings and miscommunications between the Allies regarding American military assistance to China. At that time, Chiang Kai-shek had asked the United States to send China a thousand planes a year.[3]

The Motion Picture, Broadcasting, and Recorded Sound Division

This division holds the largest and most diverse collection of war-related moving images of the period: 1,400 feature films, documentaries, and newsreels produced in Japan during the 1930s and early 1940s. The most crucial among the Japanese films are the newsreels *Asahi News* from 1935 to 1939, *Yomiuri News* from 1936 to 1940, and *Nippon News* from 1940 to 1945. In addition, the collections contain American newsreels of the period, principally *Universal Newsreel* and *News of the Day* but also *Paramount News* and *Movietone News*. Reference books in the motion picture collection provide an overview of American commercial movies produced during the war, including *The Films of World War II* (1973)[4] and the Library of Congress publication *Catalog of Copyright Entries, Motion Pictures, 1940–1949*.[5]

The finding aid, Films and Videos on China, Hong Kong and Taiwan in LC's Moving Image Collection can help researchers locate historical films such as *The Battle of China* (1944), which was the sixth film of Hollywood director Frank Capra's *Why We Fight* propaganda film series produced by the US Office of War Information. In the Motion Picture, Broadcasting, and Recorded Sound Division there are also thirty-plus original documentary films produced during the war years by westerners that possess very important research value.

Prints and Photographs Division

The Prints and Photographs Division has dozens of photo collections and albums that contain pictures of life in China and Japan during the war. One collection contains 236 photographs of *China at War: An Exhibition*, which focused on the Chinese Nationalist government and military activities of 1938–43. Part of the Office of War Information Collection is the captured Japanese albums of *Yomiuri News*, mostly containing photos of battles with detailed descriptions in Japanese. Another major collection is Photo-Documentation of the Public Career of Ch'u Min-yi (Chu Minyi) as Minister of Foreign Affairs in the Chinese Puppet Government during the Japanese Occupation, 1937–1945, which consists of eight personal photo albums illustrating, from 1931 to 1945, the early career and activities of Ch'u Min-yi, the foreign minister of the collaborationist Nanjing Nationalist Government. This collection provides rarely seen images of life in the Japanese-occupied areas in China.

Figure 16.9. Photograph of Mme. Chiang Kai-shek and Owen Lattimore, 1941, photograph from the exhibition *China at War: An Exhibition*, Prints and Photographs Division, Library of Congress.

Figure 16.10. Photograph of the laborers of minority ethnic groups in Xikang, 1938–43, from the exhibition *China at War: An Exhibition*, Prints and Photographs Division, Library of Congress.

Figure 16.11. Photograph of the Japanese bombing of Chongqing, 1938–43, from the exhibition *China at War: An Exhibition*, Prints and Photographs Division, Library of Congress.

Figure 16.12. Photograph of the Battle of Shanghai in the fall of 1937 from Japanese albums of *Yomiuri News*, Prints and Photographs Division, Library of Congress.

Figure 16.13. Photograph of the visit to Japan in 1940 by Chen Gongbo, head of the legislature of the collaborationist Nanjing government (*third from left*), and Ch'u Min-yi (*second from left*), Ch'u Min-yi Collection, Prints and Photographs Division, Library of Congress.

The Science, Technology, and Business Division

The Science, Technology, and Business Division holds extensive collections in all fields of science and technology, including the Technical Report Collection. One of the highlighted collections is the original Imperial Japan's Biological Warfare Unit (Unit 731), medical experiment documents in English based on

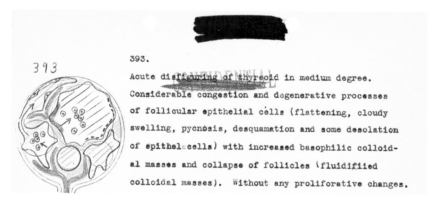

Figure 16.14. Photograph of a technical report of the Japanese medical experiments during World War II, Technical Report Collection, Science, Technology, and Business Division, Library of Congress.

the investigations of members of the Japanese Kwantung Army Water Supply and Purification Department stationed in Manchuria during the war. Unit 731 conducted notorious medical experiments using human guinea pigs on how to defend against bacteriological attacks and how to wage a biowar.

Serial and Government Publications Division

The Serial and Government Publications Division collected over 1,600 titles of U.S. and foreign newspapers published during the 1930s and 1940s, which provide useful materials for researchers. The Sino-Japanese War can be followed chronologically in one newspaper, a comparison can be made among various papers, and specific events can be researched as well.

Veterans History Project of American Folklife Center

The US Congress created the Veterans History Project of the American Folklife Center in 2000. It collects American war veterans' personal accounts, including correspondence, creative works, diaries, memoirs, photos, and audio transcripts. A search for veterans of World War II in the China-Burma-India theater results in 2,176 hits, which include audio recordings such as that of a member of Flying Tigers, "Frederick Wu-O Chiao, Major General, Air Force Veteran, China." There

Figure 16.15. Photo of American ambassador Patrick Hurley's visit to Yan'an, August 27, 1945, James C. Eaton Collection, Veterans History Project, American Folklife Center, Library of Congress.

are also important visual images in the collections such as the one in figure 16.17 showing American ambassador to China General Patrick Hurley's visit to Yan'an in the fall of 1945 for the purpose of initiating bilateral talks between the Nationalist government and the Chinese Communists after the war with Japan.

Conclusion

The history of the Sino-Japanese War (1937–45) is like a jigsaw puzzle. But with little snippets of recorded information discovered here and there, we may be able to piece together a nearly complete picture. As more primary sources are being excavated, the history of the tumultuous war period will gradually reveal itself. Hopefully the information provided in this chapter can serve as a catalyst to inspire researchers and help trail-blaze historical writing in this field.

Notes

[1] For example, Sakutaro Tachi (立作太郎). *China Incident Interpreted by International Laws (支那事變國際法論)*. Tokyo: Shokado, 1938.

[2] Wolf Schenke. *Travel on the Yellow Front: Observations of a German War Correspondent in China (Reise an der gelben Front; Beobachtungen eines deutschen Kriegsberichterstatters in China)*. Oldenburg: G. Stalling, 1940.

[3] Department of Republican History, Institute of Modern History, Chinese Academy of Social Sciences中国社会科学院近代史所民国史组编, *The Collected Official Correspondence of Hu Shih as the Chinese Ambassador to the US 胡适任驻美大使期间往来电稿* (Beijing: Zhonghua Book Co.中华书局, 1973), 44–77.

[4] Joe Morella, Edward Z. Epstein, and John Griggs. *The Films of World War II*. Secaucus, NJ: Citadel Press, 1973.

[5] Copyright Office, Library of Congress. *Catalog of Copyright Entries, Motion Pictures, 1940–1949*. Washington DC: U.S. Government Printing Office, 1953.

Bibliography

Imura, Tetsuo. *An Annotated List of Japanese Periodicals on Pre-war Asia, the Holdings of the Library of Congress (米国議会図書館所蔵戦前期アジア関係日本語逐次刊行物目録)*. Tokyo: Ajia Keizai Kenkyūjo, 1995.

Keizo, Tanpo, and Honda Yasuhiro. *Bibliography of Materials Related to the Taiwan Government General Collection at the Library of Congress in the United States* (旧台湾総督府関係資料目録: 米国議会図書館所蔵). Naruto-shi: Yagi Insatsujo, 1996.

Library of Congress. American Folklife Center Finding Aids, American Folklife Center. http://www.loc.gov/folklife/guides/findaid.html.

———. Manuscript Division Finding Aids Online, Manuscript Division. http://www.loc.gov/rr/mss/f-aids/mssfa.html.

———. Prints and Photographs Online Catalog, Prints and Photographs Division. http://www.loc.gov/pictures.

———. South Manchuria Railway Company Collection, Asian Division. https://guides.loc.gov/south-manchurian-railway.

———. Technical Reports Collections, Science, Technology, and Business Division. http://www.loc.gov/rr/scitech/trs/trscollections.html.

Tanaka, Hiromi. *A Comprehensive Catalog of Publications of the Former Imperial Army and Navy Requisitioned by the Occupation Forces and Now in the Collection of the U.S. Library of Congress* (米議会図書館所蔵占領接収旧陸海軍資料総目録). Tokyo: Toyo Shorin, 1995.

Uyehara, Cecil H. *Checklist of Archives in the Japanese Ministry of Foreign Affairs, Tokyo, Japan, 1868–1945, Microfilmed for the Library of Congress, 1949–1951.* Washington, DC: Photoduplication Service, Library of Congress, 1954.

Yoshimura, Yoshiko. *Japanese Censored Materials and Documents (pre-1956): A Checklist of the Microfilm Collection of the Library of Congress.* Tokyo: Bunsei Shoin, 2009.

Young, John. *The Research Activities of the South Manchurian Railway Company, 1907–1945: A History and Bibliography.* New York: East Asian Institute, Columbia University, 1966.

17

EAST MEETS WEST

DIGITAL HUMANITIES AT THE
UNIVERSITY OF PITTSBURGH

**Michael J. Dabrishus and Haihui Zhang,
University of Pittsburgh**

Digital humanities (DH), an area of scholarly activity at the intersection of computing or digital technologies and the disciplines of the humanities, which began as a term of consensus among a relatively small group of researchers, is now supported on a growing number of campuses by a level of funding, infrastructure, and administrative commitments that would have been unthinkable even a decade ago.[1] It is also well recognized that libraries play an important role in DH. "Librarians" need to proudly identify themselves as DHers and should fully expect to be regarded as such by peers, colleagues, faculty, and administrators and to let the broad work they do engage with that community.[2] However, for the most part, East Asian Digital Humanities (EADH) can still be considered rather new and emerging. Some of the reasons for this belatedness include the nature of the area of study, the small number of readers, language barriers, and other factors. All of these require more subject knowledge for mining, identifying, and evaluating cultural data sets, internal and external (national and international) collaborations, and special processing procedures and skills.

For more than a decade, the University Library System (ULS) at the University of Pittsburgh has been establishing long-range goals every three years, with a focus on global outreach, the creation of digital collections, and scholarly communication. In 1997, a Digital Research Library (DRL) was established to "augment the networked delivery of commercial electronic texts, as well as to create e-text projects in collaboration with faculty and graduate students."[3] Later one of the ULS goals for 2003–6 was to "digitize and deliver electronic versions of ULS print resources to a large body of users worldwide."[4] From 2007 to 2010, the ULS goal became clearer, and a specific plan was articulated to "digitize materials from our unique or endangered collections and provide innovative tools to enhance their availability, access, and continued use." To "provide the technology infrastructure and expertise to support the creation of new digital collections" became a key ULS goal.[5] In 2011, global visibility was emphasized to "increase the University's global impact by ensuring that the output of Pitt researchers was made visible to a global readership, by supporting Pitt's international research and learning programs, and by fostering worldwide sharing of knowledge."[6] Over this time and especially in recent years, to reach its consistent and explicit goals, ULS has actively supported work focused on East Asian digitization projects and achieved remarkable results. This chapter aims to review the ULS's EADH efforts, share experiences, and seek future collaboration opportunities.

Modern China Studies Pilot Project

In 2002, the ULS applied to the National Endowment for the Humanities (NEH) for a grant with which to catalog and preserve through microfilming three thousand acidic and rare books in our Chinese monograph collection. In the grant proposal, Jeanann Haas, now the head of Preservation and Special Collections, stated that "digitizing a small subgroup of these materials will offer enhanced access and provide limited searchability." It was felt that the impact of such a "virtual collection" would influence library services in the future and could lead to a network of library resources among US research libraries, which are currently limited in their access to foreign-language collections worldwide, and libraries outside the United States. The DRL had previously mounted several digitization projects to deliver English-language materials of historical significance to a global audience, including the Historic Pittsburgh and Nineteenth-Century Schoolbooks projects (http://www.digital.library.pitt.edu). "The China Studies project sought to expand its digital projects to include foreign-language material. In the wake of the digital revolution, it has been a dream of the East Asian Library (EAL) at the University of Pittsburgh to offer enhanced access to these valuable materials to scholars and researchers around the world." Upon completion of this project, the Chinese Collection will be well on its way to accomplishing preservation and accessibility worldwide. In 2003, the ULS received a two-year grant (2003–05) from NEH and was the only individual institution in the brittle books and serials category to receive an award that included a component for digitizing materials for access. This pilot project was called Modern China Studies. The ULS project became one of the first pilot digitization projects in the United States to enhance access to unique Chinese primary documents and reference books for both researchers and librarians.

These collections included works produced in the early to middle decades of the twentieth century that provide insight into political, economic, and educational conditions in China. Thirty-seven key titles (approximately 10,500 pages) formed the nucleus of this digital experiment. Project objectives included detailed analysis of the inherent structure of the texts to guide in the creation of structural metadata and pagination, romanizing bibliographic and structural portions of the texts into Pinyin, converting the text into digital image files adhering to internationally recognized imaging standards, and creating a website for the global dissemination of the texts, among other concerns. The project provided visitors with a website where they could view and print digital pages, browse the texts by subject and title, navigate a hyperlinked table of contents for each text, and search the bibliographic and structural elements of the texts. In order to facilitate the browsing, viewing, and searching of the bibliographic information in the texts, the DRL acquired and created appropriate metadata. This consisted of two key components: a MARC (Machine-Readable Cataloging) record and structural and descriptive information for each text.[7]

When the project was opened to the public, it enjoyed high usage even when only thirty-seven books were available for access on the internet. Table 17.1 presents monthly website usage for the Modern China Studies project in 2005/06.

Although the final product can't be compared with full-text searchable products today, and usage statistics decreased (see table 17.2) due to more and more Chinese e-books becoming available in the past ten years, the pilot project did enable the DRL to experiment with adapting new methodologies, tools, and techniques for creating, processing, and indexing digital library content for foreign-language materials. In their final report to NEH, Jeanann Haas and Edward Galloway, head of the Archives Service Center, stated, "The University Library System gained valuable experience participating in this pilot project to create digital access to foreign language print material. In the end, we succeeded in providing online access to the selected Chinese language texts. Never before has the Internet community had access to these works. As a result, we hope our small step will increase the dissemination of additional texts documenting Modern China."[8] The ULS has benefited from this valuable experience for future digitization projects, particularly those in foreign languages.

Table 17.1. Monthly Usage of the Modern China Studies Project 2005–2006.

	Homepage views		Full-text page views		Unique books viewed	Percentage of books viewed
	Views	Visits	Views	Visits		
May 2005	966	845	1,388	133	34	92%
Jun 2005	130	116	209	32	12	32
July 2005	69	59	39	5	4	11
Aug 2005	193	169	359	33	22	59
Sep 05	146	129	3,345	17	32	86
Oct 2005	204	182	343	29	20	54
Nov 2005	256	238	222	24	18	49
Dec 2005	172	159	466	27	16	43
Jan 2006	227	200	543	35	24	65
Feb 2006	185	166	79	10	9	24
Mar 2006	208	188	215	22	22	59
Apr 2006	263	232	139	19	12	32

Table 17.2. Quaterly Usage of the Modern China Studies Project 2012–14.

Timeframe	Pageviews (homepage only)	Unique pageviews
Q2 2012	62	57
Q3 2012	82	70
Q4 2012	60	56
Q1 2013	89	81
Q2 2013	46	37
Q3 2013	69	57
Q4 2013	212	171
Q1 2014	64	58
Q2 2014	56	51
Q3 2014	46	38
Q4 2014	44	36

Digitization of East Asian Special and Unique Collections

Due to the nature of special collections and archives—rarity, uniqueness, and limited access—special collections are increasingly becoming the focus of digital projects in museums, archives, and libraries. Thus, DH cannot simply be confined to digitizing rare books and manuscripts housed in special collections and even more challenging East Asian special collections. To begin a DH project requires defining a sustainable strategy: identification, evaluation, and selection. Institutional impact also needs to be considered.

Japanese Digitization Projects

A couple of years ago, the ULS completed two digital projects related to Japanese art. The first was titled Tsukioka Kōgyo: The Art of Noh, 1869–1927.[9] The second was the Barry Rosensteel Japanese Print Collection.[10]

Nōgaku zue 能 樂 圖 繪, or Pictures of Noh, is a spectacular series of Japanese wood-block prints by the artist Tsukioka Kōgyo 月岡耕漁.[11] Pitt owns a rare, complete set of this series, which was published in Tokyo between Meiji years 30 and 35 or 1897 to 1902. The series is comprised of five volumes containing 261 prints inspired by the plays of classical Japanese nō theater. The ULS's set of prints is located in the Special Collections Department. Over a third of a century, from the early 1890s until his premature death in 1927, Kōgyo created hundreds of paintings, prints, magazine illustrations, and postcard pictures of nō and kyōgen plays. Kōgyo also produced paintings and prints of flowers, birds, and genre and even wartime scenes, but it is for his theater paintings and prints that he is best known and remembered. In 2009 the ULS partnered with Dr. Richard J. Smethurst, a research professor of history at Pitt, to create a website focused on the ULS's set of the prints. Also key to this collaboration were several other Pitt personnel, as well as generous funding from the Toshiba International Foundation, the Japan Iron and Steel Federation, and the Mitsubishi endowments at Pitt. The key components for the ULS included scanning all the wood-block prints and creating a website. Dr. Smethurst and his colleagues created all the metadata that are part of the descriptive catalog and the contextual essays. These components are key elements of the website, which continues to draw visitors from around the world.

The Barry Rosensteel Japanese Print Collection consists of 126 wood-block prints representing works by more than forty artists and dating from the eighteenth to the early twentieth century. The images primarily portray Japanese culture through detailed depictions of portraits, landscapes, wildlife, and theatrical performances, taking into account some of Japan's rich history. A small number of prints depict Chinese scenes. The earliest print is by Kitao Shigemasa (1739–1820) and dates to 1760. The collection includes 15 works by Utagawa Toyokuni (1769–1825), whose portraits of Kabuki actors garnered much success. One of his

Figure 17.1. Kambara, fifty-three stations of the Tokaido.

Figure 17.2. The Kabuki actors Kataoka Tsuchinosuke I as Kotobuki Chitose and Kataoka Gado as Kotobuki Sanbaso, print by Yoshitaki, Utagawa (1841–99).

noteworthy pupils was Utagawa Kunisada (1786–1864), who was also known for his portraits of kabuki actors, many of which are found in the collection. While he was born in Paris, Paul Jacoulet (1902–60) spent a very large part of his life in Japan. It is thought that he created around 30,000 prints, yet fewer than 200 are known to exist, 12 of which can be found in the Rosensteel Collection. These high-quality prints were scanned and described in detail. Finally, a website was built to promote discovery and access.

Chinese Land Records

Over the past few decades in North America, the field of Chinese studies has experienced very rapid growth. Access and use of Chinese archives is crucial to advancements in academic programs. In some of fields of study, archives play an even more indispensable role in research. For reviewing the academic achievements of the "postrevolutionary" generation of Chinese political specialists in the past two decades, Dr. Elizabeth J. Perry has indicated, "Taking advantage of the two main avenues rendered accessible to foreign scholars since the 1980s, some political scientists pursued historically grounded research in government archives while many more undertook grassroots fieldwork."[12] Chinese archives have opened their collections to scholars more freely than ever before. However, access is still very limited.

Years ago the EAL purchased a significant group of Chinese land records from a private collector in China. The collection includes land deeds, property trade documents, possession draw documents, tax bills, and more. More than two hundred items span more than three hundred years from the Ming dynasty (1368–1644) to the mid-twentieth century. It is the largest collection of such documents in North America. These records are important and valuable primary documents that reflect landownership in different historical periods, land tenure changes, and the overall land management system of China. As historical records they are indispensable for the research and study of Chinese politics, economy, social life, and more. In 2014, to make the collection more accessible for research, the ULS embarked on a digitization project—Chinese Land Records—which turned out to be an interesting challenge. Certainly, it required a person who was fluent in Chinese. It also required someone who could devote his or her entire work schedule to the project, thereby eliminating members of the regular library staff as they had many other duties and responsibilities on a daily basis. As the ULS has hosted visiting librarians from China for many years, it was determined that a visiting librarian might be the answer to our personnel needs. In 2013, the ULS hosted a visiting librarian, and the digitization of Chinese land records was listed as a major task to be undertaken during his stay. The visiting librarian helped with processing the land records, recording relevant information such as location, owner, seller, and date. He also arranged the records chronologically,

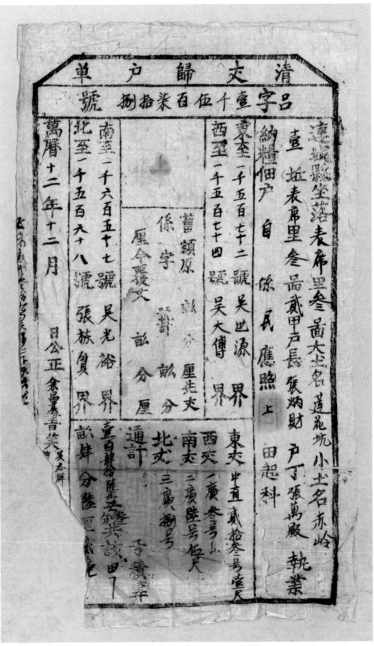

Figure 17.3. Now the digital project of China Land Records was completed and open for access. People can access it through ULS Digital Collection from the wibsite of University Library System https://digital.library. pitt.edu. This is the earliest piece in the collection, from 1584.

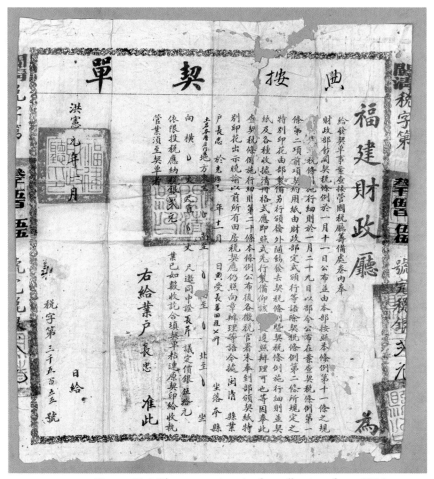

Figure 17.4. The rarest piece in the collection, from 1916.

scanned each item, and finished up by writing a guide to the collection in both English and Chinese.[13] As a result, this project provided the perfect opportunity to form a partnership among the EAL, Archives Service Center (ASC), DRL, and ULS's Special Collections departments. The end result not only offers scholars an open path to these special primary sources, but it also produced a very unique archival gem at the ULS and provided a good experience of collaboration both internationally and among the library's departments.

Szeming Sze Papers

In May 2014 the ULS received a collection of documents related to Szeming Sze 施思明donated by his descendants. Dr. Sze was a prominent Chinese medical expert who was instrumental in the creation of the World Health Organization (WHO).[14]

His father, Dr. Alfred Sao-ke Sze 施肇基,[15] was China's ambassador to Great Britain at the time, and the younger Sze spent much of his childhood in London. Sze was educated at Cambridge University and began his career by working at St. Thomas Hospital in London. He returned to China in 1934, although he traveled to the United States often. After the Japanese attack on Pearl Harbor in December 1941, Sze remained in the United States as part of the country's Lend-Lease agreement with China. He began working with the diplomat T. V. Soong and accompanied him to the 1945 United Nations Conference on International Organization, which would later become the United Nations, as part of the Chinese delegation. At the conference, Sze was one of only three medical professionals in attendance, along with Dr. Karl Evang of Norway and Dr. Geraldo de Paula Souza of Brazil. Over lunch the three men agreed that an international health organization should be established through the United Nations. When they tried to gain support and pass a resolution for such an organization, they had little success. However, during a conversation with Alger Hiss, the secretary-general of the conference, he pointed Sze in the right direction and they were able to pass a declaration calling for the creation of an international conference on health. In 1954, Sze was appointed medical director of the United Nations, and he remained in that role until his retirement in the 1960s.

The Szeming Sze Papers contain a variety of documents related to the creation of the WHO. They include correspondence, Dr. Sze's personal diaries from the 1945 United Nations conference and 1946 International Health Organization conference, official conference documents, some documents with handwritten notes by Dr. Sze and his colleagues, photographs, and one VHS tape. There are copies of Dr. Sze's personal memoirs, as well as publications from the different conferences. This collection also contains newspaper clippings on the formation of the United Nations and the WHO, as well as a later interview with Dr. Sze about his early work. In October 2014, the ULS completed the digitization of the entire collection and opened it to the public via the internet.[16] Once it was available online, the collection immediately caught the attention of scholars both nationally and internationally.

Regarding these the four digitization projects, it is clear that because their physical condition was particularly valuable and rare, the original motivation for digitizing these special collections was to provide broad access to scholars and researchers.

Overseas Chinese Student Newsletters

The ULS holds the largest collection of campus newsletters written by overseas Chinese students in North America. Altogether there are 220 titles, amounting to 1,100 issues. The earliest was published in 1964 and the latest in 1997. The majority

Figure 17.5. Szeming Sze 施思明 (April 5, 1908–October 27, 1998).

of the newsletters were published in the United States, with a few published in Canada, Hong Kong, and other countries. Most are in Chinese, although a few are in English, Vietnamese, and Korean. The newsletters were donated to the EAL by several anonymous donors who wanted to make sure that their thoughts and efforts would be preserved for future generations. The content is very rich and colorful, reflecting Chinese student life on campus; the students' enthusiasm and participation in community activities off campus; the literary and artistic creations that enriched their extracurricular lives; and their thoughts on and involvement in social, economic, and political issues in domestic and international affairs in the 1960s and 1970s, including the admission of the People's Republic of China (PRC) into the United Nations, the establishment of diplomatic relations between the PRC and the United States, Taiwan issues, and the Senkaku Islands social movement among overseas Chinese students and local Chinese communities.

Since these newsletters are not widely available, and the physical condition of most of them is not good, the EAL recognized that a digitization project could promote access while also enhancing preservation of the originals by limiting their physical handling. These newsletters are not only important historical records of Chinese student life, but, even more important, they are primary sources that contribute to research on East Asian politics, economics, culture, and sociology while also providing insight into the relations between the PRC and the

United States, the PRC and Taiwan, and the PRC and Japan. This digital project commenced in the fall of 2016 at the ACS and was completed in the spring of 2017.

Exploratory Pilot Projects

With digital technology gradually maturing, libraries will always have to face new challenges to discover, identify, and evaluate primary documents for potential digitization projects. For future library digitization projects, we must consider the following questions. First, how do libraries work with faculty members and use their subject expertise to identify the objectives of digitization projects? And, second, what is the proper way to approach faculty members who hold valuable collections that have potential for a unique digitization project that will benefit everyone in a research field? In recent years, the ASC at ULS has been attempting to work with faculty members on digitizing their special collections to provide broad access to scholars and researchers. An example is American Left Ephemera Collection, which contains materials collected by Dr. Richard Oestreicher, an associate professor of history at the University of Pittsburgh, over a thirty-five-year period, which document the history of the American Left from the 1890s to the present. The online portion of the collection was opened to the public in 2012.[17] Another example is the Wilfrid S. Sellars Papers. Dr. Sellars was a very prominent American philosopher who made significant contributions to the philosophy of science, epistemology, and many other areas within the field. He was particularly well known for his contributions to metaphysics and the philosophy of the mind. The collection consists of manuscripts of nearly all of Sellars's work (including autographed manuscripts of his texts), research notes, preliminary notes for further development, drafts of articles, working papers, correspondence, teaching materials, and lecture notes. In June 2007, digital reproduction of a major portion of the collection was completed and made available online via links within the library's finding aid, which has proven to be a very efficient method of access.[18]

Gao Archives

Experience has shown that to work with faculty members on digitizing their collections is a complex process involving many issues, including ownership of the collection, roles the library and department play, joint grant proposals, and legal and practical procedures. This is especially true when we tread the exploratory path to work with East Asian studies specialists who have special collections in non-English languages that could be potential digitization projects. Instead of describing a successful East Asian studies project in this section, we instead discuss the questions raised by referencing the Gao Archives as an example of an ongoing project.

Minglu Gao 高名潞is a research professor in the History of Art and Architecture Department (HAA) at Pitt. Gao has been an active critic, curator, and scholar of contemporary Chinese art since the mid-1980s. His exhibitions on the subject are considered among the most important ever assembled in the United States and China. His many publications explore the changing relationship between global art movements and Chinese tradition.[19]

Why is the Gao archive important? In the 1980s, Chinese contemporary art was rebellious, independent, and nongovernmental, thereby distinguishing it from the Chinese Artists Association System. From the early 1980s to the first decade of twenty-first century, accompanied by political, economic, and social changes in China, Chinese contemporary art underwent tremendous growth and change. An eyewitness to the development of Chinese contemporary art, Gao had the foresight to collect what has become a massive quantity of what are today valuable primary research materials. These include manuscripts and diaries of artists, correspondence, records created by art groups, records of historical events and debates in both visual images and texts, artworks, underground publications, exhibit catalogs, and much more. Collectively, these documents are indispensable to the study of contemporary Chinese art.

It is fair to ask why the ULS moved forward with the Gao archive project. Prior to the 1980s, research on and exhibitions of Chinese contemporary art in North America (and, indeed, around the world) were quite limited. During the past three decades, Chinese contemporary art has emerged as one of the liveliest areas of study within international contemporary art. The number of schools that offer courses and doctoral programs specializing in Chinese contemporary art has grown as well. The publication of academic monographs and articles on Chinese contemporary art has grown rapidly. All this has led to an increasing demand for broad access to relevant documentation and literature. In 2014, representatives of the ULS and HAA met with Professor Gao to let him know that his collection was well worth preserving for future generations of students and scholars and that we would welcome the opportunity to make that happen at Pitt. Certainly, preserving the original materials would be an essential step, but digitization and an online presence, including the creation of a database of contemporary Chinese art, were also subjects worth investigating. Professor Gao welcomed the overture and agreed to a collaborative project.

The project is complex and challenging. First, the majority of this archive is in a non-English language, primarily Chinese but also other languages such as French. Second, unlike many other collections that are presented in a relatively single format and stored in one place, Gao's archives, stored in his studio in both China and the United States, include a wide range of materials, as previously noted. For the archives stored in China, a special plan is required. The transfer of materials, which has already begun, will be an ongoing process. The digitization of small portions of the collection is being planned, recognizing that copyright questions must be resolved during the process. As the archive collection is coming from a faculty member who is actively involved in teaching and research, his need to have access to certain materials must be addressed. Outside financial support is also a consideration and is being investigated. Flexibility, collaboration, and cooperation among ULS departments and the donor will be critical. The project is expected to be completed over several years, so the current work is really just the beginning. To quote an old Chinese saying, the Long March begins with one step 万里长征 始于足下. We have been marching smoothly for about six months, with a survey of the collection to be completed by June 2016. This the fall of 2015, we received news that the Provost Office of the University of Pittsburgh, as part of its Year of the Humanities initiative, approved our proposal for funding that will support an exhibit of some of the Gao materials in the main library, along with a reception and presentation to recognize Professor Gao's work.

CR/10 Project

CR/10 (Cultural Revolution: 10) is an experimental oral history project supported and sponsored by the ULS and carried out by its EAL. Its primary goal is to obtain digital videos of ordinary people recounting their memories and impressions of China's Great Proletarian Cultural Revolution, which lasted from 1966 to 1976. Interviews began in December 2015 and continue into the present. Thirty-two interviews were posted on the University of Pittsburgh's Digital Collections website (http://culturalrevolution.pitt.edu) in September 2017. Additional videos will be posted in 2018. So far 118 interviews have been conducted.

Why did we initiate CR/10? History is multifaceted. A person's memory varies according to his or her experiences, geographic location, age, profession, family background, and many other factors. All these factors taken together influence an individual's understanding of historical incidents. The Cultural Revolution was a tumultuous period in China. Many of the participants in CR/10 faced extraordinary challenges—including the loss of family members and friends—in their personal lives. History cannot be quantified. The project does not focus on the number of interviews gathered or aim to assemble a vast collection of interviews that can be examined to find common ground among them. Rather, its primary goal is to record and express individuals' distinct experiences. Each interview has its own unique worth.

Since CR/10 launched, we have received a lot of positive feedback on its archival, research, and teaching value. Moreover, this project is a meaningful exploration of librarianship from warehouse to scholarship initiative. In addition to collecting, storing, preserving, and serving, librarians can also be proactive in the creative process of preserving history.

In summary, EADH is very much still under development. Due to the collection's content and languages, the digitization work is supremely representative of a team of scholars, graduate students, digitization specialists, librarians, and administrators. The challenges of discovering, identifying, and evaluating primary documents for potential digitization projects require the involvement of subject scholars and experts. Legal considerations, a need for a staff with language skills, and cultural knowledge make the process challenging yet also very interesting and rewarding. The ULS at the University of Pittsburgh has made great strides since 2000, being one of the pioneers in the digitization of East Asian research materials. It will continue to explore new developments and improvements so as to provide greater access to its unique materials, enhancing teaching and research not just on the campus of Pitt but throughout the world via its digital endeavors.

Notes

[1] *Matthew G. Kirschenbaum,* "What Is Digital Humanities and What's It Doing in English Departments?," *ADE Bulletin No. 150 (2010):55.*

[2] Micah Vandegrift and Stewart Varner, "Evolving in Common: Creating Mutually Supportive Relationships between Libraries and the Digital Humanities," *Journal of Library Administration* 53, no. 1 (2013): 67–78.

[3] ULS Goal, 1997–99.

[4] Ibid., 2003–6.

[5] Ibid., 2007–10.

[6] Ibid., 2014–17.

[7] https://digital.library.pitt.edu/collection/modern-china-studies. See Modern China Studies, University of Pittsburgh Library System

[8] Jeanann Haas and Edward Galloway, "NEH Final Performance Report," 2005.

[9] See Tsukioka Kōgyo: The Art of Noh, 1869–1927, University of Pittsburgh Library System, http://digital.library.pitt.edu/k/kogyo/index.html.

[10] See Barry Rosensteel Japanese Print Collection, University of Pittsburgh Library System, http://images.library.pitt.edu/r/rosensteel/contents.html.

[11] Tsukioka Kōgyo月岡耕漁 (1869–1927) was the preeminent graphic artist of the *nō* and *kyōgen* theaters.

[12] Elizabeth J. Perry, "Studying Chinese Politics: Farewell to Revolution?" in *A Scholarly Review of Chinese Studies in North America* (Ann Arbor, MI: Association for Asian Studies, 2013): 264–91, https://www.asianstudies.org/publications/asia-past-present/scholarly-review-of-chinese-studies-in-north-america.

[13] See Chinese Land Records, University of Pittsburgh Library System, https://digital.library.pitt.edu/collection/chinese-land-records

[14] Sze Szeming 施思明(1908–98) was a prominent Chinese diplomat and cofounder of the WHO. He was instrumental in building the organization into a specialized United Nations agency.

[15] Alfred Sao-ke Sze 施肇基 (1877–1958) was a prominent Chinese politician and diplomat during the most turbulent period in modern Chinese history.

[16] See American Left Ephemera Collection, University of Pittsburgh Library System,, http://digital.library.pitt.edu/a/americanleft.

[17] See American Left Ephemera Collection, University of Pittsburgh Library System,, http://digital.library.pitt.edu/a/americanleft.

[18] See Guide to the Wilfrid S. Sellars Papers, 1899-1990 ASP.1991.01, University of Pittsburgh Library System, https://digital.library.pitt.edu/islandora/object/pitt%3AUS-PPiU-asp199101/viewer.

[19] Dr. Minglu Gao received his PhD from Harvard University. From 1984 to 1991, he worked as a senior editor at *Meishu* (Art Monthly, Beijing). Gao has curated a number of important exhibitions of Chinese contemporary art, including, notably, *China/Avant-Garde* (Beijing, 1989) and *Inside Out: New Chinese Art* (1998, New York). For publication information, visit the HAA website, http://www.haa.pitt.edu/person/gao-minglu.

Bibliography

Kirschenbaum, Matthew G. "What Is Digital Humanities and What's It Doing in English Departments?" *ADE Bulletin No. 150* (2010): 55.

Maron, Nancy L., and Sarah Pickle. *Searching for Sustainability: Strategies for Eight Digitized Special Collections. Washington, DC: Association of Research Libraries, 2013.*

Perry, Elizabeth J. "Studying Chinese Politics: Farewell to Revolution?" In *A Scholarly Review of Chinese Studies in North America,* 264–91. Ann Arbor, MI: Association for Asian Studies, 2013, https://www.asianstudies.org/publications/asia-past-present/scholarly-review-of-chinese-studies-in-north-america

Proffitt, Merrilee, and Jennifer Schaffner. *The Impact of Digitizing Special Collections on Teaching and Scholarship: Reflections on a Symposium about Digitization and the Humanities.* Dublin, OH: OCLC Online Computer Library Center, 2008.

Vandegrift, Micah, and Stewart Varner. "Evolving in Common: Creating Mutually Supportive Relationships between Libraries and the Digital Humanities." *Journal of Library Administration* 53, no. 1 (2013): 67–78.

Index of Persons, Institutions, Collections, and Historical Events